PERCEPTIVE

Management and Supervision

Insights for
working
with people

HARRY W. HEPNER
Syracuse University
Management Consultant

PERCEPTIVE

Management and Supervision

Insights for
working
with people

Englewood Cliffs, N.J.
PRENTICE-HALL, INC.
1961

Dedicated

with warm appreciation to the following companies, their executives, and employees with whom I had the privilege of working either as a fellow employee or, in most cases, as a consultant during the past three decades. Of course this statement of appreciation does not imply that the managements of these companies, either now or at the time I was with them, agree with everything stated in this book. Each, however, contributed to my development of whatever insights I offer the reader.

The Air Preheater Corporation,
New York and Wellsville, N.Y.

The Bank for Savings,
New York.

Batten, Barton, Durstine & Osborn, Inc.,
New York and Syracuse, N.Y.

The Carborundum Company,
Niagara Falls, N.Y.

Commercial Solvents Corporation,
New York: Terre Haute, Ind.;
Peoria, Ill.; Sterlington, La.

The Crosley Corporation,
Cincinnati, Ohio.

First National Bank,
Palm Beach, Florida.

Goodyear Tire & Rubber Co.,
Akron, Ohio.

The Herald Company,
Syracuse, N.Y.

Kaufmann's Department Store,
Pittsburgh, Pa.

Merchants National Bank and Trust Co.,
Syracuse, N.Y.

Onondaga Savings Bank,
Syracuse, N.Y.

Paterson Savings & Trust Co.,
Paterson, N.J.

Philadelphia Co. & Affiliated Corporations,
Pittsburgh, Pa.

Syracuse Lighting Company,
Syracuse, N.Y.

Union Carbide & Carbon Corporation,
Sault Ste. Marie, Mich.

$\mathbf{T}$HIS BOOK HAS BEEN WRITTEN IN TERMS OF THE FOLLOWING AS-sumptions about you and your interests concerning people in business:

1. That you think of yourself as a person who intends to advance to greater responsibilities in business. Regardless of whether you are a student, a trainee, a supervisor, or a technical specialist, you are seeking further growth through your work situations. You want to be able to think with management as a member of the management team.

2. That you expect to supervise the work of others and to deal with management either as an executive or as a specialist in the performance of a business function. To be effective as an execu-tive, you recognize the importance of insight and skill in human relations. To be effective as a specialist who is trained to per-form a business function, you appreciate that the ability to deal with people is just as important for you as for the operational executive. You want to sharpen your perceptiveness in every-day human relations situations.

3. That you want to become acquainted with major findings from behavioral science studies that apply to human relations in industry. You want to know the basic principles that guide and underlie the "how to" procedures of daily practice. To fulfill this desire, most chapters include several condensations of sig-nificant reports of surveys and systematic investigations. Each of these condensed reports has been read and corrected or ap-proved by the author of the study.

Preface

End-of-chapter references and questions and problems have been classified into three groups to fit the desires of readers who have introductory or practical needs as well as those with scientific interests.

Of course, I have benefited from the help of many individuals. Certain business leaders have added to my own growth in dealing with people by giving me assignments as a management consultant. More important, however, has been the contribution they made to my insight into people's needs in their work situations. Some of these leaders deserve personal acknowledgment because of their indirect influence on the points of view expressed in this book. I want to mention particularly Maynard C. Wheeler, Alex F. Osborn, Robert M. Gates, W. F. Jetter, Hilmer Karlsson, W. E. Hammond, George Braddon, Fred B. Manchee, Lyle Purcell, Clarence Rinne, and William G. Morton. One of my faculty colleagues, Raymond G. Kuhlen, has frequently enriched my thinking through our discussions of current problems and research in the behavioral sciences. I am especially grateful to Eugene Emerson Jennings for reading the manuscript and giving me his suggestions for improving my emphases.

I am also indebted to H. P. Munger, Frank Dunbaugh, F. C. Manning, Gail Hughes, and Janet B. Tuck for reading and improving certain chapters. My secretary, Gladys K. Kennedy, not only typed and edited the manuscript but also made numerous inspections and corrections to insure accuracy.

HARRY W. HEPNER

Table of Contents

PART SIX   YOU AND YOUR ADVANCEMENT
IN BUSINESS

PART 1

Introduction

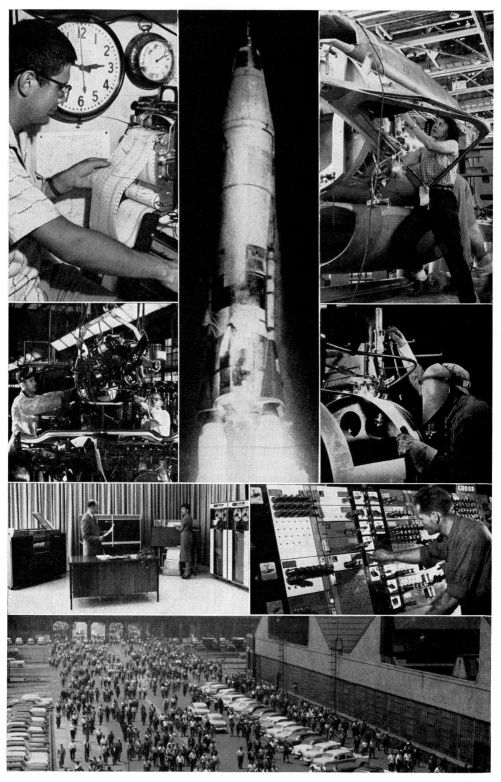

Photos courtesy Ford Motor Company, General Dynamics Corporation, The Dow Chemical Company, International Business Machines Corporation.

BASICALLY, *business is people who voluntarily cooperate to produce and distribute goods.* A business enterprise does not produce *things;* it creates products or services that have *values* for people.[1]

Perhaps you think that this definition puts too much emphasis on the human side of producing products or services, at the expense of the material and logical aspects. If so, an old truism in transportation suggests an acceptable modification: "An airline is 5 per cent metal and 95 per cent men."

For our purposes, we can define human relations in business and industry as the development of greater appreciation for the psychological and social relationships between management and the employee, the employee and management, the employee and fellow employees, and between company and customers. It implies a search for better understanding and finer skills in dealing with people. We all know that a tremendously important part of the job of the businessman, regardless of the industry or the level of his position, is getting along with people. The people with whom he deals include customers, employees, stockholders, creditors, union officials and members, politicians, fellow businessmen, and the public. In some cases, the list even includes members of the employees' families.

---

[1] See also Peter F. Drucker, "Thinking Ahead," *Harvard Business Review,* January-February 1959, p. 30.

1   Business Is People

As one company president stated: "Business problems are always problems of people—the people in business and the people with whom business is done. It is the quality of the individual in the business which measures the quality of the business itself. He, multiplied, is the business." [2]

The president of the United States Steel Corporation expressed the same idea to the students in the Executive Development Course of Texas Agricultural and Mechanical College when he said that "the most complex problems of present day management are problems in human understanding. People represent the greatest asset that any business can possess, and understanding their instincts and desires, their emotions and beliefs, their habits of thought and action, is one of the requisites to maximum industrial achievement." [3]

Alfred P. Sloan, Jr., when chairman of the board of General Motors, stated in one of his annual reports to stockholders:

> In our existing industrial economy the only difference of fundamental nature between one business and another operating in the same general field is people. The same sources of raw materials are available to all. The same equipment will be furnished to anyone who may buy. The existing standards of technology are largely a matter of common knowledge. The same markets are available with the same instrumentalities to capitalize them. The same reservoirs of capital are available to those who can qualify. All these means are open to everyone, and generally speaking, on equal terms. The one major difference is people.[4]

Certainly, our greatest wealth as a nation is not in our physical resources—our acres of fertile land, tons of ore, board feet of timber, barrels of oil, or acre-feet of water. Our wealth exists, rather, in our people— the men and women who have built America and the boys and girls who hold the future of America in their hands. And of all the resources we have, it is our human resources that are least efficiently used. It is here, also, that we have the greatest opportunity for improved economic performance in the future if we can release the full potential of people in their work.

A generation ago, our scientific research was such that we boasted of living in an electronic age. Currently, we are living in an atomic age that is on the verge of moving into an interplanetary age. But we still have to learn how to live in a human age.

The miracles of physical science are not enough to solve the problems of our day. Modern scientific developments require that the knowl-

[2] J. M. Dodge, "An Introduction to the Business of Management," The Detroit Bank & Trust Company, 1937, p. 12.

[3] *The U. S. Steel Quarterly,* February 1957, p. 5.

[4] See *Industrial Relations* (The Dartnell Corporation), April 1947, p. 44.

edge of the human mind, and the understanding of man's relationship to his fellow men, keep pace with technological advances. It is only through such dual progress that we can hope to cope with and enjoy our rapidly changing world. Our greatest asset is not usually listed on a corporation report, however. And yet, Andrew Carnegie recognized the value of this unlisted asset when he declared that, if he were stripped of all his material wealth but retained the people in his organization, his business could be rebuilt in four years. He realized that the greatest asset of any concern lies in the potential of the people who operate it.

Business executives of the current generation are keenly aware of the importance of people, people as individuals as well as the unidentified human beings who contribute to the profit or loss of the business enterprise. This awareness was indicated when *Dun's Review and Modern Industry* magazine asked the 111 company members of their Presidents' Panel about their most difficult decisions. Two out of every three respondents said that the hardest decisions they have to make are those involving people.[5]

Similarly, when the American Management Association asked 335 company presidents who were enrolled in AMA training programs about their three biggest problems, human relations problems loomed very large in their answers. Here are a few replies which bear out this point, in answer to the question: "What is your most pressing personal problem in your day-to-day business relationships?"

"Development and training of executives."

"Good men to make sound, responsible decisions."

"Developing an effective management team."

"Fully to develop the human resources of our management group so that the company may avail itself of a striking challenge which requires product and [personnel] development at almost superhuman rate."

"Development and/or acquisition of competent young executive personnel."

"Spending enough time with each man responsible to me in reviewing and criticizing his work."

The company presidents expressed an awareness of the problem of developing able successors. This was particularly true of the older men whose retirement is a prospect in the foreseeable future. The younger presidents complained of pressure from the old hands who kept them

---

[5] Kenneth Henry, "When Presidents Decide," *Dun's Review and Modern Industry,* November 1957, p. 34. Copyright © 1957 by Dun & Bradstreet Publications Corporation.

from acting as quickly or as often as they would like while the older men said that they are having difficulty developing a successor and getting the younger men to accept responsibility.

One question was, "Can you give an example of a human relations problem in your work recently and how it was solved?" Only a few examples from the presidents' replies can be quoted here:

> When I have a difficult problem with my key executives I turn over to them the investigation and recommendations; then it becomes their idea and they study the merits from their point of view.

> In a dispute between two executives of equal rank they were required to have an objective discussion with me; it developed that their differences were not so great after all and that an intelligent approach could solve what seemed to be a serious problem.

> One of my key executives became disturbed over pressures exerted on him recently; felt he should take lesser responsibility with the company; I solved it by intensive listening and a few suggestions.

> Problem—salary administration; solution—series of meetings with supervisors explaining our policy and setting up a program for regular organized review of salaries by each supervisor and his immediate supervisor with a check on such reviews by the personnel manager.

> Failure of outstanding staff executive to be effective because of intolerance and impatience; corrected by placing him in line responsibility for a year where he soaked up the understanding of frustrations and emotions affecting people and the job of getting things done.

> Problem—getting old timer VP to move over and make way for younger men; solution—finding top-flight back-up man acceptable to the old timer and employing outside management counselor to help sell need for change.

> I believe the root of nearly all human relations problems is misunderstanding, either self-misunderstanding or misunderstanding of the motives of other people; a frank, open discussion with all the people concerned has always effected a solution. . . .

> The overriding importance of an ability to get things done through people, to understand people, to communicate effectively with them, to draw out the best in them and to maximize their creativity not only as individuals but as a team is evident not only from the high rating given human relations, but by the presidents' estimate of the most important single benefit which they got from college.[6]

As one of the presidents noted, an executive's work in the final analysis "is almost nothing but solving human relations problems."

---

[6] "Top Managers' Three Biggest Problems," *Nation's Business* (Chamber of Commerce of the United States), September 1957, Vol. 45, No. 9. Original Source: "The Man in the Front Office: An Unretouched Portrait of the Company President Today," *The Management Review,* American Management Association, Inc., September 1957.

Lawrence A. Appley, president of the American Management Association and a confidant of many company presidents, described it in a somewhat different way when he called management "the art of getting things done through people."

Even though surveys of top management men indicate that people give the executive many of his most bothersome troubles, we do not assume that management men have no concern about the problems and functions of business operations such as accounting, finance, marketing, and production. Management men are men of action. Their action plans have the objectives of producing and selling goods and services at a profit. Sometimes they are preoccupied with technology, production, and the mechanics of business. Fundamentally, however, they realize that the goal of work is the satisfaction of human needs. Even though they are members of management, they are human too. They know that employees need understanding as well as security and that human dignity as well as fair wages is important to the individual. Admittedly these concepts of sound human relations in business have not become an integral part of the daily practices of all businessmen but they are accepted as objectives by the leaders.

Alfred North Whitehead, the philosopher, once defined a great society as one in which men of business "think greatly about their functions." The challenge to leaders of business today is to think greatly about developing business practices that enable people—our most valuable asset— to achieve the optimum use of their capacities and gain the fullest enjoyment of the fruits of their labors.

Stages in the development of human relations in business

It would be interesting to chronicle the recognizable stages in the concepts and objectives that have characterized the history of human relations in industry. An examination of the record in this and other countries of the world would, however, carry us too far afield for our purposes. Our purpose is not that of noting the historical development but to sense the current problems and to develop ourselves for intelligent participation in the present and the future. Suffice it to say that in earlier stages of industry's growth toward modern technology, the power of the employer was often all-controlling. Employees were looked upon as servants. They were expected to be obedient and grateful for whatever the master cared to grant to them.

Gradually the master-servant framework of thinking changed to an employer-employee concept in which the employee was recognized as having certain rights as a free man. The employee could seek work wherever he thought it would be advantageous for him to do so. Employers found it profitable to attract industrious cooperative workers. Later, some workers also protected their rights and increased their bargaining power through membership in trade unions. The pay envelope became the favorite motivational device of most employers. The economic incentive was and still is considered by certain employers to be the only incentive that appeals to the individual worker.

The modern employee is caught in a web of industrial forces which he neither controls nor knows how to utilize. He lives and works in a world he does not fully understand. Because of his confusion, he often demands more protection and fringe benefits, in the hope that the more will allay his fears. The employer too in his confusion imagines that giving more economic benefits will bring about the harmonious relations that he seeks. Managements are like the bewildered parent who realizes that his children are drifting away from him. In his ignorance of their needs, he gives them gifts in the hope that gratitude will bring about the desired happier relationships.

Our perceptual paradox

One of the great paradoxes of our time is the fact that despite the universal recognition of the importance of the human being in industry, management men and employees are still unable to fulfill the spiritual as well as the economic needs in their relationship. The men in responsible positions want to carry out the best in human relations. Employees too want to have satisfying, even enriched work relations with their employers. Each of the two parties would like to know how to live and work in a world of understanding, mutual respect, and devotion to common goals.

But each person who finds that he is a participant in a human relations difficulty tends to think that he is sensible and fair. It's the other fellow who is stupid and unfair. In the case of a strike, for example, the labor union leaders often claim that they do not want the strike and blame the pigheaded employer for causing it. The employer too claims that he does not want a strike and blames the irrational power-seeking union leaders for causing the strike. Both the labor union leaders and the employer claim that the other hates him without just cause. Rumors and suspicions abound. The misunderstandings and the erroneous perceptions flare into slowdowns, work stoppages and the full-fledged strike.

But each party to the typical conflict perceives himself as being intelligent and fair. Why the lack of agreement in perceptions?

To some extent, the typical situation in human relations in industry is similar to that of two awkward teenagers, a boy and a girl who want to get better acquainted although neither knows how to go about it. The boy likes the girl and she senses that he likes her. She likes the boy and he senses that she likes him. Each, however, waits for the other to prove his interest by acceptable action. Eventually one or the other resolves the dilemma by overtly showing his desire for friendship. Once this step has been taken, the relationship can develop normally and may lead to courtship.

The awkward teenagers exemplify an important principle for the student of human relations in business. This principle is that individuals or groups who do not know and understand each other need the experience of getting acquainted. In our example of the teenagers, it would be a mistake for some sophisticated adult to step into their situation, tell them what to do, and make overtures on their behalf. Much time and emotional wear and tear might be saved by the aid of such a do-gooder but the teenagers would miss the development which comes from the normal search for growth. The same principle applies to our human relations in industry. We cannot solve the human relations problems *for* people. We as individuals can, however, learn how to participate more intelligently in the human relationships that we ourselves experience. We can increase our understanding of ourselves and of others. We can seek development through the everyday situations that necessitate sensitivity to the perceptions and needs of others.

Contrary to accepted opinion, most people get along rather well with each other. Most employers like and respect their employees. Most employees like and respect their employers. The most extensive survey of employee opinions obtained the reactions of a half million workers of 850 companies. It showed that 86 per cent were proud of their firms and 81 per cent felt their jobs were important.[7]

The same kind of favorable reactions would also be obtained from customers in regard to the products they buy and the firms from whom they buy them. Most families like their neighbors. Most children like their parents. Most students like their fellow students and most students like their teachers. We should keep these positive reactions in mind when we discuss human relations of any kind, particularly those involved

---

[7] From *Changing Times*, The Kiplinger Magazine, October 1954. The results referred to are from surveys in many companies. The questionnaire form used is the SRA Employee Inventory, published and serviced by Science Research Associates, 57 West Grand Avenue, Chicago 10, Illinois. Further information may be had by writing to SRA's Management and Personnel Research Division.

in business. This positive perspective becomes especially important when we deal with problems and problem persons. Basically, our chief interest is not in these variations from the average or normal situation; these are of secondary importance. We are concerned primarily in learning how people now manage to work and to live satisfactorily with each other. We want to understand and extend the current favorable daily human relationships in business. We want to see how people now carry on their human relations so that we can accentuate the positive and seek possible answers for the points of friction and misunderstanding.

Learning human relations through participation in business activities

Some facts can be learned most easily from books, scientific journals, and laboratory experiments. Others can be learned best from experience. Human relations as a subject of study lends itself especially well to a combination of several major approaches to learning. Principles can be learned from the reports of scientific investigations such as the Western Electric Company's famous experiment at its Hawthorne plant (see Chapter 3); the studies conducted by the Institute for Social Research, University of Michigan (see pages 77 and 228), and other reports from investigators who have analyzed interpersonal relations systematically.

In addition to the studies conducted by trained scientists, many keen observers and leaders of business and industry have reported significant findings from their observations and personal experiences.

If the student of human relations in management and supervision develops awareness of the meanings intrinsic to his own experiences, he can enrich his social knowledge and improve his skills in dealing with the people with whom he works. He can, in fact, practice the development of alertness to human relations while he studies business and management. To learn human relations in business it is especially important to be an active participant in business, as a student, an employee, or an executive.

In the past, much study of human relations was done by the common method of studying human relations as a separate and distinct subject. This method ignores the fact that the varying nature of different business activities produces varying human relations problems. In this book, we want to study management and supervision by the human relations approach. We do not want merely to extract human relations case problems and emphasize them as isolated aspects of business. Instead, we recognize that human relations permeate every aspect of business. As

Business Is People

previously stated, "Business is people." Business and industrial procedures always involve people and the practices are modified to fit the people involved in the business situation.

Ideally, the human relationships involved in the practice of a business function such as accounting or final assembly should be taught as integral parts of the function. In real-life business practice, the two are inseparable. However, in our business and technical schools as well as in our whole educational system, we tend to compartmentalize knowledge and to stress the principles and techniques of the subject. Teachers themselves are specialists and their time is taken imparting the facts they consider essential in their field. Usually, courses in a business function such as accounting have to treat the function only. It is easier for the teacher and the student. Later, when the student has left school and become a practitioner, he finds it necessary to become conscious of the people who do the accounting as well as of the accounting as a function. The chances are that when you enter industry to perform some function as a worker no one will have pointed out the human relationships involved in the work. You will have to learn to sense them yourself, either while you are still in school or on the job. In this book, we shall offer principles and points of view that will stimulate your awareness of the human relations involved in subjects that you study in school or practice on the job, particularly those of management and supervision.

Objectives in our study of human relations

Many human relations programs have doubtful values. A few mistakenly assumed the main purpose to be largely one or more of the following:

1. To be kind to people.
2. To make everyone happy.
3. To make the worker feel important.
4. To let the worker do as he pleases.
5. To readjust the maladjusted people in business and thus help them attain a high level of psychological maturity.
6. To manipulate other people to your own ends, to get the worker to conform with what you want him to do in a calculated manner on your part. This may even include undue invasions of his privacy or an amoral concern about his emotional life.
7. To manage the lives of other people on the assumption that your intentions are good and that the other person is not managing his life in a way that is satisfactory to you.

8. To motivate people, either by some special manipulative technique or by offering extra rewards. This has been dubbed the carrot-and-stick theory.[8]
9. To study human relations for the personal satisfaction it gives you as a study. Some writers on the subject have been accused of this because they seldom put themselves into a work situation that requires special skills in the use of their own behavior with others. They suffer from ivory tower detachment. These individuals typically overemphasize a particular method of study to the extent that the method becomes an end in itself.
10. To make human relations a fad or cult. Malcolm P. McNair has discussed this aspect and called attention to the hazards as indicated by this quotation:

> There is no gainsaying the fact that a need long existed in many businesses for a much greater awareness of human relations and that, in some, perhaps in a considerable number, the need still exists. The very avidity with which people prone to fashionable thinking in business have seized on the fad of human relations itself suggests the presence of a considerable guilt complex in the minds of businessmen in regard to their dealings with people. So it is not my intent to argue that there is no need for spreading greater awareness of the human relations point of view among many businessmen. Nevertheless it is my opinion that some very real dangers threaten.
>
> The world's work has to be done, and people have to take responsibility for their own work and their own lives. Too much emphasis on human relations encourages people to feel sorry for themselves, makes it easier for them to slough off responsibility, to find excuses for failure, to act like children. When somebody falls down on a job, or does not behave in accordance with accepted codes, we look into his psychological background for factors that may be used as excuses. In these respects the cult of human relations is but part and parcel of the sloppy sentimentalism characterizing the world today.
>
> Undue preoccupation with human relations saps individual responsibility, leads us not to think about the job any more and about getting it done but only about people and their relations. I contend that discipline has its uses in any organization for accomplishing tasks. And this is especially true of self-discipline. Will power, self-control, and personal responsibility are more than ever important in a world that is in danger of wallowing in self-pity and infantilism.
>
> Most great advances are made by individuals. Devoting too much effort in business to trying to keep everybody happy results in conformity, in failure to build individuals. It has become the fashion to decry friction, but friction has its uses; without friction there are no sparks, without friction it is possible to go too far in the direction of

[8] For a description of the carrot-and-stick theory, see Auren Uris, "The New Realism in Human Relations," *The Management Review,* American Management Association, November 1957, p. 28.

Business Is People

sweetness and light, harmony, and the avoidance of all irritation. The present-day emphasis on "bringing everybody along" can easily lead to a deadly level of mediocrity.[9]

McNair and most other critics of human relations study have rightly pointed out weaknesses that should be corrected. They do not object to the proper treatment of human relations in business. They realize that human relations in business need not have the deficiencies mentioned above. Instead, they can be developed constructively—in ways that build creative values for each participant in the business activity.

We all know that many good business practices cannot be used or put into effect because of personality peculiarities of executives or employees. An executive, for example, may be so insecure that he develops an authoritarian manner that does not permit employees to make suggestions or changes. An individual employee, too, may be so fearful and defensive that he refuses to consider the adoption of new work habits.

The study of human relations will not enable us to change problem persons by means of clever techniques, but it will develop awareness of factors, positive as well as negative, to which we can adapt ourselves and our programs. Human relations means working *with* people, not doing things *to* them.

Most of the world's work is done by a team, either a definitely organized group or by individuals whose work is related to the work done by others. If each member of the team is sensitive to the human relations around him, everyone functions more easily and effectively. You can, if you wish, develop your own sensitivities through your everyday business and classroom activities. You can become a human catalyst who brings people together into common understanding and purpose.

The man or woman who wishes to become effective in his human relations in business must first of all be a competent person in the particular job or operation for which he is responsible. If he does not as yet know it thoroughly, he should be growing in his knowledge of it. If he has little or no desire for competence in some phase of business such as production, sales, finance or some other function but thinks of himself primarily as an "expert" in human relations, he's probably a politician rather than a businessman. As Malcolm P. McNair said, "An executive's ability to see, to understand, to learn, and to get comprises much more than skill in human relations."

Whenever we set up objectives for a course of study that applies to industry, we should recognize that in America we have an evolving way

---

[9] Malcolm P. McNair, "Thinking Ahead: What Price Human Relations?" *Harvard Business Review*, March-April 1957, p. 15.

of life. Our business way of life assumes that each intelligent person seeks the fulfillment of certain values for himself and for others. Typical of these values are the following:

1. To do work
2. To work productively: to improve his methods of work and to produce more today than yesterday in order that our standard of living may rise
3. To cooperate intelligently with the people who are involved in or benefit from the work. Each business organization is a social as well as an economic institution.

The objective in our study of human relations can be stated as "To learn how to work as intelligently as we possibly can with the people who are involved in or benefit from the work we do." If we pursue this objective, we shall be equipped to play our part in the evolution and improvement of our way of life in the future.

In the main, this book treats human relations in terms of the established organizational structures and common situations in business and industry. Typical problems with people are discussed or mentioned in order to help the reader develop his perspectives and insights. Some readers may even find the problems at the ends of chapters more interesting than the textual treatments.

The several chapters on the contributions of behavioral science studies in Part Two precede the chapters that deal with management, supervision, and the management and department functions. This arrangement has been made because findings from these studies concerning the psychodynamic and social influences in business have value for all managerial and supervisory functions, regardless of the level of responsibility or the specific department. The several terminal chapters of the book are devoted to certain principles that may be useful to you in your own advancement in business through the development of your social skills and your relations with the people of your work environment.

An author, at best, can provide an organizational plan and some informative materials for the student, although he hopes to allow for vision as well as guidance. Only the student can do the learning. And the student will learn best when he himself acquires and contributes new ideas to the material presented. The study of human relations offers the student splendid opportunities to add to the learning of his colleagues as well as his own. What you take with you when you leave college will be influenced greatly by what you have given of yourself while in college. You as a student can contribute by being observant and analytical of your own experiences and by sharing with your fellow students what you learn.

For All Students

Gardner, Burleigh B., and David C. Moore, *Human Relations in Industry,* 2nd ed. Homewood, Ill.: Richard D. Irwin, Inc., 1961, 1950. Treats industry from the standpoint of the people who work there.

Weimer, Arthur M., *Introduction to Business: A Management Approach.* Homewood, Ill.: Richard D. Irwin, Inc., 1958. Approaches the study of business from the viewpoint of the central figure, the manager. The business firm is treated as a key social institution of our time.

For Advanced Students

Argyris, Chris, "Human Relations: There'll Be Some Changes Made," *Management Record,* March 1959. Discusses the future of human relations.

Stroud, Peggy V., "Evaluating a Human Relations Training Program," *Personnel,* American Management Association, Inc., November-December 1959. Describes how the Bell Telephone Company of Pennsylvania tackled the problem.

For Men in Business

Drucker, Peter F., *The Practice of Management.* New York: Harper & Brothers, 1954. Presents a penetrating analysis of management. Chapters 20 and 22 are especially applicable to the content of this chapter.

Haire, Mason, *Psychology in Management.* New York: McGraw-Hill Book Company, Inc., 1956. Chapter 1 treats reasons for our not having examined our human relations in the past and the role of human factors among management's problems.

QUESTIONS ON THE CHAPTER

1. What do we mean when we say, "Business is people"?
2. What is the greatest wealth in our nation, and how well is it being used?
3. What did the AMA survey indicate was the major problem of executives? In what ways are these executives working toward its solution?
4. Describe the status of the employee in the early stages of industry's growth.
5. In what ways do employees and management often react to the confusions of the industrial world?
6. What principle can the student of human relations in business learn by recognizing the possible approaches to the problem of the awkward teenager?
7. In most situations in life, do people usually get along with each other? How does your answer apply to the business world?
8. Differentiate between the old method of studying human relations and the newer method presented in this text.

9. What dangers does Malcolm P. McNair see in an overemphasis on human relations?
10. How should a study of human relations increase our ability to deal with problem persons?
11. Explain the term, "human catalyst."
12. Name three concepts or values that the individual seeks to fulfill in his work life.
13. In order to study the people involved in business functions in terms of the human relations approach, what questions should you keep in mind?
14. State a worthy objective on the part of the individual in his study of human relations.
15. What did human relations mean to you before you read the chapter? How did your reading of the chapter modify the former meanings?

PROBLEMS AND PROJECTS

For All Students

1. No single textbook can possibly supply all the information now published in this field. As an aid to your study, examine and compare the tables of contents and prefaces of available textbooks. Compare the objectives of different authors.
2. Even though you may have had only limited experience in business, you probably have had some human relations problems with people in business situations. Describe any experiences that stimulated you to study this field.

For Advanced Students

3. Visit your library and list some of the available periodicals that should be of value to you in this field of study. Read and condense several articles that interest you. Explain how or why they stimulated your interest.
4. Some persons believe that advancements in the behavioral sciences have not kept pace with those of the physical and chemical sciences. Some have even suggested that growth in certain advanced fields should be retarded until other laggard sciences advance further. Present arguments for and against the suggestion.

For Men in Business

5. To what extent are good human relations now practiced in the company where you work? What improvements might be made? List your recommendations for changes but modify them from time to time as you read the text.
6. Give an example from your experience to illustrate the need for the principle: "Human relations means working *with* people, not doing things *to* them."

THERE ARE MANY REASONS WHY THE EDUCATED PERSON OF TODAY should study human relations in business. You, as you study or practice management or some other aspect of business, will develop your own personal reasons for doing so. Your reasons, if they are typical of those of the majority of young people who are in business or plan to enter it, will probably be expressed in terms of its personal benefits such as the contributions this study can make to an interesting and profitable career for yourself. Such reasons are, of course, worthy but ego-centered and insufficient for the man who wants to perceive human relations in terms of the larger social and economic perspectives.

As an intelligent citizen, you should be aware of the challenges in human relations that confront us in our time. You should seek to have the study enrich you as a person. In this text, we assume that you have a reasonably high level of aspiration for yourself in business. Presumably, you expect to become sufficiently competent in some phase of business to cause you to be classified as an executive or a similarly responsible worker. Certainly, you should rate yourself as a person who will have leadership responsibilities.

Leadership may be thought of in terms of pre-eminent influence. The verb "to lead" may mean "to excell, to be in advance, to be pre-eminent," or it may mean "to guide others, to govern their activities, to develop them, to hold command." The latter rather than the former meaning is implicit in our discussion.

2   Developmental Aims in Your Study of Human Relations

Of course, those who gain leadership or command in business should do so through methods that are based on a conscious respect for others and on high principles rather than on trickery. Frequently the popular image of one who has a position of leadership is that of a person lacking high cultural achievements. Television dramas, for instance, often utilize symbols for business success such as the possession of an expensive car, a large house, a luxurious office. For men in the higher levels of business, these symbols are not representative. Instead, the true leader is more likely to be the well-educated, mature, disciplined man whose possessions are incidental to a life of action rather than an aspect of ostentation. As one spokesman for industry stated:

> Industry stands for the good life, for the social and economic betterment of all, for the proposition that to produce more with the same amount of human effort is a sound social and economic objective. Industry's position in this respect rests squarely upon the ethical and moral concept of the dignity of the individual.[1]

To make this position more broadly understood is a major purpose of those business leaders who are concerned with human relations.

The hallmark of leadership is a sense of obligation in a man of character.

Goals in your study

In addition to an ability to sense the better values in the human relations of modern business, you will want to conduct your own relations with people intelligently. The developmental goals you may well strive to attain in your study are the following:

1. *To develop a broader framework for your thinking about human relations.* One aim of a text such as this is to develop in the student an increased alertness, a lively perceptiveness, in regard to practices and principles rather than to give him merely a mastery over skills or techniques. You must, if you wish to be an intelligent participant in business, sharpen your awareness of the human relations that are involved in all kinds of business situations. After you attain this mental growth and acquire an adequate background of points of view, research, and principles, you are equipped to add to your appreciation of the complex problems that you will meet in the actual business world. To repeat, the first objective is to develop an intelligent awareness of situations that call for a knowledge of human relations principles.

---

[1] Paul Garrett, "A New Dimension in Public Relations," *Public Relations Journal*, October 1956.

Your alertness should, of course, be directed toward better understanding and greater contribution to the human relations in your business life rather than the acquisition of mere book content. The breadth of view that you should seek is the kind that is expected from educated leaders in the second half of the twentieth century.

Even though you are interested in business, you may have no desire to become a policy-making major executive. You may prefer, instead, to become an expert in a specialty such as accounting or industrial engineering. As such, you will not become the management executive who directs hundreds of people but you will, nonetheless, need the background that enables you to think with the better high-level executives. No aspect of business can be treated as a specialty insulated from people. Without people, nothing much happens in business. Even the automatic machine or the "electric brain" must have human guidance.

2. *To recognize the need for helping the individual worker make and enjoy more meaningful contributions in his work life.* The members of management, the trained specialists, and educated men who have important responsibilities in business can usually find meaning, a sense of accomplishment, and the release of creativity in their work life but many employees fail to achieve these satisfactions on the job. The need for wise leadership in giving many workers creative satisfactions was revealed in vivid manner in a famous study by Abraham Zaleznik of Harvard University. He made systematic observations of the behavior of a group of workers in the machine shop of a small manufacturing plant.

Outwardly, the situation among the workers seemed to possess characteristics that often lead to friction rather than unity. The organization of the work called for little or no worker "interaction." Also, the men differed widely in social background, age, technical skill, job responsibilities, and rates of pay. Nevertheless, even though the setting and the people in it seemed unpromising, Zaleznik found a happy and congenial group. The men talked and joked among themselves, played cards together, loaned each other tools, and obviously derived considerable social satisfaction from their daily association.

On the other hand, the study produced no evidence that the men ever went beyond the bare requirements of their jobs or made any positive contributions to technical advancement. Actually, the men had plenty of ideas for improving work methods and increasing output. But this potential creativity remained untapped because they were not challenged to contribute their creativity to their jobs. Their attitude toward work improvement was purely passive. In short, the group had developed an effective social structure, but it had not achieved an ability to give its best possible contributions to the work situation.

Developmental Aims in Your Study **19**

According to Zaleznik's opinion, these findings, coupled with related evidence from other studies, point to two main hypotheses: (1) In the absence of any major restraints, a work group will spontaneously organize its relationships to achieve a minimum level of effectiveness; and (2) In the absence of any leadership challenge, the group becomes "frozen" at this minimum level and ultimately dissatisfied with the adjusted pattern of work life.

> As he saw and described it, it was doing an extraordinarily good job of surviving in its environment and of evolving those social forms required for the fulfillment of the minimum need satisfactions of its members. At this level of accommodation one could but marvel. But at the level of adaptation it lost somewhat its rosy hue. To Zaleznik its more tragic aspect was that "persons capable of so much were being asked so little," that the workers were so little involved in the new world that science and technology had produced and of which they were an essential but not a meaningful part. All they could do was to survive in an environment—certainly not hostile to them—but in which in a sense they had no meaningful place and to which they could make no significant contribution. And this was not because of any bad intentions, bad motives, or any fundamental disregard of human values by management. Far from it, this management had an unusually high regard for its workers.
>
> The central problem to which Zaleznik's hypotheses call attention is how to obtain for millions of people at all levels of life a significant and meaningful involvement in the great adventure that science and technology have introduced into the world so that they can become meaningful contributors to it and not just frozen members of it.[2]

Obviously, one of the great objectives for the man in business who seeks to improve human relations is the exercising of a kind of leadership that will facilitate the personal growth of employees through meaningful activity in their work. True leadership is characterized not by domination, but by service.

3. *To recognize the underlying human relations policies practiced in specific companies.* If you are now working in business or enter it later, you will find that many business relations activities seem to be performed on a "crisis basis." The management appears to have no guiding policies. Each decision seems to be made without reference to any policy or basic point of view.

In most business firms, policies in regard to people have not been codified or written on paper, but the policies exist, nonetheless, in the minds of the executives. They are evident in company practices. When you become informed about the more common practices and principles

---

2 From foreword by F. J. Roethlisberger in A. Zaleznik, *Worker Satisfaction and Development* (Boston: Harvard University, Division of Research, Graduate School of Business Administration, Boston, 1956), pp. x, xi.

in business and management, you will be able to recognize the underlying themes that influence the business operations in regard to people even though they are not formalized.

4. *To create an open-minded, hopeful attitude toward the efforts of those scholars in the social sciences who are trying to discover principles that are revealed through research.* The businessman of today is a man of action. He is concerned with a problem of action which he tries to solve through good judgment based on his own experience, but he should also acquire the benefits of the organized knowledge available to him.

Important advances in the practice of management and administration will undoubtedly come about as a consequence of basic research in the underlying social sciences: psychology, economics, anthropology, sociology, and political science. Thus one way in which we can move toward gradual improvement in business practices and research is to give students increased respect for the disciplines involved in our human relations.

Many contributions of outstanding and pertinent researches in this field are presented in this book in condensed form in order that the student may become as research minded toward people as he is toward material goods and processes. The possibilities of interplanetary space travel made us conscious of research in physics, but as one writer has aptly stated: "The future of the human race resides in its humanity, not in its ability to construct honeymoon motels on Venus!"

5. *To indicate the sources from which further information may be obtained.* The habit of inquiry is one of the marks of the educated man. Much information about human relations principles and practices appears regularly in the issues of journals and irregularly in numerous reports by research institutes and individual researchers. New reports are piled on the old; those who seek growth for themselves and answers to specific problems must know how to sort out the vital facts from the less useful records. A textbook can deal mainly with those points of view and principles that have been proved basic through the tests of time and experience, but the tried and true guides established in the past must be constantly supplemented by further study of more recent findings. Learning where to look for additional and current information is one of the developmental aims of the intelligent student.

6. *To acquire the factual background and analytical judgment necessary for dealing with human relations problems.* Facts are easy to learn, but the ability to evaluate the facts and to reach sound conclusions is difficult to acquire, and even more is the ability to put them into effect with people. The practitioner, however well trained and experienced he may be, is still trying to improve his ability to make sound decisions.

A survey such as this cannot give a person what years of varied experience in business can do to achieve wisdom, but it can start him on the way. This means that facts should not be learned solely in order to pass examinations but also to provide guidance for making decisions and applying skills on the problems you will meet in your business life, now and later. And the best laboratory for the study of human relations is in the persons whom we meet every day: friends, family members, fellow students, or fellow employees.

7. *To help you gain some insight into your motivations in dealing with people.* Most persons in positions of business leadership are unaware of the important underlying psychological influences that affect their interpersonal relationships. Sometimes they use people to satisfy their own unconscious needs.

Every person has had, in the course of his growth from infancy to adulthood, numerous frustrations which have developed inner needs for expression. The originating sources of these needs and the ways in which they are expressed are likely to be unknown or unappreciated by the individual. Only the experienced psychologically-trained clinician can identify them. Very few persons ever seek the services of such a clinician but many do unconsciously seek to "find themselves" and gain control over their own subconscious tendencies. Often they seek these goals by studying people as portrayed in the novel and drama. Some develop strong tendencies to advise and to help others.

The "service-to-others" tendency often develops in a person who finds himself in a predicament because his life is unsatisfying. Without being aware of his motivation, he tries to solve his own problem by attempting to alleviate the predicaments of others. The student who plans to do college teaching and then later finds that he cannot do so may adjust to his problem by helping others who are in a difficulty similar to his. This type of adjustment is, perhaps, one of the most common motivations at work in the life of the professional adviser. Executives and others who find their work unsatisfying or difficult often enter the advisory field as personnel men, counselors, or welfare workers. Such counselors usually become effective in their work, partially at least because they are sympathetic toward those who seek their advice. This kind of adjustment is both psychologically sound and socially desirable. When people make comments about a personnel man or professional counselor to the effect that he is trying to help others make better adjustments because he really is trying to help himself make better adjustments, the comments are complimentary. The motivation works out to the benefit of both the advisee and the adviser. Certainly this type of adjustment is better than the kind that is manifested in the exploitation of others.

The exploiter discharges his own anxieties and tensions by "taking it out" on others. In that case, the individual's inadequacies, frustrations, and hostilities which have accumulated over the years, are expressed through aggression. Of course all of us, at times, are guilty of this kind of aggression. As one writer stated:

> None of us is quite the fine, consistent, upright creature he believes himself to be, but each of us spends a great deal of time and effort in pretending that he is. We build involved systems of defenses to protect the idealized image of ourselves, trying to drug, distort, or deny basic conflicts in our inner life. Some seek peace of mind with a book or a bottle, others reassure themselves by bending people to their will. . . .
>
> The executive who gains insight into his need to dominate and realizes the defensive role it plays in his life, is likely to experience, at least initially, some guilt and humiliation. But this insight will open the way to greater freedom in his relationships with his subordinates.[3]

If you will develop the kind of personal insight mentioned above, you will find it easier to deal intelligently with the problem persons such as the neurotics, the belligerent employees, the domineering supervisors, and others who upset you emotionally by their cussed behavior. Many students erroneously assume that they can deal with difficult people by giving their unique behavior some designating classification such as "Oh, he's an introvert who lives within himself" or "She has an inferiority complex." Labels such as these do not help the problem person. Classifying the individual's behavior is not enough—the sensing of the dynamics involved in causing the behavior is more important.

8. *To develop the ability to deal with problem people in a calm, controlled manner.* In addition to having intellectual insight, the person who seeks to become effective in human relations must also add to his inner strength so that he maintains emotional control when he faces the problem person. This means that you should have to undergo only a minimum amount of emotional imbalance when you become the target of neurotics, belligerent employees, domineering superiors, and other problem persons who may release their maladjusted tendencies against you. This ability is very difficult for some persons to acquire. It is easy to deal with difficult people as they exist in books and courses, but the important question for you is "How effective are you when you are confronted by a cussed person in a real-life situation?"

Books and courses can provide suggestions that help to strengthen us for dealing with those whose behavior arouses our primitive tendencies to treat them as they treat us. The sarcastic person, for example, who vents his venom toward us should not be given an equally sarcastic answer. Instead, he should be viewed calmly, observed with some in-

---

[3] See Nathaniel Cantor, "The Executive as Leader," *Personnel,* American Management Association, Inc., November 1956, p. 234.

sight into his motivations, and answered in a manner that may cause him to lose his tendency toward sarcasm. The man who is truly skilled in his human relations has achieved this inner strength of character. Furthermore, he tries to treat the difficult person in a manner that may cause him to rise above his inadequacies. Many of our great business leaders have attained this level of inner growth.

9. *To help you decide whether your career shall be one of specialization in human relations.* Many students who take a course hope that it will suggest a career for them. Those who have not yet decided on their life work and wish to become further acquainted with human relations fields before making a final decision concerning their careers should find this course helpful. Once "introduced" to human relations in business, some students will make a firm decision about it as a suitable career. Others will drop the idea entirely when they fail to be stimulated by its challenges.

10. *To contribute toward the development of your personal philosophy.* Every course taken and every job held contributes in greater or lesser degree to the development of a personal philosophy. At least they help to establish one's values. The interpretation of our experiences is or should be in a continuing process of growth.

Of course some men do not rise very high in their growth curve. They congeal their judgments in regard to people on the simple level of "Men will work only for money," "Money talks," and "Every man has his price." The man whose thinking stops on this level cannot hope to become very effective in dealing with people. As one writer has well stated:

> The . . . assumption, that men will work only for money—that "every man has his price"—is so palpably false that it is extraordinary that it should persist. Our generation has seen millions of the best young men of the United States and of my own country lay down their lives for an idea; it has witnessed six to eight classes of West Point graduates virtually wiped out on Korean hillsides—not in defense of the United States, but for what we all believe is the way of freedom. Can we then turn around and tell one another that these same young men, the survivors, when they come back to our plants and offices, will work only for money? Surely there was never a greater blasphemy against the human spirit!
>
> Of course, if we tell them that the correct way to behave in business is to make their own personal advantage the primary consideration in their lives, some of them will accept this contaminating philosophy. But the best of them will not: *They* will demand an ideal, a purpose in life, which comes closer to touching what they know is best in them.[4]

---

[4] Lyndall F. Urwick, "How the Organization Affects the Man," *The Man in Management: A Personal View*, General Management Series, No. 189, American Management Association, Inc., 1957.

A similar erroneous belief on the part of many businessmen is that all people just want security, a guaranteed annual wage or high wages they do little to earn. Actually, guaranteed and high wages alone leave the individual with a feeling of frustration. Leadership in business relations is not achieved by money. Leadership is far more than a magnetic personality. That alone leads only to demagoguery and the exploiting of others for selfish ends.

Leadership in business is based on strength of character, developed through years of hard experience and the intelligent choice of values, a process that leads to a sound personal philosophy. It is creative. It lifts men's visions of themselves, not through lectures but through contacts with men of vision on the job. The employee who is encouraged to raise his performance to a high standard by a management that has high standards and a spirit of service for itself gains a new and greater respect for himself as well as his work.

As one writer, Paul Cifrino, General Manager of Supreme Markets, has well stated, "Productivity is related not to happiness but to morality—the morality of high standards." He has given some excellent examples and conclusions from his experience as an executive:

> We attempt to strike deep into the heart of a worker with the same mumbo jumbo which works so splendidly to sell tooth paste. In all this we have overlooked an important distinction. When it comes to tooth paste, the worker does not really care; it is not a matter of moral conviction. People go along with the masquerade that says you should use a given brand because it will make you look like a certain movie star. It is a harmless form of play acting. But when it is a matter of a man's work, bearing on so much of his rational nature and so much of his daily life, then he must be treated like a man. To illustrate:
>
> Supermarkets hire many teen-agers as "bundle boys." In our organization we used to follow the popular practice of handing them a little propaganda piece, starting with the theme, "Little Leaks Sink Big Ships," and going on to tell how an unnecessary bag on the floor or a light left burning might put a busy supermarket out of business. The effect on the sophisticated adolescents was impressively negligible. We have found it better to attack waste simply because it is wrong—morally wrong—not because of economic consequences. We find that our young men appreciate the compliment to their self-respect. . . .
>
> When we assume—and many of our professional personnel people do assume—that people really do not want to work and somehow must be motivated (which means manipulated) by sugar-coated pills, we not only injure their sense of integrity but do some of the very harm we are trying to avoid. There is an instinctive caution that makes people distrust techniques of manipulation when these are brought to bear on basic values. . . .
>
> Job satisfaction cannot be conditioned from above. Each employee— worker or executive—will learn it privately and for himself. Management can help best by demanding good work and spending less time stirring

up shallow enthusiasms. Such an approach imposes stern responsibilities on management; it must maintain high standards for its own performance—for "housekeeping," for supplying and maintaining capital equipment, for planning, for discipline. The moral appeal is a strong and powerful one, but it must be applied sincerely, conscientiously, and self-critically if employers and employees are to grow toward a moral partnership and a strong sense of mutual obligations.[5]

Robert W. Smuts [6] has analyzed some hundreds of reports by British productivity teams in order to discover what a wide range of these visitors concluded about the American worker.

He found a conviction that the great advantage in productivity we enjoy over most foreign nations is not due so much to better machines but to the attitude of our workers. Many of our plants, on the surface, are less efficient than their British counterparts and have older machines. But our workmen are "productivity-minded" and therein lies the difference. We do not fear technological unemployment, a European bugaboo since the early years of the industrial revolution.

"Rather than machines," wrote the coal mining team, "we should like to see injected into British industry the sense of adventurous urgency which characterizes the American attitude . . . and is found in management and men alike." Another team pointed out that, even in this country, some large investments in machinery would be uneconomic "unless the American operative was prepared to get far more output from his extensive equipment than an Englishman could anticipate." He found a feeling that America seemed to have found the way, through unions and through government, to protect the defenseless, to reduce insecurity and to disperse power, without at the same time diluting the atmosphere of self-reliant ambition in which American industry grew up.

Your attitude toward your growth

The extent to which you attain the kinds of developmental aims stated will depend upon you. You can develop an aggressive attitude toward learning more about human relations as a means toward learning more about other aspects of life and work. Or you can simply take courses.

Every June thousands of black-gowned figures line up, parade to a rostrum, accept their sheepskins, and walk back to their seats, many

---

[5] Paul Cifrino, "The Mainspring of Business Leadership," *Harvard Business Review*, September-October 1956, pp. 60-62.

[6] Robert W. Smuts, *European Impressions of the American Worker* (New York: Columbia University Press, 1933). See also Forrest H. Kirkpatrick, *Personnel Psychology*, Spring 1955, pp. 151-153.

with uncertain, sardonic smiles. To some of them, unfortunately, college has been a disappointment, a rather humorless disappointment.

In the same lines, however, there are other students whose eyes are aglow with the exciting discoveries and thrilling challenges they acquired. At the same time that they sense the challenges, they are aware of the hardships and the misunderstandings and the failures ahead, but they feel serene because they have confidence in the new resources within themselves. They have utilized their opportunities for further growth. They know that they will help to make things happen.

As someone has said, people, in regard to any subject, can be placed in three classes: the few who make things happen; the many who watch things happen; and the overwhelming majority who have no idea what has happened. It's mainly up to you to choose to which of the several categories mentioned that you wish to belong.

COLLATERAL READINGS

For All Students

Jobs in Employee Relations, Research Study 38, American Management Association, Inc., New York. Surveys executive, supervisory, and specialized positions in the field of employee relations.

Occupational Outlook Handbook, for sale by the Superintendent of Documents, U. S. Government Printing Office. (Ask for latest edition.) Provides information on the job outlook in more than 600 occupations, nature of work, and so on.

For Advanced Students

Newman, Joseph W., "Working with Behavioral Scientists," *Harvard Business Review*, July-August 1958. Discusses administrative obstacles and need for new concepts.

Spector, A. J., "Changes in Human Relations Attitudes," *Journal of Applied Psychology*, June 1958. Reports an Air Force study of a human relations training program.

For Men in Business

Perry, John, *Human Relations in Small Industry*, Small Business Management Series N. 3, Small Business Administration, Washington, D. C. A booklet.

Yoder, Dale, *Personnel Management and Industrial Relations*. Englewood Cliffs, N. J.: Prentice-Hall, Inc., 1958. Chapter 3 deals with approaches to the study.

QUESTIONS ON THE CHAPTER

1. To what kind of student is this text directed?
2. State some of the basic characteristics of leaders in business.
3. According to Zaleznik's study, what tragic aspect in the work life of workers had been neglected by those who supervised them?

4. The student who enters the business world is likely to assume that the company has no guiding policies in regard to human relations. Instead of accepting his assumption, what should he seek to do for himself?

5. What benefits may the student obtain from research reports and business journals?

6. Differentiate between the "service-to-others" tendency and the "taking it out on others" tendency of some persons in positions of business leadership.

7. Why is it wrong to assume that every man has his price?

8. What is meant by the statement: "Productivity is related not to happiness but to morality"? Why is it a poor policy to try to motivate workers by "sugar-coated" approaches? Describe a more effective approach that management can use.

9. In what respects do the reported attitudes of American and British workmen differ, and what factors of the American system have been held at least partially responsible for this?

10. What are the several categories that a student may choose for himself in regard to his part in the ways that things happen?

PROBLEMS AND PROJECTS

For All Students

1. Collect and summarize some of the published information available to you on the need for training in human relations in industry. If you wish, you may choose a specific aspect for investigation and description.

2. Give your reactions to the thought of a career for yourself in the field of human relations. Even though you do not intend to enter the field as such, can you avoid human relations entirely? How does this answer affect your thinking?

For Advanced Students

3. Examine some of the books on human relations available to you. Read the preface and table of contents of each. To what extent do they seem to duplicate or differ from the aims set forth in this chapter? Write a report on your findings.

4. Now that you have had some academic training, what challenges does past training suggest for you in the field of human relations? Choose one challenge as a possible career for yourself. What additional training would you need?

For Men in Business

5. Assuming that you are now working in business, how does Zaleznik's recommendation about enabling workers to become more creative apply to you? How are you trying to be creative in your work? Have your efforts been noted by others?

6. If you are acquainted with the production workers and the jobs in the industrial concern where you work, could Zaleznik's recommendations be put into effect for the production workers? To what extent are the production workers encouraged or discouraged in regard to their potential creativity?

Developmental Aims in Your Study

PART 2

Basic Factors:
Insights from Behavioral Studies

W HEN THE TYPICAL INDUSTRIAL EXECUTIVE FINDS THAT SOME of his employees do not cooperate in the attainment of management's objectives, he feels hurt and rebuffed, like a well-meaning father who discovers that his son prefers to assert himself as a man rather than be an obedient son. Just as a father and a son do not always see eye to eye, so management and the industrial worker often see their responsibilities in different ways.

Of course, we all know that two different individuals may perceive any situation in different ways. We have common expressions for this idea such as "If you want to understand the other fellow, put yourself in his shoes." Numerous social science studies have emphasized the importance for the industrial executive of recognizing differences in perception.[1]

This and the succeeding chapters of Part 2 present some of the findings of important behavioral studies that are significant for the executive and supervisor. These studies do not reveal the existence of wholly new or unsuspected mental processes such as perception or communication. The processes as such have been known to man ever since he became aware of the processes in his mental life. The studies do however point up for us certain very valuable *emphases* for our current thinking in human relations. We shall begin our presentation of these emphases by

---

[1] Ross Stagner, *The Psychology of Industrial Conflict* (New York: John Wiley & Sons, Inc., 1956), presents a comprehensive treatment of perception as a factor in industrial conflict.

3   Perception–The Hawthorne Studies and Their Meaning for Us

reviewing briefly the famous Hawthorne studies for their historical background and for their significance in the study of the very old problem of restriction of production by workers. The special emphasis of the Hawthorne studies for us is the importance of perceptiveness in human relations.

When workers control their output

One of the most common ways for industrial workers to show that their perceptions of the job differ from those of management is through the restriction of their production. Workers rather than management often control their output, particularly in manufacturing. Sometimes they restrict their production to an unnecessarily low level.

Usually, however, the members of a work group keep the output level at a point they consider fair to the company as well as to themselves. Most men do not want to loaf on the job. But they do want to feel that they, rather than management, control their output. They resent pressure from above, particularly pressure which they themselves have not accepted as a regular part of the work situation.

Workers generally have an informal agreement among themselves as to how many units of work they will produce. A new worker is told by the older workers what is expected of him. If he fails to produce the established output, they remind him of his obligation. If he produces considerably more than the quota they have set, they will ostracize him, hide his tools, or annoy him until he conforms. In many cases the "rate-buster" becomes a source of friction to everyone, even the foreman. The foreman, of course, wants high production but he does not want it at the expense of disrupted morale in his group.

One investigator made a study of production in twelve companies operating in several industries. The plants employed 300 to 2,500 workers. His findings showed that the average worker was not producing at a level even approaching his potential. According to the systematic observations made, the average employee could easily have done a fair day's work that would have increased the volume of his production by 25 per cent, in some cases as much as 100 per cent.[2] This kind of situation has been known to exist in most industrial plants for many years. As a result, numerous methods of stimulating employees to produce in accordance with their capacity have been developed by production analysts, experts and consultants. If you take a course in production,

---

[2] See H. Edward Wrape, "Tightening Work Standards," *Harvard Business Review,* July-August 1952, p. 64.

you will learn about many of the incentive systems developed by production experts.

THE FAMOUS HAWTHORNE STUDIES

Historically, one of the first scientific studies which caused production engineers to become especially interested in human relations was made in the Hawthorne plant of the Western Electric Company. These early studies are classics that have had a broad influence on human relations in industry. Every executive and student of industrial relations should be acquainted with them. The researches began in 1927, with the stated aim of finding "the relation between conditions of work and the incidence of fatigue and monotony among employees."[3]

Relay assembly-room experiments

In a special test room designed for the experiment, five girls assembled telephone relays at a work bench. Trays containing parts for assembly were opposite them. A sixth girl procured necessary parts for the assemblers and performed other routine duties. A male supervisor and one or two assistants sat facing the assemblers. The supervisor in charge obtained and kept numerous records relating to quantity and quality of output, reasons for temporary stops, length of time spent in bed by each girl every night, periodical medical reports of their physical condition, and other factors. Room temperatures and relative humidities were recorded hourly. The supervisor and his assistants made extensive daily notes of conversations and of the relations that developed among the workers. The workers were also occasionally interviewed in a separate room by an experienced interviewer. Furthermore, an automatic device recorded, to a fraction of a second, the instant at which each girl completed each assembled relay. Hence, a minute-to-minute record of output with supplementary information was available for each girl over a five-year period.

The five girls selected for the test room were told to work at a comfortable pace; conversation was allowed. The kinds of records that had been approved by the girls were kept, and the records they did not want were not kept. The working atmosphere was quite permissive and man-

---

[3] F. J. Roethlisberger and W. J. Dickson, *Management and the Worker* (Cambridge, Mass.: Harvard University Press, 1939), p. 5.

agement's interest in the girls was certainly much greater than in the usual worker.

Different experimental conditions of work, such as changes in the number and duration of rest pauses and in the length of the working day and week, were introduced in this relay assembly test room. For example, the investigators first introducted two five minute rests, one in the morning and one in the afternoon. Then they increased the length of these rest periods. Later they introduced the rest periods at different times of the day. Also, during one experiment period, the operators were served an especially prepared lunch. In later periods, the length of the working day was decreased by one-half hour and then by one hour. For a while, operators were given Saturday morning off. In the course of one two-year period, thirteen changes in working conditions were introduced.

In the first stages of the investigation, both the investigators and the operators were pleased because as conditions of work improved the output rate rose steadily. The early findings offered strong evidence in favor of the engineers' preconceived hypothesis that fatigue was the major factor limiting output. One investigator, however, suggested that the original conditions of work should be restored, that is, the five girls should go back to a full forty-eight-hour week without rest periods, lunches, or other aids to overcome fatigue. Instead of decreasing as expected, output strangely maintained its high level.[4]

Analysis and interpretation of the unexpected results opened a wholly new line of thought. The best interpretation became that "the responses of workers to what was happening about them were dependent upon the significance these events had for them." It became clear that the efficiency of a worker on a job is the result not only of the physical conditions of his work or the level of his wage but how he feels about his job, what he thinks of his associates, and his relations with his supervisor and with the officials above him. The Hawthorne relay assembly experiment showed that the workers were "cooperating with the experiment" and kept on doing so even after the poorer original conditions of work were restored.

How certain social relationships were analyzed

Several provocative aspects of these experiments have been described

---

[4] F. J. Roethlisberger, *Management and Morale* (Cambridge, Mass.: Harvard University Press, 1941), pp. 12, 13. Copyright © 1941 by the President and Fellows of Harvard College.

by Whitehead [5] and are here summarized because of their significance in explaining certain aspects of production.

During the five-year period there was a general increase of output. The increase, however, was not steady. Definite fluctuations took place from week to week in the quantity each girl produced.

When the production of each worker was charted in graphic form, it was found that wavelike irregularities were exhibited by each graph. Some of the waves lasted for months; others only a week or two. The output figures also showed that similar irregularities occurred with durations of as little as a minute or two.

At first it was supposed that these variations in working speed might be related to the experimental changes deliberately introduced, or possibly to other changes in physical circumstance, such as temperature or the worker's physical state. However, careful analysis of the data showed that irregularity in output failed to correlate with any known changes of physical circumstance.

The researchers next considered changes in the girls' social relationships. Study along these lines produced positive results. It was found that individual output varied markedly with changes in the sentiments entertained by the workers toward each other, toward their supervisors, and toward the group. The social history of the test room offered an explanation for the seemingly irregular fluctuations found in the graphs.

The seating arrangements of the girls at work were especially significant as indicative of the leadership and friendship structure within the group. The girl in seat No. 1 was of Polish origin, a placid follower and close friend of No. 2, of Italian origin, and the natural leader of the group. Nos. 3 and 4 were both of Polish origin and were good friends, though they had little in common besides their Polish ancestry and their proximity during most of the working time. No. 5, a Norwegian by birth, had little in common with the other girls, since she was older, was the only one married, and spoke very broken English.

Analysis of relationships in output of the individuals showed marked similarities after the girls had been working closely for 15 months. They had developed strong loyalties and common interests.

Three months later, however, a collapse of the integrated structure took place. No. 5 left the employ of the company and was replaced by 5a, selected on the recommendation of 2, a close friend. Although 5a had more in common with the other four girls than with 5, she was un-

---

[5] "Social Relationships in a Factory: a Study of an Industrial Group." This title was used by T. N. Whitehead for a paper read before Section J (Psychology) of a British Association meeting in Norwich, England, September, 1935, and later published in *The Human Factor* (National Institute of Industrial Psychology, London), Vol. IX, No. 11.

used to the group activity; and this unintegrated new member also caused a breakdown of the mutual influences in production.

Three months later, however, an even higher level of integration—the highest attained in the five-year period of study—had been achieved.

Six months later this high integration had broken down as a result of: (1) a change in seating position (the girls were arranged in a 4, 2, 5, 3, 1 order); (2) the replacement of 5a by the rehired 5. This latter action was strongly opposed by the group, and the dislike was directed to No. 5 herself. She was completely isolated. No. 2, though seated next to 5, seldom spoke to her except to snub her. The extent of 5's isolation is indicated by the fact that whenever a girl of the group had a birthday, the others gave her a present of chocolates, but No. 5 neither gave presents to nor received them from the others after her reappearance in the group.

Three months later, the group showed evidence of reintegration.

Seven months later, the output figures reflected the collapse of the developing structure after the restoration of the original seating arrangement: 1, 2, 3, 4, 5. Also by this time, a real antipathy had developed between No. 2 and No. 5, resulting in a very significant negative correlation—i.e., when one increased her production, output for the other decreased.

Ten months later, in January, 1932, at the deepening of the depression where hope had been displaced by resignation, integration was low.

The curves in production were not learning curves, because all the workers had had several years' experience in the work before they came into the test room. The plateaus and spurts in output were decidedly suggestive, and analysis showed that:

> It was the organization of human relations, rather than the organization of techniques, which accompanied spurts in these cases. This illustrates the futility of attending exclusively to the economic motivation of workers, or to their physical conditions of work. These things are of high importance; but no group of workers can be expected to remain satisfied, or co-operative, unless their social organization and sentiments are also protected at the working level.[6]

As the experiment progressed, the girls developed common interests and loyalties. The girls took their discipline out of the hands of the supervisor and supervised themselves. For example, when a girl wished to have a half day's leave she had to obtain permission from the supervisor. The girls themselves developed a custom whereby no girl would ask for such leave unless the group approved the request.

In general, the output of individual workers was directly related to

---

[6] Whitehead, "Social Relationships in a Factory," loc. cit.

their sentiments toward each other. The feelings of *approval, antagonism,* and *indifference* toward each other influenced their individual variations in output. One of Whitehead's final generalizations was the following:

> Perhaps the main conclusion to be chosen from this type of analysis is the vital importance of human relationship as a factor in the motivation of an industrial group, and in its ultimate stability. The logical motive in economic activity is financial; and endless ingenuity has been expended in devising schemes of payment, designed to secure a maximum of employee satisfaction and efficiency. But, in the last analysis, buying power is largely a means for satisfying social sentiments; and money incentives will never secure a full measure of activity and contentment until firms are organized with greater regard for the social stability of their own working groups, *at the working level.*[7]

Bank-wiring room: fifteen male workers

Another experiment conducted in the Western Electric Company involved 15 young men who did wiring, soldering, and inspecting of electrical apparatus. This study added several important findings to those obtained in the experiment with the women workers.

Nine wiremen were organized in three groups of three men. Each group of three wiremen had one solderman. Two inspectors judged the work of these 12 men, and one supervisor was in charge of the 14 employees. All 15 men worked together in a room separated from the other workers of the plant. Within the group, the supervisor had the highest official status, the inspectors ranked second, the nine wiremen third, and the three soldermen lowest. However, a more elaborate social organization soon developed. The group split into two cliques. These cliques were not divided according to social status levels but cut across one of the wiring groups and across the various occupations. Each clique or subgroup had its own leader. The members of one subgroup considered themselves superior to the members of the other clique. Each member's status within his subgroup was important to him and he would not jeopardize his status by conduct unacceptable to the other members. Interpersonal relations such as playing games, trading jobs, eating lunch with others, quarrels about opening and closing windows, and horseplay were carried on mainly with the members of the same subgroup.

---

[7] *Ibid.* The author's summary of this outstanding experiment in worker efficiency has of necessity omitted many important aspects. The reader may want to read the more complete reports listed in Roethlisberger and Dickson, *Management and the Worker.*

The customs that developed within the group related to the organization and performance of the work. Output and performance of the work were controlled through the customs which the men, rather than management, developed.

The men decided on certain levels of output from each individual. These levels were maintained through forced breakdowns, interruptions, and other behavior that wasted time. If any worker indicated that he was exceeding his allowance of work, he was "disciplined" by the others. If a man turned out too much work, he was called a "rate buster." If he turned out too little, a "chiseler." If he told a supervisor anything that would harm an associate, a "squealer." In addition to sarcasm and ridicule as a means of control, they also applied "binging," a hard blow on the muscles of the upper arm. The supervisor, too, was more or less forced to accede to the workers' control.

The wage incentive system did not function as management had planned. Output was controlled by the workers. Their control was exercised for the purpose of protecting the group from managerial interference. They jealously guarded what they believed to be their rights and privileges as workers. In a sense, the workers were not only protecting themselves against economic injustice but also against social ignorance on the part of management.

One important lesson revealed by the experiment with the 15 men is that the administrator should appear to the workers as one who is guarding and developing *their* ways of life and the emotional character of *their* group, rather than representing only the economic policies and wishes of the management. The men resisted outside threats to the integrity of *their* group.

The contrasting results in production during the experiments with the two groups of workers of the same company, the 5 girls versus the 15 men, cannot be attributed to a sex difference but rather to the fact that in the girls' group, ways and sentiments were integrated to a much greater extent with the economic purposes of the management. The girls' perceptions of their work situation differed from those of the men.

The reports of these experiments caused later investigators to pay more attention to the attitudes of workers, to the role of the subgroups within the work group, and to the social organizations within the work situations. The experiments showed that the strength of the work group can be greater than the rules and disciplines established by management. The group often operated quickly and effectively to protect itself from violations within the group as well as from the outside.

When reports of these researches were published, managements' thinking about methods of improving industrial production gradually changed. Changes in productivity were no longer assumed to be solely an effect of changes in pay, hours of work, illumination, or physical fatigue. Human relations between worker and worker as well as between manager and worker became recognized as important factors in output. The findings suggest that an executive should not only promote the efficiency of his employees but should also guard and develop their social sentiments toward each other.[8]

Obviously, incisive perception was one of the basic factors in these researches. Accurate and unbiased perception is always so important in all human relations observations that the highly descriptive adjective, "perceptive," has come into great favor when applied to the reactions of individuals in their human relations. When we wish to compliment a person in this respect, we say "He is a very perceptive man."

Effectiveness in human relations in industry requires keen perceptiveness on the part of the supervisory executive, but that ability in itself is not sufficient—it must be supplemented with creative thinking. Alert management must discover ways to improve relations with the employees. The creative thinking done after the research reports have been analyzed determines the extent of the improved productivity. Creative managements have made many improvements in productivity of employees and, at the same time, improved relations with employees. One of the newer approaches that has proven mutually beneficial in some plants is "job enlargement."

JOB ENLARGEMENT

The International Business Machines Corporation initiated an experiment in the Parts Manufacturing Department of its Endicott plant, and then extended it until it became a company-wide practice. Job enlargement was introduced in the hope that it would improve the morale of its workers.

> The management realized that the jobs in the manufacturing departments before the change were strictly those of machine operators. A part was lifted by the worker and placed in the machine. The machine was started; a cutting tool or drill did the job on the part. The machine was stopped by the operator and the part removed. All preparatory work was done by others; the machine was set up by a specially trained setup man, and the tools sharpened by other specialists. Also, when the job was completed, the part was checked by inspectors who did nothing else. Many of the operators had been at their jobs for years and had acquired the skill and the ambition to make their own setups and checkups, but they were not permitted to do so. . . . Others were either novices or

---

[8] See Whitehead, "Social Relationships in a Factory."

old hands who had acquired an "operator psychology" and either felt themselves unable to take responsibility for setup and inspection or preferred not to do so.

The department in which the job enlargement plan was first installed was equipped with the following machines: drill presses, vertical and horizontal millers, broaching machines, automatic screw machines, lathes, grinders. The job of operator on these machines, of course, requires a minimum measure of skill. Such jobs are not equivalent to the simplest of mass-production jobs like those on an automobile assembly line. A few weeks' training in machine manipulation is required.

The initial phase of the job enlargement program which affected several hundred operators was to add skills and responsibilities to the minimum skills of the single-operation worker. As a result, the job now calls for some sharpening of his own tools by the operator, and for the ability completely to set up his machine for each new order from blueprints. A knowledge of how deviations from tolerances will affect the part in subsequent machine operations is required. The ability to make a complete check and inspection of the finished part is called for. This includes a knowledge of how to use a test plate, height gauge, comparator, and other checking tools.

Installation of the plan meant the displacement of scores of setup men and inspectors whose jobs and skills had been absorbed by the operators. The problem of the replacement of these specialists was anticipated. Since the company's operations were expanding during the period of the plan's installation, no men lost their jobs with the company or suffered a reduction in pay. In the milling operations, for example, of 35 displaced setup men, 21 became operators without loss in pay; 2 voluntarily left the company; and 12 were promoted to other jobs within the company, all but one with increases in pay.

Not all setup men or inspectors were removed at once from the Manufacturing Department of the plant when the plan was initiated in 1943. For a time a certain number were retained as instructors and also to handle the work of operators not yet fully trained.

At the same time reductions were made in the inspection force, formerly considered necessary for quality control in these departments. By January 1950 all operators were doing the lion's share of their own inspection.

Benefits. The plan of course entailed certain outlays: wages of operators were raised to compensate for the exercise of their new skills, and additional inspection equipment was purchased. But these outlays have been more than offset by lower costs and other benefits.

(1) A product of better quality has resulted. In the six years following the initiation of the program company records show a substantial reduction in the losses from defects and scrap. This has been due to several factors but is substantially attributable by management to the "greater responsibility taken by the individual operator for the quality of his work."

(2) There is less idle time, both for machines and operators. The operators can set up and check with greater economy in time if they perform these duties themselves, rather than calling over setup men and inspectors to do the job for them. The cost of setting up and inspecting has been reduced 95%.

(3) Job enlargement, management insists, has "enriched the job for the worker." It introduced interest, variety, and responsibility which were not present before.[9]

Job enlargement has been developed successfully in office work by the Colonial Insurance Company, East Orange, New Jersey. In three areas of its operations management reversed the old principle of breaking jobs down into their simplest logical elements and assigning the fractionated jobs to individuals. The plan developed out of necessity when the head of Methods of the Underwriting Department was being called before management repeatedly because of a high error ratio, high turnover, and generally poor morale. Over a 20-month period in one group of four jobs, 32 people had been hired and quit.

The operation involved large volumes of work, but was not complicated. At first girls were assigned to individual jobs, each worked on a fraction of the underwriting clerical procedure of application setting up, application control, and application suspense. Operations did not improve. Extra attention was then given to supervision and to the use of psychological tests in hiring. The company tried hiring only married women for these jobs, but without success.

Finally, the head of Methods decided to try a bold experiment. Each of four girls was given the title of application control clerk. Each was made responsible for the entire policy application control procedures while the case was in the home office.

The girls who had had experience under the old system complained of the former routine and boredom. Under the new system of job enlargement the first few weeks were hectic. The girls feared they could not handle the workload. Later they adjusted to it and expressed genuine enthusiasm for it by statements such as "I wouldn't go back to the old system for anything." The error rate was lowered from 50-60 per cent to less than one per cent.

Also, the manager of one section reported that despite a raising of some job class groups to pay for increased responsibility, the unit costs had not increased. In other sections that had been reorganized there had been a reduction in unit costs with an increase in volume at no increase in personnel. Labor turnover was lower.[10]

The applicability of job enlargement in any plant is obviously dependent on the nature of the manufacturing process. It is not easily applied to an assembly-line operation where a moving conveyor arbi-

---

[9] Charles R. Walker, "The Problem of the Repetitive Job," *Harvard Business Review,* May 1950, pp. 54-58. See also a condensation of this article in *Notes and Quotes* (Connecticut General Life Insurance Co., Hartford, Conn.), November 1950.

[10] Robert H. Guest, "Job Enlargement—A Revolution in Job Design," *Personnel Administration,* March-April 1957, pp. 13-15.

Early Studies and Need for Perceptiveness

trarily limits the character of the work. It is applicable, however, to a very wide variety of machine operations where setups, tool sharpening, and inspection are called for.

The principle of job enlargement is being applied in some plants even though it may not have been formally adopted as such. Companies have been aware for some years of the penalties of over-repetitive work. For example, more than a decade ago James C. Worthy of Sears, Roebuck made this comment:

> We have found that where jobs are broken down too finely we are more likely to have both low output and low morale. Conversely, the most sustained efforts are exerted by those groups of employees who perform the more complete sets of tasks (e.g., salesmen, supervisors, master machinists, etc.) and these likewise exhibit the highest levels of morale and esprit de corps.[11]

One important result of job enlargement has been an increasing emphasis by foremen and workers alike on training and placement. Furthermore, employees who have learned to work under this policy are not fearful that they will produce so much that they will work themselves out of a job. They develop the kind of pride in craftsmanship that is found among skilled workers who feel secure in industry.

Human relations and differentials in production costs

Certainly, studies of production procedures indicate that the human relations involved in a plant are important factors in the productivity and morale of workers. Several postwar studies of this type have been reported.

In one series, cost differentials in different companies of approximately the same size and character were studied. The most striking example was that of four gas mask plants which operated until shortly before V-J Day.

> These plants had been equipped with identical government-owned facilities. Their operations were determined by the same production schedules and by the same piece rates for identical work. The government found, however, that the labor cost differed considerably in those four plants; it ranged from 52¢ to 87¢ per gas mask. It was also found that the average take-home pay was $1.17 an hour in the plant producing the

---

[11] From a paper given by James C. Worthy at the Forty-Fifth Annual Meeting of the American Sociological Society, New York City, December 29, 1949. See *Harvard Business Review*, May 1950, p. 58.

low-cost gas masks, whereas take-home was much lower (72¢ to $1.00) in the plants delivering the high-cost gas masks.

When plant operations were investigated, it developed that the reason for the cost and take-home differentials lay in the varying degree of work interest among the employees of the four plants. Supervisory know-how in "human engineering" was low in the high-cost plants, but on a relatively high plane in the low-cost plant.

As a consequence, workers responded quite differently; their output (under equal piece rates) was high or low, depending on such factors as (1) speed with which grievances were settled; (2) worker confidence in the foreman's judgment and ability; (3) ease with which the workers could bring up their problems with the foreman and (4) willingness with which the workers accepted the foreman as their boss and leader.

Other differences, not directly pertaining to the quality of supervision, existed also. The low-cost plant had a better staffed and better functioning personnel department than the others. Also, its whole industrial relations policy had been given as much attention as the technical aspects of production. "Human engineering" was recognized as an important factor in industrial operations, making for competitive advantages where cost and other conditions of doing business were the same.[12]

If you work in or study production

Presumably you will continue to study and work in some business field. Even though your major interest is not in production you should be alert to note evidences of better understanding of the people in production. Enlightened leadership will be evident in factors such as improved wage payment plans, skilled supervision, and job enlargement. These better relations with production people will have impact for the members of management and the public.

Most employees and union officials seem to agree that the responsibility for the development, maintenance, and administration of a human relations program should rest with the company. This means that the young people who plan to enter or attain leadership in business must become acquainted with and skilled in the use of techniques that elicit the full cooperation of the employees who produce products and services. Improved grievance and arbitration procedures, for example, will be developed to deal with those cases where a wage payment plan does not provide adequate incentive compensation and good will.

Industry will continue its drive for technological improvements that reduce requirements for high-effort work and manpower. The coming of the new technology with its growth of automation will affect almost

---

[12] *The Foreman's Letter*, June 5, 1946. Copyright © 1946, National Foremen's Institute, Inc., Deep River, Conn.

every production worker. It will require him to do a complete job or larger segment of the job. He will have to learn how to maintain and control machines that do the repetitive routine work for him. This means that he will need especially good instruction and supervision in order to perform effectively under job enlargement and related programs. Scientific and skilled managements will be more essential than in the past. This emerging kind of business leadership will have to come from the students who are now in college or from the alert young men in business.

COLLATERAL READINGS

For All Students

Parsons, John W., and Robert F. Peck, "Tomorrow's Production Worker: Is Industry Missing Its Best Bets?" *Personnel,* American Management Association, Inc., March 1957. Our new technology will need more high-type production workers. Intelligent young people of the kind needed are the ones who now look askance at "factory work."

Walker, Charles R., and Robert H. Guest, "The Man on the Assembly Line," *Harvard Business Review,* May-June 1952. Social and psychological problems connected with mass production are stated. In our technology, what shall we do about them?

For Advanced Students

Landsberger, Henry A., *Hawthorne Revisited.* Ithaca, N. Y.: New York State School of Industrial and Labor Relations, Cornell University, 1958. Presents a description of the methods and principal results of the Western Electric studies.

Mayo, Elton, *The Human Problem of an Industrial Civilization* and *The Social Problems of an Industrial Civilization.* Boston: Division of Research, Graduate School of Business Administration, Harvard University, 1946 and 1945. Two classics that are as enjoyable and significant today as in the time they were written.

For Men in Business

Lesieur, Frederick G., *The Scanlon Plan.* New York: The Technology Press and John Wiley & Sons, Inc., 1959. A collection of articles that evaluate and explain an unusual program for encouraging production workers and giving them participation.

Wolf, William B., *Wage Incentives as a Management Tool.* New York: Columbia University Press, 1957. This study indicates that, while incentive plans increase output and worker pay, the benefits are often attained through additions to other costs: strikes, slowdowns, grievances, and arbitration.

QUESTIONS ON THE CHAPTER

1. The author uses the term, *emphases*, for pointing up the significance of findings from the social science studies reported in the Part 2 chapters. Why?

2. Discuss briefly the aim, design, and results of the famous Hawthorne study. What benefits did the study contribute to our beliefs about important factors in worker productivity?

3. Explain the main findings from the wage incentive system among the wiremen in the Western Electric Company study. To what factors did the researchers attribute the differences found in the experiments with the men versus women?

4. Summarize the main generalizations of the Hawthorne study.

5. Objective perception is essential for effective human relations in industry but that alone is not sufficient. What must be added? Give an example.

6. What benefits were obtained from the job enlargement plan by IBM?

7. To what type of plant operation is the application of job enlargement advisable? Not advisable?

8. What were effects of "human engineering" on workers of the gas mask plants?

9. How is the growth of automation likely to affect workers of the future?

10. Of all the ideas presented in this chapter, which ones are of special interest to you in regard to their probable influence on your behavior in business?

11. What did the chapter contribute to your future relations with (a) the men who supervise your work, (b) employees whom you may supervise?

PROBLEMS AND PROJECTS

For All Students

1. Conduct a friendly interview with a factory worker or employee who does semi-skilled or skilled work. Establish rapport. Have him discuss the pay rates and the extent to which workers restrict production.

2. Conduct a similar interview with some employees of an office, bank, or store. How do their attitudes toward management, the work, and their fellow workers differ from those found among factory workers whom you know?

For Advanced Students

3. Make a systematic study of business journals that publish articles on human relations aspects of production. What are the backgrounds of the writers, the subjects treated, the emphases, and the writing styles?

4. List organizations and sources of information other than journals, that deal with human relations in production. Examples are the American Management Association, Inc., and the Federal Small Business Administration in Washington.

For Men in Business

5. One of the major purposes of this chapter is to emphasize the differences in the perceptions of workers and members of management. Think of some of the supervisors under whom you have worked: how did their perceptions of you and your fellow workers differ from those of the supervisors?

6. Apply the idea of job enlargement to the production practices where you now work or have worked. To what extent would it be feasible? Do some of the supervisors where you work now practice job enlargement? How?

A HUSBAND CAME HOME FROM WORK ONE EVENING, KISSED HIS wife in the usual perfunctory manner, ate the dinner she had prepared, and sat down in his favorite chair in the living room to enjoy his pipe and the evening paper. After she had done the dishes, the wife came into the living room and said: "What do you think of getting new linoleum for the kitchen, my dear?"

"Sure, it's Okay with me," said the husband as he continued to read the paper. After a few moments, she said: "What kind do you think we ought to get?"

"Oh, any kind you want," was his answer. She continued: "Well, how much do you think we ought to pay for it?"

The husband, impatiently: "Oh, heck, get any kind you want and pay whatever you have to pay. I don't care. That's your job —to run the house as you wish, not mine."

Then the wife snapped: "You inconsiderate brute, you! You're not interested in our home," and so on and on.

The next day, the baffled husband confided in his fellow worker: "How can you please a woman? Last night, my wife wanted to know whether she should buy new linoleum for the kitchen. I told her to get whatever she wants and pay whatever she has to pay and still she got mad. Now I ask you, how can a man please a woman?"

Psychologically, the wife was right. The husband should have recognized that she did not want his advice or approval—she just wanted him to show that he was an active participant, a

4   Enhancing Participation
                                         by Employees

colleague, in their home life. He should have laid down his paper, taken his pipe out of his mouth, and asked: "What kind would you like to get? Where would you like to buy it," and so on. Then she would have bought what *she* wanted, not what he suggested, but she would have felt better about it.

Many employees are in a similar situation. They do not want to receive or give advice about great problems of the business, but they do want to feel that management thinks of them as colleagues—that the two, the executive and the employee, are active, respected participants in the business, that they are working together toward the same goals.

Participation may be defined as a management practice that encourages employees to have mental and emotional involvement in their work situations. It is sought by pursuing the practice of enabling the employee to share responsibility for choosing goals (solutions to business problems) and contributing to their attainment. The term usually applies to the members of the organization below the supervisory levels.

The idea of participation has developed in America as a phase of our cultural emphasis on the use of democratic rather than authoritarian principles. Legally, we believe that all men are equal before the law. We believe in respect for the individual regardless of his social or economic status. We assume that his ideas as well as those of his supervisory superiors should be given consideration. We believe in the right of appeal in regard to any important treatment that involves justice. Our managements as well as our courts are, to some extent, controlled by the belief in the right of the individual to participate in attaining decisions, plans, and actions.

In former generations, executives, particularly owners of business, followed the practice of choosing business goals and determining plans without very much regard for the wishes of the employees. Employees were expected to do as they were told. This kind of authoritarian philosophy does not fit our contemporary culture very well. We now are in a process of cultural evolution in employee relations and we shall therefore evaluate some of the newer participative procedures, their benefits, and limitations.

Many employees of today have a level of ability which in an earlier time would have enabled them to become owners. Self-employment is not impossible today, but conditions have changed so that a larger proportion of members of our population are employees rather than owners. This shift in outlets for men of ability has intensified the pressure for the use of democratic processes in business management. As Lawrence A. Appley, President of the American Management Association, has well stated:

We talk today about the shift from the autocratic, one-man type of operation to the democratic, consultative type of supervision. What we are talking about is the person who exercises judgment versus the person who gets others to exercise judgment. We talk about centralization versus decentralization. What we are referring to is having all the decisions made in one place versus having them made at many places by people in much better positions to make them.[1]

Managements have learned that the effective supervisor tries to organize his work and relations with workers so that they will perform their jobs as productively as possible by contributing their know-how and ideas as well as those of the supervisor. An effective supervisor cannot hope to tell each employee exactly what to do, when, and how. The employee must be encouraged to contribute the special knowledge and judgment that he possesses as the one person who performs the task. Every employee has some knowledge or skill that he can contribute to do the job more quickly, more easily, or with less cost and effort than the boss.

Anyone who becomes acquainted with employees' after-hours activities will discover that some carry on do-it-yourself hobbies or other recreational projects that require imagination and high intelligence. The supervisor of such an employee wonders why he does not demonstrate the same level of ingenuity on the job. The answer is, in most cases, the supervisor has failed to give the employee a sense of real participation in the job.

Pseudo-participation

As in many techniques that involve a social evolution, the philosophy of participation is, at times, practiced in a nongenuine manner. A few management men imagine that they practice participation with employees when they are merely putting on an act. When, for example, a meeting is held by such men, it is held in a manner which indicates that management has already made the decision. If the employees vote in a contrary manner, this type of management man uses persuasion to bring about a vote in line with the previously-made decision. Sometimes management just disregards the opinion of the majority, does as it had planned, and gives no explanations. Naturally, workers are not fooled by a pseudo-participative procedure. They are just as smart as this kind of management.

---

[1] Lawrence A. Appley, "It's More Difficult," *Management News*, American Management Association, Inc., February 1959.

Participative techniques are more difficult to put into effect than many executives realize. When a typical executive of today finds that some important improvement must be made, he has an intellectual recognition of the need for participation on the part of the employees involved in bringing about the desired change. He usually invites the department heads and key employees to a meeting where he explains the needs for the desired improvement, asks for their suggestions for bringing about the change, and gets each to commit himself as to the actions he will take. Later, he presses the department heads and reminds them of their commitments. He keeps the heat on. Progress meetings are held. Between meetings, the pressure is maintained by means of office memos in order that assurances given will be kept.

In spite of all the pressure and effort, the results obtained are seldom completely satisfying to the manager. Frictions develop. Anxieties are accentuated. Wasted efforts are evident. All these and other disappointments occur in spite of the management man's assumption that he practiced participative procedures with his subordinates.

Modern managements are under constant pressure for the development of procedures that are better than their conventional ones because they frequently hear expressions which indicate the need for participation. Examples are:

"I don't like changes which I don't understand and that's why I'm not going along with this one."

"Some of the fellows say there is a gimmick in it. We'll have to work harder and then the brass will eliminate a lot of the jobs."

"These changes you want to make were dreamt up by a bunch of whiz kids in engineering. Our foreman doesn't even know what it's all about."

The effective practice of participation involves more than holding meetings or tacking up some suggestion boxes, good as they may be. It requires a basic theme of thinking. It becomes a kind of operating philosophy. The management men who have not as yet learned this theme, require courage to depart from traditional procedures to search for newer better managerial practices. Skill and imagination are needed to draw from employees on routine jobs their best suggestions and their assistance in making a profit for the company. Managements usually find it difficult, at first, to give employees a genuine sense of participation. Of course, to be genuine, "participation" must be consistent with what is feasible and sensible. Workers should not be asked to "decide" questions which are beyond their experience or interest unless the decision and the putting into effect of the decision is part of their work.

Comparative studies in participative leadership

The most frequently quoted experiment in this field is one conducted at the Harwood Manufacturing Company, Marion, Virginia, under the direction of Alfred J. Marrow, President. The experiment concerned work groups in a clothing factory.

One of the big problems faced by the company (it manufactured ladies' undergarments and pajamas) was the reluctance of employees to adapt themselves to new methods in production. Changes in style constantly plague the ladies' garment industry. This means frequent overhauling of the production process. Workers have to relearn their operations and this "relearning" is costly. A girl operator may take three to six months to reach a level of output that will net a profit on the product. Marrow noted that even the most experienced operators often took longer to learn a new stitch or fold than the newcomers. Accordingly he hired social scientists to aid in tackling the problems: (1) why do workers resist change and (2) how to get the employees to relearn faster.

A real-life action experiment was designed to study the problems. Three experimental groups and one control group of transfer employees were set up.

1. The *control group* went through the usual factory routine. The production department modified the job, and a new piece-rate was set. A group meeting was then held in which the control group was told that the change was necessary because of competitive conditions, and that a new piece-rate had been set. This rate was thoroughly explained by the time-study man, questions were answered, and the meeting dismissed.

2. In *Experimental Group 1*, the change was made differently. Before any changes took place, a group meeting was held with all the operators. The need for the change was presented as dramatically as possible. The employees were shown two identical garments. One sold for 100 per cent more than the other. The group was asked to identify the cheaper garment. It couldn't. This made the group aware of the problem of cost reduction. Management then asked for suggestions on how these economies could be made. The management then presented a plan to set the new job and piece-rate. This plan was essentially the same as the usual one except for one important modification—a few representatives of the group were elected to help the management to work out the new method and the new rate. These few participated not only in developing the new pay rate and the new method but also assisted in training their co-workers in the new method.

3. *Experimental Groups 2* and *3* went through much the same kind of change meetings. However, since the groups were smaller, all operators were chosen as "special" operators; that is, they were all to participate directly in the designing of the new jobs, were all to be studied by the time-study man. These employees made so many suggestions in the meetings that the stenographer had difficulty in recording them.[2]

The figure below shows what happened.

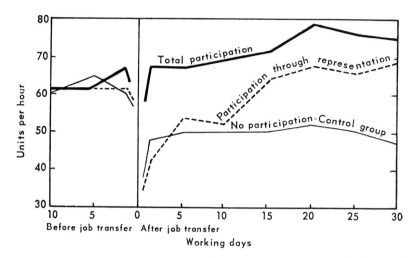

Employee participation in decisions about a job change eliminated the usual drop in productivity. SOURCE: *L. Coch and J. R. P. French, Jr., "Overcoming Resistance to Change,"* Human Relations (1948). *This chart was adapted for* Some Applications of Behavioural Research, *edited by Rensis Likert and Samuel P. Hayes, Jr.* (UNESCO, 1957), *p. 53.*

The results of the experiment were fairly clear. The control group dropped in production immediately upon change, and by the end of the experiment showed no appreciable amount of recovery. Resistance developed almost immediately. There were marked instances of aggression against management, deliberate restriction of production, lack of cooperation with the supervisor. Nine per cent quit during the first 15 days after the change. Grievances were filed about the piece-rate which, upon checking, was found to be even a little "loose."

The recoveries for Groups 2 and 3 were dramatic. Both groups recovered to their pre-change level of production the second day after change, and by the end of the experiment they had actually surpassed their pre-change level by about 14 per cent. They worked cooperatively with their

[2] See Stanley E. Seashore, "Administrative Leadership and Leadership and Organizational Effectiveness," in Rensis Likert and Samuel P. Hayes, Jr., eds., *Some Applications of Behavioural Research* (New York, Paris: UNESCO, 1957), Chapter 2, pp. 51, 52. For complete and exact wording of this material, see L. Coch and J. R. P. French, Jr., "Overcoming Resistance to Change," *Human Relations,* 1948, pp. 512-32.

supervisors, there was no indication of aggression, and there were no quits during the 15-day period.

Group 1 required more time to recover (possibly because of an unavoidable operational problem), but reached the pre-change level by the 14th day after change, and by the end of the experiment had exceeded its pre-change level. Here, too, no quits were recorded. One act of aggression was observed which was neither prolonged nor serious. . . .

The success of the experiment seemed to be attributable largely to the fact that experimental transfers were given the opportunity to participate in planning the change, in planning their own work future. Thus, where such external motivating forces as monetary rewards, management pressure, and other means had failed, group involvement and decision developed internalized motivation for the accomplishment of a goal mutually desirable to management and worker.[3]

Employee turnover and participation

Frederic R. Wickert made a study of turnover and morale among some 600 young women employees of the Michigan Bell Telephone Company. He compared the characteristics of those who remained against the data for those who quit. His findings indicated that turnover was significantly related to the employees lack of feeling of participation and ego-involvement in the day-to-day operations of the company.

First, he made an analysis of the factors that personnel researchers traditionally associate with turnover. He found that neither biographical data from the application blank nor scores on tests taken at the time of employment were of any help in identifying the turnover-prone employee. Wages and supervision showed little or no relationship. Even neurotic tendency, as measured by scores on some personality test items, failed to show any relationship to turnover.

The main point of difference between those who stayed with the company and those who left was the greater feeling of ego-involvement on the part of the employee in the day-to-day operations of the company among those who stayed. Those who stayed with the company tended to say that (1) they had a chance to make decisions on the job, and (2) they felt they were making an important contribution to the success of the company. The girls who stayed had greater ego-involvement in their work because they felt they had the opportunity to make decisions on the job.[4]

---

[3] Alfred J. Marrow, "Human Factors in Production," *Personnel,* March 1949, pp. 343-44.

[4] See Frederic R. Wickert, "Turnover, and Employees' Feelings of Ego-involvement in the Day-to-Day Operations of a Company," *Personnel Psychology,* Summer 1951.

Several investigations show that many workers feel deprived of an opportunity to apply their skill and knowledge in full measure to their jobs. A series of interviews conducted by the Survey Research Center of the University of Michigan among nearly 600 employees in a typical company revealed that over 75 per cent of them wanted more opportunity to help decide things. Of the remaining 25 per cent, half were already making decisions and felt they had responsibility enough; only 11 per cent, all told, made no decisions at all and were content not to do so.

In one survey of a large plant typical of heavy industry 5,700 workers were interviewed.

> Over fifty per cent of them stated that they would like to have more to say about the way their work was done. Sixty-eight per cent felt that, as things stood, they had little or nothing to say. Sixty-three per cent thought the work would be better done if the men could freely make suggestions about such things as design, setups, and the layout of the work. When pressed further as to why the men did not openly volunteer their opinions, fifty per cent of the workers stated that "men don't get credit for suggestions," and twenty-eight per cent expressed a belief that top management would not use the ideas offered.[5]

Managements often discover the values of participation when they realize that employees can make special contributions. One company, for example, reported that when management contemplated rearranging the foundry and the installing of new equipment, a drawing board plan was laid out for examination by the employees. The employees made numerous beneficial suggestions which could be made only by persons who were closer to the operations than management or engineers.

An impressive example has been reported by the action of the employees of the Chesapeake & Ohio Railroad:

> This week, a batch of Chesapeake & Ohio Ry. employees traipsed into the plush meeting room of the road's board to demonstrate their pride and joy: a big-scale model of how they think the Huntington (W.Va.) shops should be remodeled.
> The model was a labor of love run up during six weeks' intensive work —a lot of it on their own time—by some 60 blacksmiths, electricians, carpenters, metalsmiths, engine hostlers, and apprentices. One measure of the scope of their effort: C&O brass had figured that a similar planning job would take from 30 months to three years.
> The idea sprouted when C&O realized it would have to re-do the 60-acre facility at Huntington to take care of Diesel locomotives. Man in the 11-acre shop building—it houses the wheel, electric, coach, blacksmith, battery, and related shops—began talking over the project at their lunch hour.
> They were fed up with the existing setup, built in 1928 and poorly

---

[5] See "Attitudes and Opinions of Hourly Employees," University of Michigan Survey Research Center Report, Ann Arbor, Michigan, August 1950.

laid out in the first place, according to E. E. Slack, the supervisor. One example: The wheel shop was half a mile from the optimum site, wheels had to be trundled that distance.

That [sic] noon talks soon got down to cases, everyone told how he would cure the bugs in his own setup. Slack, the boss, listened and took notes. He had a draftsman get the ideas down on paper, then invited all hands to get in on the mass planning. The end product was the scale model that was shown to the directors this week.

There are some pretty persuasive arguments in favor of the plan, quite apart from the fact that it would make the workers happy. For one thing, estimated costs of the whole conversion job are around $2.5-million. That's a more heartening prospect than the $10-million to $15-million that management had expected to have to spend.[6]

Several training programs have utilized participation of former trainees on the assumption that current trainees will take more kindly to procedures recommended by men of their own age and status. In these training sessions, the new trainees meet as a group but have former trainees available for counseling and guidance of individuals. Emphasis is given to "training by the trained." Selected graduates from the previous training program play a leading role in training the new group.

The graduates also contribute their ideas and influence in planning the detailed training program for the new group. They help select topics, lectures, and discussion material which they found from their own experience to be especially helpful. These trained people take a leading part in conducting the instructional meetings. This kind of program has produced results that appear to facilitate the learning process of beginners.[7]

In the field of sales management, workshops that involve everyone are frequently used. In one company, for instance, six months prior to the workshop, all workshop alumni receive a questionnaire in the mail. Each alumnus is asked to check the five items that are currently his biggest problems. All salesmen who attend the workshop know that the problems to be treated have been chosen by the men themselves.

The findings by Wickert and others are substantiated by a whole series of studies made by the Institute for Social Research, University of Michigan, as found in a systematic investigation about participation in one company:

1. In work groups where morale was highest, a high percentage of employees felt that the company took considerable interest in their ideas and suggestions. Very few in low-morale groups felt this way.

---

6 From "Workers in Ancient C&O Shop Lay Out Plans for Remodeling," *Business Week*, November 14, 1953. Reprinted by special permission.

7 See Jack W. Hoyt and Bernard Silver, "Training by the Trained," *Personnel Journal*, September 1957.

2. In high-morale groups, most employees felt that group discussions with their supervisors were worth while. Not so in low-morale groups.

3. Both supervisors and employees felt that group meetings resulted in increased job interest and the group's working together more as a team.

4. Supervisors who held meetings with employees which employees felt were worth while in general looked on their supervisor as being good at handling people. If the supervisors held meetings, but employees didn't think them worth while, they generally felt their supervisor wasn't good at handling people.

5. In work groups having low absence rates, employees felt relatively free to discuss job and personal problems with their supervisor. In low-absence groups, the employees thought their work group had high group pride and good team spirit.

6. Supervisors who are given quite a good deal of "say" in spending money budgeted to them are more cost-conscious than those who don't have much "say."

7. Supervisors who were appraised by their superiors as doing a good job, and who were considered best qualified for promotion, met frequently with their employees and, in turn, participated frequently in decisions with their superiors.[8]

These findings are similar to those obtained in other studies on the nature and value of participation.

Involvement rather than facts convince people

When John R. P. French, Jr., psychologist, was director of research for the Harwood Manufacturing Company he wanted to convince staff members that women over 30 possess the kind of skill required in this factory. At a number of staff meetings he cited scientific proof. The staff listened attentively, but its attitude remained unaffected. More talks and more evidence were supplied, but this bias against employing women over 30 withstood every assault of reason and logic.

French finally recognized that offering more data would contribute little to changing this attitude and that it was necessary for the members of the staff to unlearn their mistaken beliefs.

Accordingly, the psychologist set up a plan that would involve the top staff members in a research project on their own. The project suggested was that if older workers were inefficient, it would be advisable to determine how much money the company was losing by continuing the employment of older women already in the plant.

---

[8] Rensis Likert, "Motivation: The Core of Management," *Personnel Series,* No. 155, American Management Association, 1953, p. 37.

The staff members analyzed the production records very carefully. Gradually, they discovered that older women not only equalled but surpassed younger women in work performance. The data also showed that the older workers learned new skills more rapidly. Comparisons of absenteeism and turnover data were in favor of the older workers.

When the staff members were faced with a conflict between prejudice and facts analyzed by themselves, they trusted the facts they themselves had developed.[9] This illustrates the old principle that the typical employee has most confidence in verdicts when he himself exercises his judgment. He believes that he knows how he arrives at his opinion; he does not know how the other person, even though he is an expert, arrives at his opinion.

Participation decreases defensiveness

The effects of nonparticipation often appear in the reactions to a kindhearted employer's good intentions. It is most evident in cases when the benign management decides to do something "nice" for the employees. Management may, for example, decide to pipe music into the office, cafeteria, or shop. To management's surprise the main reaction from the employees is one of faultfinding. They do not like the programs, the hours the music is played, or some other aspect. Why should they? They were not consulted. They were simply informed that a broadcast system was being installed and that music would be played at certain intervals throughout the work day.

When management has an employee relations problem such as having too many employees of the plant washing up too soon, the responsible executive often calls a meeting and "lays down the law." Everyone present immediately becomes defensive. Some feel that they have been unfairly accused. Without true participation, they merely carry out a new regulation for a short time. If they have no real involvement in selecting the plan, they do not feel responsible for its implementation. If, on the other hand, the executive does not state a criticism but simply describes the problem and asks for solutions, he is likely to get cooperation. Some of the employees will develop corrective plans and will feel responsible for putting them into effect. They will also encourage the rebels to follow the practice of the majority.

---

[9] See Alfred J. Marrow, *Making Management Human* (New York: McGraw-Hill Book Company, 1957), pp. 92, 93.

Multiple management

Multiple management is a participative practice started by Charles P. McCormick in 1932 at McCormick & Co., Inc., Baltimore. Previously the company had been managed as a one-man business by its founder, W. M. McCormick. Since then the plan has been used successfully in hundreds of companies, both unionized and nonunionized. The subordinate boards of directors consist of executives, supervisors, and younger men in the organization who show real management potential. These subordinate boards are given opportunities to study any company problem and to recommend courses of action. Membership on the boards is maintained through performance as measured by semi-annual merit ratings. The subordinate boards must drop three members each at the end of each six-month term. Continued membership is possible only through outstanding performance. Senior executives do not attend meetings except by invitation or give indirect control. Recommendations are made to the corporate board of directors. Only those on which there is unanimous agreement are passed to the company's board of directors. A recommendation does not become effective until the president or the company's board approves it.

Generally, the recommendations made by the subordinate boards are accepted. In 27 years of multiple management experience, less than 2 per cent of recommendations have been turned down.

In large companies multiple management may use several specialized junior boards, such as sales and office employee boards as well as factory employee boards.

Multiple management has proved itself especially effective in the development of middle managers, and its spirit permeates an entire organization. It trains men for the responsibilities of top management. It not only implements the latent creativity of middle managers and specialists but also brings about stronger identification with the company. Benefits accrue to all members of the business: management, stockholders, employees, and customers. At its best, all become participants. When multiple management is, however, adopted by a top management that gives the plan only lip service without genuine support, it usually fails. Thus far, the number of failures has been relatively small. Few managements adopt the plan unless they believe in its potential benefits and want to make it suceed.

Limitations of the participative approach

We must not assume, however, that all studies of leadership demonstrate the superiority of participative over authoritarian techniques. The literature on the subject shows that the benefits of participative leadership did not always take place as expected.

In one study, for example, the company faced a competitive situation which, in the judgment of its top officials, required it to undertake a program of substantial cost reduction. Inasmuch as the management was encouraging the use of participative methods in meeting its problems, it was decided to employ these methods to reduce costs. The management held a series of committee meetings, extending over a period of months. Managerial and supervisory staff members attended. At these meetings, the conditions which made cost reduction imperative were explained, current costs were analyzed, and many suggestions for reducing costs were discussed. As a result, some improvement in cost reduction was made, but not as much as was anticipated nor as much as the situation required.

The situation was overcome, however, by an official who used the older, more authoritarian, methods. He conducted committee meetings, forcefully explained the need for cost reduction, and gave personal and specific instructions to individuals on how and where they should cut costs.

The supervisory and managerial staff members were put under pressure. His methods achieved the desired purpose but they also aroused much antagonism, anxiety and resentment. Definite disruptive effects were produced throughout the organization.

This case was discussed by a seminar group of experts who themselves favored the participative approach. They considered the crisis aspect of the situation, the conditions under which participative methods are likely to prove effective, their inherent advantages and their limitations.

They concluded that this company's experience did not demonstrate that authoritarian methods are necessarily more effective than participative methods, even in a crisis, but they agreed that to make participative leadership work, certain principles must be followed:

> 1. Before an effective group decision or action can be reached, the group must accept the necessity of reaching a decision or taking appropriate action. In addition, there must be group recognition and acceptance of the hard, objective realities which establish the problems to be solved and the limits of freedom of decision by the group. In the case of this company, the requirements of the situation were a cost reduction of a given magnitude to be achieved within a specified time; these had to be met in any solution which could be regarded as acceptable.

Enhancing Participation by Employees

2. It is the responsibility of individual leaders to see that the requirements of the situation, including the need for action, are made clear to subordinate groups. It is not inconsistent with participative leadership that objectives and limiting conditions should be set by higher authority.

3. Discussion alone is not enough, although formal meetings and informal discussions are an essential part of the participative leadership process. Discussion is useful only if it leads to agreement, decision and action.

4. Decisions reached by means of participative leadership will not lead to effective action or change unless there is understanding of the goals sought and unless members commit themselves to specific action.

5. The effectiveness of participative leadership practices depends on who is allowed to participate. The process of participation and group decision should ordinarily extend throughout the organization and include all those who will be affected by a decision and whose understanding and help are needed.

6. The responsibility of a group engaged in participative leadership does not end with agreement or decision, but includes deciding upon responsibility for follow-up, review, and appraisal of progress toward the agreed-on goals.

Did the company's programme for cost reduction through participative leadership methods include these essential features? It was not possible during the seminar period and with the information at hand to make an appraisal of this particular company's use of participative leadership practices. However, it appeared to the group that the company's programme, even though conducted with evident sincerity and considerable expenditure of time and energy, may have been deficient in several important respects. . . .

A final—and critical—observation of the seminar participants was that committee meetings were carried down to the foreman level, but not to the workers' level. Yet the co-operation of the workers with whatever programmes were developed to meet the crisis was plainly essential. It was they who would have to take some of the action for reducing costs. They were sure to be affected by many of the cost-reduction measures likely to be adopted—for example, lay-offs and work re-assignment. Their understanding and acceptance of such measures and their active co-operation were certainly important.[10]

The seminar members agreed that the participative approach has its limitations. It will not accomplish miracles. Considerable skill is required to make it work effectively. In some situations, participative methods are inappropriate.

The extent of employees' readiness to accept and expect participative leadership methods influences its effectiveness. The degree of effectiveness may depend upon the history of the organization. Many organizations are moving gradually toward greater reliance on participation.

---

[10] Stanley E. Seashore, "Administrative Leadership and Organizational Effectiveness," in Resis Likert and Samuel P. Hayes, Jr., eds., *Some Applications of Behavioural Research* (Paris and New York: UNESCO, 1957), Chapter 2.

Those which are moving too rapidly toward large-scale employee participation, may find that their employees are not yet ready to take on the unexpected responsibilities.

Participative methods require greater leadership skills on the part of management than do other more conventional kinds of leadership.

A great many executives simply do not want to bother with a participative procedure. It takes too much time. Other executives are not psychologically capable of sharing problems and accepting recommendations made by subordinates. This was one of the major difficulties found by Robert N. McMurry, senior partner of McMurry, Hamstra and Co., personnel consultants. After he had participated in a study of nearly 1,000 top-level and middle-management executives, he concluded that the hard-driving men at the top have had to keep the power in their own hands to rise. These top-level men do not want the system.[11]

Clearly, management men, supervisors, and employees need time and practice to learn these more complex skills and to develop the climate in an organization essential for the effective functioning of participative methods.

Principles and purposes in the use of participation

Participation in regard to problems must be made reciprocal—employees can easily give numerous problems to management. If management merely solves the problem, no participative action takes place. If, on the other hand, management asks for suggested solutions to the problems dumped into management's lap, participation is likely to develop.

Participation varies in degree.

1. It is low when the employee is merely informed about policies which directly affect him.
2. It is increased when information regarding the reasons for action or a policy are added.
3. It increases even more when the employee is invited to make suggestions on handling a problem situation.
4. It becomes dynamic when the employee is involved in the action plan to the extent that he feels responsible for the outcome.

Many problems are beyond the scope of the average worker. He cannot participate in dealing with major financial, managerial problems.

---

[11] See Robert N. McMurry, "Case for Benevolent Autocracy," *Harvard Business Review*, January-February 1958.

He can deal effectively only with those problems that he understands, problems within his area of work.

The modern management practice of making employees participants in the business has purposes more important than those of merely building up the egos of employees by asking them to express their opinions. The greater purposes are those of helping them to develop their judgment and to add the kind of judgment which only they, because of their close contact with the work, can give management. They become genuine colleagues in doing the work in the most productive manner that is feasible.

COLLATERAL READINGS

For All Students

Harvard Business Review, September-October 1958, pp. 143f, discusses the idealistic thinking of many of the leading researchers in human relations.

Schoenfeld, Erwin, "Authoritarian Management: A Reviving Concept," *Personnel*, American Management Association, Inc., January-February 1959. Discusses the benefits of firm directive leadership in times of crisis.

For Advanced Students

Craf, J. R., *Junior Boards of Executives: A Management Training Procedure.* New York: Harper & Brothers, 1958. Reports findings from a survey of some twenty enterprises that have had junior boards of executives.

Rensis Likert and Samuel P. Hayes, Jr., eds., *Science and Society, Some Applications of Behavioural Research.* UNESCO, 1957. The Foundation for Research on Human Behavior, which is devoted to promoting behavioral research and encouraging its application in business, government, and other organizations, contributed heavily to this work by placing material at the disposal of the investigators.

For Men in Business

Davis, Keith, "Management by Participation—Its Place in the Business World Today," *The Management Review*, American Management Association, Inc., February 1957. Discusses five participative plans: consultative supervision, democratic supervision, production committees, suggestion programs, and multiple management.

Lawrence, Paul R., "How To Deal with Resistance to Change," *Harvard Business Review*, May-June 1954. The author raises the typical management questions: "Why do workers resist change?" and "Is there an easy way for management to make the countless little changes that spell progress?" Participative procedures are stressed as answers.

1. Define participation. To whom does the term participation usually apply?
2. Why is America a logical place for the idea of participation to develop?
3. Why are suggestion boxes not a fully effective practice of participation?
4. In the Harwood Manufacturing Company study what explanation is given for the difference in production rates between the control group and the experimental groups?
5. Explain the effect of the ego-involvement factor in the Wickert study.
6. What does the story of the Chesapeake & Ohio Railroad employees illustrate for management?
7. What is meant by the "training by the trained" principle?
8. How do high-morale and low-morale groups differ in their attitude toward employee-supervision group discussions?
9. What should an executive do instead of "laying down the law" in a problem situation?
10. How does multiple management, the junior board of executives, type of plan function?
11. Discuss some of the limitations of the participative approach as reported by Stanley E. Seashore and others.
12. What are three principles which should be followed in order to make participative leadership work?
13. Of the ideas presented in the chapter, which ones are of special interest or value to you?
14. What did the chapter contribute to your future relations with (a) the men who supervise your work, (b) employees whom you may supervise?

PROBLEMS AND PROJECTS

For All Students

1. What differences can you note between the use of participation on the part of students in the classroom and by employees of a business? Should the teacher ask students what they wish to study? Does management ask employees what products they wish to make? What are some of the advantages and disadvantages of having students participate frequently in classroom discussions?

2. Describe the ways in which you intend to use participative procedures in your family life. At what age do you think that children can benefit from participation in making decisions that involve the family? An example might be the decision as to where the family will spend a vacation or the determination of the kind of automobile that is to be purchased.

3. Utilize the resources of your library in examining the benefits and limitations of "Brainstorming" as a method of encouraging employees to contribute their suggestions for dealing with specific business problems. You might begin with "Brainstorming: Cure or Curse," *Business Week,* December 29, 1956.

4. Utilize the resources of your library to find out which labor unions do and which do not practice participation in regard to union affairs. Which unions appear to be the stronger? Which ones contribute the more to the development of the member as a person in industry?

For Men in Business

5. One important factor in the effectiveness of participation by employees is their readiness to accept participative leadership methods. Evaluate the readiness for such methods on the part of executives and employees of a company where you know both the executives and the employees.

6. Consider several individual executives whom you know. Which ones would be able to use participative methods effectively? How do they differ from the others? Which type of executive would you rather have supervise your work? Why?

THE SPIRIT OF AN ORGANIZATION CAN BE GAUGED, TO SOME EXTENT, by the percentage of employees who habitually refer to the company as "we" instead of "they." If the pronoun commonly used is "they," the employee implies that members of management, not he or his associates, are responsible for the company's products, policies, profits, losses, and so on. If he says "we," he identifies with the organization and implies that he too is partially responsible for the company's successes and failures. He of course also uses these pronouns when he refers to subgroups within the total company group.

The term *group dynamics* refers to the forces operating in groups: factors that give rise to them, conditions that modify them, and ways in which they may be directed by leaders who are aware of these influences.

The systematic study of group dynamics has come about, in part, because experience in business has frequently shown that the important contacts and interpersonal influences in a company do not follow the pattern called for in the organization chart. The formal structure does not usually indicate the informal lines of communication or the ways in which decision-making takes place nor the ways in which work gets done. People just simply do not follow in their entirety the relationships visualized by the chart makers.

Anyone who works in the business world soon senses that the members of some groups "hang together" very tightly; members

5

Group Dynamics
and Teamwork

of other groups seem to function as isolated individuals. Leaders are aware of these differences.

A group may be cohesive or disruptive in influence on its members. A method of determining the interrelations that operate in any group was developed by Dr. J. L. Moreno, a psychiatrist and the founder of "sociometry."

The method he originated is still widely used in research studies of group relations. When used in industry, it consists of questioning each member as to his attitude toward the other members in his work group: *Whom does he like and whom does he dislike? With whom does he prefer to work, to eat, to live beside, to take his troubles to, and whom does he prefer to avoid?* By means of this kind of information, the researcher can construct a simple diagram, called a "sociogram" which shows how members of the group feel about one another. The patterns of likes, dislikes, and indifferences indicate the interconnections in the influences at work in the group. It is easy to see which group members are popular, which ones are unpopular, who is the most powerful as a leader, and which persons are "isolates." In large groups, cliques are easily recognized.

Experience in watching how groups function indicates that the isolates and peripheral members are likely to get less satisfaction from their jobs than those who are liked. Isolates feel that they do not belong and are likely to quit their jobs sooner than those who feel that they do belong. These isolates tend to leave the group under pressure and are disruptive.

Moreno's sociograms are useful in predicting group behavior. He made sociograms of the interpersonal relations in a reformatory for girls at Hudson, New York. He found that 14 girls who ran away within a few weeks were members of a network. Apparently each girl in the same network prodded and emulated the other members of her group. The reformatory had an epidemic of attempted escapes. On the other hand, girls who were "isolates" and ran away did not stimulate others to follow their example.[1]

An instance has been reported of a corporation president who discovered, after dealing for two years with the same group of research engineers, that he could predict their individual votes on alternative decision problems with such high accuracy that he was tempted to dissolve the group. It could tell him nothing he could not find out without consulting it.

Of course people often act differently in different groups and when

---

[1] See Alfred J. Marrow, *Making Management Human* (New York: McGraw-Hill Book Company, Inc., 1957), pp. 60-62.

playing different roles. Their relations with different groups or with different individuals within a group change from group to group. However, "a good deal is now known about the dynamics of small groups—three to six people . . . and executives who attempt to deal with individuals only on the basis of their individual psychologies, without reference to group motives and pressures, are passing up half the balls pitched to them without even swinging." [2]

In some companies, a high percentage of the members of one group do not like the members of another group. This is more or less frequent in the attitudes of members of the engineering department toward the members of the shop. To overcome the antagonism, some managements appoint a tactful old shop man of good technical training to act as liaison between engineering and the shop. Similarly, in newspaper offices, the clerical workers are likely to think of the members of the editorial room as a bunch of lazy reporters who come and go as they please while the accounting department employees work. Publishers try to overcome the disruptive influence by appointing members of both groups to committees that require the two to work together.

These attitudinal relationships in business are so important that when a new employee is to be hired or an old employee is to be transferred, three questions are likely to be asked: (1) "Can he do the work?" (2) "How well would he get along with the people where he would work?" and (3) "How well would he get along with the other groups whose work is related to that of his group?" Some managers do not say so publicly but they follow a policy of hiring new employees from all available religious and racial affiliations. They believe that "mixtures" help to overcome the development of cliques and increase cooperation.

Why people belong to groups

Obviously, there are many reasons why the individual belongs to groups. He could hardly function effectively in our kind of civilization as a hermit or an isolate. In addition to the need from the functioning standpoint, the normal individual gains feelings of security and belongingness from his membership in a school club, neighborhood gang, church, political party, union, or business organization. He feels more complete when he knows that he is accepted as a person by members of groups whom he likes. Alfred J. Marrow has reported an incident in

---

[2] Alfred G. Larke, "Group as Well as Person Shapes the Executive," *Dun's Review and Modern Industry*, November 1956, p. 111. Copyright © by Dun & Bradstreet Publications Corporation.

an English oil refinery where the workers wanted an increase in pay because the plant was being automated. They referred to the desired extra pay as "lonely money," a compensation for their losing the companionship of workmates.[3]

It is also probable that when a workman can gain little satisfaction as a craftsman because of the growth of large scale industry with its automated operations, he feels more dependent upon his fellow workers. He needs extra emotional satisfactions to compensate for loss of ego-maximation that he might have had through craftsmanship. To the worker on an assembly line system, the sense of worthwhileness must come as a group member, not as an independent individual.

Shared beliefs often cause groups. A collection of people develop group feelings from shared views about work, politics, or other interests. The sharing of ideas and beliefs is called "social closeness" in contrast to physical closeness.

As in physical space, there is also social space. When we are members of a group of people who talk about topics of no interest or when they express opinions distasteful to us, we are socially distant. We do not enjoy full group membership. "Social space affects behavior and is a force affecting the feeling of group membership." [4]

Numerous studies are being conducted concerning group behavior. Some of the early studies have dealt with easily-measured factors such as the optimum size of a group to give each member full in-groupness feeling. For some purposes such as discussion, five is the optimal number. Factions begin to appear when the group becomes larger than twelve.

Outstanding research in the field of group dynamics is being conducted by the Institute for Social Research of the University of Michigan.[5] The Institute is composed of two research centers, the Survey Research Center and the Research Center for Group Dynamics.

---

[3] *Op. cit.*, pp. 53-56.

[4] See Eugene Emerson Jennings, "Forces That Transform a Collection into a Group," *Personnel Journal*, September 1956.

[5] The Institute was conceived as a mechanism by which sustained research programs could be conducted in a variety of academic disciplines, with resources permitting the conduct of studies of considerable size.

The Survey Research Center is concerned primarily with the utilization and development of the sample survey in advancing theory and knowledge in the social sciences. The Center has active research programs in the fields of economic behavior and attitudes, organizational behavior and human relations, communication and influence, political behavior, and mental health.

The Research Center for Group Dynamics is engaged in the development of a basic science of groups. Through an integrated program of social research, theories and techniques are being developed for studying such properties of groups as cohesiveness, communication, norms, leadership, decision-making, and productivity. The Center uses a variety of methods in its investigations of group behavior. Studies are made of natural groups such as those found in communities, schools, or industry as well

Van Zelst's use of sociometric procedures with construction workers

The building trades are especially well adapted to the use of sociometric procedures because they are not subject to the same limitations that are typical of mass industry where a regrouping of workers means that each worker must learn an entirely new job. The subjects of this study by Raymond H. Van Zelst were four total work groups: a carpenter group of 20 members, another carpenter group of 18 members and two separate groups of bricklayers, each having 16 members. These men were working on the same housing project, but were split into two separate groups by a highway running through the middle of the site. In housing construction the foreman normally assigns men arbitrarily to work crews, but in Van Zelst's study he asked the men to indicate their first, second and third choices as to preference for teammates. The foreman assigned workers into these new groups, respecting each man's choices as far as possible.

The graphs on the next page show the results in terms of costs. The savings in both materials and labor are quite evident. Furthermore, the men liked the new system much better than the old. The experiment showed that the use of sociometric procedures resulted in increased satisfaction for the workers and greater financial returns for management. The company's chief construction engineer in his report to management revealed that the savings due to this psychological procedure exceeded those of any previous work saving device that had been tried by the management. The financial benefits were such that the company could construct every 29th building entirely from savings in labor and material costs.[6]

Walker's study of thirty men and a machine

Production executives of today are keenly interested in the reactions of employees to automation. Automation is one of the most significant trends of our time but few serious studies have been made of the actual impact on workers and work groups of a major technological innovation.

---

as of groups assembled for experimental purposes. In addition to its efforts to develop a basic understanding of group life, the work of the Center has had practical implications for programs of human relations in business, government, education, religion, and the community.

[6] See Raymond H. Van Zelst, "Validation of a Sociometric Regrouping Procedure," *Supplement to the Journal of Abnormal and Social Psychology*, April 1952.

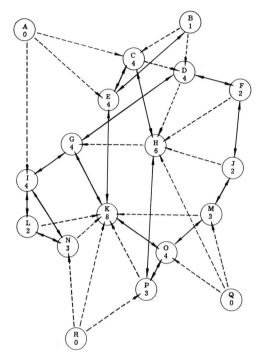

This sociogram shows a work group of eighteen carpenters, from data collected by Raymond H. Van Zelst. Each circle represents one man. Each member of the group was requested to nominate the three men with whom he would most like to work. Arrows indicate the direction of choice; broken lines indicate one-way preferences; solid lines indicate mutual choices. Total number of votes for each individual is shown in the circle. "R" chose "N," "K," and "P." "R" is an isolate because no one chose him. SOURCE: *Raymond H. Van Zelst, "An Interpersonal Relations Technique for Industry," Personnel (American Management Association, July 1952), pp. 68-77.*

Fluctuations between experimental and control groups on materials costs compared for entire three-month period

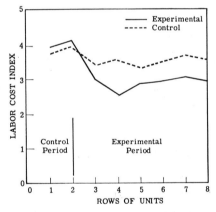

Fluctuations between experimental and control groups on labor costs compared for entire three-month period

These figures show cost differences in the work done by an experimental group on which sociometric procedures were used and a control group where these procedures were not used. Both groups worked on the same housing project during the same time. They were separated from each other by a highway. Note that the cost indexes for both materials and labor were lower in the experimental group—the one which received the benefit of sociometric techniques. SOURCE: *Raymond H. Van Zelst, "An Interpersonal Relations Technique for Industry," Personnel (American Management Association, July 1952). See also "Validation of a Sociometric Regrouping Procedure," from Supplement to the Journal of Abnormal and Social Psychology (April 1952).*

A notable new contribution to the literature has been made by Charles R. Walker.[7] He reported a three-year study of the mechanical, social, and human difficulties encountered in "getting the bugs out" of a new semi-automatic plant of the United States Steel Corporation.

One of the most striking findings that emerged from this report of "a three-year battle between 30 men and a machine" is that many of the human relations troubles arose from management's tendency to view the workers in the new mill as a collection of individuals rather than as members of a team. Thus when, after 17 months, an incentive plan was finally announced, it was indignantly rejected because it eliminated two men from each of the three crews and covered only the crew operators. After management offered to retrain and find new jobs for the six men and broadened the plan to include indirect labor, production rose sharply, only to slump again when the old mill shut down and several crew members in the new mill were "bumped" out of their jobs. Almost three years were needed to achieve a state of high productivity and good morale. As Mr. Walker pointed out, a better understanding of the plant as a work community and a social system might have avoided much of the conflict and confusion along the way.

Much grief might have been avoided by giving employees a more extended technical and psychological preparation for the change. In the early critical months, the men did not believe that the mill would reach estimated capacity or that it would ever earn, for them, as much as they had made in the old type of mill. They felt that their job security was only temporary and that either all or some of them would soon be out of work. Even though events proved that all these fears were unfounded, the worry about security persisted. Even at the end of the study period, the men were not sure in their own minds that the new mill represented progress *for them*.

While the workers welcomed the relief from their former physical drudgery, they were concerned about the fact that an operating crew in the new mill consisted of nine men, instead of the 20 or 30 who had been needed in the old mill. In the event of a depression, they reasoned, they might lose three days' work out of four because the new mill turned out four times as much as the old. There were fewer job classes, and hence fewer opportunities for promotion. None of them had any hope of rising in the mill hierarchy—the better jobs, they felt, would henceforth to "college boys." In general, there was a feeling that the company was getting much more out of increased production than the men were sharing.

---

[7] Charles R. Walker, *Toward the Automatic Factory, A Case Study of Men and Machines* (New Haven: Yale University Press), 1957.

The study points up the kinds of difficulties that will be encountered increasingly as automation gathers momentum. The adoption of automation puts a burden on management and labor leaders alike, to prove that technological progress really means progress for everyone—or, in Mr. Walker's words, "to make it so, if it isn't." [8]

Workers' restriction of production

Perhaps the most poignant interest in group dynamics on the part of management men has arisen as a result of workers' restriction of production. Anyone who examines records of production by factory workers is likely to find that their output does not fluctuate from day to day. One would expect that each worker would have some good days and some bad days. Instead, their output remains fixed for months. Those on piece work usually turn out an exact number of units every day. This means that the workers have established a level which they can attain on poor days. This level is in line with what management expects or what in-plant custom has determined. (See pages 32-38.)

Workers on a piece-rate or other incentive system often limit their own wages by restricting production. Many would like to earn more money but they seek satisfactions which are more important than money. Each prefers to maintain his status as an accepted member of the group. When the group members have an informal agreement among themselves on a fair day's output, most members will conform to that standard. If an overzealous "eager beaver" tries to violate the code, the others will subject him to ridicule, threats of physical harm, and perhaps actual harm.

In our social system, the urge to conform generally wins out over the urge to excel, especially among wage earners. A worker might like to get more money for producing more, but he normally holds back if his co-workers take a dim view of superior accomplishment on the job. He usually decides that the extra pay is not worth the extra effort or, perhaps, the extra risk.

This group influence is not wholly bad. Group solidarity also provides important benefits to the individual worker. The group often protects its weakest members. If the weakest cannot do as well as the best, the best may voluntarily restrict their production so that the differences in earnings cannot be used as a reason for discharging or transferring the weakest. This is especially likely to occur when the weakest are socially

---

[8] See *Personnel*, American Management Association, Inc., January-February 1958, pp. 5, 6.

EFFECT OF GROUP EXPECTATIONS ON MEMBER PRODUCTIVITY
(Sewing Factory)

GROUP RESTRICTION OF PRODUCTION

Obviously, the attitude of the individual worker toward the amount of work he should produce is often influenced by the members of the group with whom he works. Performance of the individual worker is often controlled by what the group members believe to be fair. The effect of such social influence on the worker is illustrated by the above figure. In this case, the output of a girl increased greatly when group pressure was removed. As stated by Lippitt from the study by Coch and French at the Harwood Manufacturing company:

> We see the day-by-day production curve of a girl belonging to a work group with a group production level of 50 units per hour represented by the dotted line. On the 11th and 12th days her production began to rise noticeably above the group standard and when she on the 13th day, hit standard production of 60 (a psychologically very important deviation for the other members) she became a scapegoat of the group with a great deal of social aggression directed toward her. Under this pressure her production decreased toward the level of the other group members. After 20 days the work group had to be broken up and the members transferred to various other units. The scapegoated operator remained on the same job, alone. As can be seen, her production shot up from about 45 to 96 units per hour in a period of 4 days. Her production stabilized at a level of about 92 and stayed there for the remainder of the 20 days. Clearly the induced forces on behavior from a strong subgroup may be more powerful than those induced by a progressive friendly management, and by personal needs for economic reward.

Evidence that the group influence often restricts the production of the individual members is available in almost every factory, but we should not assume that the group influence is restrictive only. Sometimes it aids productivity very decidedly. This has been proved by several laboratory experiments where group members participated wholeheartedly in the solution of complex problems such as code problems. Group effort was found to be more productive than solitary effort. The benefits of group participation are pronounced when problems require originality, insight, and the rejection of incorrect ideas. SOURCE: *Lester Coch and J. R. P. French, Jr., "Overcoming Resistance to Change,"* Human Relations, *Vol. I, No. 4 (1948), after Ronald Lippitt,* Current Trends in Social Psychology *(U. of Pittsburgh, reprinted 1951).*

Group Dynamics and Teamwork 73

popular. Any supervisor who has wanted to identify the employee who has made a serious error knows how difficult it is to be sure of the way the error occurred and who was responsible. The employees protect each other by giving the supervisor dubious information.

The group as a whole may work slowly to create the impression that the piece-rate is too low. This is likely to occur whenever the union is asking for a higher rate. Management, of course, usually knows what the workers are doing but the power of the group is often greater than that of management.

Responsiveness to group pressures differs among individuals

The evident influences of group dynamics in industry should not cause us to imagine that every member of the group is equally susceptible to group pressures.[9] In any industrial group, certain employees will invariably go along with majority opinion; others tend to identify and side with management in so far as they can without antagonizing their colleagues. Some few will even choose management's points of view at the risk of losing the friendship of their colleagues.

In factory production, every large employee group also contains a few isolates who are so individualistic that they do not care for the good will of the group. Many of these men are "experts" who achieve status through unique skills. Mechanics of this category typically demonstrate their superiority by handling intricate assignments with ease. They do not enter into group affairs. They do not compete for informal leadership. They satisfy their limited needs for group acceptance through job skills which other employees cannot or do not care to attain. Smart supervisors recognize the contributions of these isolates and give them special places to work, privileges to use certain restricted kinds of instruments, and recognitions that are not accorded to other workers. The other workers classify these isolates as "special" members who are not required to conform to all their group practices. Needless to say, these special workers lead a more lonely work life than the others.

---

[9] Solomon E. Asch, "Opinions and Social Pressure," *Scientific American*, November 1955, pp. 31-35, presents an excellent report on studies of differences in reaction to social pressure on the part of college students.

Informal groups and factional leaders

Employees normally develop certain interpersonal work relations which management has not specifically planned. They borrow tools from each other, give or withhold information to certain associates, counsel certain fellow workers, and they associate with some employees and ignore others during the non-work hours and days. They are attracted to some and repelled by other employees of the job environment. As a result of these and other influences, factions develop. As one writer has well stated in regard to the social satisfaction of the clique:

> Belonging to a clique affords certain social satisfactions and a sense of status. The office boys matching pennies in the stock room feel a kinship based upon mutual distaste for their betters in other departments who order them around. The executive secretaries find special satisfaction in being identified with their bosses who are deferred to by others in important positions. The typists can enjoy a sense of superiority over the file clerks, and they in turn are keenly aware of the social distance separating them from the messengers or office boys.
>
> These cliques have considerable influence over their members—sometimes more than the formal organization has; and they can invoke disciplinary measures.[10]

Some managements who discover the presence of strong cliques try to overcome their influence by transferring clique members to other departments. Others accept them and try to align them toward company goals.

An oft-mentioned example of informal leadership is the situation that arose when a new social worker came to work with juveniles of a settlement house. The social worker was conducting a recreational program in the building the first evening on the job. He could handle the juveniles in the building but his efforts were repeatedly thwarted by a few boys on the outside who purposely made noise and disturbed the indoor program. The social worker came out several times and appealed to the individual boys to let up because they were disturbing the others inside. The boys persisted in making a disturbance. Finally, a local oldtimer in the settlement house decided to put a stop to the nuisance. He came out to the boys, quickly recognized the leader of the group, and gave him responsibility for controlling the other boys of the group. The disturbance ended immediately. Factional leaders can be utilized to accomplish ends of benefit to the group and to related larger groups. Generally, most managements accept the fact that cliques exist and

---

[10] George S. Odiorne, "The Clique—A Frontier in Personnel Management," *Personnel,* American Management Association, Inc., September-October 1957, pp. 38-44.

cannot be ordered to disband even though they may be gradually weakened.

In nonunion plants, the cliques are watched in order to see whether a clique is becoming the nucleus of a formal union that will spearhead group hostility to management. If such cliques are developing, it usually means that management has failed in its communication responsibilities. The employees have not been given a participative relationship with management. Progressive managements therefore avoid making abrupt changes which affect the social organizations of the employees. Changes are planned to enlist the support of the cliques. Management also considers the physical facilities such as office space and telephones in regard to their significance to employees. These status symbols often have important bearings on the feelings of clique members.

The factional leader is looked to as the informal leader. To some extent he functions as a "big brother" in a family setting. He is expected to get action or follow through with the supervisor on problems or wishes of the group. He is an unofficial spokesman. Giving him special status symbols will add to his position as the informal leader.

Most managements expect each supervisor to know the cliques in his group. He should know his people well enough to identify each clique and its leaders.

The foreman who is socially alert realizes that he must get spontaneity of cooperation through the informal groups and their leaders. If he ignores their existence because they are not mentioned on the organization charts, he will become the victim of extra resistance. If he introduces technical changes or new methods of work without any attention to their effects on group relations, he will find that his employees are likely to develop mannerisms and attitudes which indicate that they harbor the feeling that they are being "pushed around." Those who have the feeling invariably discover ways of pushing in the opposite direction to that desired by management. They can slow down the production rate, lose tools, damage equipment, or "forget" to perform tasks which they would ordinarily perform.

According to the findings of Zaleznik's study of group behavior in a factory, work groups tend to provide themselves with stable social structures. To Zaleznik, it looked as if in the "work group" as in the "body" there is a "wisdom" greater than that which resides in any one of its parts.

> In the particular group he observed, for example, the intricate social patterns of behavior that had evolved and that seemed to be helping to resolve the potential sources of conflict that were present, seemed to him to have in them a wisdom far greater than anything management could have "cooked up."

This hypothesis has, of course, tremendous implications for management and administration. From it one could conclude that those managements who are overly concerned with what *they* can do to improve the productivity and satisfaction of work groups are not taking full advantage of what the groups, if not interfered with too much, can do better and more wisely themselves.

But let us not jump to this conclusion too quickly. Although it contains a half truth—and even perhaps a little more than half—it still does not quite entirely state the whole story . . . it is astonishing how most work groups accommodate themselves to the reality in which they have to survive and live. But this very adjustment may be also from the point of view of *adaptation* a failure in growth and development. Thus work groups that are "adjusted" at one level may also be "frozen" at another.[11]

This suggests that to overcome the dangers of a static social organization it is necessary for leadership to introduce challenges into the group. Furthermore, new members who come into the group, new equipment, and new supervisors as well as new work objectives are essential to overcoming "frozenness."

Group cohesiveness

Groups differ greatly in their "cohesiveness," the attraction they have for their members. Some are loosely-bound. Members drift in and out. The group may even disintegrate and vanish. Other groups are strong and command the active support of most members.

In a "high-cohesive" group, one strongly attractive to its members, the pressure to conform will be much greater than in a "low-cohesive" group.

Anyone who walks through a plant may observe in one department, that the men there are hostile to one another. They quarrel frequently. When an employee needs help, no one offers to assist him. If he asks for help, he gets the answer: "Yes, it's tough for you. You worry about it."

In contrast, the employees of a nearby department work together cheerfully. They help each other. They consult about ways to do the work. The employees obviously are enjoying the day's activities. They like each other. They are members of a cohesive or closely-knit group.

Some groups are more closely-knit than others. Formerly, it was assumed that a highly-cohesive or closely-knit group is likely to be more productive than a loosely-knit group.

The Institute for Social Research, University of Michigan, has made

---

[11] From F. J. Roethlisberger's Foreword in A. Zaleznik, *Worker Satisfaction and Development* (Boston: Harvard University, 1956), Division of Research, Graduate School of Business Administration.

outstanding research investigations which have thrown new light on this assumption. One approach has been to study the characteristics and performances of high-producing and low-producing work groups. In one series of researches the degrees of cohesiveness of different work groups were studied by asking each employee questions like: "Would you rather remain in this work group than move to another one even if you can get the same pay and do the same kind of work?"

Strangely, one of the findings from the study of cohesiveness was that the productivity of the cohesive work groups was only slightly higher than that of the groups that were not cohesive. Some of the closely-knit groups showed both very high and very low extremes of productivity.

Subsequent analysis showed that attitude toward their company was a key factor in understanding the exceptions to the teamwork rule. When highly cohesive work groups were convinced that the company really had their interests at heart, that they could rely on what they were told, and that achieving the company's goals would help them, they showed exceptional productivity.

Just the opposite happened when a cohesive working team felt insecure about its company. Robert L. Kahn, director of the Center's Organizational Behavior Program, amplifies this point: "We now recognize that a highly cohesive group can motivate its members to work toward whatever the group has defined as its goal. If the group has accepted high productivity as its goal, then its members will be high producers. But if the group is hostile to management, then its cohesiveness will be a most effective means of reducing and restricting productivity of its members." [12]

Every teacher who has taught many classes of students has recognized that some groups are much easier to teach than others. The members of the groups that are easy to teach usually have pleasant feelings toward each other and the institution. Team spirit, of course, is less strong in college than in business groups. It is most evident in industrial and military groups. When a supervisor has good teamwork, the group produces well and has good morale. Leadership is a pleasure.

Supervisory practices that have been found effective in developing teamwork in plants are: insisting that foremen shall listen patiently to individual workers; having employees participate in deciding which day each individual may have as his day "off"; making sure that each employee is content with his work; not transferring or lending employees

---

[12] See *Modern Management* (The Bureau of National Affairs, Inc., Washington, D.C.), Aug. 15, 1955, p. 2. The most comprehensive report of the Program's work in this area is Stanley Seashore, *Group Cohesiveness in the Industrial Work Group*, Monograph Series #14, Survey Research Center, The University of Michigan, December 1955.

to other departments; letting employees control their own rest-pause system; consulting and discussing the work with the employees; and giving them a sense of mutual responsibility and teamwork.[13]

The wise supervisor lets his men feel that they are important in getting the work done. He lets them feel that they are responsible for getting the work done. When possible he gives credit to the entire team. When errors occur, he does not pin the blame on any one person but lets the group know that he expects the men to help each other in preventing errors. If output of individuals can be measured, he encourages each individual to outstrip his own best performance rather than that of a teammate.[14]

One deterrent to teamwork is evident when individual employees engage in "petty politics" for the purpose of getting ahead. An executive dislikes the idea of people "buttering him up" because he knows that when employees are willing to sabotage each other in order to get ahead, team spirit has declined.

Developing company group feelings

Some subgroups within a company have strong group spirit but relatively little identification with or group feeling toward the company. Most managements like to have a strong company-group as well as subgroup feelings. They prefer to have employees feel that they belong to the company and gain a sense of security and satisfaction from membership in the total organization.

Generally, company-group feeling is not likely to be strong if members of subgroups have closed ranks against other subgroups such as departments. A company group cannot successfully compete with subgroups for the loyalty of their members. Management can, however, encourage cooperation among the subgroups. Company group feeling will be weak if the subgroups are in conflict. This means that management cannot build a strong company group by attacking or attempting to undermine an employee group such as the union. If management uses this kind of strategy, the employee groups will close ranks in opposition and the company-group feeling will be further weakened.

Company-group feeling will not be developed if management be-

---

[13] See Elton Mayo and George F. F. Lombard, *Teamwork and Labor Turnover in the Aircraft Industry of Southern California* (Boston: Bureau of Business Research, Harvard University Graduate School of Business Administration). Copyright © 1944 by the President and Fellows of Harvard College.

[14] See Robert Hershey, "Individualism vs. Teamwork," *The Management Review*, American Management Association, Inc., November 1957.

lieves that its objective is to do something *to* or *for* employees. Instead, management must give employees a sense of participation in dealing with company problems and of working toward the achievements that benefit everyone.

Disaster is an important influence in developing positive company-group feelings. When a chemical company, for example, has an explosion that wrecks the plant, the workers respond willingly above and beyond the requirements of their regular jobs. Some of our finest demonstrations of loyalty and helpfulness occur when a company suffers a disaster.

Production employees should be encouraged to work happily with other vitally important groups as the junior executives, salesmen, engineers, office workers, and supervisors.[15]

Companies that have strong company-group feelings among employees usually have executives and department heads who like each other. Routine problems have a way of solving themselves at the lower levels of the organization when the department heads enjoy working with each other.

In unionized plants, the management cannot usually blame the union when company group feeling is poor. Company loyalty varies among nonunion as well as among union plants. Management and employee groups are hostile to each other in unorganized as well as in organized plants. The results are equally costly. True, employees who are hostile often unionize before a strike. But low productivity, high labor turnover, and other products of dissatisfaction with the company probably cost American industry more than strikes.

The management that wants to instill the "we" feeling if it does not exist, cannot follow any simple formula. It develops naturally when the conditions are favorable. First of all, the members of top management must genuinely feel that they want the help of every person in the organization, that they are concerned about helping each employee achieve his purposes. When management provides that kind of leadership, the workers will feel very quickly that they and their work are important. They will work together to solve company problems and will identify their own happiness and welfare with the prosperity of the organization. They will trust and believe in the management that believes and trusts in them. The "we" spirit is a byproduct.

---

[15] See John Perry, "Human Relations in Small Industry" (Small Business Administration, Washington, D.C.), March 1954, pp. 15, 16.

Criticisms of the group emphasis

Certain leaders in industrial relations have criticized personnel programs and policies in industry today that are heavily group oriented. They fear that the need for individual recognition has almost disappeared from corporate thinking. They would like to have team spirit without losing individual identity.

A sociologist has voiced fears that our society has gone overboard in its reliance upon the group.[16] He sees in it the seeds of a new totalitarianism. He states:

> For the individual faced with a difficult decision or problem which requires careful thought, it is always much easier to join a group and throw the responsibility for deciding what to do on a leader. Since the whole group agrees, the decision receives the added sanction of social approval. . . . It is precisely the making of decisions by consensus, rather than by individual thought, that constitutes the danger of the worship of the group. It leads ominously to conformity and the feeling that the right opinion is the one the group thinks is right. Carried far enough, it leads to the identification of mental health with group conformity.

A typical reviewer of the situation has concluded, however, that it hardly seems fair to condemn group participation as a sinister device to secure group conformity and to submerge the individual. Rather, most observers of management in this country would agree that we have hardly gone far enough in our efforts to tap the thinking of the group.[17]

In actual practice, most American business managements are still emphasizing the individual in their personnel relations. They have increased fringe benefits such as group insurance and union relations, but the individual has not been forgotten. After all, the executive still selects a specific employee rather than a group for promotion. Of the two approaches for the improvement of employee relations, the group and the individual, the factors in effective group behavior have been the ones neglected far more than those that treat the employee as an individual.

You can sharpen your perceptiveness of group dynamics

As previously stated, one of the main objectives in your study of human relations is the acquiring of an increased sensitivity to the forces

---

[16] Edward Gross, "Group Worship—The New Orthodoxy?" *Adult Leadership,* April 1956.

[17] See Julius E. Eitington, "On the Line," *Personnel Administration,* July-August 1956, pp. 41, 42.

in the behavior of others. This increased sensitivity is just as essential in regard to the dynamics in group as in individual behavior. If you have this objective in mind as you study people in business you will see many examples of group dynamics and thereby enrich the ways in which you function with others.

As stated in the early part of the chapter, people do not follow in entirety the relationships visualized by the chart makers, but this does not mean that organizational charts have no value. The better view is that good organizational structure is basic to effective functioning but you should be alert to observe the ways in which group dynamics function in accordance with the charts and the situations when they do not. Reports of many helpful studies of the subject appear in our journals from time to time.

COLLATERAL READINGS

For All Students

Hershey, Robert, "Individualism vs. Teamwork," *The Management Review*, American Management Association, Inc., November 1957. Members of the group must be given sufficient incentive to have them adapt their goals to the good of the organization.

McHugh, Keith S., "Developing the Management Team," *The Management Review*, American Management Association, Inc., January 1958. The author discusses college recruitment, the boss as coach, leadership, and job-related vs. "new horizon" courses.

For Advanced Students

Leavitt, Harold J., *Managerial Psychology: An Introduction to Individuals, Pairs, and Groups in Organization*. Chicago: The University of Chicago Press, 1958. An analysis of the psychology of these units from the managerial standpoint.

Stogdill, Ralph M., *Individual Behavior and Group Achievement*. New York: Oxford University Press, 1959. Presents an integration of the scattered literature concerning group influences on behavior. Develops a theory of organization achievement.

For Men in Business

Sayles, Leonard R., *Behavior of Industrial Work Groups: Prediction and Control*. New York: John Wiley & Sons, Inc., 1958. A field study of 300 work groups shows why some groups are "always troublesome" while others are cooperative, and suggests ways management can predetermine worker reaction to supervision.

Stanley, J. D., "How to Live with Worker Cliques," *Personnel Journal*, June 1958. Informal groups are constantly exerting substantial influence upon the performance of personnel functions. Describes countermeasures that may be used.

1. Define the term group dynamics. How has study of the subject come about?
2. What are sociograms and how are they useful in interpreting group behavior studies? Who is the founder of "sociometry"?
3. List some reasons why people belong to groups.
4. Describe the functions of the Research Center for Group Dynamics, University of Michigan.
5. In the Walker study of the steel plant, what factor was found to be one of the main reasons for worker dissatisfaction with the introduction of automation?
6. What are the functions of the factional leader of a group?
7. How do workers limit production when they wish to do so?
8. What is meant by group cohesiveness? In what ways do high-cohesive and low-cohesive groups differ in production performance?
9. In what ways should a company encourage or discourage the formation and behavior of subgroups among the employees?
10. According to one sociologist, what is a danger of overemphasis on the group in our present society?
11. Name some of the supervisory practices that have been found effective in developing teamwork.
12. Of all the ideas presented in the chapter, which ones are of special interest or value to you?
13. What did the chapter contribute to your future relations with (a) the men who supervise your work, (b) employees whom you may supervise?

PROBLEMS AND PROJECTS

For All Students

1. Make a study of the psychological relationships that exist between the members of some group that you know well. Use the sociometric technique. If you were to supervise these members, how would your knowledge be of value to you?
2. Think of the students whom you know. Which ones are factional leaders? How do they exert their informal leaderships? Contrast them with some isolates.

For Advanced Students

3. Search the available literature for additional studies of group dynamics. Look particularly for reports by the Research Center for Group Dynamics, University of Michigan. Scan the tables of contents of business journals for recent articles.
4. The National Training Laboratories has been developing its unique approach to leadership growth. Reports of their conferences are published periodically. You may also wish to write to them at the Na-

tional Education Association, 1201 16th St., N.W., Washington 6, D.C., for available booklets and bibliographies.

For Men in Business

5. It is easy for an alert employee in industry to recognize the groups in his company. Here is a list of questions supplied by one writer: [18]

(a) How many groups and subgroups can you think of in your own business organization?

(1) The entire company	(11) The natives of the community
(2) Top management	
(3) The office staff	(12) The oldtimers
(4) The office girls	(13) The female factory employees
(5) The salesmen	
(6) Junior executives	(14) The men who bowl together
(7) Foremen	
(8) Union members	(15) The members of the same church
(9) Members of factions within the union	
	(16) The shop stewards
(10) Employees in each department (welders, cutters, etc.)	(17) The ex-G.I.'s
	(18) Others?

(b) How many groups and subgroups can you think of to which you belong, inside the plant and out?

(c) How would you rate each of these groups, so far as each concerns you personally?

(1) "Belonging" is essential to me. Can't think of anything that would drive me out.

(2) "Belonging" is very important. It would take something really big to drive me out.

(3) I want very much to "belong," but I can think of some possibilities that would make me willing to get out.

(4) "Belonging" is a good idea.

(5) Don't care much one way or the other.

(6) I'm not sure I really "belong" there anyway.

---

[18] John Perry, *Human Relations in Small Industry,* published by Small Business Administration, Washington, D.C., March 1954.

Whenever you as a stranger come into a new group of people such as factory or office workers, the people there are likely to react to you by saying to themselves, "Is he one of us?" And when you come into a new clubroom, religious congregation, or student body, the people there have the same kind of question as part of their feelings toward you.

If they were able to verbalize their feelings more fully, they would say, "What are his identifications—do his feelings really make him one of us?"

Identification means that the individual feels that he is part of another person, situation, or institution. In some cases, he feels that he is part of the purpose of the institution, activity, or person. The process is one of feeling rather than of intellect.

When you attend a football game, you not only cheer for your favorite team but you also "play" the game—you "become" the player who is carrying the ball. You do the things the team is trying to do.

When you are in the theater, you identify yourself with the hero, fight his battles, endure his hardships, conquer the villain, and finally marry the heroine. You are, for the time being, more than a mere observer or onlooker—you are the admired character in the picture or the play, psychologically speaking. If instruments were attached to your body to measure your bodily reactions, they would show that you make many incipient movements that give reality to your imaginary acting.

6

Identification
and Status Symbols

Every person in business, particularly the leader, should be conscious of the psychodynamic influences of identification. It is essential to certain needs of the individual such as the sense of belongingness and achievement by membership in a group, or on a team. Every sport fan knows that the successful team is the one in which the members identify themselves with the team as a whole. Each player does not play an individual game but integrates his playing with that of the entire team. Even though business is not a game, the team spirit and the ability of individual members of the team to identify with the team are important. Employees then use the pronouns "we" and "our" rather than "they" and "their" when they refer to the company.

Through the achievements of other persons, groups of persons, and institutions, the individual may reduce tensions arising from his own inadequacies. Identification may be made with social and political organizations or reform movements. An individual may also identify himself with his material possessions, as exemplified by the housewife who cleans and protects her home so well that it becomes uncomfortable to others. Possessions such as the house, clothing, automobile, office desk, or factory machine may be used to gain many subconscious satisfactions as well as obvious prestige values.

Positive identification is one of human nature's most valuable means for enjoyment. It is a recognizable theme in the development of every well-balanced happy person; it is absent from the mental lives of certain patients in hospitals for the mentally ill. In other patients, the identifications appear in an extreme form as in those who identify themselves so fully with heroes or villains that they become "Napoleons," "Messiahs," "Hitlers," or "Jesse Jameses." The well-adjusted person is one who has learned the art of identifying himself intelligently with the people and the tasks of his daily contacts. The factors that involve growth in his mental life are integrated into an effective working unit. He feels at home with his associates, his supervisors, his community, his family. Unlike the cynic, he finds the world in which he lives reasonably admirable because he has identified himself with its admirable aspects.

Identification is fundamental to a happy marriage and married life. Ideally and typically, two people marry, not mainly for sexual gratification but for more complete identification of their emotional and spiritual selves. In the course of the evolution of man, mankind has developed many institutions in order to enable its members to identify themselves with satisfying personalities. In addition to marriage, we have the church, which aims to have the individual identify himself with the cosmic mind.

The good citizen identifies himself with his community and his nation. The well-adjusted student identifies himself with his college, his fellow students, and his teachers. In business, the happy effective employee identifies with his fellow workers, his supervisor, the management, the customers, and the company as a whole.

Intelligent business executives try to assist their employees in identifying themselves not only with the company, but also with the community in which they live, the institutions of which they are a part, and the social groups in which they are nurtured and have received their racial heritage. The true business leader of men not only directs employees' work efforts but he also helps them to appreciate their place in the scheme of things. He does this by pointing out the trends in the business, changes in methods, and the problems of today that challenge them to excel in their development of new and better products. He enables them to realize that the benefits of the mechanisms and activities of business enlarge their perspectives and enrich their lives through service to customers. People live more happily as a result of ego involvement in the products or services they help to produce and sell.

How identifications are acquired

Numerous and complex influences enter into the development of a person's identifications and no one can explain every phase in their development. When we want to help a person develop positive identifications with a company or a person, we can contribute toward that end by means of the following procedures:

1. We must provide goals for the individual that are worthwhile to him. When management talks about the things that interest management—higher profits, lower costs, and better competitive position—the employee is not impressed. Such goals are not especially worthwhile to him as an employee. To make the goals worthwhile, they should be stated in terms such as the greater number of people, usually customers, who are benefited by the bigger production and lower costs.

2. The people who benefit should be the kind whom the worker likes or respects, usually people who are similar to himself—workers rather than stockholders. This principle has proven its value time and again in advertising. Housewives who view television commercials identify readily with other housewives of refinement but not with society matrons, crude comic characters, or sexy models. Children lose interest in programs when there is an emphasis on adults. Instead, they like to hear children's voices and to see children of their own age participating in children's activities.

The parent who tells stories to a child knows that the boy or girl wants to hear about children of the same age. The child wants to identify himself with someone not older, nor markedly younger, but a personality like himself.

Similarly, television commercials that sell men's products should portray masculine men rather than "eggheads." If the viewer or reader can identify himself with the users of the product, if he can see himself in the situation portrayed in the advertising, then his feelings become involved and the process works toward believability and acceptance. It is identification that makes it "for me."

3. Identification is developed through shared experiences. Its strongest forms are often brought about through personal sacrifice as in the case of soldiers who have been together in combat or in rigorous training as exemplified in our Marine Corps. Their shared hardships cause them to identify firmly with members of their group. In like manner, children who are reared in families where all members of the family share to the point of personal sacrifice for the family life often have deeper family loyalty than children of families where the parents do all the sacrificing. In business, the executive who inspires employees to sacrifice their own comfort in order to make a contribution to the business develops far stronger identification of the employees with the company than the executive who thinks mainly in terms of what he or the company can do for the employees. The identifications of most persons are intensified when they learn how to "give of themselves" to ideals, persons, and institutions outside themselves. Employees who buy stock in the employing company usually improve the strength of their identification.

This means that management must give the employee ego involvement on the part of the employee toward the products and services of the company. One method is to challenge the employee to make or help make the best pies, or television receivers, or whatever the company makes, that have ever been made. Most workers want to be good craftsmen and worthwhile members of society. We fail them when we do not supervise them in that spirit. Business and profits must be thought of in this manner by management.

Of course this means that managements have to learn how to give the worker a feeling of colleagueship in the business, not as an "expense" that can be eliminated. The inability of managements to give the employee emotional as well as economic identification with the company has been a strong influence in causing employees to form associations of their own and through those associations, to compel employers to bargain with them.

When an employee identifies with his company, he learns to realize that the management is similar to the head of a family—the head must withhold some desired rewards and earnings in order to distribute the available income where it is needed most. The head of a family cannot afford to give each child everything he wants, nor can a management give each employee everything he wants.

4. Constant communication and participation are essential to the development of strong identification with a company. That is one reason why managements give attention to such programs. The frequent exchange of information between the company and the employee are necessary for strengthened identification.

5. Symbols of identification are helpful. Think of all the badges, diplomas, and titles which are sought and treasured by the people in business. This topic is so large and varied in its implications that special attention will be given to it in this chapter. We should, however, also recognize some of the dangers in the misuse or overemphasis of identification before we treat the topic of symbols in business.

Limitations and dangers in identification

The able executive who has insight into the processes of identification among his employees is careful to see that they clearly differentiate between interest in him and interest in their work. The executive who enables employees to identify themselves with his personality should also help them to transfer their identifications to other tasks, persons, and institutions. He may direct them so well that they wish to become a boss "like him." Later, the employees may find they are really interested not in the intrinsic values of their tasks but in the person who happened to supervise them. Each worker should be led to find the intrinsic values of his work and to feel that his work makes him a worthwhile member of the organization to which he belongs.

Those workers who identify too blindly with a superior and fail to develop themselves in relation to the work are likely to be among the first laid off in a recession. Generally, the weaker men in a department are the ones laid off first but their weakness as employees may be the result of overidentification. Such men cater to the department head as a person. They coast in their work because they feel secure in their relationship with the chief. In contrast, the man who consistently does very good work is likely to find that he is needed regardless of recessions and organizational changes that may occur. Catering to the boss as a person and coasting in regard to the work seldom provide as much security as doing good work.

When men are chosen for supervisory positions, consideration is given to the directions of their strongest identifications in employee-management relations. Anyone who observes the degrees of identification between an executive and his foreman will notice that some foremen identify strongly with their boss but keep their subordinates at a distance. They tend to be critical of the workers and feel that the workers are not trying to do a good job. Such a foreman is not interested in his employees as individuals. They, in turn, sense that he is aloof and disinterested in them. When they are in his office or associate socially with him, they feel uncomfortable. They notice that he seeks contacts with his superiors when on company premises as well as at outside community social affairs. Sociologists often use the term, "social distance" to describe these relationships between the executive, the foreman, and the employees. Ideally, of course, all three identify with each other—the social distances between them can be minimal.

When a college senior is interviewed as an applicant for a management training program, the directions of the applicant's identifications are considered. If the senior identifies only with workers or those whom he considers underprivileged, there is little value in hiring him as a management trainee. On the other hand, if he identifies with management so strongly that he lacks any genuine interest in workers, he might develop into a good controller but a poor supervisor or personnel manager. The direction of a person's identifications help to shape his career and should be recognized early by the individual who wants to enjoy his life in business.

How can a person recognize his identifications? The answer is "The same ways in which a skilled employment interviewer recognizes them in an applicant." He knows from answers to questions such as the following: "With whom or with what people have you associated in the past?" "What kinds of people do you like to work with on the job?" "Where would you like to live?" "To what organizations do you now belong and which ones do you intend to join?" "What kind of job do you expect to hold ten years hence? Twenty years from now?" "What diplomas, badges or symbols of achievement do you hope to earn in the years ahead?"

SYMBOLS

A man's identifications are often revealed by the symbols he desires. Symbols play a far greater role in the mental life than most persons appreciate. Actually, people think and react in terms of symbols rather than logical ideas. Ideas stated in the abstract are meaningful to only the select few who have trained themselves to analyze and evaluate abstractions in the field to which the abstractions apply. The "select few" are exemplified by the researcher who has specialized in a specific science. Ability to think in the abstract is limited to the area in which the thinker has specialized. That is one reason why a trained scientist can, for example, think well in the field of physics, but in the field of politics he may react with little regard for facts, and base his thinking mostly on symbols and his own unconscious motivations.

Symbols are also necessary for logical thinking as in mathematics. The educated and the noneducated need them. If we hear or see the words "United States," we visualize the term as a map or a flag. *Peace* is often symbolized by a dove, *innocence* by a happy child, and *silence* by a forest scene. A flag is a dyed piece of cloth and an engagement ring is a metal band on a girl's left hand, but we attach deep emotions to them because of what they symbolize. Each person acquires his own unique set of symbols but certain symbols are so common and significant in human relations in business that we should become aware of them.

The symbols of executive status in most business concerns are the following:

1. An organization chart that bears his name
2. Name listed in company telephone directory
3. A private office
4. Stenographic help
5. Access to rooms for holding meetings and private conversations with subordinates
6. No requirement to punch a time clock
7. Invitations to meet with other management members at conferences, dinners, social events, etc.
8. Opportunities to attend conventions, visit other plants, etc., to enlarge knowledge and grasp of his job
9. Introduction to plant visitors
10. Facilities comparable to those of other management members with respect to parking, dining, and washrooms.

In a lighter vein, "A Ready Guide for Evaulating Executives," by K. B. Bernhardt, Director of Personnel, Monsanto Chemical Company, is shown on page 92. Among the outward and visible signs of achievement at different organizational levels listed in this "guide" are briefcases, office desks, office tables, carpeting, plant stands, vacuum water bottles, library, shoe-shine service, parking spaces, and luncheon menus. No mention is made of salary, titles or clothes. Lists of this kind are, for the most part, not intended to be taken seriously, but the importance of such signs of status is well recognized—the very fact that they are ridiculed testifies to this. Even though the individuals in an organization

VISIBLE APPURTENANCES	TOP DOGS	V.I.P.s	BRASS	NO. 2s	EAGER BEAVERS	HOI POLLOI
BRIEF CASES	None -- they ask the questions	Use backs of envelopes	Someone goes along to carry theirs	Carry their own -- empty	Daily, carry their own filled with work	Too poor to own one
DESKS, Office	Custom Made (to order)	Executive Style (to order)	Type A "Director"	Type B "Manager"	Cast-offs from No. 2s	Yellow Oak -- or cast-offs from Eager Beavers
TABLES, Office	Coffee tables	End tables or decorative wall tables	Matching tables Type A	Matching tables Type B	Plain work table	None -- lucky to have own desk
CARPETING	Nylon-- 1 inch pile	Nylon-- 1 inch pile	Wool-Twist (with pad)	Wool-Twist (without pad)	Used wool pieces--sewed	Asphalt tile
PLANT STANDS	Several -- Kept filled with strange exotic plants		Two -- Repotted whenever they take a trip	One medium-sized Repotted annually during vacation	Small Repotted when plant dies	May have one in the department or bring their own from home
VACUUM WATER BOTTLES	Silver	Silver	Chromium	Plain painted	Coke machine	Water fountains
LIBRARY	Private collection	Autographed or complimentary books and reports	Selected references	Impressive titles on covers	Books everywhere	Dictionary
SHOE SHINE SERVICE	Every morning at 10:00	Every morning at 10:15	Every day at 9:00 or 11:00	Every other day	Once a week	Shine their own
PARKING SPACE	Private in front of office	In plant garage	In company garage- if enough seniority	In company properties-some- where	On the parking lot	Anywhere they can find a space -- if they can afford a car
LUNCHEON MENU	Cream Cheese on Whole Wheat Buttermilk and Indigestion Tablets	Cream of Celery Soup Chicken Sandwich (White Meat) Milk	Fruit Cup - Spinach Lamb Chop - Peas Ice Cream - Tea	Orange Juice Minute Steak French Fries - Salad Fruit Cup - Coffee	Tomato Juice Chicken Croquettes Mashed Potatoes Peas - Bread Chocolate Cream Pie Coffee	Clam Chowder Frankfurter & Beans Rolls and Butter Raisin Pie A'la Mode Two Cups of Coffee

often ridicule them, they are evident and highly valued within most organizations.

Salary is an outstanding indicator of status in the organization. According to an American Management Association survey of executive compensation, when the president's salary is used as a base of 100 per cent, salary of the top marketing executive is 60 per cent; the top financial executive, about 55 per cent; the top production executive gets around 50 per cent; and the industrial relations executive receives, on the average, 27 per cent of the salary paid his company's president.[1]

Titles are important in giving a person appropriate recognition in regard to his job. Each company has its unique method of determining job titles but in most companies, the use of *General* before another title as exemplified in *General Manager,* indicates superior status. *Director* is often applied to a staff rather than a line position, and is in some cases analogous in status to *General.*

Titles are often established to satisfy the ego needs of specific department heads. If the head of a department believes that other people in the company downgrade his department in their thinking, he is apt to ask management to change the name of his department and to give him a high-sounding title. Every large organization is likely to experience special requests of this kind. Some department heads will request a change in title for a subordinate in order that he may be granted a salary increase. Others give the subordinate a better title *instead* of a pay increase. Many executives, too, prefer to have a title such as vice president, rather than receive a substantial raise with no title change. Using status symbols in this respect often creates problems, however, as evidenced by the reorganization that one large company made in its newly decentralized areas.[2] In order to bolster the feeling of individual responsibility, they renamed the heads of the areas and their functional subordinates divisional presidents and vice presidents, respectively. In time, the "presidents" became more and more independent in their work, and serious interdivisional problems arose. Top management hesitated to enforce the authority it had more or less abdicated, because of its possible demoralizing effect on the status-conscious divisional presidents. As a result, the company suffered great losses before a new chief executive regained proper control of the subordinate units.

Certainly, many titles are not indicative of the true ability or status of the holder. The only safe procedure for a newcomer to a company

---

[1] See *Personnel*, American Management Association, Inc., March-April 1958, p. 4.

[2] See Arch Patton, "What Makes Executives Run?" *Dun's Review and Modern Industry*, September 1957, p. 36f. Copyright © 1957 by Dun & Bradstreet Publications Corporation. See also *The Management Review*, American Management Association, Inc., November 1957.

is to inquire about the functions of individuals who hold various titles. Even then, the inconsistencies are likely to be more pronounced than the consistencies. Most difficult of all, some top managements avoid the use of any titles as much as possible.

White-collar versus blue-collar

Office and shop employees are easily distinguished on the streets as well as on the company premises. When we walk on a street of a northern city, we note that the responsible office and professional worker tends to wear heavy shoes, padded coat, white shirt, drab-colored suit, and a constricting necktie. These clues to his status indicate that he thinks of himself as a person of responsibility. In contrast, the worker who wears slacks and other clothing suitable for the factory rather than the office is assumed to be a wage-earner rather than a salaried employee. Clothes indicate a level of achievement, or at least the general occupational level with which the wearer identifies himself.

White-collar people are expected to dress somewhat somberly; their working attire is not a uniform, nor is it different from clothing generally suitable for street wear. Management men often "dress down" for those occasions when their attire might cause others to think of them as snobs. This occurs at company picnics and mixed social affairs. Also when a labor union contract is signed, the newspaper pictures of the signing often show the union representatives dressed in somber "Sunday best" suits, white shirts, and ties, but the company men are seen without their coats and with their sleeves rolled up. Apparently, the union representatives try to establish their equality by dressing as they think their management counterparts do. The management representatives, on the other hand, "dress down" for the occasion in order to avoid giving any impression that they think of themselves as superior to the workers.[3]

The new employee soon senses the kinds of clothes appropriate for him to wear. He realizes that he may remain an outsider if, unknowingly, he violates the group norm. Very few managements have ever attempted to encourage or enforce the wearing of any specific clothing except for safety purposes—executives realize that each employee will adopt the group norm. If he deviates markedly from the norm, he indicates that he identifies himself with those occupational classes whose symbols he chooses.

---

[3] See Frank J. Jasinski, "How They Dress on the Job: Clues to the Informal Organization," *Personnel*, American Management Association, Inc., November-December 1957.

Payroll classifications often indicate status. Generally, executives, staff specialists, office workers, foremen and supervisors are on a salary basis. In some companies, executives are paid once a month; office workers twice a month; and factory workers once a week. Those who are on the monthly payroll need not punch a time clock. Some differentiation may also be made as to whether the salaried employee is on the home office or on the local plant payroll. Those on the home office payroll usually have the more important positions and greater job security. A beginner in the company may progress from an hourly payroll to a weekly, to a semimonthly, to a monthly at the local plant, and finally to a monthly payroll of the home or main office. Complaints about pay and requests for higher rates often indicate a desire for greater recognition as to the payroll classification—higher status—rather than a need for more money.

Tools and tool boxes of factory workers indicate status. Zaleznik in his study of workers in an instrument factory found that job title and pay rate were not the only symbols of difference in job status among the men. In the machinist trade, the tradition for expressing job status differences through the kind of tool box the machinist owns is evident. A first-rate experienced machinist owns a tool box filled with various hand tools and instruments. It is usually located conveniently near his most frequent work position. The machinist's work coat or apron may also indicate status.[4]

Authority symbols and fear of authority

Many a worker fears every individual who symbolizes authority. Logically, there is no need for the fear; psychologically there is. The fearful worker does not fear the general manager as a person but what the general manager represents. He is a symbol of authority. As a symbol, he represents the power of giving and withholding privileges, even imposing punishment.

The desire to please others and to avoid punishment is learned by children long before they become employees. The child is rewarded, admonished, and punished by parents and other adults through thousands of instances that eventually condition him against all symbols of authority. The child soon learns that he must please authority to get what he wants. Eventually this idea becomes an integral and a partially unconscious influence in his character. It carries over into adult life. Even though the boss is a genial, easygoing person, this kind of employee

---

[4] See A. Zaleznik, *Worker Satisfaction and Development* (Boston: Harvard Business School, Division of Research, 1956), pp. 20, 21.

feels that he must please the boss to get a promotion and obtain desired privileges such as a trip to an industry convention.

The influences of authority symbols and fears of authority are often discussed in relation to political life. In World War II, these predisposing influences were analyzed and reported in journals and newspapers. German Nazis and anti-Nazis were studied by psychiatrists. One study, for example, found that anti-Nazis oftener than not grew up in families where the maternal influence was stronger than the paternal. An Army psychiatrist who had made extensive studies in postwar Germany conducted three- to four-hour, or sometimes longer, interviews with 150 German men, 90 of whom were presumptive anti-Nazis, 40 confessed Nazis, and the remainder borderline cases. He investigated family and other influences which make men either total conformists ready to accept authoritarian leadership, or individuals capable of forming their own judgments and acting accordingly.

According to this psychiatrist, the average German father is a "respektsperson"—a term used frequently by Nazis in describing their own fathers. As one Nazi said: "With one look in his eye he made us children obey him." Corporal punishment, administered almost as a ritual by the father, was the rule rather than the exception in the German home.[5]

Obviously, home influences such as these are likely to have some bearing on a person's reactions to authority and authority symbols.

"Status anxiety"

Certain individuals on all levels in industry are constantly in a state of emotional disturbance over their status. They compare their position relative to others. An inadequately adjusted, worrisome person of this kind notes whether a colleague gets more recognition from the boss than he does. He expects others to recognize his proper status, to use his correct title whenever possible, and to confer with him about every problem that is even remotely related to his functions. This kind of tense individual is likely to be an ambitious person who has failed to achieve the level he thinks he deserves. As a frustrated person, he is apt to exhibit various nervous disorders such as insomnia and feelings of persecution.

Of course the effects of these anxieties become evident to others.

---

[5] See Dorothy Dunbar Bromley, "Maternal Influence Seen Factor in Creating German Anti-Nazis," *New York Herald Tribune*, April 28, 1946.

Executives tend to withhold additional responsibilities from such persons. Indeed, one of the most common questions asked about an individual who is under consideration for advancement to additional responsibility is, "Can he take it in stride or would the extra responsibility increase his anxieties too greatly?"

Top executives note the ways in which junior executives react to and use the titles they have earned in the past.

Jim Bright, for example, is proud of the fact that he has been given the title of Assistant Traffic Manager of his company. If someone asks him, in the presence of his boss, what his job is, he will be expected to say, "Oh, I help Mr. Bye in purchasing." Jim's direct mention of his own title would indicate too much anxiety about its importance.

Many top executives grant titles to subordinates, but assume that the titles will be taken seriously only by the holder's wife! Franklin J. Lunding, Jewel Tea Co. chairman, has been reported as once remarking that if he found a manager in the organization markedly interested in his own title, "then he doesn't work here any more."

The junior executive should play down his own title, but he may, under certain circumstances, play up the titles and prerogatives of others, particularly those persons who suffer from status anxiety. Most mature, well-adjusted executives are unconcerned about their own titles; when titles are emphasized, they are annoyed rather than pleased.

The smart junior executive who functions for his boss at such times as vacation periods is always careful to make known that he is only acting for the boss temporarily. He keeps himself in the background and the boss in the foreground. After all, the boss, not the temporary fill-in, is responsible for whatever goes wrong as well as for what happens during his absence.

Prestige symbols of the public

Symbols of success or failure are highly personal, vary with the individual, and change from one generation to the next. In former generations, the presence of a maid in the home was a status symbol; later, it was the ownership of a piano. Then the automobile became the number-one status symbol. However, a car is no longer the prestige item it was years ago. When 1,100 advertising executives were asked whether the automobile is losing its role as a status symbol, slightly more than half (51%) said yes, but 40 per cent insisted that a car is still number one among status symbols. The remaining 9 per cent believed that the

Evolution of an ad man
(1940 to   )

1940 ...the publication's fault about the key address.

Sincerely,

SMITH, JONES, INC.

J. P. Shmart

J. P. Shmart, Copy Dept.

1948 ...due to the inexperience of a cub copywriter.

Very truly yours,

SMITH, JONES, INC.

Joseph P. Shmart

Joseph P. Shmart, Chief Copywriter

1955 ...and will get the copy chief on the ball.

Cordially yours,

SMITH, JONES, INC.

J. Purloine Shmart

J. Purloine Shmart, Acc't. Executive

1959 ...to assure you a new man on the account.

Cordially,

SMITH, JONES, SHMART, INC.

Jos. P. Shmart

Jos. P. Shmart, Vice-President

LAST ...agree that we need new faces on the board.

Best Regards to Your Wife,

SHMART, SMITH, JONES, INC.

Hunter   *Jos. P. Shmart by E.L.*

Jos. P. Shmart, President

SOURCE: *by Hunter,* Printers' Ink (*December 11, 1953*), p. 39.

automobile is still a status symbol but in another form—the prestige comes in owning a sports car, a foreign car, or in being a two-car family.[6] Ownership of a smart-looking late-model car is the rule rather than the exception in America. Hence, consumers are turning to other products

---

[6] See *Tide,* January 25, 1957, p. 33.

or services for status symbols such as beautiful suburban homes, power boats, hi-fi sets, expensive furs, and travel.

These prestige symbols are mostly possessions or privileges of a material nature. In addition, the public also recognizes prestige symbols of a nonmaterial nature such as achievements in the professions and the fine arts. These are rated higher than those dependent upon income.

Can businessmen minimize the importance of minor-value prestige symbols?

Many executives realize that the public and employees overemphasize the values of prestige symbols. They would prefer that recognition should be given to true achievement rather than symbols of achievement. After all, certain symbols are often acquired more or less accidentally and without demonstration of great merit. This is a very common situation in the universities—certain possessors of degrees have fulfilled the formal requirements for the degree but have failed to get an education.

A few business leaders try to overcome the spurious values of status symbols by ignoring the prestige privileges they have earned. One corporation president, for example, each morning pilots his car into the least desirable spot in the company's parking lot—a place reserved for him at his own request.

The chairman of a giant midwestern company guides his conspicuously old low-priced car past the rows of gleaming new models, owned by his subordinates, to his regular space.

These and other top executives are trying to downgrade that much maligned but omnipresent appurtenance of corporate power—the status symbol. They are fighting a losing battle.[7]

Most members of the public and employees have deepseated psychological needs for status symbols. Many corporate leaders also defend them as an aid to discipline and operating efficiency. Status symbols in business underscore the lines of authority and indicate to employees where power and responsibility are centered. In addition, status privileges provide "fringe benefits" for executives and employees, benefits which may be more attractive than taxable increases in pay.

Even though symbols have significance only in accordance with the meanings that the seekers and holders give them, they are essential to the emotional well-being of most members of the human race. It is neces-

---

[7] See "The Rising Status of Status Symbols," *The Management Review,* American Management Association, Inc., December 1957, p. 32.

sary, therefore, for the supervisor to become perceptive in regard to what specific symbols mean to the individuals with whom he works.

COLLATERAL READINGS

For All Students

Dubin, Robert, editor, *Human Relations in Administration.* Englewood Cliffs, N.J.: Prentice-Hall, Inc., 1951. Chapter 15, "Functions of Status Systems in Formal Organizations," by Chester I. Barnard, is a classic in its field.

Smith, Henry Clay, *Psychology of Industrial Behavior.* New York: McGraw-Hill Book Company, Inc., 1955. Pages 58-68 deal with status in terms of man's belonging needs.

For Advanced Students

Boulding, Kenneth E., "Symbols for Capitalism," *Harvard Business Review,* January-February 1959. Discusses the need for changing the meanings of certain capitalistic symbols if we want to strengthen our present politico-economic system.

Dubin, Robert, *The World of Work.* Englewood Cliffs, N.J.: Prentice-Hall, Inc., 1958. Chapters 2 and 5 describe some power and status relations in business. The ends of chapters list helpful annotated bibliographies for behavioral science studies.

For Men in Business

Cantor, D. C., "Setting Up and Maintaining an Effective Job-Title Program," *Personnel,* American Management Association, Inc., November-December 1957. Presents principles for management in setting up job title programs.

Foegen, Joseph H., "Time to Scrap 'Rank and File'?" *Personnel Journal,* March 1957. The author suggests "production workers" as a substitute and gives his reasons.

QUESTIONS ON THE CHAPTER

1. How does identification affect the behavior of the individual?
2. Discuss the relationship between shared experiences and identification in connection with business.
3. Why do management interviewers consider an applicant's identifications when he is being considered for hiring?
4. Comment on some dangers of overidentification.
5. Is it possible for an individual to know his identifications? If so, how?
6. Why are titles in many companies not indicative of true ability or status?
7. In what respects do payroll classifications indicate status?
8. Why do some adults fear individuals who symbolize authority?
9. Describe some characteristics of an individual suffering from "status anxiety."

10. How should a junior executive react to the use of his own title?
11. Explain the two classifications of prestige symbols.
12. Why are prestige and status symbols essential to most individuals?
13. Of the ideas presented in the chapter, which ones are of special interest or value to you?
14. What did the chapter contribute to your future relations with (a) the men who supervise your work, (b) employees whom you may supervise?

PROBLEMS AND PROJECTS

For All Students

1. Identification involves feelings that are deeper than admiration or respect. A mother identifies with her son even though she may not admire his behavior. She usually remains loyal to her identification. Can you apply this idea to a business concern or institution that has some personal meanings for you?
2. Discuss status symbols sought by students of your institution. Are the students who seek the status symbols more loyal to the institution than those who do not seek them? What are some of the disadvantages of status symbols?

For Advanced Students

3. Make a study of status symbols found in authoritarian *versus* those in democratic forms of governments. Do status symbols seem to enable the holders to flaunt power? Do your findings offer suggestions for business managements?
4. Some studies of people who live in suburban communities indicate that they are especially active in community organizations. Many of the members work for large companies and are moved about frequently. As a result they lack roots. Activity in the local organizations gives them roots. Make a study of this thesis.

For Men in Business

5. Which departments or employees of a specific company you know are downgraded in the thinking of some executives and employees? What factors brought it about? Do these downgraded departments have any outstanding executives with whom employees can identify themselves? How might the situation be improved?
6. The supervisor who lacks identification with his management is likely to show it when he explains to an employee that management denied his request such as the desire for a title or increased pay. He blames the top management. Give an example from your experiences with supervisors to describe the difference between the supervisor who does identify with management and the one who does not.

COMMUNICATION IS MORE THAN TALKING WITH OR WRITING TO people—it is the exchange of meanings. It uses many media and methods: face-to-face conversations, telephone calls, memoranda, publications, speeches, group conferences, newspapers, radio, television, and posters, among others. The extent to which it takes place depends upon factors such as the psychological climate, mental sets of individuals, face-to-face relationships, semantics, and the channels for transmitting the message.

Nonverbal communication

People communicate with each other not only by means of words but by facial expression, gesture, and their actions as well as through symbolic and practical objects. In everyday life a large part of social interaction is not verbalized. Visual observation is essential for the full comprehension of communicative behavior. Every time you meet anyone, he not only hears your words but he also observes and reacts to nonverbal cues. He notes your approximate age, body structure, glasses, wristwatch, necktie, clothes, car, facial expression, body posture, tone of voice, muscular tension, and other signs and symbols of what you are and do. He looks for cues to feelings as well as statements. All human beings spontaneously look for and react to

7

Communication
with Employees

these nonverbal cues in order to identify the person and to sense his underlying motives. These may be more revealing than his words.

Listening is more than hearing words. It includes the hearer's estimate as to whether the speaker is sincere or merely trying to put something over to his advantage. The employee who is listening to his boss speak about the company looks for meanings in what is not said as well as in what is said. Does the boss imagine that he is clever or is he honestly trying to explain the subject in a sincere way? Does he himself really believe what he says? Is he speaking in terms of his own biases only or is he objective? Sometimes silence is more eloquent than words.

Both the sender and the receiver must be active participants in the communication process. The receiver may appear to be a passive participant. Actually, communication is a dynamic process in which both parties participate. The best example of good communication is that of a man-to-man discussion, in which both parties alternately speak and listen, answer questions, correct misconceptions, agree on the extent to which they agree or disagree, and plan an appropriate course of action.

Communication in itself is not an end or a goal. Rather, it is a tool for conveying meaning and, in the business world, a basic factor in inducing action. Without it, management could not coordinate the various elements that make a business enterprise out of men, materials, and money. Management must give instructions so that employees and other people understand and act on them. In industry, the channels of communication are of three kinds: up-line, down-line, and cross-line, depending on the direction from the source to the ultimate recipient of the message.

COMMUNICATION WITH EMPLOYEES

The supervisor as an agent in communication

Communication with employees has been of increasing concern to management. If it is to be a mutual process in which the employees are active participants, organized ways must be provided to enable them to express their ideas in their everyday relations with management. Furthermore, they must be confident that management is listening.

Surveys of employee opinion indicate that management does not always know the employees' attitudes toward their work, the job, and the company. Management tends to assume that they are, or should be, the same as management's.

Management wants employees to have respect for the company and the men at the top. Certainly the old policy whereby management thought it could win the employee's respect by being the victor in a last-ditch fight between labor and management is no longer sensible.

Most companies rely upon the foremen to be the active communicator of management's policies and objectives to the employees. The foremen are in close relation with the workers and should be able to pass on management's directives, answer their questions, and provide explanations. Unfortunately, many foremen are not as articulate as management wishes. To overcome the problem, the more alert managements seek additional avenues for keeping employees informed. In some cases, the personnel department is assigned the responsibility for communications, not only those of the routine variety such as posting changes in rules or policies on the bulletin boards, but also those of the educational type that require the organizing of special meetings and the writing of instruction booklets.

"Accentuate The Positive." By reshuffling a few phrases and rephrasing a few words, a safety man in a railway yard cut accidents in half. He simply took the usual safety slogans and translated them into more personal and positive terms. Here are his revisions:

- "Remove your gloves when operating this machine" was changed to: "Save your fingers—and your income—by removing your gloves."
- "Danger! High voltage" was given this addition: "Even 240 volts can kill; there are 660 volts here."
- "Wear goggles at this grinder" was revised to read: "Eyes aren't replaceable; goggles are. Please use both at this machine."
- "No smoking" was expanded to: "Lighted cigarettes cause fires, damage and death. Please—don't light up."
- "Pick up those tools" was changed to a less bossy and more informal: "Scattered tools cause accidents. Pick up your tools and save your conscience."
- Over the wrench stand he put the sign: "There's the right wrench—and the wrong one. Use the right one first."
- On doors he cautioned: "Careful now: Danger may be on the other side of this door."

Most signs outlive their usefulness after a while. They become part of the walls they are stuck on and are no longer noticed. This is the fate of all danger signs, no matter how startling their message. Frequent change of position, design and phrasing is a good method for keeping signs effective.

Source: *The Foreman's Letter*, March 22, 1950.

The foreman, in spite of his limitations, remains the key agent in bringing about communication in both directions, up and down. Some supervisors make it easy for employees to bring their complaints, suggestions, and even their personal problems to them. Management must, however, select and train foremen to perform effectively in two-way communication. If their interest in the problem is only casual or occasional, the effectiveness of communication is uncertain and intermittent. One of the most common indicators of a supervisor's failure to communicate effectively takes place when a supervisor loses a good employee and says: "Why didn't he come in and talk to me before he quit—we could have straightened out the problem!" The fact that a supervisor associates or even fraternizes with his employees does not mean that employees will communicate fully with him. They may know him so well that they realize he does not want to hear about certain problems nor discuss them. They usually know what topics are "off-limits" in his thinking.

To be a good communicator, management must provide special training for the supervisor. He must be stimulated to act on management's messages. The supervisor must be led to appreciate that without a sound communications system, a top executive operates partially in the dark. The supervisor should realize that he communicates the top manager's ideas, feelings, purposes, and goals, indeed his whole personality.

BARRIERS TO COMMUNICATION

Almost all persons are "touchy" about certain topics. Think of all the people with whom you would not start a discussion on religion, politics, race, family ancestry, higher education, etiquette, and a host of other topics about which a specific individual may be especially, though often unnecessarily, sensitive.

Certain persons in a company are touchy subjects—the kind that people discuss only with persons whom they trust. Perhaps the most common example is the unique personality of a key executive. He may be a man of considerable ability, highly respected, and competent but his idiosyncrasies are irritating or bothersome to some associates and subordinates. Remarks about him are likely to be answered by "He's just that kind of a guy and there's nothing anyone can do about him—so let's not talk about him."

Certain subjects, too, are avoided because a member of management has fixed ideas about them. The plant manager, for example, who spends several years in developing a bonus system for the shop may be so loyal to his brainchild that no one has the courage to suggest changes in the bonus system.

Executives recognize that employees are overly sensitive about certain topics. They maintain "zones of silence" as indicated by these typical comments: (a) "If we speak up, our message will be called propaganda," (b) "The union wouldn't like it," (c) "Let sleeping dogs alone—discussion is too risky. Employees will ask questions we can't answer the way they want them answered," and (d) "That's a topic that always gets the person into trouble when he talks about it. 'Never wrestle with a pig, you'll both get dirty.'" [1]

Generally, the management that wants to inform employees about its policies and plans can do so. And the management that is tightlipped cannot be helped by setting up a formal plan or by hiring a communications expert.

On the assumption that people who engage in communication may have some insights, The National Industrial Conference Board asked this question of more than 750 company members whose general level of responsibility places them in the management category: "What are the barriers to communication within a company?"

The barriers cited by these management representatives were found to fall into three major groups:

> Barriers arising from the fact that individuals are involved in communication—and individuals differ. These might be called pre-existing barriers to communication, which a company inherits because they are common to society.
> Barriers arising from the company's "climate," or atmosphere, which tend to stultify communication.
> Barriers that are largely mechanical in the sense that they stem from lack of proper facilities or means of communication. [2]

Status relationships as a barrier to communication are in the first category. People who are in subordinate or superior positions tend to slow down the free interchange of information. The typical subordinate likes to tell his boss only what the latter is interested in hearing. He prefers to cover up mistakes, failures, and bad news. He modifies or withholds information going up. He wants to anticipate what the boss wants to know or what he may want to know later. He tries to present things in such a way that his boss will feel that the situation is not too bad. He prefers to give good news.

The superior, in turn, cannot always describe his problem to his subordinate. Some information such as the names of persons selected for promotion and details about new products and organizational plans must

---

[1] See C. J. Dover, "Silence—An Employee Relations Pitfall," *Advanced Management,* September 1957.

[2] "Barriers to Communication," *Management Record,* National Industrial Conference Board, January 1958.

be withheld until the time is propitious. As a result, the subordinate interprets and misinterprets actions and attitudes of his superior.

Of course, distortion and filtering of information both up and down the line is lessened when there is an atmosphere of permissiveness and where the team spirit is so strong that criticism can be given and taken without rancor.[3]

Mental sets of men of management and unions

"*Mental set*" is often defined as "a readiness to think or respond in a predetermined way." We all note a person's mental set at any given time by his posture, tone of voice, muscular tension, and facial expression. Even though he says no words, we note whether he is resistant or receptive to an idea. A mental set often becomes a hindrance to change. A set may be so fixed, that it does not permit the possibility of change. Many people have developed so rigid a pattern of thinking and living that we no longer attempt to introduce new ideas to them.[4]

Some of the established tendencies in a person's thinking can be ascertained or deduced by means of word association tests.

The best known word association test was invented by Sir Francis Galton in 1879 and was popularized by Carl Jung around the turn of the century. It is still used to discover tendencies in a person's thinking.

The first major effort to standardize the free word association method is now a classic document in this field of psychological research; this is a book by two authors, Kent and Rosanoff, which contains standard tables of free word association responses for 100 selected words, obtained from 1000 normal subjects. One of the interesting findings over the years is that the most frequent associations to test words have not changed much in more than a half century. Words like "table" still produce the top association of "chair," the word "man" produces the top association "woman," "bread" brings "butter," "whiskey," "drink" and so on. This usually holds true, too, for the top ten most frequent associations to a word. On the average, about seven or eight of the top ten associations to a Kent-Rosanoff word in the year 1900 still remain in the top ten today.[5]

---

[3] See Schuyler Dean Hoslett, "Barriers to Communication," *Personnel*, American Management Association, Inc., September 1951.

[4] See Roger M. Bellows, "Personnel Frontiers," *Personnel Administration*, March-April 1957, pp. 44, 45.

[5] See James M. Vicary, "The Psychology of Seasons," *The Changing Consumer*, Contributed Papers to an Advertising Conference of the Department of Journalism, University of Michigan, 1955, p. 76.

Communication with Employees

Experiments indicate that a single adjective may reorganize the whole view of a person described, its effect going far beyond the simple, logical relevancy of the word and, in addition, such a reorganization modifies other aspects of the observer's behavior toward the subject.

Mason Haire, for example has reported an experiment in which the subjects were 76 members of a Central Labor Council and 108 representatives of management—industrial relations or personnel men from plants or employers' organizations. All members of both groups lived and worked in the San Francisco Bay area. Many members of these two groups (though not necessarily all) had bargained with one another.

> The test materials consisted of two pictures and four descriptions. The pictures were chosen in an attempt to represent "ordinary people"; they were middle-aged, moderately dressed men, with no particular expression on their faces. The four descriptions were made up in the following manner: all four descriptions contained the information that (1) the person was almost 46, (2) was healthy, (3) had been married for a long time and had a family, (4) had held several jobs, all successfully, (5) had few hobbies or interests outside of family and work, and (6) read newspapers and fixed things around the house. In half the cases these items were arranged in different order so that it did not sound like the identical man, though in fact the same items were present. Further, in half the cases the man pictured was described as "local manager of a small plant which is a branch of a large manufacturing concern," and in the other half as "Secretary-Treasurer of his Union." . . .
>
> The subjects were told that this was part of a research project to see how well people could analyze personality on the basis of a few facts. They were given one minute to study the picture and description, then were told to turn the page where they found a list of 290 adjectives relating to personality. At the head were the following instructions:
>
> *Directions:* A number of common adjectives are listed below. Please read them over quickly and check all those you would consider to apply to the man in the photograph. Don't worry about duplications, contradictions, etc. Work quickly and do not spend much time on any one adjective. Check your first impression of each adjective. You may check as many or as few as you like.[6]

The most striking result is as follows: when a member of either group (management or labor) describes a person, the description varies markedly depending on the role of the person described, although the facts and the pictures are identical. Thus, 74 per cent of the subjects in the managerial group chose the word "honest" as descriptive of Mr. A, *when he was identified as manager*. The same managerial subjects, however, chose the word "honest" to describe Mr. A only 50 per cent of the time when he was identified as a representative of the union.

---

[6] Mason Haire, "Role-Perceptions in Labor-Management Relations: An Experimental Approach," *Industrial and Labor Relations Review*, January 1955.

The experiment showed, in this particular instance, that a single person looks very different depending on whether he is seen as a manager or a union secretary. Moreover, the nature of this difference depends on whether he is thus seen *by* a manager or a union man.

In summary, from looking at these data, we can say:

(1) The general impression of a person is radically different when he is seen as a member of management than when he is seen as a representative of labor.

(2) Further, the change effected by membership is different when it is seen by members of management and labor. The kind of effect of such a characteristic or group membership is influenced by the group membership of the perceiver himself.

(3) Management and labor each sees the other as less dependable than himself.

(4) Management and labor each sees the other as less appreciative of the other's position than he himself is.

(5) Management and labor each sees the other as deficient in thinking, emotional characteristics, and interpersonal relations in comparison with himself. . . .

On the basis of these data it seems clear that labor and management are not talking to the same people when they confer with one another. Labor sees itself and management so differently and management sees itself and labor so differently that, although they are [the] only two people in the room, four people seem to be involved in the conversation. Consider, for example, the meaning of a statement like "we are anxious to work with you." Let us suppose it is made by Mr. B., a labor representative. He is seen by labor to be honest, dependable, and efficient. However, by management he is seen as persistent, opinionated, argumentative, and outspoken. He is seen by labor to have high thinking ability, to be dependable, and to see the other's side of the problem. He is seen by management to be a less clear thinker than management is, to be relatively undependable, and to fail to see management's side of the problem. Under these circumstances, it seems hardly possible that the statement can mean the same thing to both parties. Though only one man speaks, the masks through which the statement comes are so different that it is hardly the same thing any longer.[7]

Research studies of this kind confirm what we know from daily experience with people in business—mental set causes members of management and of labor to perceive each other in terms of their own characteristic reactions. It is also involved in the way a subordinate perceives his superior and the superior perceives his subordinate. All persons have mental sets that color their perceptions of others in the family and in school as well as in business life.

The number of barriers to communication is so great that extended study is necessary to appreciate them. One phase of communication,

---

[7] *Ibid.*

the grapevine, is often treated as a barrier. Actually, it is a symptom of inadequate communication.

The grapevine

Every company has one or more "rumor mills" or centers from which rumors are passed on to employees by means of a communications procedure, ordinarily called the grapevine. Its information is often distorted, at best, incomplete.

If management ignores the grapevine and it is allowed to operate unchecked, it may cause discord, layoffs, or even strikes. At its worst, it may damage unjustly the reputations of innocent individuals. Some managements ignore the grapevine, particularly during a strike period. In a period of labor tension the union involved will usually distribute, openly or by grapevine, information favorable to the union while management remains silent.

Some companies are grapevine riddled, year in and year out. Common rumors are that the plant is going to be closed down and its operations merged with another factory, that pay scales will be raised, that pay will be cut, that the president is going to resign, and so on and on. The origin of such rumors may be in the misinterpretation of an overheard telephone conversation or someone's overactive imagination.

One source of rumors is the personnel who operate duplicating equipment in an office. Some of the operators cannot understand or interpret simple information when they read it. The duplicating machine operator who sees the first copy giving news of a management decision may tip off his or her friends days before copies of the release are distributed to others. Even though he is given instructions to maintain secrecy, the mimeograph operator may be unable to control his urge to tell "inside dope" that will excite others.

A few managements have duplicating equipment installed in the executive office suite and train a reliable secretary to operate it, so that confidential matters may be kept confidential until the time of official release. Dictating records and transcriptions also require extra control. All those who take part in processing information as well as the sender and the receiver are participants. Those who should not receive the message are also participants in a sense. In modern business, a very important party to many routine transmissions of memos and letters is the person who should receive a carbon copy.

Several executives have advocated using the grapevine for spreading plant information. They think of the "grapevine" as a medium of communication. Actually, as more experienced writers have pointed out, the "grapevine is only a measure of the vacuum that exists in a communication system." When anyone attempts to use it as a channel for sending information to employees, he will find that he has no control over the content of the message once the "leak" is made and when made, no assurance that the message will go to the right people.[8]

Management should not, however, use the public address system to debunk a rumor because this method seems to make the rumor better remembered than the refutation.

A rumor should be interpreted as a psychiatrist would a symptom: "What anxiety or attitude does this rumor reflect?" The cause of the anxiety, rather than the rumor per se, should be corrected.[9]

Whenever a company finds itself in competition with a "rumor factory" going full blast among its plant employees, it means that normal communication channels are not open and available. Rumors flourish most in the absence of reliable information.

Supervisors can be taught to be attentive to the questions and complaints of their employees and to relay distortions of fact that might create trouble later. The management that keeps its employees informed at regular and frequent intervals about its plans and problems is likely to have little trouble with the grapevine.

Few rumors arise when each worker feels secure, regards himself as a member of a team, and knows facts and plans that involve him. Rumors arise and are spread when employees do not know the facts.

Participation is the most effective form of communication

For the employee to believe in his employer, he needs more than words, kindness, or managerial integrity. This has been discovered by certain corporation executives who assumed that the publishing of an annual financial report on the business, including the percentage of profit on the sales dollar, would convince employees that the employer was fair in the amount of the income shared with the employees.

Surveys made after financial reports had been published, showed that

---

[8] See Lester R. Bittel, "Human Relations," *Factory Management and Maintenance,* July 1957, p. 129.

[9] See "Washington Report," U. S. Chamber of Commerce, December 21, 1956. See also *The Management Review,* American Management Association, Inc., March 1957, p. 45.

employees read the financial reports but still said: "The company makes too much money!" So a few executives decided they could convince the employees of the company's fair dealings by asking each employee by means of an unsigned questionnaire how much profit he would expect on each sales dollar if he were to invest ten thousand dollars of his money in a business. Their answers mostly were to the effect that they would, in their own business, expect to make at least 25 cents on the sales dollar. Quite logically the employer said: "You say that you would want a profit of 25 per cent if you were in business for yourself. Look at the company's financial statement. We make a profit of only four per cent. Don't you think that we are generous to you, the employee, when we make much less profit than you yourself would expect if you were the employer?"

The reaction of employees to this kind of explanation about corporate profits was a loud and emphatic: "The company makes too much money!"

Upon getting the same old answer from the employees, most of these employers threw up their hands and said: "What the hell! If employees can't be convinced after all the proofs and logical explanations we have given them, they just can't be convinced. We'll do the best we can and quit trying to convince them about the fairness of our treatment of them."

Fortunately, a few employers did not quit trying. They analyzed the situation further and came up with the rediscovery of a very old psychological principle, namely: *People believe in the extent to which they participate.*[10]

Certain managements do convince their employees of the company's fairness by giving them a sense of participation in the business. This has been done by explaining the company's plans and problems to the employees and getting them to help solve the small and the ordinary everyday problems. Employees are given more than information—they are asked as colleagues to help by doing their own work more easily and profitably. Most of this has been done successfully without benefit of either a formal suggestion or a profit-sharing system. The supervisors have learned to practice this philosophy because the executives above them believe in and practice it. The vital factor has been the application of the American philosophy of thinking of employees as colleagues rather than subordinates.

When the employees are taken behind the scenes in the management of the company and sincerely given participation in those problems

---

[10] See Ross G. Walker, "The Misinformed Employee," *Harvard Business Review,* May 1948.

Communication with Employees

within the range of their abilities, the doubts and misgivings about the employer's fairness in management disappear. The employees come to believe in the employer and the business when they understand, through participation, management's problems. In a sense, they feel that they sit in the president's office every day.

The best communication technique is usually direct face-to-face oral communication between people. The use of this technique is even possible in a large modern company where management is genuinely anxious to communicate with its employees.

Harry D. Kolb, Manager of the Employee Communication Division, Esso Standard Oil Company, has described how it can be done. He defines communication in industry not as a device to sell, convert, or attack, but rather as a process of exchanging ideas, feelings, and information. Further, a good communications system should stem from the belief that the employees have a right to hear and be heard.

As an example, Kolb cited the work of one of his plants of 1,700. In contrast to an old attitude of keeping business secrets for a chosen few, they began with the attitude that, as one of their own executives put it, "We have no business secrets that we need to keep from our people." Their first step was to hold a forum-type meeting of supervisors and employees. Nineteen groups met and discussed past records, present situations, and future plans. As a result, 4,000 questions were presented, which the top men then attempted to fully answer.

They did not stop there. Instead, following this, there were a large number of face-to-face group discussions between and within all levels. For example, weekly staff meetings were held not only by the top management, but also by the lower echelon groups, too. In the line of printed communications, bi-weekly bulletins were circulated among the supervisors. In addition, a four-page tabloid, edited by a trained man, was distributed throughout the plant.

The meetings not only demonstrated the leader's interest in his men, but also stimulated positive reactions and a feeling of participation on the part of the employees. In addition, groups accomplished more when they had looked into their goals and problems and attempted to tackle them together. Thus, it was found that only frank and open communication can minimize suspicions, correct misunderstandings, and build the teamwork essential to the continuing success of a company.

Kolb emphasized that all this and more was done to maintain a steady and timely flow of information. Of course, each company must adopt the best methods for its own situation. When properly organized and carried out, a good communications system builds a sense of colleagueship among employees in all strata. Each individual then realizes that he does play an important and active part in the daily operations of business.[11]

This suggests that everyone in business should be concerned about his media commonly used for distributing information to employees. The media usually utilized for this purpose are employee magazines, bulletin boards, moving pictures, and meetings. Helpful suggestions are offered in numerous books and articles published on the subject. In the remainder of this chapter, we shall give attention to those communication procedures of special interest to the student of human relations who expects to work in management circles.

Meetings for communicating with executives and with other staff members of the organization are so much a part of American business that it is important to give some attention to them in the remainder of this chapter.

COMMUNICATION IN MANAGERIAL AND STAFF CIRCLES

Meetings

The terms "conference," "committee meeting," and "meeting" are often used interchangeably. Generally, a *conference* in business is called by one or more executives to get information in order that the executives may make a decision or develop a plan. A *committee* is usually charged with responsibility for making a recommendation or carrying out an action plan. The individuals chosen for a committee are also likely to be chosen with more care than the members of a conference. A *conference* is, by definition, "a formal consultation . . . an interchange of ideas." A *meeting* may be distinguished from a conference as being less formal.

Many American executives feel harassed by the practice of holding meetings. When an executive is told that a conference is to be held to discuss a problem, his answer is likely to be something like this:

"Oh, no! Not another meeting. I've had to attend fifteen meetings in less than a week. As a result, I've had to stay late every evening this week to get my work done."

Many meetings are unproductive and wasteful of time. In spite of their unpopularity, they continue to be used. When rightly planned and

---

[11] See Harry D. Kolb, "Creating the Organizational 'Atmosphere' For Improved Communication," *Personnel,* American Management Association, Inc., May 1954, pp. 482-87.

conducted, they can be very productive. To be productive, the meeting should have a purpose of interest to all who attend.

A meeting that does not keep to its purpose becomes dull and unproductive. Without control, irrelevant matters are brought up and a few people take up the time of the others discussing a subject of interest only to them. Matters are brought up that frequently can't be settled. Or someone wants to talk about a subject that must be discussed later because someone concerned is not present at the meeting.

In business a meeting is usually run by the man who calls it. A time limit should be set in advance. The shorter the time, the better. A meeting lasting up to 90 minutes is likely to be productive. After that, the time-work ratio declines. For some chairmen, participation is their main problem. Their usual procedure is to make a statement and say: "Anybody have any questions?"

Generally, only silence follows, and the meeting ends without discussion. But some of the people who remained silent *had* questions. They were reluctant to ask them. Perhaps the man who presided gave the impression that he really did not want questions. If the chairman genuinely desires questions, he asks in an inquiring tone. He turns to someone and asks: "What do you think about it?" or "How can we handle this problem?"

Group members who do not ask questions or express opinions in some cases may exclaim to another member afterwards, "It's no use talking to him—he knows it all," or "He doesn't really want our ideas. Did you notice that he looked down his nose at us at the same time that he was asking the questions?"

Sometimes the chairman gets plenty of questions and opinions of the argumentative variety. As the chairman he would like to develop enlightening discussion without useless argument. Carl R. Rogers, a psychologist, has suggested an effective technique for avoiding the kinds of arguments that change no one's opinion and for bringing about, instead, a real listening and understanding when conflict prevails. The technique recommended is for the leader of the meeting to stop the heated debate and get everyone to agree that no one will speak until he has first restated the ideas and feelings of the person who has last spoken. He must do this accurately and to that person's reasonable satisfaction. The meeting does not go on until this is done.

This rule is often difficult to put into effect, but it does require each speaker, before presenting his own opinion, to listen receptively enough to "get" the previous speaker's opinion, and the thinking behind it. It means that each speaker must clearly comprehend and state what the other has said. It usually reduces emotional tensions; "The heat goes out of the argument," as Rogers has put it. Of course the speaker whose ideas have been paraphrased may also modify his original statement. The main point is that effective communication requires a conscious effort on the part of every member to get at the meaning of the other person's feelings.[12]

Committees

For many persons in responsible positions, attending committee meetings is one of their most time-consuming activities. Department heads, for example, spend as much as 20 per cent of their time in committee. The amount of time spent in committees seems to be increasing. Some managements are so addicted to this kind of communication that almost every problem of importance is treated by a committee before a decision is made. Strangely, in certain companies that adhere to the committee idea, the president himself usually attends, and he always sits as a majority of one!

Committees as a management tool or procedure have serious weaknesses such as the tendency of weak executives to use them to avoid the risks of decision making. Strong executives, in contrast, may use them to get rubber-stamp approval for their decisions.

The fact that several men of sound judgment come into an office for a conference does not mean that they combine their thinking and develop more sound judgment than anyone alone would do. A group may cause each one to rely on the opinions of the others and to exert less individual care himself. The greater the confidence in his colleagues, the stronger this tendency. Sometimes a group of competent executives will make mistakes that no one of them would commit alone.

When responsibility is spread across a committee, no one person feels responsible for a decision. Committees not only avoid responsibility by making a decision an action of a committee but a committee can also be a whipping boy that enables the individual members to escape chastisement for bad action.

Certainly, many good ideas get lost in committees. As Charles F. Kettering, General Motors' research chief, stated: "The surest way to kill a valuable new proposal is to lay it before the average committee." President Griswold of Yale has been quoted as having asked: "Could Hamlet have been written by a committee? Or the Mona Lisa painted by a club?"

One reason for the failure of a committee to function well is in the

---

[12] See Alfred J. Marrow, *Making Management Human* (New York: McGraw-Hill Book Company, Inc., 1957), p. 169.

Communication with Employees

psychological peculiarities of some members. Every committee is likely to have at least one member who knows nothing about the subject presented to the committee. This individual is apt to feel that he ought to justify his membership by comment on the proposal. It is easier to call attention to dangers in the proposal than to comment on it constructively. He therefore criticizes and helps to kill what may be a good idea.[13]

The astute chairman wants those present to participate, but he knows there are several kinds of participators. There is the kind of involvement with others present which makes a member of the group feel important. Such a person is more conscious of his own needs than of the problem under discussion. The satisfaction of his need for prestige or self-regard is his main objective. This kind of participation is called *ego-involvement*.

Some persons present wish to be participants but are unable to express themselves in regard to the major topic or to contribute to the exchange of ideas. They go through the verbal motions of participating but are obviously unable to do more than repeat words. This kind of participation is called *verbal-involvement*. The wise chairman seeks responses which show that the members of the group are thinking about the problem rather than their own psychological needs.[14]

After studying hundreds of committees in operation, several researchers have set seven members as the top limit for efficiency. Beyond that point, "low participators" tend to stop talking to each other. Certain "top men" do most of the talking; and when low participators do talk, it is likely to be to the top men only.

On being a good participant in a meeting

The main requirement for intelligent participation in any meeting is a genuine interest in the problem under discussion. At the same time that one presents his ideas and learns those of other members of the group, he must also recognize the human relations situations involved in the people present. Almost every conference group has at least one defensive member, the kind of individual who has an urge to impress others. Or there may be the perennial critic who always finds a flaw in the conclusion reached by the others. Such a person cannot be cured —he can only be held in check by the chairman and endured by the

[13] See *Management Briefs*, No. 76 (Rogers, Slade & Hill, New York). See also *The Management Review*, American Management Association, Inc., January 1957, p. 9.

[14] See Eugene Emerson Jennings, "Forces that Transform a Collection into a Group," *Personnel Journal*, September 1956.

others. Intelligent, mature persons who attend meetings rise above the annoyances imposed upon them by the emotionally immature members of the group.

The young ambitious employee who is invited to attend an important conference of executives is likely to feel somewhat self-conscious and betray it by either talking too much or not at all. He can overcome such tendencies on his part by means of the following principles:

1. Be prepared. When executives invite a bright young man to sit in on a conference, they are giving him an opportunity to get acquainted with the organization and its problems but they also hope that he will contribute tactfully to the discussion. He can find out the topic for discussion and prepare his ideas in advance. He can ask his associates for their ideas, get facts and figures, and plan his presentation.
2. Be on time. The executive who invites the bright young man expects him to be sufficiently respectful of his responsibilities to be on time. The old college classroom habit of wandering in when the spirit moves is not tolerated by most executives.
3. Be courteous toward other members of the group. This means staying awake, looking interested, and asking sensible questions. Listen respectfully to the ideas of others, but do not try to flatter anyone or give compliments. Mature men do not need them from a youngster. Anyone who uses the conference table to make a testimonial speech to flatter the boss is not likely to get much respect from the boss and none from the others. The nearest to giving a compliment that is possible for the young man is to nod his head in approval of what someone says.
4. Avoid showing up anyone even if he is wrong. No one likes to be made to appear stupid or ridiculous even if the evidence might prove it. No one in a conference should be forced to lose face.
5. Skip all the clever jokes or funny stories that come to mind during the meeting. Do not tell them unless they are very brief and pointed to the problem under discussion. Executives do not like to waste their time listening to long stories. Only the presiding member is expected to use humor to liven the meeting.
6. Respect the confidences of other members of the group. Matters of a semi-secret nature are often mentioned in conferences. One mark of the responsible business executive is the ability to keep quiet when he is unable to answer a question without revealing confidential information.[15]

---

[15] Adapted from Frank M. Kleiler, "Etiquette for Business Bull Sessions," *The Office Economist*, June 1957. Copyright © 1957, Art Metal Construction Company, Jamestown, N.Y.

Communication with Employees

For All Students

Newcomb, Robert, and Marg Sammons, "Management Tries Some Straight Talk," *Dun's Review and Modern Industry,* November 1958. How some companies present economic facts to employees to make them aware of what factors really make jobs secure.

Stessin, Lawrence, "The Gimmick Craze in Employee Communications," *The Management Review,* American Management Association, Inc., September 1957. Discusses clichés of management such as that of the executive who says: "My door is always open to any employee."

For Advanced Students

Jennings, Eugene Emerson, "Forces That Lead to Group Agreement and Decision," *Personnel Journal,* September through December, 1956. The author presents excellent summaries of some of the outstanding research done in this field.

Hovland, Carl, Irving Janis, and Harold Kelley, *Communication and Persuasion.* New Haven: Yale University Press, 1953. Presents basic findings from a Yale Communication Research Program indicating that opinions of people persist unless they undergo some new learning experience. Suggests approaches to the learning.

For Men in Business

Hackett, Herbert, and others, *Understanding and Being Understood.* New York: Longmans, Green and Co., 1957. A primer on effective communication for businessmen.

Ingram, K. C., *Talk That Gets Results.* New York: McGraw-Hill Book Company, Inc., 1957. The author draws upon his experiences as a journalist and as an executive with Southern Pacific Railroad to produce a useful, readable book on communication.

QUESTIONS ON THE CHAPTER

1. What is communication? How does nonverbal communication take place?
2. What is the function of communication in the business world?
3. Who is the key agent in bringing about communication in industry, both up and down?
4. What are three groups of communication barriers within a company, according to a National Industrial Conference Board survey?
5. What method is often used to ascertain the mental set of a person? Describe the findings of Mason Haire in his study of the perceptions of labor union leaders and of representatives of management.
6. In what ways may the grapevine be considered a barrier and an aid to communication?
7. Explain the situations in which rumors are most apt to arise.

8. What is the best communication technique and how has Harry Kolb described a way that it can be carried out?

9. Differentiate between a conference, a committee meeting and a meeting.

10. How much time do department heads spend in committee meetings?

11. What two types of participators should a committee leader be able to recognize?

12. In what respects is preparation important to committee work?

13. Name four principles that would be advantageous for a young employee to follow in executive committee meetings.

14. Of the ideas presented in the chapter, which ones are of special interest or value to you?

15. What did the chapter contribute to your future relations with (a) the men who supervise your work, (b) employees whom you may supervise?

PROBLEMS AND PROJECTS

For All Students

1. Articles on the subject of communications appear from time to time in many business and scientific journals. Examine available copies, particularly *Business Week* and *Dun's Review and Modern Industry*. State some of the new ideas you learned that are not covered in the text.

2. Attend a meeting as an observer. Evaluate the chairman's leadership and the participation by members. Describe what happened. Were there any examples of the subjects covered in this chapter? What specific suggestions did you get for yourself for your acting as chairman in the future?

For Advanced Students

3. Examine some of the behavioral science textbooks available to you—your own and those of fellow students. What information do they contain about communication?

4. Test yourself in regard to the ability to write an article for an employee magazine on the subject of current economic or political trends. Is your style appropriate for employees of a factory? Show your finished article to several persons who work in industry. What are their reactions to your article?

For Men in Business

5. Obtain copies of various company publications for employees. Study their contents and the themes of the articles by management. How do they differ from publications put out by unions?

6. Some companies subscribe to a poster or bulletin service for employees. These services usually admonish the employee in regard to safety, thrift, and other virtues. How do you evaluate such services?

A COMPANY IS MORE THAN AN OFFICE, A PRODUCTION OR SERVICE building, and some machines. It is a personality. Its product (or service) has a personality.

The "corporate image" is what people see in their mind's eye when the name of the company is seen or heard. It varies with individuals and their relations to the company: employees, customers, suppliers, dealers, stockholders, and nonusers of the company's product.

An image can be defined as all the ideas and visual symbols which are associated with or suggested by mention of a company, product, or brand. These ideas and visual symbols arouse and carry characteristic meanings whenever a company or its product is mentioned or seen. Visual symbols communicate much faster than word descriptions because they involve less mental effort than thinking in terms of words. Images simplify our existence.

Alert managements are keenly interested in their corporate and product or brand images. Research firms are conducting costly "image building" programs with continuous surveys of their image problems. These companies have discovered that the impression which employees and customers have of them is not always what management thinks it is. One manufacturer of household appliances, for example, found that most people had an image of the company as being a solid, unexciting, heavy goods producer of electrical equipment. The image of the company's principal and financially more successful competitor, in

8   The Corporate Image and
Public Relations

contrast, was that of being an alert, progressive company that creates products of advanced design.

A corporate image reflects the character of a corporation. And when that corporate image is an especially good one, it not only sells merchandise, it can help do a lot of other things. For example . . .

A corporate image tends to make the busiest of men find time to see you when you call.

A corporate image creates confidence in any product that bears your company's name.

A corporate image helps assure you of acceptance for a new product, in advance.

A corporate image gives your company an edge in attracting good talent.

A corporate image helps keep the people at your company feeling it's a good place to work.

A corporate image helps attract capital to your company at favorable terms.

A corporate image causes a stockholder to seek out your stock and select it over another.

A corporate image gives your company an edge with dependable sources of supply . . . helps you secure efficient, profitable distribution.

A corporate image can be the difference between a lawmaker's "yes" and "no."

A corporate image helps a community understand a company, accept it as a good neighbor.

SOURCE: From a house advertisement by Time Inc., publishers of *Life, Time, Fortune, Sports Illustrated, House & Home, Architectural Forum, International Editions* of *Time* and *Life;* published in *Time,* June 9, 1958. Quoted by special permission.

Brand images are stronger and more durable than corporate images because the customer knows more about the brand than about the company but the corporate image, when known, is merged with that of the brand.

The more favorable the image, the more active people are in recommending a company's products to friends. This is shown by a study made of 12 companies that market consumer goods. When the customers of these firms were grouped according to their image of the companies, the proportion of each group which had recommended the companies' products in the last year increased as the favorableness of the corporate image rose. The results of the study [1] can be summarized as follows:

[1] *Executive Control of the Corporate Image,* The Public Opinion Index for Industry (Opinion Research Corporation, Princeton, N.J.), July 1958, p. 5.

```
Least favorable image  ........  13%
More  favorable  .............  21%
More  favorable  .............  35%
More  favorable  .............  46%
Most favorable image  .........  54%
```

Corporate images tend to be self-propagating through word-of-mouth, become part of the people's tradition. The old monopoly charge against Standard Oil, and Ford's $5 a day wage, still influence public thinking. Hence the need to create favorable images and continually to reinforce them through a flow of fresh experience and exciting information.

How company images are estimated

Research firms that specialize in the study of company and brand images use several techniques in their surveys. Some techniques involve skilled depth interviewing. The techniques more commonly used are likely to involve the following:

1. A simple question may be asked such as "What does the name, (company or brand) suggest to you?" Anything that is answered is considered as part of the image.
2. The respondent may be given an incomplete sentence and asked to complete it: "Mr. A works for Company X. He probably works there because he ———."
3. The respondent may be given a cartoon which has a partly empty balloon emanating from the mouth of a figure. The incomplete statement in the balloon may have the words: "I ought to work for Company X if I ——————."
4. Pictures of various kinds may be used; the respondent is asked to invent certain kinds of stories appropriate to the picture. Of course, many persons are unable to fill in anything simply because they have no imagery associated with the company or its products. This too is significant—it means that the management has failed to build any image whatsoever.

The questions can be framed to elicit ideas as to the kinds of persons who would be most likely to work for a company: alert, intelligent, unambitious, or dull people. Also, the kinds of people who would be most likely to use the company's products might be found to be professionals, executives, manual workers, old folks, sickly customers, alert young men, or others.

The use of these and more incisive techniques requires special training in the social sciences. Our major attempt here is not to describe these techniques but to cause those who enter or work in business to become aware of the importance of mental images in business, to seek to know more about the images associated with a given company, and to contribute toward the development of desirable corporate and brand images. Every executive, employee, salesman, friend, enemy, and acquaintance of a company helps to build its image.

What kinds of images do managements seek to develop?

Dun's Review and Modern Industry asked the presidents of 162 companies, three fourths of them among the 500 largest in this country, about the kind of company impression they want to make on their various publics—employees, customers, stockholders, and others. In most answers, these company presidents said the image they try to create in the public mind is that of a company making and selling a reliable product at a fair price.

The consensus was that company prestige begins with the product itself—its quality, reliability, and constant improvement.

Some presidents, however, seek to develop recognition for certain additional qualities for which they want their companies to be known. These are personality characteristics such as competence, leadership, integrity, friendliness, vigor, forthrightness, warmth, reliability, progressiveness, and so on.

Only 4 per cent of the presidents think their companies are doing an "excellent" job of achieving a positive public identity. At the other extreme, 4 per cent admitted that they are doing a "poor" job. But three fourths of the companies believed they are doing a "good," "fair," or "satisfactory" job.[2]

The need for building more accurate imagery

The fact that top management men want their company to be known as producing good products and conducting their businesses in a spirit of responsible service does not mean that most people think of them in that manner. When, for example, Gilbert Youth Research Co. con-

[2] See Kenneth Henry, "Creating and Selling Your Corporate Image," *Dun's Review and Modern Industry,* July 1958; copyright © 1958 by Dun & Bradstreet Publications Corporation.

ducted a survey of 1,923 teen-agers of 42 cities, the attitude of many could be summed up in the statement: "Big businesses run everything in America—they have all the money."

Asked to express whatever came into their minds when they heard the phrase "big business," 31 per cent responded by picturing a sort of giant monopoly spread across all America. Many feared that in the future all free enterprise would be swallowed up in one or two gigantic trusts.

One third of the young people believed that electric and telephone companies make between 25 and 49 cents on every dollar of income; one out of 10 thought they make 50 cents or more. Only 29 per cent of the teen-agers could even vaguely define common stock or had any idea of the number of stockholders in large companies.[3]

Even though capitalism is an important part of our business way of

SOURCE: *by Al Kaufman,* The Management Review *(January 1958), pp. 32-33. Courtesy American Management Association, Inc.*

life, many adults think of it in negative terms only. Douglas Williams reported this example:

> We once tested a film for a company, fortunately while it was still in unfinished form. The intent of the film was to demonstrate to the employes that the company stock was widely held by people in all walks of life—not restricted to a few secluded, wealthy people.
>
> Our procedure was to show this film to employes, then ask them what they thought of it. Almost universally, the first response was a question: "What's the purpose of this film?"
>
> That pretty well sums up how far the film had missed its target.
>
> I remember one girl who said she did learn some things from seeing the film. She said she now realized that a newspaper boy, an elderly couple, the corner grocer, and similar people owned stock in the com-

[3] Reported in *Industrial Relations News* (230 West 41 Street, New York 36), October 20, 1956. See also *The Management Review,* American Management Association, Inc., March 1957, p. 35.

pany. So they could, she supposed, be thought of as capitalists. Nevertheless, she said: "I don't want anybody ever to call me a capitalist."

It was a dirty name in her mind.

If management had appreciated her image of capitalism, it would have used a different approach.[4]

When the United States Chamber of Commerce analyzed returns from a questionnaire submitted to 1,443 high school students in 13 schools in a typical industrial county, organized labor was rated by 56 per cent of the students as having done most to improve living standards; business management, by 16 per cent; government, by 14 per cent; and 14 per cent had no opinion.

The average score on questions about basic facts of the American economic system was 47.1 out of a possible 100. The following examples point up some typical "blind spots":

Only 11 per cent knew that the average profit on sales was between 3 per cent and 6 per cent; most thought it was over 10 per cent. Though one third of all corporations show no net income every year, fully 77 per cent of the students thought few companies operated at a loss. More than half felt that of each dollar divided between company and employees, the larger share went to the owners.

More students (49 per cent) thought a strong and able union afforded better protection for job security than the employer's ability to meet competition (31 per cent). Productivity as a factor in raising living standards was rated low by 71 per cent of the students, who answered "No" to the question: "Should the worker produce all he can?" Asked what was the "most practical way for workers to increase their living standards," 66 per cent of the respondents said, "Get more of the company's money"; only 34 per cent said, "Produce more."[5]

Interestingly, many people, old as well as young, visualize big business as an ogre even though they, at the same time, admire certain big companies. Some companies are perceived as progressive-minded, efficient, and modern. They are felt to be warm and friendly. The managements are described as fair, considerate, and public spirited.

An examination of the purposes of the image-building programs indicates that they vary from an emphasis on leadership in atomic development to getting along well with labor unions.

The Metropolitan Life Insurance Company is a big company, but it has built a favorable image. Management started with the definite ob-

---

[4] Douglas Williams was interviewed in "Six Policies Increase Will To Work," *Nation's Business,* November 1958. Copyright © 1958 by *Nation's Business—the Chamber of Commerce of the United States.*

[5] *Industrial Relations News* (230 West 41 Street, New York 36, N. Y.), February 26, 1955. See also *The Management Review,* American Management Association, Inc., May 1955, p. 342.

jective of equating itself with leadership in health rather than in leadership in death. At the time, this was contrary to the common practice. The company really sells death insurance, not life insurance, and in England it is still called death insurance. However, the company has put forth extra effort to promote all kinds of measures that cut down the death rate.

General Electric has given the public fascinating "progress reports." The company spends time and money to publish and broadcast information about bridges and radar equipment that no individual consumer buys personally. This, however, causes members of the public to feel favorably disposed toward the company and indirectly causes many buyers of smaller appliances and items to choose the GE brand.

One automotive manufacturer for years has sought to spread a prestige aura over the entire product family.

Another manufacturer tries to picture his firm as the one company that makes the housewife's life easier.

A manufacturer of farm products builds his image as one of helpfulness to the farmer.

One reason for building a strong corporate image is to attract potential investors. Of course, when that is a major purpose, financial and investment publications get a large part of the advertising.

The merged company and its image

Many large companies have to define who they are and what they make because mergers, acquisitions, and interchanges of divisions have left the public confused as to the products made. In the case of mergers, management must find out what comes first with a customer—his confidence in the product or his confidence in the company behind the product. The good reputation of one can support the other.

One important decision for the management of a merged corporation involves the question as to which company—the parent or the subsidiary —should be featured in the image-building program. When a company with a reputation for precision engineering acquires several subsidiaries doing less exacting, price-competitive work, should all the companies be lumped together? Should the parent company continue to maintain the identity of a subsidiary? Instead of using an all-embracing, identifying family name for all products, should they follow a policy of individual product identity and promotion for each company?

If the company name already has strong association or imagery woven around it—of fashion, mechanical precision, or homey wholesomeness—

Out of Union Carbide research come products for the modern home: shower curtains and fibres for clothing . . .

metal alloys and antifreeze for snowy weather . . .

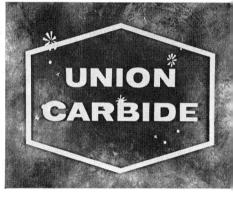

from the infinite universe and bearing

. . . the trade symbol of Union Carbide

Union Carbide Corporation manufactures and sells thousands of different products for industry and the consumer. When the company dropped its old name and adopted the present one, management had to decide how to present one corporate image to the public.

It was decided to use animation in television commercials. The viewer is taken on a whirlwind tour of one day at home and at work, where many everyday items are revealed as having sprung from a common source—the universe and Union Carbide research labs. The cartoon characters are subordinated to symbolic patterns which are constantly rearranging themselves into the dominant hexagonal shape—the Union Carbide symbol. The frenetic musical score matches the visual pace of the color-splashed message. (See Printers' Ink, January 24, 1958, pp. 50-51.) Courtesy Union Carbide Corporation.

that image-rich name can be used to promote the products of a new and dissimilar subdivision.

The broadcast personality

In recent years, the person used in television and radio advertising has often become symbolical of a company and its products. Examples can be seen on the television screen every day.

The well-chosen broadcast personality delivers the commercials with a straight-forward sales pitch that tells more than words. These individuals perform not only salesmanship functions but also provide public relations values. The television announcer becomes the personification of the corporate personality. For most people he is the personal contact personality for the company. Television announcers are among the best known personalities of our time. A hundred million people will see a company's announcer in the course of a year. His personality adds believability to the sales message. Some corporations think that he should be considered a member of the corporate executive staff and be accorded the same treatment as a top management executive.

The broadcast personality has, to some extent, displaced the old testimonial writer. Testimonials are still, however, effective in much advertising because we want to copy those whom we deem superior in taste, knowledge, or experience. We respect those whom we consider authorities or admirable even though they talk about a prosaic product.

Advertising men, copy writers, and artists not only plan the advertising to maintain continuity of character by means of specific styling, but they also guide the design of the product and the package in accordance with the essential character desired for the brand. This character is as fully developed and recorded as a character in a play. In a play, the concept of the character guides the director, the costume designer, and the actor. Each interprets the character under varying conditions. In like manner, successful managements strive to create individual characters for their products in the eyes of the consumers whom they wish to reach.

The airline that inaugurated "Executive Flights" gave facts about its transportation but added atmosphere: cigars, filet mignon, no women allowed on the flight, and a red carpet as the passengers leave the plane.

When the Marlboro cigarette had become known as a high-style cigarette for women, it was decided to change the brand image to make the cigarette attractive to men. The strategy used was:

1. No women were featured in the magazine illustrations or television commercials—only men.
2. All the models were nonprofessionals of the virile type: cowboys, mechanics, outdoor workers, etc.
3. Each man had a plainly visible tattoo on his hand. The tattoo was one of the standard U.S. Navy tattoos. The personalities portrayed in the art work were symbols of meanings that could not be expressed in words. And yet, the men were of the masculine types that appeal to women—he-men, virile, and self-confident.

Just as the rugged tattooed man in the Marlboro cigarette advertisements symbolized the cigarette's new brand personality more effectively than words, so images often speak volumes for companies and their products.

PUBLIC RELATIONS

Every employee of a company is, in a sense, a member of the public relations department.

A large oil company in the Midwest made a survey several years ago in the communities where its plants were located, in order to find out what people in the community thought of the company. The most interesting finding was that 77 per cent of the people who held favorable opinions of the company had received their good impressions from talking with one or more satisfied employees. Conversely, 56 per cent of those who held unfavorable opinions about the company had talked with one or more dissatisfied employees.

The study provided startling proof of the importance of satisfied employees to any public relations program. On the basis of this and similar studies it seems plain that while good employee relations may be possible without good public relations, it is not possible to have good public relations without having good employee relations.[6]

Fundamentally, public relations is not a program, but a philosophy. It is not a kind of "lotion" which can be applied when needed. It is a point of view or an attitude that permeates all of a corporation's activities. It is a way of business life that demonstrates a continuing sense of responsibility toward every institution and person who is directly or indirectly related to the company. It seeks to earn and maintain the confidence and respect of people. Respect and confidence must be de-

---

[6] *Public Relations Journal,* Vol. VIII, No. 9. See also *The Management Review,* American Management Association, Inc., January 1953, p. 11.

served—not acquired by a program of publicity. Modern management realizes that it must have a full awareness of the public judgments which will be passed on actions when they are known.

The man responsible for public relations in any company is the president. As executive officer, he has the responsibility of chief decision maker. All members of the public relations department must be really helpful to the president and other executives who give their leadership to the company and the community.

Many people imagine that public opinion can be purchased. A common delusion is that if a company has enough money to pay for printing, advertising, and "propaganda," peoples' minds can be changed. This is not so as Earl Newsom, a leader in the field, points out in the following statement:

> You may remember the effort made some years ago to make Cincinnati "United Nations conscious." During a six-months campaign almost 13,000 people were reached directly through the PTA; every school child took home literature on the UN programs; 10,000 in the Catholic PTA were exhorted by the Archbishop to support the UN; club women sent 1,000 letters and 1,350 telegrams to the American delegation; local radio stations averaged more than 150 spots a week. There were newspaper features, club speakers, and car cards. In all, more than 59,000 pieces of literature were distributed.
>
> At the end of the six months, only half as many people considered the United Nations a means of preventing war as thought so at the beginning. There was almost no change in the number of those who thought the UN should take an active part in world affairs. At the beginning, 76 per cent of Cincinnatians were in favor of the United States joining a movement for an international police force; at the close 73 per cent. Fewer people favored UN control of atomic bombs. There was no change in the number of those feeling the U.S. should trade more with other countries. There was no improvement in those knowing what the UN is and how it works. Criticism of the record of the UN actually increased during the campaign.
>
> Why did people respond in this way? Perhaps because most of us tend to resist when somebody tries to *sell* us something that is going to change our views. But I suspect that the people in Cincinnati during that six months got their chief impressions of the United Nations, not from the campaign but from their observations of what was happening at the UN during that particular time. Corporate managements are fast learning that their public behavior in times of crisis and trial does far more to create public attitudes toward them than most of the "literature" they develop to "educate the public" in between times.[7]

---

[7] "A Philosophy of Corporate Public Relations," a report of an interview conducted by editors John H. Smith, Jr. and Edwin C. Kepler in Mr. Newsom's office in New York on March 1. *pr* (*Quarterly Review of Public Relations;* 1010 Vermont Ave., N.W., Washington, D.C.), April 1957, pp. 7-14.

Purposes of public relations programs

Certain managements assume that a company's publics should be "educated" to understand and go along with the company in attaining its objectives. The management thinks mainly in terms of interpreting the company to the public through education. Such programs often fail. Companies that seek to educate their publics so that they will be more sympathetic toward the company are likely to be disappointed. Educational programs can perform some important functions as in giving information about matters that affect the public directly such as airline flight schedules, safety precautions, and services available, but deep-seated convictions and attitudes are not often changed merely by giving information.

Employees who lack what the company considers to be a fair attitude toward the company's goals and profits will not have their attitude changed by a formal information program. They need a changed management framework of thinking from that of the old master-servant relationship to one of participation.

Realistic-minded managements do not seek to change basic attitudes of employees or members of the general public such as voters. Instead, their public relations programs have more feasible purposes such as seeing to it that the company is a good member of the community where a plant is located, that it carries out the company's responsibilities as a "citizen," and works with every one of its publics to their mutual advantage. A sound public relations program is a "two-way street" and includes as a major purpose interpreting the public to the management.

Some managements claim that they have no public relations program. In actuality, every company has public relations whether or not it wants to. It deals with people. The value of a "formal program" is that people become conscious that an effort is being made and they give credit accordingly. Many managements are doing some things quite well but they are not getting credit for them from their people. They have not formalized their efforts, clarified them, and made people conscious of them.

Big business

Most companies, particularly big corporations, need more friends. This is indicated in a report made by Erwin O. Smigel, sociology professor at Indiana University. He found that a person forced by unusual circumstances to steal from an organization would probably pick a big business as his victim. More than 60 per cent of those questioned would pick on big business ahead of small business and government. The reason most commonly given: Big corporations "can afford it best." The study also showed that while most disapprove of stealing in any form, they feel strongly opposed to cheating small businesses.[8]

The well-known attitude of hostility toward bigness has caused corporations to utilize advertising. This kind of advertising has the purpose of building in the minds of millions of readers a mental image of the company as a friendly group of people who are good neighbors, good citizens, and good customers. Managements of big companies realize that they must do more than make good products at reasonable prices and build industrial plants which are necessary in national defense—they also have to make themselves liked as a company and be looked upon as a friend.[9]

Community leaders

One of the most effective points of entry into a community is through the persons of top levels of status and authority. Every community has certain informal leaders who have influence in manipulating rumor and opinion. Company managements supply the leadership to many progressive communities.

Sometimes we can appreciate this most easily when we see its evidence in the negative form—the lack of real leadership. A business magazine, for example, described the situation in one large Midwestern city in these terms:

> Lagging economically behind competing cities, its efforts to keep pace are hampered by lack of dynamic leaders, business hesitancy in a labor-run town, caution of capital.
>
> Downtown's decline has been hastened by the failure of the city to attract outside risk capital, by the conservatism of its own third and fourth generation wealth, and by the slowness of its public improvements. . . .
>
> . . . But this year, when the Civic Progress group hoped to replace the 1914 city charter with one that would weaken the ward politicians and strengthen the mayor, they failed. . . .
>
> "It may be," a sociologist says, "that our businessmen are afraid to stick their necks out in a labor-run town."
>
> Other reasons, too—other influences, quite likely, also are at work:

---

[8] See *Business Week,* January 19, 1957, p. 174.

[9] See G. D. Crain, Jr., "Big Business Needs Friends," *Advertising Age,* February 4, 1957, p. 72.

By scattering to several suburbs, businessmen may have broken the links that held them together

Increasingly, as firms sell out or merge, [this particular city] is becoming a city of absentee-controlled companies. A man who yesterday ran his own firm today is only a vice-president of a larger one from out of town. His [local] stature is downgraded.[10]

Participation in community affairs by management involves some obvious dangers. When a company takes sides in a controversial issue, some enemies are made. The company is also accused of running the town. As a result, some companies discourage their local managers from becoming active in civic affairs. They are not allowed to contribute personal leadership, time or money to local causes. The home office management may also fear that when their local manager becomes involved in the community, he will not be a good manager because he will let his feelings toward the community interfere with his business judgment. Eventually such a policy brings more problems than solutions—the company is looked upon as an exploiting force rather than a friendly neighbor. In spite of the dangers of misinterpretation of management's good intentions, progressive companies want the management and the employees to become integral parts of the community. Management men can participate in civic affairs, give financial support, and offer leadership without being accused of running the town or imposing political domination for the company's financial benefit.

The people of most communities today take an intense interest in the affairs of business concerns that affect them, their friends, and their neighbors. This development can be attributed, at least in part, to the fact that as corporate businesses grow, more and more people, as employees, suppliers, customers, investors, and as neighbors, are directly and indirectly affected by what the corporation does and how it does it. Sensible managements recognize this mutuality of relationships. When a survey of public opinion was made in a Midwestern industrial city, opinions toward seven corporations were evaluated. The findings showed that the company that paid the highest wages was not considered the best place to work. Instead, the most respected and best-liked companies were those that had transmitted to their neighbors the feeling that they were something more than profit-making machines. Over the years, they had convinced the residents of the community that management wanted to help create better lives for those who worked and lived there.[11]

One of the most striking developments in modern business is the concern of top executives with plant-community relations. The explanation

---

[10] *Business Week,* August 24, 1957, pp. 56-68.
[11] See *The Management Review,* American Management Association, Inc., June 1957, pp. 44, 45.

How to work with your neighbors to protect your home and community

Community crowded?

Neighborhoods decaying?

Housing deteriorating?

In neighborhoods throughout the nation today, citizen groups by the score are tackling, and licking, the manifold problems of modern community growth.

They are people just like you. They have found strength and success in numbers . . . by keeping up their own homes . . . by joining with their neighbors in community improvement projects and thereby gaining better living conditions for all.

You will find that *everyone* is interested in bettering his way of life. You will find it easier to gain better living conditions when neighbors join forces. By forming, or joining, a local community improvement group you gain many personal benefits yourself.

Keep up your home — work with your neighbors

Keep up your own home. Then talk with your friends, local business leaders, neighbors. Discuss this message with them. If conditions in your community need correction, *get together to get things done.* Get the facts, set practical goals and act. Your group might begin by undertaking special neighborhood projects: clean-up campaigns, street or sidewalk repairs, gaining and upholding better housing and zoning laws. Today you might want improved garbage collections. Tomorrow your group could spearhead a combined community conservation, rehabilitation and slum-clearance program.

ACTION and many local agencies can assist you

Cooperation is the key to success. Work with the many private groups which already exist. Talk to your city, county or state officials. They can help *you*—your group can help *them*.

Use the points at right as a basic organization and operating guide. For further information, write ACTION—the American Council To Improve Our Neighborhoods.

It is a national citizen organization dedicated to home and neighborhood improvement. It can help you by sending suggestions, ideas and success stories on how other community improvement groups began, what they have done, and how they did it.

Use coupon to send for free publications

Fill in the coupon below to receive the following booklets and reports:

1. Time for ACTION
2. The Complete ACTION Catalogue of Publications.
3. The ACTION Reporter, a monthly newsletter.

For information on a specific home-improvement or group project, write a letter explaining the exact situation to ACTION.

How to conduct a successful group

1. Organize systematic methods for getting the facts . . . household surveys, meetings with key officials, employment of expert counsel.
2. Present the facts to the people, your civic leaders, the local authorities.
3. Work with other local groups and official agencies.
4. Plan long and short-range objectives . . . each with a concrete beginning, middle and end.
5. Maintain a continuing program. Vary it. Make membership easy, keep it representative.

Some things your group can do

1. Keep up your own homes, encourage others by sharing your experiences in housing improvement with them.
2. Organize neighborhood and block groups to handle their own problems.
3. Undertake special neighborhood projects: clean-up campaigns, planting trees, converting vacant lots into pleasant playgrounds.
4. Be the "watchdog" on city services and facilities, guard against violations of housing or zoning codes.
5. Publicize community improvement projects and maintain contact with national groups such as ACTION.
6. Hold periodic Community Conferences, invite civic officials to explain local laws and answer neighborhood questions.

GOOD NEIGHBORHOODS ARE OUR NATION'S STRENGTH

ACTION

American **C**ouncil **T**o **I**mprove **O**ur **N**eighborhoods

ACTION:
American Council To Improve Our Neighborhoods
Box 462, Radio City Station, New York 20, N. Y.

Please send me special ACTION material that will help me organize, join or conduct a Community Improvement Group.

Name_____

Address_____

City_____ State_____

Organization (if any)_____

for this concern is not quite so simple as critics sometimes make it out to be. Critics may think it lies solely in the profit motive, but when executives are questioned about it, they often reveal that they are interested in a good plant-community relations program not simply because it is "good business" but also because they think it is "right"—a fitting and proper aspect of the activities of a responsible business.[12]

The "good neighbor" policy of any company in its community relations is best implemented not by a formal program of economic arguments, but by a sensitivity to the feelings of the people in the community. Here is an example:

> The Texas and Pacific Railway has lines only in Texas, Louisiana and New Mexico. W. G. Vollmer has been T & P's president since 1945. Since then the old T & P has become very human indeed. One day—for instance—the Dallas office got a heartbroken letter from a little girl along the railroad's line: "Your big train killed my black cat named Cinder. He had one white whisker and I loved him very much. Marlene W—-." T & P folks spent a lot of time locating another black cat with one white whisker and a lot more time patiently negotiating with a little boy and persuading him to swap the cat for a puppy. But one morning the same "big train" that had run over Cinder I stopped at Marlene's home. The engineer climbed down and put Cinder II in her arms. There wasn't a dry eye on the train.[13]

Plant tours for employees

One way of increasing a community's knowledge about the activities of a local business is through a program of tours of a company's plants and grounds. These may be either for the employees or for members of the community. Plant tours for employees are highly beneficial in companies of almost every size. The employees in a company of only 50 people may be just as remote from management as those in companies having thousands of employees.

Plant tours for employees are easily conducted. Usually, a director of the tours is appointed from the personnel department. He asks each department head to select one employee for the next tour. The director invites those chosen to spend an hour as a group with him. He briefs the employees on where they will go, what they should try to see, and whom they will meet. He tells them that the group will meet the president (or other top level executive) in his office for an hour or two at which time he will try to discuss topics of interest to them.

---

[12] Adapted from editorial comments about the work of Hazel C. Benjamin, *Harvard Business Review*, September-October 1956, p. 22.

[13] "The Human Side—Working for the T & P," *Sales Management*, September 1, 1953, p. 8.

In advance of the tour and while still in the group meeting for briefing, each member of the group writes out a question which he would like the president to answer. The suggested questions are discussed openly and the group decides which questions are to be submitted to the president. The chosen questions in written form are given to the president before the tour begins. He mentally prepares himself for his session with the tour members.

A time and place for the start of the tour are agreed upon. As the tour group visits each department, a member of the tour group who works in that department acts as a guide to the group. He takes care of questions about the department and makes the introductions essential to a friendly visit. When all departments have been visited, the tour group enters the president's office. The president then becomes the host, discusses the questions submitted in advance, and explains his current goals for the business.

The costs of these tours are negligible but the results obtained from this simple procedure have been markedly successful. The plan can be adapted to and used by any company. Employees like it because they get a chance to ask questions, to visit departments they would like to see in order to note how the work of other employees ties in with their own, and they get a chance to sit in the president's office while he talks to them about the business.

Plant tours for community members

Members of the public learn and accept new ideas slowly and—even more important—what they learn is often by interaction of neighbor on neighbor without a formal program. On the basis of the flow of ideas, the American public can be stratified into three categories: idea starters, idea spreaders, and the very large group of inert citizens, the idea users.[14]

The idea spreaders are most easily recognized. As an example, barbers are community opinion spreaders. A few companies pay special attention to them by holding an annual "Barbers' Day" at the plant. Every barber in the area is invited to a plant tour. Color movies and discussions with top brass are on the agenda.[15]

Plant tours and open house days for other idea-spreader groups are arranged by many companies. Certain occupational groups may be especially invited such as teachers, ministers, newspaper editors, engineers,

---

[14] See *Personnel Journal*, November 1956, p. 235.

[15] See "Who Are Today's 'Liberals'?" *The Management Review*, American Management Association, Inc., January 1951, p. 3.

civic officials, and key customers. An open house program should have a theme. The theme should be dramatized. One company that had just constructed a new building chose accessibility to the city as its theme. This was dramatized by having several clients arrive simultaneously by different means: one group came by cruiser, another by helicopter, others by car and plane. Newspapers played up the story with three-column headlines: "Visitors Arrive by Land, Sea, Air."

By tradition, top management men stay in the background at an open house. They are available and usually constitute a receiving line. If the number of guests is large, however, the company officials show by special signs that their offices are open to any visitors. Tour guides may introduce them in the course of the tour.

Relations with the press

Newspaper reporters are always on the alert for stories of news value. The reporter who has heard about a layoff, a labor dispute, or a proposed management reorganization, assumes that he has a right to know all about it. Unfortunately, too many reporters are more anxious to present in screaming headlines something that is wrong than to explain calmly the things that are right. Even though all the facts are given a reporter, the emphasis in his write-up is more likely to be faultfinding than strictly factual. Hence, top management should appoint a contact man to the press. The contact man will learn how to get along with the local newsmen and give them what they want with a minimum of danger to the company's good relations with the public.

The contact man will learn that he cannot threaten, scold, or pressure newsmen. Newsmen do not want to think that personal friendship influences their evaluation of a story's news interest. They also think that being an advertiser should have no bearing on whether a story is published or how it is written. If the news is bad, they want to present it as they wish.

Generally, most smart contact men know how to handle publicity of an unpleasant nature—they face up to it. They present to the press all the bad news in a complete package and deliver it to the papers immediately. Under no circumstances do they permit unfavorable news to be withheld and reported at a later day. The policy of airlines, railroads and industry in general is "get the bad news off the front page the first day."

Top management, not the specialists, must control the corporate image

Most college students who are considering public relations as a career assume that a company's public relations should be controlled by the public relations director and his department. This is an erroneous assumption. A company's public relations should always be under the control of the top management. The specialist in public relations suggests objectives and programs and puts the approved ones into effect *after* they have been approved by top management. The chief executive must synthesize the public relations into a consistent image of the whole company. The public relations specialist is a staff man, not a line executive. His thinking must be integrated with that of management. As someone has said: "Public relations, like war, is much too important to leave to the specialists."

COLLATERAL READINGS

For All Students

Gellerman, Saul W., "The Company Personality: What It Is, How It Got That Way, and What To Do About It," *The Management Review,* American Management Association, Inc., March 1959. The title explains the content of the article.

Martineau, Pierre, "Sharper Focus for the Corporate Image," *Harvard Business Review,* November-December 1958. The author is a recognized leader in motivation research as applied to marketing. Describes unconscious factors in corporate images.

For Advanced Students

Finn, David, "Struggle for Ethics in Public Relations," *Harvard Business Review,* January-February 1959. Discusses whether business should respect the right of people to make up their own minds rather than attempt to engineer consent.

Bayton, James A., "Researching the Corporate Image," *pr, The Quarterly Review of Public Relations,* October 1959. In corporate image research the company is transformed into a humanlike entity. Human personality traits adhere to it.

For Men in Business

Hodges, Wayne, *Company and Community.* New York: Harper & Brothers, 1958. Supplies a wealth of information on the ideals, aims, and techniques of industrial community relations for use by executives in planning long-range community relations.

Gellerman, Saul W., "The Company Employment Image: Attracting People of the Caliber You Want," *The Management Review,* American Management Association, Inc., March 1960. Discusses employment images as an aspect of corporate planning.

1. What is meant by the term "corporate image"? What benefits may a favorable image give a company?
2. Differentiate between brand image and corporate image.
3. In the survey of company presidents, where did the majority feel that company prestige began?
4. What methods are used for estimating corporate images?
5. Mention some of the persons and factors that build a company's corporate image.
6. Why should public relations be considered a philosophy and not a program?
7. What may be learned from the results of the movement to make Cincinnati "United Nations conscious"?
8. Explain why a sound public relations program is considered to be a two-way street.
9. Why do progressive companies want both management and employees to actively participate in civic affairs?
10. Why are plant tours valuable for companies of all sizes?
11. What principle lies behind an occasion such as "Barbers' Day?"
12. Who should control a company's public relations? Why?
13. Of all the ideas presented in the chapter, which ones are of special interest or value to you?
14. What did the chapter contribute to your future relations with (a) the men who supervise your work, (b) employees whom you may supervise?

PROBLEMS AND PROJECTS

For All Students

1. Collect several advertisements that were designed to help build a corporate image for the company. Ask several friends to state the image which they think each of the advertisers is trying to build. Compare the answers for each company.
2. Assume that you have been placed in charge of public relations for the institution you are attending. State the problems and your objectives. Do you wish to overcome the negative or build the positive? To whom are you directing your program?

For Advanced Students

3. Many students look forward to a career in public relations but have only vague ideas about it. Examine the available literature in order to clarify the purposes and techniques of modern public relations. Describe the work from the career standpoint.
4. Some persons think that absentee-owned companies take less interest in the community than locally owned companies and that when executives of a company are moved from plant to plant, they have

less interest in the community. Make a study of these two questions. You might begin by reading *Business Week,* January 17, 1959, p. 49.

For Men in Business

5. Describe the corporate image of a company that you know well. Does the company have a formal or planned program? If it does, describe it. If it does not, suggest suitable objectives and procedures for building a worthy image.

6. Interview several employees and ask each to describe the image of the company for whom he works. Ask each to assume that a friend is thinking of applying to the company for a job. How would he describe the company to the friend?

Whenever you visit several homes or educational institutions, you will, if you are alert, note that each has a distinctive psychological atmosphere.[1] Every company, too, has a climate of its own. Each department or work group may have a unique climate. The atmosphere of one, for example, is tense because of the presence of an authoritarian boss and a lot of neurotic employees. In another place, the pervading atmosphere is cheerful and friendly because the boss is an emotionally mature leader and the employees are relaxed and cooperative. The people, not the buildings or the furnishings, determine the atmosphere of a place.

The psychological climate in industry is so important that every student and supervisor should be aware of its influences. He should be sensitive to it whenever he enters an office or a factory. He should observe it, not merely to evaluate it, but for ways in which he can contribute to a positive psychological climate wherever he goes. No one has ever found a perfect climate, geographically speaking, and no one will ever find a company that always has a perfect psychological climate. We can, however, note factors that add to or detract from its benefi-

---

[1] The psychological climates and their influences on students of several colleges have been measured and described in systematic studies by C. Robert Pace and George Stern, "An Approach to the Measurement of Psychological Characteristics of College Environments," and by Donald L. Thistlethwaite, "College Press and Student Achievement," and "College Press and Changes in Study Plans," in *The Journal of Educational Psychology*, issues of October 1958, October 1959 and August 1960.

9 The Psychological Climate in a Company

cent aspects and intelligently play our own role in its sunlight or its shadow.

Many of the factors that are influential in producing the climate within a company have been discussed in the preceding chapters. In this chapter we want to increase our awareness of various kinds of psychological climates and sharpen our abilities to distinguish them. The alert member of industry who visits or works in different companies soon learns to sense the climate of each firm. Here are several examples:

A very large public utility operates under close government regulation and entrenched labor union influence. The employee setup is highly mechanized. The personnel department is rigidly limited in making its decisions. Even the hiring is automatic when the formal specifications are fulfilled by the applicant. The employees who work in this atmosphere merely need to know and follow the rules. Individual initiative is quite circumscribed. Only those who seek life-long security and are willing to conform to the operational climate tend to remain with the company. Few have any strong desire to grow. Their motto, "Nobody here ever sticks his neck out," is not hung in a frame on the wall of each office—it's so evident that it need not be put into words.

In contrast with this public utility, a large retail clothing company is fast paced—decisions on style selection are proved right or wrong in a few weeks. Executives tend to hire employees who also are fast-paced. Here the members of the personnel have to function far more rapidly than in the public utility where decisions must wait months for approval from regulatory agencies.

In a certain company of another industry, the dominant climate is cold and logical. Engineering knowledge is essential to corporate effectiveness. Everyone seems to think or try to think in a mathematically precise manner. Logic rather than feeling is dominant. Management men have come from the engineering staff.

A metal manufacturing concern is still under the control of a fatherly founder who runs the place in a paternalistic manner. Executives and employees have to be careful not to disagree with or hurt the feelings of "The Old Man."

Obviously, the personalities of controlling executives will always have considerable influence on a company's climate. In addition, the larger environmental settings in which the company operates also have some important influences on the climate.

1. *What extra-company environmental influences should be noted?*

Social scientists who study "climatic" influences from outside the company are especially interested in cultures. *Culture* may be defined as a "body of learned behavior," a collection of beliefs, habits, practices, and traditions, shared by a group of people (a society) and successively learned by new members who enter the society. Cultures are found in nations, communities, and companies. The older the institution, the more certain the likelihood of finding such a body of learned behavior. A culture is more than a collection of loose, disconnected ideas. Rather, it is a somewhat unified whole, no element of which can be disturbed without repercussions on a wide scale. If, for example, an American agricultural specialist is assigned to improve the economic well-being of the people of a foreign undeveloped area, his natural tendency is to attempt to organize the land areas in fields sufficiently large for the use of agricultural machinery. To accomplish this, he may have to take account of graves, shrines, dowries, and sex habits as well as rights of way, inheritances, and property laws. Failure to recognize these cultural influences is likely to bring about firm resistance. People who believe in their own cultural heritages will sabotage a program even though it would undoubtedly bring about economic benefits for them.

Cultural factors may also cause a management to refuse to go into a financially profitable venture. An example has been cited of an American businessman who proposed to the heads of a British firm of silversmiths that they consider the financial advantages of legally avoiding American import duties on finished silverware by shipping American-owned silver into England, performing the finishing operations there, and then shipping the finished goods back duty-free. The immediate reaction of the British firm was one of rejection because of the fact that in England a silversmith company that works on silver it does not own occupies a much lower social status than a company that owns the silver it fabricates.[2]

Cultural differences in regions of this country are often influential. Many supervisors believe that persons reared in rural areas are likely to have somewhat different attitudes toward work than those reared in the city. Rural-reared employees are more willing to accept and attempt to fulfill management's work expectations. Generally, morale surveys of

---

[2] See J. M. Juran, "Improving the Relationship Between Staff and Line," *Personnel,* American Management Association, Inc., May 1956, p. 522.

industrial firms indicate that the attitudes of employees toward management are relatively better in the South than in the older industrial centers of the East.

The mores of the people of one geographical location often differ from those of another region. Studies have shown, for example, that the Tennessee Valley Authority had certain supervisory problems because southern workers were not accustomed to the rough-and-ready language of those foremen whose previous work experience had been in the North.[3]

2. *What is the dominant orientation of the management?*

One of the most easily noted orientations of a management is in the relative importance of production in comparison with that of sales. In a production-oriented company, the management is especially concerned with the manufacturing equipment, the shop employees, and the engineering staff. Quality control is a popular topic in management meetings. And a frequently-stated criticism is that the sales department makes too many ridiculous promises to customers in regard to delivery dates. Executives are likely to be pessimistic about what the product will do. To make the production easier and technically more correct, this kind of management likes to get large, long-term contracts with the big merchandising firms such as the Chicago mail order houses. That kind of arrangement makes it easy to put production on a stable, efficient basis.

In contrast, management in a sales-minded firm usually prefers small contracts with many customers. Selling, not production, is fun. The popular topics in management meetings are marketing and advertising. Executives try to find out what the customers want by means of expensive market researches. They are apt to assure the customer who buys that the product will do or be just what he wants. And they are optimistic about the quality of the product.

In some companies, the significance of the sales volume to the top management men is especially important. Sales volume may be sought to build high salary-paying practices and retirement benefits for the major executives, to earn profits for important stockholders, or to satisfy status needs. Fortunately, most professional management men have a desire to develop a bigger and stronger company because of the chal-

---

[3] See Milton M. Mandell, "The Effect of Organizational Environment on Personnel Selection," *Personnel*, American Management Association, Inc., July 1953, p. 14.

The Psychological Climate

lenge, and not for the sake of special benefits to any one interest group.

In small companies, wholly or largely owned by one man, the basic orientation may be toward the building up of an estate for the benefit of heirs. Few profits are spent for research or further growth. Instead, the policy is usually described in such words as "The old man is milking the company in order to take care of his incompetent heirs." The owner of such a company may have one or two competent assistants but most employees are chosen because they can do a passable job and are willing to work for below-average pay. No one is selected for employment because he has excellent potentials for growth or because he eventually will become a first-rate aggressive executive. If, by chance, a young man of drive and high aspiration is employed in such a company, he soon leaves for a better job in a growth company where the psychological climate is more favorable.

3. Is the management expansion minded?

The average industrial employee is likely to prefer to work in a climate of stability, a place where few changes take place. The ambitious young man, in contrast, usually prefers to work in a less stabilized place, one where the growth of the company is more important than piling up cash. Relatively few managements like to pile up profits into cash reserves. They prefer to invest their profits in expansion programs. Historically, the contrasts between cash-rich and expansion-minded managements are often studied by comparing the earlier development of Montgomery Ward under Sewell Avery, and of Sears, Roebuck and Company under General Woods. Avery followed a policy of piling up cash. Woods used cash for expansion. Later, Montgomery Ward management recognized that profits are most productive when put to work.

Most American executives subconsciously think of expansion first and profits second. Business boom and growth are more thrilling to the aggressive executive than money in the bank. Many have sought expansion for the sake of expansion with little regard for profit. Certain managements find this necessary, at times, for competitive reasons. Short-term return on money invested in expansion may be less important than ultimate survival. The history of automobile manufacturing offers examples of this kind of need for disinterest in profits in one year for the sake of later corporate health.

An important need for survival expansion arises when the company's main product is declining in sales simply because it is approaching the end of its life cycle. New products are like people—they are born, grow slowly, reach the vigor of maturity, decline, and eventually die. Alert managements therefore seek to retain their corporate vigor by expanding their activities toward the acquisition of other products and companies, often through mergers.

A company may have any of several reasons for seeking to bring another firm into its own organization: to strengthen product lines, to join forces with another firm that deals in the same product, to build a vertically integrated unit as exemplified by the textile maker who buys a clothing manufacturing company; to diversify its products and to bring about operating savings. In some cases, the competitive position may be improved through the acquisition of a larger sales force or a better geographical distribution of sales offices.

A common reason for mergers is the need for high-grade management. Perhaps the management of the acquiring company consists of old men, while that of the acquired company has a crop of capable young executives.

One of the benefits for the small companies is that they may have a chance to grow under the umbrella of a large organization.

Fundamentally, however, expansion is a part of our business way of life. If growth through further enlargement of the company's current activities is no longer feasible, expansion must be made into unrelated lines. The company diversifies. Some of these diversifications may be organized in a manner that brings about integration—others merely bring about a polyglot collection of companies.

> The typical polyglot is a company that has diversified through acquisition until it is no longer a single operation or group of related operations but a collection of widely varied activities related only by the common management at the top.[4]

Many merged companies suffer severe varieties of "indigestion" before the added segments become profitably integrated with the parent company. Some never seem to reach stable profits and growth. This suggests that the growth-minded man who chooses a company for its expansion mindedness should also try to note whether the executives are as able and versatile as the expansion program requires.

On the human relations side, personality clashes and conflicts of interest often arise between members of the acquiring and the acquired managements. The controlling company's management may make decisions which the acquired company's executives know to be wrong. Or the latter may give only lip service to the central management's programs while running the operations in a manner that produces only mediocre results. Members of a central management and those of a

---

[4] "Polyglots—and a Touch of Babel," *Business Week,* September 21, 1957.

The Psychological Climate

subordinate management need years of experience with each other in order to develop mutual confidence and wholehearted cooperation. Until such time as they have gone through tribulations together, they lack identification with each other and remain a polyglot collection in spirit as well as in structure. The psychological climates of merged companies often remain varied and uncertain until their members have experienced suffering and success with each other.

4. Is decision-making centralized or decentralized?

Every large company, whether resulting from a merger or not, can be viewed as a grouping of smaller business units. Decision-making may be so highly centralized that no subordinate can act on his own until he has got a signal from someone up the line. Initiative on the part of middle management men is stalled. Personal growth is difficult because of hampering red tape.

Emphasis on decentralized decision-making has increased and is a direct result of the desire to improve human relations in the large organization. The current policy in some large companies is to create a small business atmosphere by dividing the company into a number of smaller units, each headed by a man who has broad responsibilities. The concept, as Harlow H. Curtice of General Motors has expressed it, is:

> . . . to divide the business into as many parts as consistently as [sic] can be done, place in charge of each part the most capable executive that can be found, and develop a system of coordination so that each part may strengthen and support each other part; thus not only welding all parts together in the common interests of a joint enterprise, but importantly developing ability and initiative through the instrumentalities of responsibility and ambition—developing men and giving them an opportunity to exercise their talents, both in their own interests as well as in that of the business.[5]

One of the best ways to utilize human relations for business success is through the delegation of the decision-making power, as Curtice has pointed out. Henry Ford almost lost his business as a result of failure in this realm.

Anyone who has risen to top levels in management, whether as the owner-manager or as a driving member of a large organization, is likely

---

[5] Harlow H. Curtice, *The Development and Growth of General Motors,* Statement before Subcommittee on Antitrust and Monopoly of the U.S. Senate Committee on the Judiciary, Dec. 2, 1955. From Alan C. Filley, "Human Relations in the Growing Company," *Personnel,* American Management Association, Inc., September-October 1957.

to feel that the success of the business is due to his efforts. It is difficult for him to let others make important decisions because he learned to depend upon himself rather than others. To develop his subordinates, however, he must learn how to allow them to make mistakes. Generally, executives who really want their subordinates to grow do so by choosing the goals but letting them decide how the goals will be attained. For the ambitious young man, the extent to which he will have the privilege of decision-making in regard to operational procedures is one of the most important aspects of a company's psychological climate.

5. Who are the controlling personalities in the company?

The formal head is not necessarily the most influential leader in a company. The man in the president's chair may in reality be a figure-head—some other executive may be setting up the goals, pushing the sales, and directing the organization. He, rather than the formal head, also may be looked to as the leader by the customers.

In some companies, the financial powers may be the controlling influences. These may be represented by very intelligent, forward-looking men who know how to select and inspire the company's leaders. Or they may be conservative old fuddy-duddies who try to hang on to a traditional dividend rate.

The fact that a company is under the financial control of a banking group or a foundation does not mean that the management provides a good or a poor climate, one that is favorable or unfavorable for the young man who wants to grow. If he knows, however, who the controlling personalities are, he can evaluate their influence more accurately.

If the founder of the business has, in his old age, turned the company over to a charitable foundation for control, the climate is likely to be one of conservatism, and a conservatism that leads to the decline and eventual death of the company. Continuity of family control is often safeguarded by the placing of large blocks of stock in the hands of a trust which retains them for the benefit of the original owners' children and grandchildren.

If an heir remains at the helm, the management may be competent or incompetent, probably competent because the founder usually trains able assistants who can guide the heir. In many cases, too, the founder puts the heir through years of strenuous training for later responsibilities. If the heir does not achieve an acceptable level of ability, the board of directors quietly arranges for his departure from the company. The members of the board and other executives are likely to have so great an investment in time and money in the company that they will not allow a weak scion to jeopardize their investment through poor management. In American business, dynastic succession is less prevalent than popular fancy imagines. A survey of public opinion on the subject, made by The Psychological Corporation, indicated that almost one third of the public believes that most of industry is run by a few wealthy families like the Rockefellers, du Ponts, and Fords. Yet careful analysis of the top command echelons of the 500 largest publicly owned corporations of the United States revealed only a 14 per cent incidence of dynastic relationships, much of it at secondary levels. Relatively few managements take a fixed stand on the question of nepotism—the showing of too much favor by one in power to his relatives. Informally, many companies do not employ relatives. Even though they have no established policy, they feel that hiring relatives tends to mean trouble. Also, many able young men refuse to work in their fathers' companies because they want to earn their titles and responsible positions. Besides, some sons know the father too well!

Many heirs are sons of forceful fathers. Such fathers are apt to be exceedingly demanding and intensely critical of their sons' performances. Many fathers are still at the height of their own powers when their sons reach adulthood. "In the very best of circumstances, sonship in dynastic industrial families is no bed of roses. The pressure can be intense, and an heir's opportunity to spread his wings may be long delayed." [6]

6. What are the ages of the top management men?

Boards of directors usually want the management to have some young men rather than a management group of old men only. The perpetuation of the company is a basic responsibility of a board. They like to be able to refer to the management as "young and aggressive." Of course a company that has young men only may be as weak as one that has only old men.

Age is a poor criterion of managerial ability. Many of our most competent top executives are in their fifties and sixties. Some are even older. Generally, top management men need judicial wisdom that has developed from years of experience. Their greatest contribution is in guiding the younger, more aggressive members of middle management. "Judgment ripens as the hair whitens." The fact that a management

---

[6] See "Heirs at the Helm," Forbes, November 15, 1957, pp. 63-72.

can be described as "young and aggressive" does not necessarily mean that it is efficient and successful.[7]

The full development of a personality often takes place in the later years of life. Maturity means that the emotional roadblocks of youth have been overcome so that energies are fully released for constructive activities. Of course when senility is evident, its ability to influence management should be, and usually is, reduced.

Actually, the continuation of executives in jobs which they are no longer able to fulfill is not management's most serious problem in regard to age. Instead a greater difficulty centers in the presence of old men on all levels who have become embittered through the years. Their unhappiness tends to permeate the department or division to such an extent that they create a psychological climate of pessimism, frustration, and criticism. Top management is usually aware of their negative influence on the younger employees but does not want to be so unkind as to remove them. It is up to the younger person, therefore, to evaluate objectively the pessimism of the disgruntled old employees and plan his career without letting their soured outlook affect him.

7. Do the personalities at the top mesh together?

Many students who read the literature on human relations in business gain the impression that the ideal climate for a company is one where no frictions can be found—only sweetness and light. This is not true. We should not look for a complete absence of friction because that may mean that the members of the organization are not thinking aggressively, but just coasting.

Growth companies, those noted for their growth in sales over the years, can be characterized by their vigorous management spirit. Their management men have an enthusiasm for achievement. They like to accomplish things. They like to take the lead in making changes.

Growth companies have organized programs of corporate planning, product research and development, market research, and diversification. They plan their programs with recognition of an accelerating rate of economic and technological change and an accelerating intensity of business competition.[8]

---

[7] See Ralph A. Bing, "The Fallacy of 'Young Management,'" *The Analysts Journal,* August 1957.

[8] See Robert W. Smith, "Management Spirit: The Big Intangible in Corporate Growth," *Sales Management,* April 18, 1958. Smith is Assistant Director, Economics Research Division, Stanford Research Institute, Menlo Park, Calif. This article presents preliminary findings from a study of 210 apparently "gifted" companies, selected for having exceptional growth histories as measured by growth in sales.

Management spirit is a tremendously important factor in corporate growth. When individual executives have a strong drive to achieve, and are dynamic and imaginative in their thinking, they are bound to develop some frictions with their colleagues. But their frictions usually occur in regard to objectives and the means of attaining them, not in regard to petty or personal differences. Good management men do have conflicts with each other but the conflicts have corporate purpose and result in a meshing of personalities and common enthusiasms.

When a smart management man realizes that his own personality limitations are a handicap to his associates and subordinates, he selects a colleague who provides for the gaps in his own personality pattern. One well-known American corporation is headed by a man of driving ambition and pride. He is meticulous in attire and in speech but mercurial in temper and is abrupt with people. He has become so aware of his negative characteristics with people that he has delegated most human relations responsibilities to a fellow executive who is of great ability but the opposite of himself in attire, manner, and speech.[9]

PEOPLE WANT TO WORK FOR A COMPANY THEY CAN RESPECT

They want to be proud of their organization—its reputation, its product or service, its worth-whileness in the community. If they are asked where they work, they want to be able to reply with the name of an outfit with a good standing.

If a company departs from ethical standards in any of its dealings—not only with employes, but with customers, suppliers, stockholders, neighbors in the community, and so on—low employe morale results. This extends to matters such as a company not keeping up its equipment, or letting the appearance of its buildings go downhill.

I can think of a plant which was starting to allow poor quality goods to get out into the market. This seriously affected employe attitudes there. Conditions of pay, working conditions, work required, all stayed the same—and by this I mean in a favorable sense—but the defection on quality hurt employe spirit.

I know of another company, about the same size, making a similar product. The president could be described as just plain tough. Fair, but really tough. And employes griped about the work that was returned to them because Quality Control set such high standards.

But their morale was higher than in the other plant. They were able to take pride in their company's product. And tough though he was, they respected the president. He was able, and he was on the level.

SOURCE: Douglas Williams as interviewed in "Six Policies Increase Will to Work," *Nation's Business*, November 1958; copyright © 1958 by *Nation's Business—the Chamber of Commerce of the United States.*

---

[9] See *Fortune*, August 1957, p. 112.

The Psychological Climate

How companies acquire good climates

Very few managements can hope to acquire a favorable climate by issuing directives or by hiring outside experts to produce it. If, for example, the president is upward-oriented in the direction of spending most of his time and thinking to gain the good will of financial interests while he neglects his associates and subordinates, the climate is not likely to change until he takes a sincere interest in the members of the organization. In time, when he has solved the company's financial problems, he or his successor can modify the climate by concentrating on giving the employees greater psychic income. He will organize programs and direct his colleagues in ways that will provide for the employees' emotional participation in the business. He will treat all members of the organization as colleagues whom he likes. He will conduct himself in accordance with high ethical standards and he will hold employees to high work standards. The systems he installs will be backed up by his continuing efforts to work with his people. As someone has stated: "Today's weather is tomorrow's climate."

A superior top management not only sends its junior executives to special institutes to take management courses but also realizes that courses will not change a company's climate. Further, alert managements realize that subordinates cannot put into effect any new practices they learn which contradict those of their superiors. The middle-level man who learns sound principles in a course knows that it is unwise for him to do his work in a manner that is markedly different from what his superior expects. Wise managements know that middle-level leadership of, say, the participative variety cannot function with top-level leadership of another variety, such as the authoritarian. The climate of an organization will not be changed by a few injections of some new philosophy of leadership.

A good climate is more likely to develop when there is a normal growth pattern of structural changes in the organization. Rapid changes disrupt the climate. An organization may be rather loose-knit by design. After all, the structural organization is less important than its spirit. Frequent reorganizations tend to destroy the spirit. Structural changes, when made, should be minor, and evolve slowly over the years. They should bend to the requirements of growth, not be imposed suddenly. Climate is likely to be favorable when the company has a record of steady growth and a low percentage of personnel turnover.

Climate is developed when employees know that management is sincerely interested in their welfare. Every executive should spend a large part of his time in close individual contact with employees in

The Psychological Climate 153

regard to their work. Each employee should feel that the boss is interested in helping him to do his work, not merely inspecting him or his work. The functions of a supervisor are to evaluate the job the employee is doing and to help him do a better job.

One clue to the extent that a management is vitally interested in employees as human beings is the company's effort or lack of effort in finding jobs for capable employees in other organizations if management cannot, in its own company, provide opportunities that will use the employee to the full. Few employers follow this policy, and yet this policy not only attracts superior men but also causes many of those who have left to come back with experience and loyalty that could not be obtained otherwise. Some managements also assist laid-off employees in locating positions elsewhere. They do more than offer good wishes— they make vigorous effort to help them find new positions.

Another clue to the climate encouraged by a management is indicated by the way members of the organization preface explanations of new ideas. If they present them in an extremely apologetic manner as "Now I know this sounds silly," or "This is just off the top of my head," the climate within the organization probably does not stimulate growth through individual initiative. An employee should voice respect for his colleagues but he should not have to apologize for an idea which he believes might be helpful. If executives have indoctrinated subordinates with the dictum, "Don't open your mouth until you are sure of what you are saying," they are promoting second-guessing rather than original thinking. The test of an idea is to see it in action. The employee who presents only sure-fire ideas is not a creator—only a describer of old ideas.

The company that has a good psychological climate is likely to have many executives who are always accessible to the employees. Employees can easily identify themselves with them because they are true leaders who practice participative methods. Men of great character and good will usually enjoy and contribute to the positive psychological climates wherever they go.

The supervisor's influence on the climate

Even though many members of an organization contribute to its climate the supervisor is in a key position of influence. If he is lacking in emotional control, he is likely to have many employees who feel that they are working under intense pressures. A tense atmosphere prevails. The typical tense supervisor is demanding in his directives. Emergencies seem to take place every few minutes. Urgently needed materials have not arrived. A machine breakdown is slowing production. Defective products have been returned by a customer, and so on.

"Of course I want it back today! If I had wanted it tomorrow, I would have called you tomorrow."
SOURCE: *by Interlander,* Advertising Agency Magazine (*September 27, 1957*).

Some work groups have many tense members. Sometimes the cause for their presence may be found in a selection bias practiced by the personnel manager—he just happens to like people whom he designates as the "ulcer type." In a tense group, whatever the causes of the continuing strain, the supervisor usually looks tired. The typical harried supervisor says that he cannot trust anyone to do anything right. He claims that he cannot hire good men these days. Either they do not know their jobs or they do not do an honest day's work for their pay, and so on ad infinitum.

The emotionally mature supervisor has few of these problems or convictions. Instead, he likes his employees and speaks well of them. He has few crises because his employees help him to plan ahead and to anticipate problems. He stimulates productivity because he has developed a climate where people are genuinely interested in the work problems and in doing good work. They know that the boss likes them and respects them and their abilities. Good work climates do not develop by chance. Instead, they are produced by leaders of good will and competence.

The Psychological Climate

For All Students

"The Motivation to Work: Some New Insights," *Personnel,* American Management Association, Inc., Sept.-Oct., 1960, p. 5. Summarizes studies of factors in employees' work satisfaction as reported by Frederick Herzberg and his associates.

Perry, John, "Human Relations in Small Industry," Small Business Administration, Washington, D. C., March 1954. Gives excellent examples of good versus poor climates and describes influences involved.

For Advanced Students

Argyris, Chris, "The Organization: What Makes It Healthy?" *Harvard Business Review,* November-December 1958. Study of a company organization, pronounced "healthy" by management and workers, but which on probing examination turned out to have certain perplexing contradictions. Presents a tentative theory for regarding the contradictions.

Schutz, William C., "Interpersonal Underworld," *Harvard Business Review,* July-August 1958. Presents research studies that seem to offer a new and better way to pick combinations of people who will work well together.

For Men in Business

"Checklist of Factors Affecting the Business Climate," Economic Research Department, Chamber of Commerce of U. S., 1615 H Street, N. W., Washington, D. C. Designed to aid leaders in identifying factors that affect the climate and in planning a program of constructive action. Free booklet.

Deutsch & Shea, Inc., Consultants, "Company Climate and Creativity," *Industrial Relations News,* 1959. Report of a survey of 105 scientists and administrators on their views concerning climate and aspects of control by management.

QUESTIONS ON THE CHAPTER

1. What factors are influential in determining the atmosphere of a home, schoolroom or company?
2. Differentiate between the production-oriented and the sales-oriented company.
3. How do regional differences affect the attitudes of employees?
4. Which is the more important to most American executives, profits or expansion?
5. What are some reasons for company mergers?
6. Discuss possible effects on company climate of the ages of top management men.
7. Explain the current emphasis on decentralized decision-making.
8. What is the danger of turning a company over to the control of a charitable foundation?

The Psychological Climate

9. Differentiate between the public belief and the actual percentages in regard to the frequency of dynastic relationships in industry.
10. What are some characteristics of the executive who tends to make a work atmosphere one of tension?
11. Describe ways in which executives may develop a good company climate.
12. Of the ideas presented in the chapter, which ones are of special interest or value to you?
13. What did the chapter contribute toward your future relations with (a) the men who supervise your work, (b) the employees whom you may supervise?

PROBLEMS AND PROJECTS

For All Students

1. Describe some of the psychological climates that you have experienced in living centers or classrooms. What key personalities were influential? Did you try to improve any negative or depressing climates? How?
2. When you enter the business world as a worker, you will note the climate of the new work environment. If you try to contribute to its favorable aspects, what dangers should be recognized? Must a contributor be more tactful than a noncontributor?

For Advanced Students

3. Examine the available literature on growth companies. Note their main characteristics. Begin by reading Philip Marvin, "What Makes a Growth Company," *The Management Review,* American Management Association, Inc., October 1958.
4. If you are interested in rating scales for personality traits of individuals, try to develop a rating scale for measuring psychological climates of companies. Little research has been done in this field but checklists are available.

For Men in Business

5. Describe the climates in some of the departments or companies where you have worked. If the climate changed in the course of time, describe probable causes. Did you change in your reactions to it or did the climate really change?
6. Perhaps you have worked in a company where the advent of a new executive head changed the climate. Describe the before-and-after situations. How did the changes affect you? Were you able to contribute to any improvements?

PART 3

Management, Supervision, and Management Functions

If YOU VISIT THE HOME OFFICE OF A CORPORATION AND TALK with a member of the upper echelon of management, you may find an organization chart hanging on the wall. The executive also probably has a loose-leaf book that describes the company's formal organization: the chain of command, the span of control, and the formal policies. The book will also describe certain specialized functions and define their place in departmental relationships.

The mentally alert person who takes a job in a large company is especially anxious to see the organization charts and any accompanying descriptions of their meanings. The charts will orient him in regard to any subsidiary companies, major divisions, and departments. The charts show how the company is structured as an organization. The chain of command is indicated from the stockholders down through the board of directors, the president, vice presidents, department heads, foremen, and the operating personnel.

Managerial practices in regard to charting the organization vary. Some companies have elaborate and detailed organization charts. They may even have an expert who devotes all of his time to the study and planning of new chartings. Other companies may have no charts hanging on the walls and no descriptions filed in executive desk drawers. All companies do, however, have some kind of framework within which their activities are organized. That is why many courses and books on management

10

Management:
Its Upper Levels

give so much attention to organizational structure. Of course, the formal organization is of itself without significance except as human beings give it meaning and value. The meanings and values that are expressed by the people who work in the organizational framework are part of the informal organization. In this book, we are devoting most of our thought to the informal organization, but we must also appreciate the need for the formal organization.

The formal structure delineates the duties, obligations, and work rights of each member. It reveals to whom and for whom each member is accountable in the performance of his functions. It provides a base that sets forth the expectations of the members as to the extent that each person may look to or expect designated persons to carry out assigned tasks. Lines of communication and work channels are indicated.

Some experts in company organization believe that organizational structuring should be done on a strictly logical basis. They think of it as essentially an engineered system or framework into which people will fit themselves. There is, of course, need for logic in planning a company's organizational structure. Textbooks and courses in management treat the topic in terms of necessary logical work relations.

The need for a formal organization

In a small business, the head can oversee and direct every operation. He himself can supervise and train his few employees as he works with them in his shop. He may wrap shipments and take them to the post office. He can keep his records, write his checks, and make the bank deposits. He may even write the advertising and put the stamps on the outgoing mail. He can, however, keep sole control of the operations only as long as the business is small. As the business expands, he must delegate more and more responsibility. In time, he must have department heads who supervise the performance of certain designated functions. If the business grows still more, departments become major divisions or subsidiary companies. Eventually so many problems arise that a formal organization must be planned in a logical manner.

A formal organization develops because the setting of objectives, planning, and coordinating of resources, technical and human, can be achieved only when some persons are given authority to direct the work of others. The area of authority usually needs definition. Persons accountable for specific functions and operations must be designated.

The top coordinating authority cedes to subordinates parts of his authority. These in turn yield parts of their authority to lower echelons of management and supervision. Theoretically, the level of ability to manage decreases in the flow of authority from top to bottom. The individual at the top is always responsible for those under his direction regardless of how remote they may be. Even though he has never seen them, he is still their operational superior. The president of a corporation having a hundred thousand employees who live in various countries and cities is their organizational head regardless of the number of managerial levels between him and them. The productiveness of employees on all levels may be helped or hindered by the formal organization, but the informal relations are likely to be even more important. If you know the informal functioning of management, you will find any future study of the formal organizations more fruitful.

The type of product sold, size of the company, method of distribution, and selling policies of the company are all factors which help determine the type of formal organization a company develops. The formal organization is, however, constantly modified by the human beings in the organization. Some executives are more competent and more ambitious to grab additional responsibilities from others. As a result, the formal framework is warped to fit the strong and the weak people in the organization. To appreciate some of these formal and informal relations we shall discuss them in terms of the formal structure as indicated by the usual line of authority from the board of directors downward.

Top management consists of the policy-making executives who are responsible for the over-all direction of all company activities. These include the chairman of the board of directors, the president, vice presidents in charge of major divisions or functions, officers of the company, and the more responsible key executives. They develop the broad plans for the organization's future activities. Middle management puts them into effect through procedures that implement the plans. Lower management, often called supervision, puts the procedures into effect on the operational level through personal supervision of line workers.

Boards of directors

A board of directors is an official body of persons who direct the corporation. They have important legal status and certain responsibilities. They give the corporation perpetuity. They function as a balancing influence between the operating management and the stockholders. They have the responsibility of protecting the stockholders' investment. They are expected to direct the company so that investors gain an adequate return on their investment. They may or may not hold positions on the boards of other corporations. Some are paid for their services; others are not paid. The board has the responsibilities of electing the management, borrowing money, approving major capitalization expenditures, acquiring other companies as in mergers, declaring dividends, approving salaries of major management men, overseeing basic corporate affairs, and establishing corporate policies and objectives. They evaluate and approve or disapprove the president's long-range plans and deviations from past policies.

In fiction and drama, directors are often pictured as dopey old men of wealth who somehow fell into membership on the board, usually as a result of inheritance or family connections. Actually, most members of boards are intelligent and conscientious and take seriously their responsibilities. Most are able men whose abilities as business leaders have been proven. Generally, they work with the operating management as advisors, as controls, and as stimulators.

Their personal contacts with members of the organization are mostly with the president and other officials such as the treasurer. They rarely express opinions or give directions to any member of the operating personnel. Minutes of their meetings are circulated among few persons other than themselves and anyone who sees their minutes is expected to keep in strict confidence any knowledge of their plans and problems.

In theory, they hire and fire the members of top management, particularly the president. In actual practice, the president often selects the men who are to become members of the directorate. In some companies, the president functions under a hand-picked board that looks to him for counsel and instruction in regard to the board's actions. Obviously, the president who has such a board is the key controlling member of the entire company. If he is a man of outstanding ability, the company prospers. If he is of mediocre ability, the company is likely to drag along with passing success until such time as the president retires or dies, or the board decides that the management should be changed.

The effect on a company's vitality of a hand-picked board often depends upon the kinds of persons with whom the president likes to associate in business and in his social relations. If he enjoys friendly social relations with financial men, such as heads of banking firms, he naturally selects financial men for membership on his company's board. A board made up of the president's friends may be, but is not necessarily, a rubber-stamp for the president. When a man becomes a member of the board of a large corporation, his sense of responsibility to the company usually takes precedence over personal friendship.

Also, we should recognize that a president may have a hand-picked board because the president himself is a strong character. He is an individualist, knows the business well, and is determined to run the company as he sees fit. He usually chooses men who know some phase of the business that he does not care to deal with himself. He may even choose very able men whom he is trying to develop for future needs of the company. He, too, wants a board that will approve his plans but he retains the presidency because he is the ablest man in the management. A company under such a president is likely to be successful as long as he remains vigorous. He, however, is likely to hold on to the presidency too long and thus cause the business to decline. Furthermore, he seldom develops men who are as strong as he. He is likely to be so strong a manager himself, and so individualistic, that he is unable to build men who can take his place as soon as his energy and leadership ability begin to decline. Sometimes he is removed from the presidency in a proxy fight, but usually he keeps control of enough stock to enable him to have himself re-elected as long as he wishes.

Some boards consist of the company's leading stockholders only. If each member owns stock and the directors are appointed because of their stock holdings, the board members are likely to give the affairs of the company regular attention.

If several financial firms have invested heavily in a company's stock, they naturally wish to be represented on the board. These "bankers on the board," as they are usually called, are likely to know very little about the company's products, how to make or sell them. They do know how to read financial statements. They are likely to be poor leaders of men because they have learned how to develop the respect of other financial men, but not the respect of operating executives or employees. Strangely, many of these financial men on boards are not so greatly concerned about whether the company makes money as about their continued membership on the board. Membership on a number of boards gives the prestige-hungry financier about the same kind of satisfaction as that which is enjoyed by the academic man who likes to be a member of many committees of professional organizations.

Fortunately, those financiers who seek membership on as many boards as possible do not usually express a drive for power by imposing their will on executives or employees. After they have helped to select the top executive of a company, they deal with him, and he may manage the company as he wishes—so long as he produces profits or can satisfactorily explain why profits are not being made.

Another type of board consists of major executives of the company. These men are not financiers. Each is an experienced, tested member of top management. Some of our largest and most successful companies have boards of this kind. These are full-time, not part-time boards. They meet every working day. Some investors prefer to invest their money in companies that have a board made up of executives who own large amounts of stock. The president of such a board is likely to be an able leader who knows how to build and direct a team of able men.

A good board of directors is made up of men of ability—men who look upon their membership as a serious responsibility. They give the company their best in counsel and direction.

The president

Fortunately, most presidents of America's corporations are men of ability. They think of managing as a profession that requires special abilities in the functions of management: organizing, planning, staffing, executing, and appraising. As the chief executive officer, they realize that they are expected to strike equitable balances among the conflicting interests of employees, customers, stockholders, and the general public. They have a deep sense of responsibility for their office.

One approach to the understanding of the young corporation president is via reports concerning the Young Presidents Organization. To be a member, the president must have become the boss of a substantial company before age 39. When 393 members of the YPO participated in a self-analysis survey, some findings about the "typical" young president were:

His company employs 235 people.
He has 7 scheduled appointments each day.
He works more than 58 hours a week.
He spends 80 per cent of his business day "just talking to people." [1]

The typical president associates with other businessmen and attends meetings in order to keep in touch with trends that affect his business. He may not be especially sociable for the mere purpose of being with people. When he goes to a meeting, he goes to learn rather than to fraternize with associates. He of course identifies himself with other successful leaders in business. He wants their good will but he wants to earn it by their respect for the kind of business he directs.

He reads the financial pages, the business journals, and newsletters in order to give himself the background needed to do his job. He is mentally alert in regard to all matters that affect his company and the industry of which the company is a part. He is informed about national and world affairs. He thinks of his company in terms of its setting in the affairs of business and society. He constantly improves his per-

---

[1] See *Sales Management*, April 15, 1954, p. 67.

spectives. He wants to be able to interpret the courses of events and predict how his company will be affected so that he can take appropriate action.

In many cases, the man chosen for the presidency is the executive vice president or one of the other vice presidents. If the members of the board of directors have been foresighted, they have directed the staffing of the company with able management men so that the office of the president can be filled whenever the president retires or leaves.

The usual fictional description of the way men are selected for the presidency is one of intense rivalry between vice presidents. Each candidate is portrayed as using chicanery to gain ascendance over his rivals. The most ruthless man supposedly wins! This kind of situation does occur, but only rarely. Far more commonly, the board of directors studies the company's needs to increase its chances for future success. If the company's finances have been weak or too limited, the directors may decide that the next president should be a financial man who has the ability to influence other financial men and institutions that can strengthen the company's financial resources.

If the company's greatest need appears to be the reducing of production costs, an able production man may be chosen. If the sales record has been disappointing, an effective sales manager may be the choice. If the research and development of new products has been too slow to meet competition, the man chosen is likely to be an executive who has a successful record in that function, and so on. The company needs that seem to be the greatest are a dominant influence in the kind of man the board members elect. Sometimes the board members choose an "interim president," someone who can build up the company in regard to what is believed to be a short-term need such as establishing more workable relations with labor unions. This type of man is likely to be near retirement age and the directors tell him about their hopes and expectations so that he can prepare a successor for the long-term needs of the company. Presidents, in short, are chosen in a businesslike manner —not to provide drama that will entertain spectators.

Human relations problems of presidents

The main human relations problem of a president is his own personality—how he feels about people. His attitudes toward people are basic. If he has had so many failures in getting along with people that he is sour on much of the human race, he will unconsciously transmit that feeling to others. If he is so unsure of his ability to handle people that he deals with them in a mechanical manner, people will think of him as a cold fish and look elsewhere for understanding. If he is so insecure that he protects himself from others by developing an armor-plating of dignity that causes people to keep their distance, people will treat him with awe but consider him a stuffed shirt. No matter how many fine speeches he makes, his real personality will be communicated to others. They will not tell him their honest reactions, but they will think them and act accordingly.

Fortunately, many a president realizes his own personality shortcomings and he therefore chooses colleagues in management who offset his weaknesses. He chooses an executive vice president, general manager, or assistant who provides the warmth and personal leadership that he lacks. If he realizes that certain people dislike him, he may arrange to have a "buffer" personality on his staff.

Generally, a president functions in either one of two ways: by limiting his contacts almost exclusively to his vice presidents and top executives or by personally knowing and exerting influence to and through many members of the company. The former type is characteristic of large bureaucratic organizations such as those of the government and large corporations, the latter of companies where the president is a true leader of men rather than an impersonal delegator of assignments.

Presidents recognize their own human relations problems. They discuss them with other presidents and consultants. The kinds of problems that concern them were indicated in one of the American Management Association's "Presidents' Round Tables."

These meetings are a strictly off-the-record affair, attended by a score of chief executives of companies with sales ranging from a few million dollars a year to hundreds of millions annually. Each chief executive has an opportunity to share his confidential problems and innermost thoughts with others of equal rank and to get their joint comments, advice, and suggestions.

One of the chief headaches discussed in a recent meeting was the problem of *judging the performance of a company's management personnel.* The presidents wanted to know how best to size up the results of their executives' actions, how to appraise the individual executive, and what measuring sticks to use.

Another and related problem which the participants were eager to hear about was how their colleagues get measurements of their own personal performance as a president.

As one would expect, a question that struck sparks was, *"How can I know what's really going on in my company?* What system of review can I set up that will warn me of trouble before it gets too serious?"

A group of problems that interested these men revolved around *the art and science of delegation.* The round table participants wanted the other presidents' advice on where to draw the line between too much and too little delegation; which matters a president can delegate to others and which he cannot; how he can tell when he is delegating properly; and how he can delegate and still participate in company operations as much as he thinks he should.

Other high-interest topics included ways of improving communications between departments; getting the most out of research and development; building the right kind of board of directors; and developing broad, constructive, and creative thinking about the company on the part of all its management men. Along with these came other human relations questions:

> Whom do you put in charge when the company's chief executive is away?
> Is the failure to designate someone a sign of poor organization?
> Should you let people in the company know whether you have chosen your successor—and who he is?
> When should an executive retire?
> What, if any, are the advantages of filling top management jobs from outside the company as against promotion from within?
> How can you get the feeling of management as a professional activity to pervade your organization?
> When a man is being considered for a position, how much weight, if any, should be given to the kind of wife he has? [2]

These and related daily problems of presidents as well as those of other members of management have resulted in the common definition of management as "the art of getting things done through people."

Assistants to the president

The pressures on a president are numerous and the responsibilities varied. Quite often, he realizes that he should be in two or more places at the same time. Also, he may have some work that he does not want to entrust to a female secretary. One solution for his needs is to appoint one or more staff assistants who are given the title of "Assistant to the President," "Executive Assistant," or "Administrative Assistant." Generally, the assistant has staff rather than line responsibility. If he has line responsibility, he is called "Assistant" rather than "Assistant to." The "Assistant to" is not held accountable for operating results. His functions are limited to furnishing services of a specialized nature.

---

[2] For full details of this report, see Harwood F. Merrill, "The Listening Post," *Management News*, September 1957, p. 6.

One of the arguments for the appointment of assistants to the president is that the job gives the appointees training and development for greater responsibility. The position enables the incumbents to share the boss's problems and to gain top management perspective. Many an executive needs one or more assistants who are trained in his way of doing things, men whose loyalty can be depended upon. Certain presidents could not function effectively without such assistants.

Other presidents believe that the position of "Assistant to" should not exist. If a man is to be trained for line or other major responsibility he should hold a line job and be an assistant who can be held directly responsible for operating results. The way to learn to manage is to manage. A man must direct employees and have employees look to him for direction, not to someone above him, if he is to be developed for management. He must be on his own rather than have his thinking dominated by that of a chief whom he serves so closely that only the chief's thinking appears to be right.[3]

The trend in management practices is to have the president or other manager appoint a subordinate manager, a next-in-command man, rather than install an assistant to himself. If a top executive needs a subordinate to take over during his absence, the next-in-command type of executive assumes the full role of the executive whose position he fills temporarily.

Vice presidents

Men who have important responsibilities near the top management level and do an especially good job may be given the title of vice president. They have major responsibilities such as heading production or sales. Generally, the title is earned rather than acquired as the result of nepotism. In many companies the executive vice president is chosen from the vice presidential group. This is a highly-sought position, not only because of its extra responsibility, but also because it suggests the possibility that the executive vice president is in line for the presidency.

In some industries, particularly in communications and banking, the title of vice president may not involve executive responsibilities. The title may merely mean that the holder is a customer contact man who needs the title in order to deal more effectively with clients or customers.

---

[3] See Louis A. Allen, "Can You Eliminate Assistants?" *Dun's Review and Modern Industry,* December 1956.

Span of control

In some companies, the president may have as many as 20 subordinates reporting to him; in others, only the executive vice president is directly accountable to him. Most companies have a span of control for executives of eight or less.[4] Generally, the concept of span of control is applied to the highest operating officer of a company or the head of a major division.

Most top executives try to limit their span of control to six or eight subordinates. The directing executive wants to be able to keep in close touch with each subordinate executive's operations and accomplishments. He must, however, do more than keep himself informed in a factual manner. He must also give each executive personal attention on a continuing basis. He must enable each subordinate to feel that he is important as a person and that his superior is so keenly interested in his work that the work is constantly checked regarding its current progress and how management may help him do his job as expected.

"He simply refuses to delegate authority!" SOURCE: by Dale Mc-Featters, courtesy Publishers Syndicate (30 North LaSalle, Chicago).

[4] James H. Healey, "Coordination and Control of Executive Functions," *Personnel*, American Management Association, Inc., September 1956. See also *Executive Coordination and Control*, The Bureau of Business Research, The Ohio State University, 1956.

The informal organization

Many students who study management structure are inclined to think of authority and responsibility as if they were physical entities. This, of course, is not true. Organizational structures should be thought of in terms of the individual perceptions and mutual expectations of the members of an organization. If these do not agree with the lines on the organization chart and its corresponding manual, the chart and the manual are mostly window dressing. Only the human relations as they really are give the organizational structure its true meaning.

Many of the daily activities of employees are not defined or sanctioned. We note everyday examples when employees treat the boss in terms of their feelings toward him rather than in accordance with the authority vested in his position, when employees cater to a certain member of management in order to get his good will even though he has no supervisory responsibility for their work, when employees make "understood" agreements with rate-setters and inspectors by adjusting machines to operate so as to keep production within the limits determined by the employees, and when employees help an old or sick supervisor whom they like by doing his work for him so that he may continue to hold his job.

Anyone who works in the business world knows that almost every employee interacts with other employees and executives who have no charted relationship with them. The coordination of work activities requires it. These interaction relationships are not so vague or surreptitious that they cannot be recognized. Instead, the newcomer to an organization who has studied the formal organizational structure learns, if he is smart, to look for the informal relationships. These can be identified by the alert observer.[5]

The person who wants to be an intelligent participant in business will seek to learn about the logical planning of organizational structures but he will find his study of a company more interesting when he asks questions such as "Is the official (usually the president) shown at the top of the chart really the controlling personality or is he a figurehead?" Is a given corporate framework a kind of strait jacket that restrains initiative, spontaneity, and imagination, or is it one that stimulates individual and company growth?"

---

[5] See Ralph M. Stogdill, "The Sociometry of Working Relationships in Formal Organizations," *Sociometry*, August 1949, pp. 276, 286. Also, Ralph M. Stogdill and Carroll L. Shartle, *Methods in the Study of Administrative Leadership*, Monograph No. 80, The Ohio State University, Bureau of Business Research, 1955. Describes a technique for identifying informal working relationships.

THE OHIO STATE LEADERSHIP STUDIES

PERSONNEL RESEARCH BOARD
OHIO STATE UNIVERSITY

The formal organization chart is shown in solid lines with the pattern of interpersonal relationships in checked lines. The checked lines show the first two choices; that is, the two persons within the group with whom most time is spent. The arrow points in the direction of the person named. Thus, number 51 named number 1 and number 511, and number 1 named number 2 and number 51. One can see what are sometimes called "violations" of the organization chart. The studies of various staffs suggest that "violations" are a normal activity. The informal or interpersonal work structure represents day-to-day relationships. Staffs are usually fairly familiar with the organization chart, but little has been done to acquaint staff members with an understanding of the "interpersonal chart."—The informal structure is one index of the dynamics of getting work done, and it appears that for efficiency it will necessarily deviate from the formal structure. Extreme deviations, however, may hamper rather than promote efficiency.—In the organizations studied thus far, executives who devote a relatively large amount of their time to planning rank high in being chosen as ones "with whom most time is spent in getting work done." In eight out of ten organizations studied, those executives who were frequently chosen attempted to delegate a comparatively high degree of authority to subordinates. It thus appears in the staffs studied that high sociometric ratings, planning activities, and delegation of authority go together. SOURCE: Carroll L. Shartle, "Leadership and Executive Performance," Personnel, American Management Association (March 1949), pp. 370-380.

"Is the organizational structure master or servant?"

"Does the structuring unify the activities of the people who are now in the organization and make them more effective in their work? Or is the structure designed for theoretically ideal people rather than real ones?"

"Is the framework so designed that it enables a dominant personality such as an owner-manager to continue to dominate the organization by keeping control in his hands? Or is it designed to give many subordinates a chance to grow?"

An organization chart is not a substitute for competent men of good will who get together and work at the jobs to be done. Nor does it protect the company against stupidity at the top, in the middle, or at the bottom of the organization. It does, however, aid in attaining objectives.

Appraising a management

Managements of companies are frequently appraised by members of the company, by financial analysts, by consultants, and by others. There is, however, no generally accepted method.

Of course, financial men examine thousands of management records to note whether a specific corporation is making or losing money, how much, and for how long. Their opinions, as the result of their findings, are expressed to some extent in the price they are willing to pay for the company's stock. Many appraisals of both incorporated and non-incorporated companies are made by bankers, especially when the company seeks to borrow money.

A determining factor in the appraisal of a company's financial worth is the management. Prospective investors especially want to know the quality of the management. One financial writer expressed the investor's interest by the question, "Is your money riding with a top management team?" Another used a similar question, "Is it a 'pace-setter' or an 'also-ran' type of management?"

Of the total of some 300,000 industrial firms in the United States approximately 30,000 are believed to have management of high quality.[6] Even though the quality of management cannot always be measured statistically, the best judgment indicates that these 30,000 firms are members of a very select group.

In some of the remaining 270,000 firms, the quality of management is so obviously poor that astute judgments are not necessary. Lack of quality can be recognized by failure to hold a proper share of the market, by the slowdown or decline in growth, and by lack of drive among executives in the top management levels.

Weakness or excellence of management is likely to be in direct proportion to the amount of deadwood at the top. When deadwood executives hold the best positions, able young men of ambition do not wait

---

[6] See W. Arnold Hosmer, "Small Manufacturing Enterprises," *Harvard Business Review*, November-December 1957.

until they can take over more responsibility—they move to other companies.

Generally, graybeards must give way to crewcuts but a company may also have too high a proportion of crewcuts. The management evaluator wants to know whether the crewcuts are merely young and riding high

Management: Its Upper Levels

on the momentum given the company by the old men or whether the young men have acquired the lusty risk-taking powers of the old heads that built the business. The mere presence of young men in management is not enough to impress the seasoned evaluator of managements. He wants to know whether the intrinsic strengths of the old pioneers have been transmitted to the younger generation of executives. Years are of less significance than the degree of strength of the dynamic leadership attained by the successors.

Family-run enterprises are suspect as to the quality of management. Most families want to have increasingly higher dividends. They do not want to give up dividends in order to pay for new equipment or high salaries of able staff members. As a result, they often have outmoded equipment, go-as-you-please production methods, sketchy accounting, skimpy advertising budgets, inadequately-paid salesmen, and high-cost uncoordinated operations. Nor are they likely to hire outside consultants who might put them on a sound basis. They just continue to coast along until dividends decline to the point where the family members decide they had better sell out and take whatever they can get before bankruptcy.

Islands of autonomy exist in many large organizations. Clusters of executives and employees who "grew up together" understand each other and they function well but they are apt to function with a certain disregard for the other divisions of the organization. This kind of situation is especially likely to occur when one large company buys another company and transfers the personnel from the purchased to the purchasing company. The transferees naturally know and trust each other to a greater extent than they do members of the company that has absorbed them.

Some islands of autonomy also develop because the head of a division is unusually able. He hires men who admire him and they become more loyal to him than to the organization as a whole. When a number of these islands develop in a company, division heads whose offices are on the same floor may not confer with other heads in regard to mutual problems. They may even compete with each other to the extent of buying supplies outside the company rather than from divisions of their own firm. Tie-in sales that might be made are given to outsiders. In one chemical company, for example, the division heads of one office rarely conferred with related heads who happened to have offices in another building only two blocks away. As a result, these two blocks were called the "longest distance in the chemical business." [7]

Depth of management is a criterion applied to large companies. A

---

[7] See *Business Week,* June 1, 1957, p. 71.

In management, too...

Borg-Warner plans for the future

Like any team, a company's management is strengthened by the depth of its reserves. Accordingly, Borg-Warner several years ago initiated a program of building Management in Depth—to assure a continuing supply of capable executive manpower at all supervisory levels.

Basis of this activity is an intensive executive training program involving concentrated study of all company operations, and such management problems as maintaining a sound corporate structure, new product development, cost reduction, labor relations, communications, and similar subjects.

That the program is successful is evidenced by the fact that during the past few years many young but highly qualified men have been advanced to more important executive positions, and their places capably filled by others trained to succeed them.

Presently pursuing this program with increased effectiveness, Borg-Warner plans for the future confident that its management structure will continue strong.

DESIGN IT BETTER *MAKE IT BETTER*

BORG-WARNER.

310 S. MICHIGAN AVENUE • CHICAGO 4, ILLINOIS

To provide management in depth, most growth companies set up special training programs. And many ambitious young men investigate an employer's management training before taking a position with the firm. Other ambitious young men, however, think that they have better chances for advancement in a company that has no formal training program for young men, all competing with each other as members of a trainee group. Seniors who apply for their first long-term employment should consider the prospective employer's policy of management in depth as well as their own best potentials in regard to a formal or an informal training plan.

management may have able men in each top job but few or no replacements. Or the replacements that are available may be of a decidedly lower grade than the members of the top echelon. Hence, the death or retirement of a few men may weaken the organization to a dangerous extent. To overcome this danger, some leaders in management teach their subordinates that the test of a good executive is that he's not afraid to have a second man who's a real challenge to him. To be strong, a management must be built in depth. The men directly under the top men should be as good as, if not better than, the top men.

Top executives function in a "lonely" manner

Napoleon is supposed to have stated: "There's something awful in the loneliness of supreme command." One of the loneliest of men in a large corporation is the president. Even though he is by nature a friendly person, his position insulates him from others. He is not one of them in the fullest sense. His social life is largely limited to persons of similar station in life.

If the business is very large, the information that comes to him is likely to be prepared for him. People who come to see him plan their approach. He cannot learn how other people really feel and think through ordinary everyday contacts where everyone is natural. He spends most of his time in talking to people but he cannot talk about his own personal problems. And yet he must win the loyalties and respect of those who depend on him for leadership.

The top level executive cannot discuss some of his own thoughts and plans with his subordinates. He cannot, for example, "think out loud" as to which of several men he ought to promote to an important vacancy. If he mentions their names to someone else, his mention is likely to be construed and reported as though he had made a final choice.

He cannot discuss financial problems, new product plans, negotiations for purchase of plant sites, and a host of other topics until his own thinking has reached an appropriate stage. He must even consider the effects on others when he goes to lunch with subordinates. "Lunch with the boss" may imply significance in regard to an impending promotion to an existing vacancy and arouse apprehension on the part of those not invited.

The higher the executive in the hierarchy of management, the more insulated and lonely his position makes him. As a result, he may turn to consultants for counsel and business companionship.

Management men often hire a consultant in order to check their own evaluations of their business situation. As one executive stated: "I hire a consultant's services on a regular basis because if he can tell me something I haven't already known, I have been asleep!"

The Increasing Use Of Management Consultation

The most serious problem in many businesses today is the shortage of skilled managers. Sometimes this shortage is recognized only when a key executive retires and no acceptable replacement is at hand. More often, however, in these days of rapid industrial growth and frequent shifts of product lines the shortage is chronic. Management needs expert guidance in a hurry — to solve a commercial problem, to analyze the market for a new product, to diagnose the reasons for declining sales, to reorganize a production line.

Few businesses — even among the largest firms — have enough available management talent to cope effectively with such emergency problems. Few of the better managements, in fact, try to live wholly within themselves. They have learned that it is more economical and often more effective to call in specialized outside talent to cope with emergencies and to supplement the company's own thinking about new problems. And the hundreds of medium-sized and small businesses, faced with a critical competitive problem or with a desire to grow, are turning to experienced, reputable management consulting firms to help them solve these problems. It is the one practical way open to them to have available the array of talents and specialized services which they need in order to meet skillfully and promptly an emergency situation.

If you have an immediate problem on which you need specialized guidance you may find it advisable to discuss it with a management consulting firm. You will find that there are many excellent firms available for consultation on a wide range of administrative problems.

BARRINGTON ASSOCIATES, INC.

Business Research and Management Consultation Since 1926

230 PARK AVENUE • NEW YORK 17, N.Y.

SALES POLICIES AND METHODS • SALES COMPENSATION • SALES ORGANIZATION • MANAGEMENT CONTROLS
PERSONNEL AND LABOR RELATIONS • ORGANIZATION ANALYSIS AND PLANNING • MANUFACTURING METHODS
SYSTEMS AND PROCEDURES • OPERATIONS RESEARCH • WORK STANDARDS

Member — Association of Consulting Management Engineers

Consulting organizations such as this one and evaluations of their services are often discussed by members of the top echelons of management. Ambitious students who wish to become professional counselors in business should become acquainted with consulting firms. They enable the trained specialist to have an interesting career by serving a wide variety of companies.

Management: Its Upper Levels   **179**

Consultants feel at home in the top echelons of management. They customarily associate with men of ability. Top management executives know that the consultant has management's perspectives. The consultant is free from the ties which executives of the company have toward each other when they have worked side by side for many years. Men who work together cannot be entirely frank with each other because each knows the other man's blind spots, idiosyncrasies, and emotional needs. The consultant is a newcomer to these personal ties. He can be more objective than personal friendship may permit.

The ways in which a corporation president or top executive must function suggest that he should not usually be treated with awe. Instead, a friendly manner resulting from appreciation of his psychological situation is likely to be more appropriate.

COLLATERAL READINGS

For All Students

Davies, Daniel R., and Robert T. Livingston, *You and Management.* New York: Harper & Brothers, 1958. A practical introduction to the management field designed for those who are interested in careers as managers. Includes checklists and guides.

Henry, Kenneth, "Company Presidents Size Up the Board," and "The Board of Directors at Work," *Dun's Review and Modern Industry,* November and December, 1958. Describes interactions between the boards and presidents of several companies.

For Advanced Students

Gilson, Thomas Q., "Some Significant Projects in Recent Management Research," *Personnel,* American Management Association, Inc., September-October 1958. Describes the work of the four leading research groups in this field.

Glaser, Edward M., "Psychological Consultation with Executives: A Clinical Approach, *The American Psychologist,* August 1958. Psychology in action at the executive level. How one group of clinically oriented consultants functions.

For Men in Business

Write to the Association of Consulting Management Engineers, 347 Madison Ave., New York 17, N.Y. and ask for free booklets on what a management consultant does and how to go about hiring one. "How the Management Consulting Profession Serves American Business" is a recent title.

Also read the booklet "How Management Consultants Help Small Business," in the Federal Small Business Administration's *Management Aids for Small Business,* Annual No. 1, Washington, D.C.

Write to the American Management Association, Inc., 1515 Broadway, Times Square, New York 36, N.Y. for a *Directory of Consultant Members,* compiled biennially by the Management Information Service.

QUESTIONS ON THE CHAPTER

1. Differentiate between the formal and informal organizations.
2. Why is a formal organization necessary?
3. What are the functions of the three main levels of management?
4. Describe the general duties of a board of directors.
5. What is meant by "rubber-stamp board of directors?"
6. According to a YPO survey, what are some characteristics of a "typical" young president?
7. How are presidents often described fictionally?
8. What are the arguments for and against having "assistants to the president"?
9. To whom does the concept of span of control generally apply, and what is the average span in most companies?
10. What is a determining factor in the appraisal of a company's financial worth?
11. What is meant by the phrase that "to be strong, a management must be built in depth"?
12. Of all the ideas presented in the chapter, which ones were of special interest to you?
13. What did the chapter contribute toward your future relations with (a) the men who supervise your work, (b) the employees whom you may supervise?

PROBLEMS AND PROJECTS

For All Students

1. One famous industrialist stated: "Good management consists in showing average people how to do the work of superior people." This is a fine adage. How would you put it into effect? Apply it to a situation with which you are acquainted.
2. Would you like to become a member of a board of directors? How can a person became a member? For reference, see E. Everett Smith, "The Neglected Board of Directors," *Harvard Business Review,* May-June 1958 or other sources.

For Advanced Students

3. Examine the available literature regarding psychological factors involved in management's actions. An example might be Melville Dalton, *Men Who Manage: Fusions of Feeling and Theory in Administration.* New York: John Wiley & Sons, Inc., 1959.
4. Consultants and outside specialists can disrupt an organization. Make a study of some of the likely hazards in their use. Consult W. L. K. Schwartz, "What to Do Till the Doctor Comes," *The Management Review,* August 1958.

5. When out-of-town members of top management visit a plant, it is cleaned and spruced up before they arrive. This is a poor concept of top management. How can such visitors be given more positive meanings for the employees?

6. Some executives who retire go into consulting work. Does consulting demand skills that differ from those of the typical executive? Describe your own experiences with consultants, particularly those of the retired executive variety.

O F ALL THE DYNAMIC INFLUENCES THAT BRING ABOUT CHANGES in an organization, one of the strongest is that of the upward pressures exerted by the ambitious members of the *middle management group*. The executives who function on levels of responsibility between the top policymakers and the plant foremen or office supervisors constitute middle management. Examples are heads of the larger departments, managers of small plants, the chief accountant, the chief product development engineer, and the regional sales manager. Many of these men are so important to management that they, as well as the members of top management, are given annual bonuses.

Members of top management of the more progressive companies take an active interest in the morale and development of the men in the middle management group. As the men mature, the most able move up the line into the top management positions. The training and experience of these men represent a heavy investment. Many perform key operations in the business. Some have important direct personal contacts with customers. Top managements try to avoid loss of members of middle management. If several leave for better jobs elsewhere, their going is of deep concern and top executives try to correct the causes that bring about their departure. They are difficult to replace.

Their importance as a source of top management positions is indicated by the likelihood that about one half of the top level

11

Middle Management
and the Effects on People
of Changes in Management

executives in the course of a decade leave because of retirement, disability, or death. Generally, companies prefer to find replacements from the middle management group. Their development is of vital importance to the continued vitality of the enterprise. To move to the top, these men must become acquainted with the company's over-all situation. They must learn through daily job experience how to delegate authority in order to get results from their subordinate supervisors.

The attainment of middle management positions is fairly easy for the intelligent, well-trained individual. Most college graduates can do it if they wish. They need not acquire many new personality patterns nor do they have to learn how to assume responsibilities that are markedly beyond those found in many jobs on the lower levels. However, only a relatively few middle management men have the drive needed for advancement to the top levels where executives set general policies, develop broad plans, and establish business contacts with other top level men. Most middle management people prefer to remain where they are. They know that they have important positions and that their work translates top management's general policies and broad plans into practicable procedures. They have the satisfaction of knowing that they put plans into effect. Some are content because they prefer to enjoy life without the pressures and extra responsibilities inherent in the many top management jobs within their view. These men and women are the backbone of American industry and within themselves they know it, even though their job titles are not as shiny as those of the higher-ups. A business magazine editorial has paid tribute to them as follows:

> Everything must have a top and a bottom, and the middle is presumed to be a place of active movement, from which talent seeks its right level. Actually, some roads do not lead to the top. There are many able men of creative skills, of scientific bent, of philosophic perspective who have neither the gift of leadership nor the desire to assume it. These men serve in the middle management levels of industry. Often they are unselfish, and dedicated to the assignment of helping others get ahead, even at their own expense. Whether they stay in the second or third layers of authority may be a matter of personal choice, or of management decision based on a sensible appraisal of the individual and the circumstances.
>
> What is more important is that top executives recognize the "middle" men in management and show the proper sense of appreciation for services rendered. Who is this man who lingers at the half- or three-quarters post while younger men pass him, many of them grateful in after-years for coaching and guidance, a few of them callous and forgetful of the help freely given? He can be located in such diverse posts as department heads, regional sales manager, accounting supervisor, credit executive, traffic manager. He may be the scientist, the chemist, the mathematician, or just the jack-of-all-trades who is given all the ornery assignments where tact, skill, and common sense are basic requirements. Often this in-

dispensable person is a woman who has more management information at her fingertips than the president or the treasurer.

The years slip by, and the personality of the company and the individual merge in a common identity. Even the customers are aware of these key middle management people, and know how to pass routines and red tape by a letter or a phone call to them. Some eventually rub elbows with the brass and even give it a little extra polish; but others just carry on a day-long public relations job, internally and externally, without benefit of title.

There is some justification for sentiment when we think of these veterans on lower shelves of authority, but sometimes their services are taken for granted. They are treated like members of the family, especially members who never complain and are ignored because of this. Every company has these loyal servants who couldn't be top executives and have sense enough to know it, but they are responsive to praise, and equally sensitive, if quiet, in neglect.[1]

The more able middle management men are, in their thinking, oriented both upward and downward. They are oriented *downward* in the sense that they are concerned about operations, particularly with getting production out through the line workers.

They are oriented *upward* in the sense that they keep upper levels of management informed about production: reasons for inability to ship a customer's order on schedule, need for new equipment, serious causes of dissatisfaction on the part of the workmen, and so on. One of the signs of the lower levels of management is in their lack of orientation beyond the department.

Many members of middle management, though ambitious to advance, have much difficulty in reorienting their thinking beyond the department level. The skills, habits, and perspectives that enabled them to rise to middle management are not sufficient for top management functions. Some find it hard to understand why promotions and salary increases no longer come their way. The ability and energy that carried them to the midway stage in business are not sufficient to go to the top. Middle management men, to become effective members of top management, need special training to help them shift their thinking upward. One of the arts of management is not to let men grow stale.

Training managers

Middle management training is not as common as employee and foreman training in industry, but it is gaining increased recognition. A

---

[1] Editorial, "'Middle' Management Men," *Dun's Review and Modern Industry*, December 1956, p. 134. Copyright © 1956 by Dun & Bradstreet Publications Corporation.

survey of 250 members of the Society for Advancement of Management, characteristically middle management men, found that two out of three of those under 35, and one out of three of those over that age, were still taking formal training of some sort. Most members had plans for further improvement. The survey also revealed that 77 per cent of these executives felt that getting along with people was the paramount factor in gaining advancement. Most of this group felt their primary need was for more social skills. They wanted training in encouraging staff teamwork, in gaining the confidence of others, and in conference leadership. About 40 per cent felt the need of further study in such fields as engineering, accounting, business law, and production, though many wanted more knowledge of business economics and finance.[2]

One of the oldest executive development programs for middle management men is conducted by the Alfred P. Sloan Foundation at the Massachusetts Institute of Technology. This is a one-year program, started in 1931. About 30 men annually earn Master of Science in Industrial Management degrees. The year is packed with classes and reading, dinners and talking, field trips, thesis writing, and parties. It is neither a vacation nor a business trip. When the members of one graduating class were asked their reactions to the program, their answers boiled down to:

The Biggest Gain—They felt that more than anything else, the year had built self-confidence into them. They felt better equipped to get along with people, to formulate ideas readily, make decisions quickly, and to understand the complex of activity within a company.

Most agreed that self-confidence was what they needed, and they said theirs got an extra boosting from MIT's dinner meetings, where, over cocktails and food in a small room, the men met and talked straight from the shoulder with visiting top executives.

Said one student: "You told yourself, 'I can develop into that man's position.' In other cases you felt, 'I could be that man tomorrow.'"

Counter-Currents—Reactions were not all rosy. One aspect of the yearlong course drew criticism, and another led to uneasiness.

The undercurrent of uneasiness was put tersely by one of the students: "We've been playing marbles for fun here, not for keeps. I'm wondering what's been going on back at the company." This was a general reaction. They felt that they had been away a little too long—despite the opportunity the MIT course might give them for advancing within their companies.

Sharper Attitudes—But, in the end, what seemed to count most was the way the course refined their attitudes toward their jobs, and these were some of the comments they made on this:

"I know now there is no single best way to solve a problem."

---

[2] See *Personnel Executives' Newsletter*, Deutsch & Shea, Inc., November 30, 1953. (The name of this publication has since been changed to *Industrial Relations News*.)

"Your job as an executive is not to impose on people, but rather to persuade them to do things."

"You usually get more fruitful conclusions out of group or committee discussion than from single-handed thinking."

"We have a greater desire for responsibility—also for a higher standard of living. We want to get in and see what we can contribute."

"I don't think it's bravado, but we're not awed by top management any more." [3]

In 1951 Mr. Cordiner, President of General Electric Company, instituted a research program into the factors involved in the development of management people. The project cost something over a million dollars. Participants were a dozen General Electric men and such consultants as Peter Drucker, Zip Reilley of McKinsey and Company, three men from Harvard Business School, and others. One of the basic principles that emerged from the four years of research was that

> *All development is self-development.* Development is not something you do *to* a man. The whole drive, and the desire and willingness to pay the price—because there is a price for development—must come from within the individual. *You* can't develop anybody but yourself.
>
> This suggests that every incumbent manager in any enterprise should undertake to develop himself, no matter what his age, no matter what his exalted position in the social structure of business; that we are all of us operating somewhere around half, or less, of our potential, so there is great possibility for self-development of everyone, in any organization, at any age, of any status. . . .
>
> Our studies have shown that *managing* is a separate, distinct and professional kind of work which can be taught and can be learned, and that the quality of the managerial talent in an enterprise is of the greatest importance.[4]

The problem of developing executives is one of the most pressing problems facing top management today. The first logical step in the actual process of guiding the development of the individual to become a manager is guided experience, or coaching on-the-job. The best way for a man to learn how to manage a big job is to let him get the experience of managing a lesser job. He cannot read a book or look over someone else's shoulder only. He must learn by doing under the guidance of a manager who can stimulate, praise, and reprimand him. Generally, one of the best measures of a manager is his ability to develop managers. The factors that make for success or failure in a management job are more an art than a science. A management that finds it necessary always

---

[3] "The Pay-Off Is Confidence," *Business Week,* June 18, 1955.

[4] Moorhead Wright, "Development of Men," in Papers from the 38th Annual Meeting, American Association of Advertising Agencies, 420 Lexington Avenue, New York 17, N.Y.

to go outside the company to get its managers is not likely to be a strong management. Some outside blood may help the "body economic" but too little growth from within indicates a basic weakness.

Could you fill the president's shoes? Executives at Tom Houston Peanut Company, Columbus, Georgia, get a chance to try every Monday night. As participants in a unique "Executive Course," developed to teach "executive technique," each man attempts to solve the same problems the president of the company might face. Object of the course is to give each of the twenty-man executive team an over-all view of the company's total operations.

The course, developed by Southern Institute of Management and American Institute of Management, runs five months with a total of sixteen sessions of two to three hours each. Emphasis is laid on executive technique. SIM and AIM, after a two-year survey, have come up with a four-point formula for the successful executive, which can be taught to others, according to Howard Bowles, SIM vice-president. Four points, as outlined by Bowles, are "(1) to constantly create in his executive mind the ever-changing over-all picture of his own operations and the surrounding world affecting it; (2) to see this picture with 'driver's seat' vision—a sense of directional responsibility; (3) to decide and prescribe for the parts of this over-all picture—internally and externally; (4) to compare results of his decisions in terms of all parts of the company as well as dollars." SOURCE: Sales Meetings (May 3, 1957).

Training

William B. Given, Jr., Chairman of the Board, American Brake Shoe Company, has spent many years in helping to develop managers. Some of his findings about training are summarized as follows:

> What are the qualities that make a manager—a man who can move from department to department, from company to company, even from industry to industry—and do well wherever he goes?
>
> The first is *wisdom*—also known as common sense. The story is told of a woman who hired an electrician to wire her house in India. He ran to her for instructions on every detail. Finally she said, "Why don't you use your common sense?" "Madam," he answered, "common sense is a rare gift of God. All I have is a technical education."
>
> Our company requires technically trained men, but we do not depend merely on the training they bring us. Nor do we find common sense limited to a gifted few. We believe that in the course of their work, men's minds can be both stretched and stimulated.
>
> A second essential attribute is *integrity*. Over the long haul, the man who rates the confidence and cooperation of his associates is the man who is known to present facts honestly, though he might be vitally interested in the decision; to give full credit to others when he might safely grab it for himself; to discuss his mistakes as openly as his successes.
>
> An executive needs *courage*—not physical courage, but the courage to gamble on a decision, even if it may mean his job. And with this courage he must combine loyalty—to the company, to his associates, above all to his subordinates. Men will perform seeming miracles for a superior who will fight for them.[5]

The "game approach" to training executives

For years the Armed Forces have used simulated "battles" as a basis for training in analysis and performance under various situations. Recently the concept has been adopted to developing business men and labeled "the game approach," or simply "the game." Simulations of reality are now being used as a tool for teaching more effective analysis and decision-making in the business environment.

One of the first large-scale games was devised by the American Management Association.[6] At their Saranac Lake, New York, location, they

---

[5] William B. Given, Jr., "Must Managers Specialize? The Case for Executive Versatility," *The Management Review*, American Management Association, Inc., November 1956, p. 976.

[6] *Top Management Decision Simulation*, American Management Association, Inc., 1958. See also, "Fun-Even for Busy Executives," *Business Week*, May 4, 1957, pp. 165-170.

organize several teams of executives into "companies" that battle for two days for a common market. Their simulated work is divided into imaginary quarters and spans an imaginary ten- to twenty-year period. Each "company" makes decisions for the next three months on pricing, marketing, production, research, development, and the like. Each team strives to increase its assets, but the real objective is to learn the techniques of figuring out why certain decisions produced gains and others losses. Another objective is to show the interrelationship of decisions among management functions—for instance, the effect of a pricing decision on production, or of a financial decision on research and development.

With the aid of an IBM computer, complex details become organized results after each quarter; and at the end, the winner—the team representing the company that has amassed the most assets—is announced. No individual loses, however, no matter what decisions his team made during the game. Instead, it has been found that each participant gains in knowledge and insight that he not only uses himself in the future, but also shares with members of his company. The benefits of a situation like this are immeasurable, for there is much hashing among the members of the teams for long hours after the decisions are made and the results are in.

This method of teaching as applied to business is organized and designed to give practices in analysis, decision-making, human relations development, and broadening the points of view of the executives who are in training by this technique. In some uses of the game, the conclusions reached in the "student's" thinking are manually tabulated.

The game approach in business, by using quick answer calculators, tries to create the environment of time pressure for those who make the decisions. Educators of academic institutions, however, believe that their allowance for greater time and analysis with emphasis on background knowledge is more realistic for learning. Most educators believe that the pauses allowed between "plays" in conventional college teaching permit the "players" to discuss and digest issues at hand and thus acquire "assimilated" knowledge in the process of learning.[7]

The gaming theory in education is now used almost exclusively on the graduate or seminar level, but it may sift down to the undergraduate level in perhaps a more simplified state in the future. This method cannot substitute for other tools of learning, but when used along with them, may become of use to certain students who must tackle practical situations in the dynamic world of business after graduation.

---

[7] See Albert N. Schrieber, "The Theory and Application of the Management Game Approach to Teaching Business Policy," *The Journal of the Academy of Management*, August 1958, pp. 51-57.

Of course, the training of middle managers and other members of the personnel have great impact on the organizational structure and operations of a company. Training accentuates the "upward thrust" of the ambitious people in a company. In addition, several other influences such as mergers and reorganizations also have pronounced effects on employees.

Reasons, other than mergers, for changes in the organization

When the organizational structure of a company is changed, many employees are emotionally disturbed before, during, and after the change. The changes are disturbing because they often require the employee to modify his work habits, to accept a new executive as his supervisor, and to wonder whether he can meet the expectations of those who work with him. Many employees prefer an organization to remain static. This, of course, is not possible for many reasons, some of which are the following:

1. A company must grow or perish. New products and new services must be developed to fit the changes in the market.
2. Some members of management die or move to other companies. Their replacements change the organizational set-up because they believe that they can work more productively in a structure that they like.
3. The ambitious young people who come into an organization want new outlets for their energies and ideas. The men above them do not retire, die, or leave as fast as the ambitious young men prefer. They are ready to handle bigger jobs and top management recognizes that they are ready. One way to capitalize on their potentials is for management to buy a new company, add some new products, or set up corporate objectives that challenge the able men who want to get ahead. Companies grow from the upward surge of young executives.
4. Some corporate structures must be reorganized because too many executives and other members of the personnel have grown antiquated in their thinking and are slow-moving and incapable of meeting competition. The old executives need not be fired—they can be given fancy new titles that sound well but prevent them from functioning in the old ways that retarded growth.
5. Conversely, when certain aggressive members of the organization

try to outrun the company as a whole, they ignore teamwork in order to increase their individual power. "Empire-building" takes place. These empire-builders set up goals of their own. They are often efficient and productive. Top management may allow them to continue their empire-building for a time. Eventually these aggressive power seekers go too far and top management reorganizes the company structure in order to keep them under control.

6. Companies that are family controlled are likely to collect so many barnacles in the form of incompetent staff members that a reorganization with new executive heads may be necessary to displace the deadwood at the top.

Generally, reorganizations are made in order to enable a company to move faster, to meet competitive threats, to produce new and better products, or to take advantage of an opportunity to merge with another company. The influences that cause reorganizations to be made are numerous and varied. The causal factors are of less interest to us than the effects of the changes on the people who are involved. The impacts on people are so great and so easily recognized that the board of directors of one of America's largest corporations has an unwritten policy of selecting a new president who is not more than 55 years of age. Their reasoning is that the first five years of a new president's term of office are needed in order to enable the other executives to learn to accept him and to work with him. Thus, if he retires at age 65, he has only five years of effective cooperation to do his job well.

One of the most important effects of a change in structure that results from placing a new man at the head of a company or business is the displacement of the old "favorites of the court." In royalty, every king has his favorite counselors and friends. Even though a corporation president thinks that he rules impartially, the members of the management circle know who his favorites are. When a new managerial "king" comes to the throne, the favorites of the old one are usually replaced by a new set. The typical American top executive would probably deny that he has any special favorites in the company—all, he claims, are treated impartially. All may be treated impartially in regard to privileges and prerequisites but he speaks in a more friendly tone to some than to others. His face lights up more when he meets certain individuals. He asks their opinions more often. He gives them special assignments that involve extra confidences. He does all these and other things that reveal his deeper liking for them. The nonfavorite members of his staff soon learn to identify the boss' favorites and accept without complaint their own places in the circle. Those who find themselves on the outer fringes of the select few and resent their positions are usually glad to see a new head appointed—maybe things will be different for them.

Most employees know whether their own supervisor rates high, low, or medium with top management. (In very large companies having several plants, "top management" often means the plant manager.) The employees sense his status by the number of times their own chief attends top level conferences, by the ability levels of the men with whom he associates, and by the way he acts when he returns to his office after visits to the superior's office. If his manner is cheerful or depressed on his return, the employees notice it and gradually develop a pretty good estimate as to whether he is in the center or on the fringe of those who count at the top.

Besides, the chief has a secretary—she probably tells her best friends in the washroom about certain incidents which indicate how her boss feels and acts. At any rate, the acceptance status and the pronounced emotional ups and downs of a department head are often sensed and known by his subordinates.

Possible effects of changing the department head

When a department head is changed, the employees expect the new boss to make changes in the operations and the personnel. Some employees look forward to the changes they hope he will make, others fear the effects. Much depends upon how keenly they are interested in their work and on how well they know and like the new head. Normally, they assume that the new head will try to give the functions and the operations some new emphases. They try to forecast his probable emphases by noting his experience background.

A good example of the effects of a change in department heads as influenced by the experience of each head occurred in a well-known company that has a marketing department which employs more than a dozen college graduates. The man who developed the department was an executive whose experience had been in the marketing of Product A. He was succeeded by a man who had a background of experience in marketing Product B. These two department heads, 1 and 2, not only differed in their experience backgrounds but they also differed in their emphases in the work of the department.

Department Head 1 placed the offices of the men who were most important in his thinking near his own office. When he left, the new de-

DEPT. HEAD #1 Product Background (A)	MARKETING MAN Product (A)	MARKETING MAN Product (A)	MARKETING MAN Product (A)	MARKETING MAN Product (A)	MARKETING MAN Product (A)
MARKETING MAN Product (A)	MARKETING MAN Product (A)	MARKETING MAN Product (A)	OFFICE MACHINE ROOM	STATISTICIANS	
MARKETING MAN Product [B]	MARKETING MAN Product [B]	MARKETING MAN Product [B]	MARKETING MAN Product [B]	MARKETING MAN Product [B]	

SECOND LAYOUT (one month later)

DEPT. HEAD #2 Product Background [B]	MARKETING MAN Product [B]	MARKETING MAN Product [B]	MARKETING MAN Product [B]	MARKETING MAN Product [B]	MARKETING MAN Product [B]
MARKETING MAN Product [B]	MARKETING MAN Product [B]	MARKETING MAN Product [B]	OFFICE MACHINE ROOM	STATISTICIANS	
MARKETING MAN Product (A)	MARKETING MAN Product (A)	MARKETING MAN Product (A)	MARKETING MAN Product (A)	MARKETING MAN Product (A)	

Note that department head #1 had an A product background and that he placed A men in offices near his own. Contrast this floor layout with that of a month later when department head #2, B background, placed B men in offices near the corner office. The B men were moved near the controlling center of the department.

partment head, 2, in the course of one month, moved the offices of the men most important in his thinking near his own office. He also discharged several Product A men and hired more Product B men. (See floor diagrams above.) Naturally, the discharged Product A men resented the sudden change in their status.

An objective evaluation of the effects on the personnel by the changed emphases in the department was that the weaker men in the department were the ones who were discharged. These men had catered to Department Head 1 as a person. They also had coasted in their work because they felt secure in their relationship with the chief.

What the discharged men had failed to appreciate can be stated in terms of two basic principles:

(a) Anyone who studies business intelligently soon learns that the dynamic influences at work in business compel us to expect and prepare ourselves for changed emphases in the growth of a business.

(b) The man who consistently does very good work is likely to find that he is needed regardless of organizational changes that may occur. Catering to the boss as a person and coasting seldom provide as much security as doing good work.

Dynamics in the line-staff relations

One of the organizational points of friction in human relations often occurs in the changes made in the evolving line-staff working relations. We can appreciate the likelihood of such frictions arising when we understand the functional connections between line and staff.

Certain departments in any large company are responsible for making and distributing its products or services. They are usually considered to have line organization functions. Production and sales are examples. Other departments and individuals of the company such as accounting have no direct responsibility for making or distributing the company's product and are called staff divisions of the organization. A department of the line organization may have staff divisions to offer advice and give assistance in the performance of line responsibilities. The sales department, for example, may have need for the benefits of market research, usually considered a staff function. Staff departments are often shown on a formal organization chart by placing its name on the side of the direct flow of authority from top to bottom.

A staff man helps top executives and line personnel to carry out their operating responsibilities. He supplements but does not displace the line men.

Staff specialists give procedural, legal, and financial counsel. They coordinate sales with production schedules. They audit records. They inspect the product. They do research and have departments of their own such as employment, insurance, research, and accounting.

The functions of the staff are often described as providing the line with counsel, control, and service. Staff members collect and present information, determine the degrees to which policies and plans are carried out, and perform other services that enable line people to perform their functions more quickly and productively. This indicates that staff specialists are subordinate to the line. Many staff men are intel-

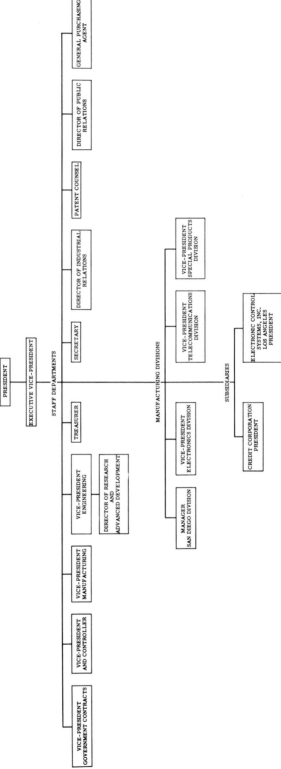

The over-all organization of line and staff personnel required for the operation of Stromberg-Carlson, a division of General Dynamics Corporation. It will be noted that the three manufacturing divisions are headed by individual vice presidents. Each of these divisions maintains its own production engineering, production control, purchasing, inspection and quality control, manufacturing personnel, and manufacturing areas departments, all of which report to the production manager in charge. SOURCE: Miles G. Agan, "Purchasing," Line-Staff Relationships in Production, Special Report No. 18 (American Management Association, Inc., 1957), p. 81.

lectually inclined and technically well trained but they can only make recommendations—they do not actually have responsibility for putting recommendations into effect. At the same time, they are often blamed for failures when line men say that they did what the staff recommended. Perhaps the counsel given was good but the line's execution was weak or faulty?

Small wonder that heated discussions take place between line and staff. Conflicts between the two are so common that top managements have to realign the organizational relationships from time to time.

Theoretically, staff people cannot tell line people what to do. Actually, line executives often give specialists instruction to carry out certain policies. Also, staff people interpret policies, measure results, and make reports to management of their findings in regard to the line's achievements or lack of achievement.

Obviously, confusion and disputes arise as to boundaries of function and authority. If a staff or a line man has empire-building tendencies, conflicts are especially likely to arise.

The line man is, according to the staff specialist, supposed to accept and adapt himself to the recommendations made by the staff. The line man may believe that certain recommendations are unrealistic—theoretically good but practically worthless. The staff man, in turn, may think that the line man is too stupid or too unconcerned to put the suggested program into effect. Line men are wont to say that staff men should mind their own business and not stick their noses into operating decisions or supervision of their personnel.

The kinds of situations that give rise to conflict are exemplified by these three instances:

1. While walking through the plant, the safety engineer of a manufacturing company noticed a machine guard out of place. He went over, adjusted the safety device correctly, and criticized the careless worker. The foreman immediately came up and said angrily, "Who are you to be pushing my men around? This damn safety business gives me a pain in the neck, anyway. No wonder we never get anything done around here!"

2. A department superintendent gave the personnel officer the names of two men he wanted for a particular job. They did not measure up to specified job requirements, so the personnel officer turned them both down and sent two other candidates instead. The supervisor angrily burst in, asking "Who's running my department, anyway? The hell with the your fancy tests—I guess I know what kind of men I want to hire for my shop, and I've been around here long enough to know a good worker when I see one."

3. The design engineer who created and developed a new product kept moving in on the production line after the item had been turned over for manufacture. He talked to his old associates who had been trans-

ferred to production, made adjustments, criticized quality, and gave instructions to employees. The supervisor soon found that the employees were turning to the engineer for their orders.[8]

As American business managements hire more and more specialists, frictions tend to increase. Even though the functions of line and staff men are supposedly well defined, problems continue to develop. Interactions between the two are necessary and continuous. They are bound to continue because staff men often have greater technical knowledge and are likely to be more ambitious. Some are also forceful. A few are more skilled in supervising people than the typical line supervisor. When the specialist proposes the making of changes, the line man may feel threatened—perhaps top management has more confidence in the specialist than in the line supervisor.

Staff people must be generous in giving credit for improvements to the line. If, for example, a methods engineer develops an improvement in operations, credit for the improvement cannot be given to the methods man alone. Credit must be shared with the line foreman even though he played a relatively small part or even exerted an inhibiting influence in effecting the change.

Management cannot turn back the clock of progress and eliminate the staff specialists. Rather, their numbers are likely to increase; statistically they are on the rise in relation to line jobs. New production techniques and new machines of the automation variety call for an ever-increasing number of engineering and staff specialists. They must work with and for line personnel. Line and staff complement each other.

The Bureau of Business Research of Ohio State University reported the results of a survey of 211 manufacturing establishments in Ohio. The survey revealed that the average manufacturing company, regardless of size, requires 75 additional indirect workers for every 100 direct workers employed.[9] The two will have to learn how to work together harmoniously. Staff men will have to learn how to educate line men by tactful rather than authoritative techniques. Line men will have to learn how to accept and utilize staff assistance. Both will have to learn that they seek the same objectives. And top managements will have to learn how to give credit and blame to both staff and line men rather than to line men alone.[10]

---

[8] *Acme Reporter* (Association of Consulting Management Engineers, Inc.), No. 2, 1957. See also "Line and Staff—Conflict or Cooperation?" *The Management Review,* American Management Association, Inc., September 1957, p. 26.

[9] See Mathew J. Beecher, Manager, Manufacturing Division, *Line-Staff Relationships in Production,* Special Report, No. 18, American Management Association, Inc., 1957.

[10] See Edward C. Schleh, "Make Your Staff Pay Its Way," *Harvard Business Review,* March-April 1957.

Admittedly, these are "nice" recommendations which are more easily made on paper than put into effect in real life. Staff versus line arguments are never-ending. They seem to be as much a part of business as frictions in a happy marriage. Also, frictions frequently arise between line and line as exemplified by the criticisms of the production department when the sales department makes promises which production cannot possibly meet. All these frictions, whatever their cause, cannot be eliminated as long as human beings remain as they are, but we as individuals can seek to learn to recognize and to deal with them intelligently whenever and wherever possible.

The tendency to overemphasize power politics as a factor in change

Politics exists in all organized societies; perhaps even when authority is accepted as hereditary, politics is more intense than ever. It is found in religious groups, schools, hospitals, and in trade unions as well as in the civil service. Almost everyone becomes acquainted with power seeking as practiced by some of history's political leaders. He also hears about power seekers in politics and in business. After he gets a job in a business organization, he notes the machinations of certain ambitious employees who are referred to as "empire builders," "eager beavers," or "crown princes, self-appointed." These men function at first as factional leaders. They are likely to move into any group situation where the group lacks leadership or where a power vacuum exists. Power politics in the work situation exists in many companies and the new employee must become sensitive to the effects. If he becomes a party to the influence in its worst forms, he is likely to develop certain crafty qualities which may at first appear to give him advantage over his associates.

As one writer has stated, there are several different types of power seekers. Some operate only in a relatively small group. They use various methods. A few, but not all, are ruthless. The empire builder may acquire his empire by any one of several beneficial procedures:

(a) by skillful maneuver when others fail or retire or both, or
(b) by sheer ability and applied imagination, being two or three jumps ahead of his colleagues, or
(c) by being multi-functional in his work. The more departments he controls the greater his effectiveness.[11]

---

[11] See John Marsh, "Power Politics and Power Politicians," *Personnel Administration*, July-August 1957.

Generally, these procedures benefit the company and the employees. If they are likely to have more harmful than good effects, top management controls the power seeker.

We must not imagine that only ruthless power seekers advance in business. Those are likely to be more conspicuous than the more representative men who advance in business through unselfish service. There are, in every large company, certain good sound men whose aggressiveness is objective and sensible. They are able men who are usually well adjusted as personalities. They have not sought power—it has come to them because they learned to seek *power with* rather than *power over* others. They have vision. They have ability. They help others get ahead. But the dominating center of their thinking is the work, the job to be done. They do not perceive themselves as ends in the attainment of self-centered power but as agents in getting things done well. Finally, every member of an organization should realize that change, even painful change, is as necessary for the growth of a company as for the development and progress of a human being. This means that the individual employee in industry should perceive the changes taking place, adapt himself to them, and view them with pleasure, not fear.

COLLATERAL READINGS

For All Students

Janney, J. Elliott, "What Makes a Business Builder," *Dun's Review and Modern Industry,* January 1959. A management psychologist describes several successful entrepreneurs—men who built business successes on daring and imagination.

Porter, L. W., "Differential Self-Perceptions of Management Personnel and Line Workers," *Journal of Applied Psychology,* April 1958. Management men tended to describe themselves in terms of leadership traits, line workers in cooperative follower terms.

For Advanced Students

Bradford, Leland P., "A Look at Management Growth and Development," *Journal of the American Society of Training Directors,* July 1958. Recent research projects indicate that organization charts should relate staff team to staff team.

Luce, R. Duncan, and Howard Raiffa, *Games and Decisions: Introduction and Critical Survey.* New York: John Wiley & Sons, Inc., 1957. Aimed toward those readers working in the behavioral sciences. Surveys central ideas and results of game theory.

For Men in Business

Dyer, Frederick C., *Executive's Guide to Handling People.* Englewood Cliffs, N.J.: Prentice-Hall, Inc., 1958. Written for the executive at or near the top. Practical advice on developing a positive "executive style" and having effective human relations.

Stanley, John D., "Your Informal Organization: Dealing With It Successfully," *Personnel Journal*, July-August 1956. Offers four "guides to
action" for dealing with the informal organization. Includes a check-
list for evaluating its influence.

QUESTIONS ON THE CHAPTER

1. Which executives are classified in the middle management group?
2. Describe the upward and downward orientations of middle management men.
3. What did the General Electric Company study conclude about the
development of managers?
4. How can a management find out whether a man is capable of managing a big job?
5. How do the attitudes of business men and educators differ concerning the game approach?
6. What is empire-building and how can it be controlled?
7. Who are the "favorites of the court" and how are they affected by
change?
8. How does one firm of management consultants feel that the phrase
"People make jobs and profits" should be applied to organizing methods?
9. Differentiate between line and staff divisions of an organization. How
can staff men gain the cooperation of line men?
10. What are the characteristics of the men who seek power *with* rather
than power *over* others?
11. Of all the ideas presented in the chapter, which ones were of special
interest or value to you?
12. What did the chapter contribute toward your future relations with
(a) the men who supervise your work, (b) the employees whom you
may supervise?

PROBLEMS AND PROJECTS

For All Students

1. Interview an executive whom you know. Ask him to describe his
developmental history, and his formal and informal training. Also
ask him to tell of the persons who were especially influential in his
advancement to major executive responsibilities.
2. Interview several employees in regard to the effects on employees of
having middle management men move up to top management. Who
benefited and who lost in the change? Did some employees leave
because of the change?

For Advanced Students

3. Read a biography or an autobiography of a successful businessman.
Note the developmental influences in his life history. Did the writer

have insight into his development? What suggestions did you gain for yourself from the reading?

4. Examine available current literature on the use of simulation (business games) for management training. Publications of the American Management Association should be especially helpful. Compare findings with those of this text.

For Men in Business

5. Think of several middle management executives whom you know. Why are certain ones obviously moving toward top management levels while others seem to prefer to remain in middle management? Is it lack of drive or intelligence?

6. If you have had several years' experience in business, you may have seen how the job importance of certain employees has risen or fallen with changes in management. Describe one of the transitions. What kinds of employees gained? What kinds lost? What did you learn for yourself from the occasion?

WHAT IS AN EXECUTIVE? ONE HUMORIST DEFINED HIM AS "someone who can hand a letter back to a redheaded secretary for a third retyping." The president of The American Arbitration Association described the boss as "a fellow who has worked his way up to where most of the headaches are." Another described him as "a person who goes out to find work, finds someone willing to pay for having it done, and then hires somebody to do it." A more acceptable definition is "Any person who is charged with administrative work or the management of a business function." Generally, "manager" is more likely to be used than "executive" when the function or operation is specified, for example, "sales manager" contrasted to "executive vice president." The two terms, "manager" and "executive" are, however, often used interchangeably. In this chapter we shall use "executive" because we shall discuss him as a person in an administrative situation, not as an official who has been appointed to perform specific functions.

The *public image* of the business executive is shaped, to some extent, by the fiction writers. In "business novels," the executive characters rarely do any specific work. Many appear to spend most of their time trying to defeat each other in some underhanded manner in a race for promotion. If, as happens occasionally, they are depicted as strong characters, they are pictured as resisting pressure to conform to some unethical corporate requirement. The details of their jobs are nebulous,

The Executive

but their sexual frustrations are likely to be elaborated in detail. If any heroes are presented in the play, they are government officials or heads of charitable foundations. The typical executive is portrayed in fiction as a rascal, rogue, or weakling. Very few executives could recognize themselves or their colleagues in terms of these dramatic portrayals, written by authors who wish to entertain rather than inform.[1]

Systematic studies of executive characteristics

Fortunately, some serious studies have been made of real rather than fictional executives and the factors that seem to make them successful. The studies indicate that no one or two characteristics determine an individual's chances for success as an executive, but significant patterns of characteristics are evident. One of the studies used the case-history approach. The "whole" executive, past and present, was studied systematically in relation to his work situation. The investigators used interviews, questionnaires, and psychological tests. A total of 33 executives from 29 organizations completed the diagnostic materials of the study.

These findings apply to the typical top-level executive in terms of where he came from, the nature of his psychological equipment, and, in general, how he has developed.

1. Some of the general conclusions that are supported by the findings of this investigation are the following:

(1) The educational level completed by the typical executives is far above the average of the general population.
(2) He takes full advantage of varied educational opportunities.
(3) He is an active participant in and leader of social organizations during childhood and throughout his career as a worker.
(4) He is interested in religion as a force toward developing high moral and ethical standards.
(5) He has experienced and continues to experience good health.
(6) He is interested in people—particularly in selling them on the idea of fundamental cooperation. He is interested in the written and spoken word as a means of communicating his ideas. He is not preoccupied with the technical phases of his work, but rather with promoting harmonious human relationships.
(7) He possesses very superior mental and analytical ability.
(8) He is serious and conscientious in his approach to work. He is willing to take risks only after full consideration of the available facts.
(9) He is forceful and intense, actively seeking new work to be done and new methods of doing it.

---

[1] See "The Fiction-Eye View of Business," *Business Week*, October 12, 1957, p. 187.

Brown's Job

Brown is gone, and many men in the trade are wondering who is going to get Brown's job. There has been considerable speculation about this. Brown's job was reputed to be a good job. Brown's former employers, wise, gray-eyed men, have had to sit still and repress amazement, as they listened to bright, ambitious young men and dignified old ones seriously apply for Brown's job.

Brown had a big chair and a wide, flat-topped desk covered with a sheet of glass. Under the glass was a map of the United States. Brown had a salary of thirty thousand dollars a year. And twice a year Brown made a "trip to the coast" and called on every one of the firm's distributors.

He never tried to sell anything. Brown wasn't exactly in the sales department. He visited with the distributors, called on a few dealers, once in a while made a little talk to a bunch of salesmen. Back at the office he answered most of the important complaints, although Brown's job wasn't to handle complaints.

Brown wasn't in the credit department either, but vital questions of credit usually got to Brown, somehow or other, and Brown would smoke and talk and tell a joke, and untwist his telephone cord and tell the credit manager what to do.

Whenever Mr. Wythe, the impulsive little president, working like a beaver, would pick up a bunch of papers and peer into a particularly troublesome and messy subject, he had a way of saying, "What does Brown say? What does Brown say? What the hell does Brown say? —Well, why don't you do it, then?"

And **that** was disposed.

Or when there was a difficulty that required quick action and lots of it, together with tact and lots of that, Mr. Wythe would say, "Brown, you handle that."

And then one day, the directors met unofficially and decided to fire the superintendent of No. 2 Mill. Brown didn't hear of this until the day after the letter had gone. "What do you think of it, Brown?" asked Mr. Wythe. Brown said, "That's all right. The letter won't be delivered until tomorrow morning, and I'll get him on the wire and have him start East tonight. Then I'll have his stenographer send the letter back here and I'll destroy it before he sees it."

The others agreed, "That's the thing to do."

Brown knew the business he was in. He knew the men he worked with. He had a whole lot of sense, which he apparently used without consciously summoning his judgment to his assistance. He seemed to think good sense.

Brown is gone, and men are now applying for Brown's job. Others are asking who is going to get Brown's job—bright, ambitious young men, dignified older men.

Men who are not the son of Brown's mother, nor the husband of Brown's wife, nor the product of Brown's childhood—men who never suffered Brown's sorrows nor felt his joys, men who never loved the things that Brown loved nor feared the things he feared—are asking for Brown's job.

Don't they know that Brown's chair and his desk, with the map under the glass top, and his pay envelope, are not Brown's job? Don't they know that they might as well apply to the Methodist Church for John Wesley's job?

Brown's former employers know it. Brown's job is where Brown is.

Batten, Barton, Durstine & Osborn
Incorporated

ADVERTISING
383 Madison Avenue, New York

SOURCE: The Wedge, *with special permission of Batten, Barton, Durstine & Osborn, Inc., 383 Madison Avenue, New York 17, N. Y.*

(10) He is objective in facing his personal problems, frank and straightforward in his dealings with people, and spontaneous in his interpersonal relationships.

(11) He is ambitious and able to identify his ambitions with those of his company to an outstanding degree. . . .

If there is one broad implication to be drawn from this study, it is that an executive to be successful must feel himself an integral part of his organization and be vitally interested in the people around him. The executives studied were found to have recognized the importance of the human element and to have identified themselves with their various activities at every turn of the road—from early life on. Hence, the man who can identify himself with his company to the degree that his greatest motivation and satisfaction stem from increased business development, and who has appropriate qualifications otherwise, will be a good bet for executive training.[2]

2. *Dun's Review and Modern Industry* queried in confidence a panel of 110 presidents of key companies in regard to themselves and their jobs. One part of the study dealt with the problems they worry about when not at work. Regardless of the time, at work or at home, they worry most often, three times out of ten, about people—the people they have and the people they need. One man's answer: To get young people to have the same enthusiasm and to work as hard as he did years ago so that they too may qualify for advancement and the taking over of key positions. The selection, development, and stimulation of people was frequently mentioned as a problem.[3]

Of course the presidents who head the 110 Panel companies of this study are aware of many of their own flaws. Four out of ten men think they are too impatient, intolerant, or reluctant to delegate responsibility.

Eighteen of the presidents called impatience their main weakness— "Impatience with mediocrity," impatience "with slow motion in others," and impatience "with those supposed to be competent." In contrast, another five presidents consider themselves over-patient, too lenient, or too "softhearted." Eight men feel they are intolerant or overcritical of others, and one said his chief personal difficulty is "unconsciously setting a pace which may be difficult for my associates to follow." Next to impatience, the most frequently mentioned personal shortcoming was the "desire to do things myself and failure to delegate properly."[4]

3. Several investigators have used motivational research techniques in order to gain insight into the deepseated psychological characteristics

---

[2] Robert M. Wald and Roy A. Doty, "The Top Executive—a Firsthand Profile," *Harvard Business Review*, July-August 1954, p. 53.

[3] Kenneth Henry, "110 Leaders of Industry Look at Their Jobs—and the Future," *Dun's Review and Modern Industry*, July 1957, p. 32. Copyright © 1957 by Dun & Bradstreet Publications Corporation.

[4] *Ibid.*

The Executive

of executives. An excellent study of this kind was made by William E. Henry and his associates, the Committee on Human Development, at the University of Chicago. Over 100 business men took various psychological tests and participated in a short undirected interview. Despite uniqueness in personality that was clearly present, all the executives studied had in common a certain general personality pattern:

1. *Achievement desires:* Successful executives show high drive and achievement desire. They conceive of themselves as hard-working and achieving persons who must accomplish in order to be happy. They get satisfaction from doing rather than from merely contemplating the completed product. Real to them is the continual stimulation that derives from the pleasure of immediate accomplishment.

2. *Mobility drives:* All successful executives tested have strong upward mobility drives. They feel the necessity of moving continually upward and of accumulating the rewards of increased accomplishment. There are two groups: For some, the sense of successful mobility comes through the achieving of competence on the job. These men struggle for increased responsibility and derive a strong feeling of satisfaction from completing a task. The second group relies more upon the social prestige of increased status in their home communities or within the organizational hierarchy. Satisfaction for them comes from social reputation, not from the personal feeling that necessary work has been well done. The first group seems generally to be the more successful.

3. *The idea of authority:* The successful executive posits authority as a controlling but helpful relationship to superiors. He looks to his superiors as persons with more advanced training and experience, whom he can consult on special problems and who issue to him certain guiding directives. He does not see the authority in his environment as destructive or prohibitive forces.

4. *Organization and its implications:* While executives who are successful vary considerably in their intelligence test ratings, all of them have a high degree of ability to organize unstructured situations. They can also see the implications of their organization. This implies that they have the ability to take several seemingly isolated events or facts and see relationships that exist between them. This ability to organize is not always good, however, for it may result in forced organization. Among the less successful there is a tendency to apply the mold to every situation. This means that there is a strong tendency to rely on techniques they know will work and to resist situations which do not readily fit the mold.

5. *Decisiveness:* These executives have the ability to come to a decision among several alternative courses of action. Whether this is done on the spot or after detailed consideration is unimportant. What does matter is that they can reach a decision. Very seldom does this ability fail. Nothing is too difficult for them to tackle, and at least try to solve. The role of the executive demands conviction and certainty.

6. *Strong self-structuring:* The men know what they are and what they want and have well developed techniques for getting what they want.

In general, they maintain considerable flexibility and adaptability within the bounds of desire and the often rather narrow possibilities of their own organizations.

7. *Activity and aggression:* The executive is essentially an active, striving, aggressive person. This activity and aggressiveness are always well channeled into work or struggles for status and prestige—which implies a constant need to keep moving, to do something, to be active. Physical movement is not necessary as long as they are continually mentally and emotionally alert and active.

8. *Apprehension and the fear of failure:* If one is continually active and always trying to solve problems and to arrive at decisions, any inability to do so successfully may well result in feelings of frustration. This seems to be true of the executives. In spite of their firmness of character and their drive to activity, they also harbor a rather pervasive feeling that they will not really succeed and be able to do the things they want to.

This means that there is always some place to go, but no defined point at which to stop. The executive is self propelled and needs to keep moving always to another goal ever ahead. This suggests that a cessation of mobility and of struggling for new achievement will be accompanied by an inversion of this constant energy. It will be inverted into other channels—e.g. psychosomatic ailments, disfunctions, or defenses.

9. *Strong reality orientation:* Successful executives are strongly oriented to immediate realities and their implications. They are directly interested in the practical, the immediate and the direct. This is, of course, generally good for the immediate business situation though the executive with an over-developed sense of reality may cease to be a man of vision, for a man of vision must get above reality to plan and even dream about future possibilities.

10. *The attitude toward parents:* In a sense, the successful executive is a "man who has left home." He feels and acts as though he were on his own, as though emotional ties and obligations to his parents were severed. It seems to be most crucial that he has not retained resentment of his parents, but rather simply broken their emotional hold on him and been left psychologically free to make his own decisions. In general his relationship to his mother has been the most clearly broken tie. The tie to his father remains positive in the sense that he sees the father as a helpful but not a restraining figure.[5]

The student who hopes to become an executive can, from these and other studies, gain much insight into the personal qualities that are needed to attain such responsibility. He will have some difficulty, however, in evaluating his characteristics in comparison with those of the patterns reported. One approach to the evaluation of himself in regard

---

[5] William E. Henry, "The Business Executive: The Psychodynamics of a Social Role," *American Journal of Sociology*, January 1949, pp. 286-291. The advanced student who wishes to amplify the above findings should refer to the reports of Ephraim Rosen and L. Huttner, mentioned at the end of this chapter, page 223.

to his characteristics as a possible future executive is to note the personal profile of the typical executive in terms of work factors such as his vacation, after-hour work, plans for the future, and how he feels about his job. A study of this kind by the American Management Association obtained answers from 335 presidents.

Work patterns of executives

As to *vacations*, the vast majority take two weeks or more but business is likely to intrude. Many take their vacations by traveling or touring because of their constant concern about the business. Two men out of five conduct some business while away on vacation. Some of this is briefcase and dictaphone work, but more is convention-going and customer visiting.[6]

About one half take less than the total amount of vacation time allocated to them. Some take no vacation at all.[7]

In regard to the *work week*, a high percentage of executives take work home from the office. This practice, however, varies with the industry. Of one thing we can be certain—executives are not members of a leisure class. Manual workers of today have far more leisure than any occupational group such as executives. Men who are in the highest social status groups usually have the least amount of leisure time.

One of the major conclusions from one survey of management executives was that for a top executive, overtime does not mean overwork. When asked why they worked overtime, many respondents gave answers such as "Lots to do—and interesting," and "I like to accomplish what I feel is necessary." Most had a gratifying sense of responsibility. The largest single portion of a typical executive's time goes into planning and thinking for his company.

Company meetings take up a large portion of the working time. Generally, the more meetings an executive attends, the longer the hours he is likely to work. The one respondent who attended the largest number of meetings per week stated that the greatest single waste of his time is "listening to people take an hour to say what could be said in 10 minutes."

Of internal meetings and conferences two-thirds or more are con-

---

[6] See Lydia Strong, "The Man in the Front Office," *The Management Review*, American Management Association, Inc., September 1957.

[7] Elizabeth R. Floyd, "Research and Information," *Management News Letter*, American Management Association, Inc., August 1957.

Executive on Vacation

"Here are your reservations."

"Cancel those appointments."

"The ball's in your court, boys."

"Don't update me on anything."

"I'm giving the whole thing up for three weeks."

"Let's not take worries with us . . ."

"Just gonna relax . . ."

SOURCE: *Booth*, Tide (*January 25, 1957*).

ducted partly or wholly for the purpose of decision-making. Half the executives feel that some of these decisions could have been reached as effectively by a single individual. But the gospel of group thinking has taken so strong a hold that few have an inclination to pass the decision-making back to the individual. Group participation on many decisions is believed to be necessary for purposes of cooperation, communication, and morale. One company president sums it up: "I believe in the management team concept and practice group discussion even though very often an individual could or in effect does make the decision." [8]

In addition to spending a large portion of his time in planning and decision making, the typical executive is future-action-minded. He is not interested in analysis as a mental exercise nor in pinning blame for wrongs committed. Rather, he thinks in terms of action for the future. The effective executive does not merely react to situations; rather he acts to make things happen. Top managements that are most successful in using job challenge as a primary motivation for their executives and supervisors obtain a high degree of productivity from the top and middle management executives. The job challenge motivation is more significant than the kind of activity that results from fear of discipline such as the withholding of promotion for failure. [9]

The desire for high status and earnings is not a strong motivating influence in the lives of great executives. Opportunities for creative thinking, solving problems, making decisions, and a liking for new and varied experiences are more likely to characterize the great executive than the desire for money or title. Money and title, when they are attained, are attained as byproducts rather than as ends in themselves. Central to the work of creativity, people play an important role in their satisfactions.

Effective executives enjoy their jobs because of, not in spite of, people. They like and identify with the people and the organization of people which they direct. The closer a man is to the top of the organization, the more likely he is to identify himself with the company organization, all the people in the company. The farther he is away from the top of the organization, the more likely one is to find that he makes statements such as "I don't own the joint. I just work here." [10]

---

[8] See Lydia Strong, "Of Time and Top Management," *The Management Review,* American Management Association, Inc., June 1956.

[9] See Arch Patton, "What Makes Executives Run?" *Dun's Review and Modern Industry,* September 1957, pp. 36-38. Copyright © 1957 by Dun & Bradstreet Publications Corporation.

[10] See J. Elliott Janney, "Company Presidents Look at Themselves," *Harvard Business Review,* May-June 1952.

Non-financial compensations

Very few business executives work for salary alone. Many go from a well-paying position in one company to a job in another company that pays less but offers more opportunity. Opportunity usually means that the executive expects to have more voice in the management of the new employing company. In many cases he expects to have more independence of action in discharging his responsibilities.

A true executive wants to be treated as an executive: he wants responsibility for getting work done, competent men to direct in doing the work, a voice in determining policies, privilege of making decisions, and a chance to set up goals for the company.

Even though the salary with a new employer may be higher, the increase is more likely to be a token of appreciation than extra take-home pay. Some managements expect each executive to be a substantial shareholder so that he will find a part of his recompense in helping to increase the value of the company's stock and its yield through the higher profits which he helps to bring about.

Money alone does not enable corporations to hire and keep executive talent. The tax bite taken out of high-bracket incomes is now so great that a raise in salary is virtually meaningless. Many companies therefore offer the hope for more reward by means of the stock option plan.[11] These offers usually go to members of top-level management.

Most top managements think of the executive as a human resource. They want him to be as well paid as he would be in a similar job in another company. They realize that salary alone will not enable him to be efficient and comfortable. They therefore supply extra satisfactions in the form of attractive offices. The offices are often decorated by a professional interior decorator or by companies that specialize in office designs. Many of the new offices resemble a living room more than a conventional office. The less formal decor is especially likely to be the design for an executive who spends most of his time in conferring and reading. For him, conversation areas with armchairs and coffee tables are more appropriate.[12]

Expense accounts are a symbol of status in the business world: most employees have no expense account privileges, some have specific allowances or reimbursement privileges, and certain others liberal allow-

---

[11] Under a stock option plan, company stock is sold to the executive at a special price, usually 95 per cent of the market value of the stock at the time the option is granted. For further information, see *Financial World*, April 17, 1957, p. 7.

[12] See *Business Week*, March 30, 1957, pp. 172-175. See also *The Management Review*, American Management Association, Inc., July 1957.

ances, the degree of liberality depending upon the policies of top management. Some top managements are generous, others stingy in regard to expenditures such as trips to annual industry conventions, visits to foreign branches, and entertainment for customers. Relatively few have use of a company limousine or plane!

The most popular way to handle the executive's expenses is by direct reimbursement for expenditures made on the company's behalf. Executive expenses are under the control of some official even though policies are liberal. Managements recognize that spending habits of the men at the top set an example for the entire organization. They are expected to have the same consideration for the company's money as other employees.

Executives generally have highly developed consciences about the company's money. The idea of claiming reimbursement for money they did not actually spend is repugnant to an overwhelming majority. The psychological effect of a discretionary accounting procedure sets their already proven honesty on a still firmer foundation: "If the company takes our word for it and trusts us to use our own good judgment, how can we take advantage of that trust and turn it to personal gain?" [13]

The executive's relations with upper management

The individual executive, depending somewhat on his rank, is likely to have close associations with the management men above him. Of those relations to which he must give special thought, the getting of approval for his plans is probably most important. He must defend ideas and plans in which he believes but he must also accept good suggestions from others. Ever present in his mind is the realization that his management is responsible for making a profit and that he must develop plans for contributing to the profit making.

In addition to preparing major plans for future action, he also carries out certain practices that help to improve his relations with management. These usually are:

1. Keeps members of management informed about accomplishments and failures in his area of responsibility. He lets his colleagues and superiors know what is going on in his department and why he has adopted policies and practices that involve other executives.

---

[13] See "Executive Expense Accounts: A Survey of Company Practices," *American Business*, January 1957. For a report of a survey on executives and their use of expense accounts, see Edward E. Furash, "Expense Accounts," *Harvard Business Review*, March-April 1960, pp. 6f.

2. Provides *a well-organized budget message* including (a) results of the current year's program, (b) analysis of next year's objectives, (c) specific goals for the future, (d) an explanation as to the methods for achieving the goals, (e) the reasoning behind the method and (f) a listing of the estimated costs for the recommended program.
3. Gives his superiors *a carefully planned presentation* of his budget, including, in some companies, (a) the use of visual illustrations and (b) a reading aloud of the budget message in the presence of management.[14]

Psychological roles of the executive

Almost every executive must work with other people and get them to work with him. This means that he must have their respect and confidence. His personal habits as well as his ability bear importantly upon how well he is able to establish effective work relationships.

To the employees whom he directs, he is far more than an assigner of tasks. He also fulfills certain vital roles of an unconscious nature. As he acquires years of experience in dealing with people, he realizes that to certain individual employees he is an *authority figure, impartial judge, target of affection, target for hostility, confidant, catalyst,* or a *tone-setter.* He must meet or help to fulfill the deeper psychological needs of people, needs of which they themselves are not aware. His most important functions are likely to be in the symbolic meanings that he represents for each of his employees. In some cases, failure of a given executive can be directly traced to his inability to fill successfully the role expected by the employee.[15] He is sensitive to the deeper psychological needs of people (see Chapter 24), and he is likely to increase his skills in becoming the kind of role symbol that makes his leadership effective.

The executive who has developed an acute sensitivity to the feelings of others toward him realizes that he communicates and receives feelings as well as ideas. What he says in words is often less significant than the feelings which he transmits and receives. When, for example, he feels that a subordinate is not very important, he realizes that his feelings are transmitted to the subordinate even though his verbal behavior does not state the message.

---

[14] See Raymond P. Wiggers, "How To Work Better with Other Departments of Your Company," *Industrial Marketing,* December 1956.
[15] See Norman H. Martin, "Practical Politics in Administration," *Personnel Administration,* July-August 1957.

He knows that covert hostility is expressed toward him by subordinates through behavior such as excessive absenteeism, tardiness, resistance to his suggestions, and subtle blocking of his program. These and other forms of opposition often stem from difficulties that have their origins in symbolical as well as in unexpressed difficulties that remain covert. Some executives who sense these covert influences in interpersonal relationships believe that the best way to overcome them is to bring them out into the open. Sometimes a frank exchange of feelings, even though somewhat bitter, may clear the air and improve the situation.[16]

One of the factors that often develops or is involved in covert resistance is the difference in social rank between the executive and the subordinate. If either the subordinate or the executive is conscious of a difference, adjustment for the employee may be difficult. Fortunately for most executives, many a shop employee has just as much respect for his craftsmanship and the importance of his job as for the executive and his ability. When the executive-employee relations are in line with basic American democracy, neither the boss nor the subordinate is awed by the other "partner" in the work situation. One of the gratifying experiences in business is to see the kind of relationship between executive and employee where each has a genuine liking and respect for the other. Relatively few modern executives think of employees as subordinates—they are colleagues who occupy a different position in the organization structure. In terms of feelings, the high-grade executive does not think of the employee's position as an inferior one. Each of the two has certain functions to perform, appropriate to the individual's abilities, and each is worthy of the other's respect.

The executive as an exemplar

The top executive has certain responsibilities in regard to his daily human relations. He is under close observation by those with whom he works: superiors, subordinates, associates, and the public. One of the main parts of his job is example-setting.[17] He is aware of the effects of his own conduct in relation to what he asks of his employees. If, for example, his superiors issue instructions to curtail annual leave

---

[16] For a more comprehensive treatment of these covert interpersonal relations, see William C. Schutz, "The Interpersonal Underworld," *Harvard Business Review*, July-August 1958.

[17] See G. W. Peak, "The More 'Personal' Responsibilities of the Top Executive," *Advanced Management*, December 1957.

during a heavy work period, he realizes that he himself cannot take his vacation while his employees are denied theirs.

Many everyday decisions involve basic ethical principles. Even though the situations are casual, he cannot overlook the moral judgment required. If he does, he will encourage a cynical attitude on the part of employees, customers, and the public. Now and then he must decide big questions of an ethical nature as in these two examples:

1. If he is the president, threatened with a proxy fight by financial interests who seek personal gain rather than the giving of long-term economic leadership, should he attack the insurgents on a personal basis?

2. If a labor union head promises labor peace in exchange for under-the-table payments, should he go along with the offer so that his employees may go back to work much sooner than they could if he were to hold to his principles? [18]

The man who is basically honest, however, does not acquire a reputation for integrity as a result of a few big decisions. That comes from little daily decisions as to how employees and customers shall be treated. Nor does he turn his principles off and on as situations arise—he lives within a basic ethical framework that is part of himself.

Each executive attracts some people and repels others

Many students of management assume that every executive should have or try to acquire a standard personality pattern or, at least a standard pattern of behavior in dealing with people. The inexperienced person imagines that the human relations techniques used by executives are or should be as standardized as the techniques of a surgeon. This kind of developmental objective for the student is impracticable. Managing men is an art that is an integral part of the personality of the individual manager. He cannot conform or try to conform to a specific pattern—he must be himself. Of course he can improve his techniques. He can learn from others and from his own errors and successes, but he must still function as a genuine person, not as an imitator or as one who seeks to conform to a pattern that is unnatural for him.

This means that his personality and his techniques in dealing with

---

[18] See Wayne G. Broehl, Jr., "Ethics and the Executive: The Small Decisions that Count," *Dun's Review and Modern Industry*, May 1957. Copyright © 1957 by Dun & Bradstreet Publications Corporation.

people will attract some persons and repel others. Those who are attracted will tend to remain with him. Those who are repelled will tend to leave his department or company.

An alert observer who visits a department or company headed by a specific executive can often see a relationship between the chief and the employees under his direction. This does not mean that the employees are near-duplicates of the chief's personality. Instead, the executive in charge unconsciously symbolizes answers to basic needs on their part. If he is a domineering person, he is likely to have many employees who feel more secure when they work for an autocrat. If he is the teacher type of executive, he is likely to have many employees who like to be treated as intelligent colleagues.

We must not assume however that all employees at any one time are there because the personality of the boss and the employee complement each other. Certain employees, those of superior psychological qualities, may remain for several years under the direction of a repellent personality because of interest in the work itself. These stronger persons usually have definite career objectives and they will "put up with" or ignore the characteristics of an executive who repels them. These exceptional individuals usually remain only as long as necessary to gain a desired amount of experience or other objective that fits their specific needs. Then they move on.

The health of executives

Surveys indicate that many executives take short or inadequate vacations, that they usually take too much of their work home with them at night, and that at lunch they do more shop-talking than eating.[19] If an executive achieves success for his company, it is often believed that he does so at considerable personal cost.

When an ambitious young man hears adverse comments and reads reports about the hazards in executive responsibility, he may conclude: "Success as an executive is too hazardous—I'd rather settle for less and live longer."

Certainly, the ambitious young man who is considering a career as an executive should know the findings of the best researches available on health probabilities.

The best available research indicates that tension comes from within a man, not primarily from his job. Tension is not inherent in an execu-

---

[19] See William C. Menninger, and Harry Levinson, *Personnel,* American Management Association, Inc., September 1955, pp. 95, 96.

tive's job. When a businessman feels that he is under constant pressure, it is more likely to be the fault of his own personality development or of problems outside business, than of the job itself. This conclusion was reached by the Life Extension Foundation, Inc., after compiling answers given anonymously by 6,013 businessmen in 179 companies. The foundation is part of Life Extention Examiners, the medical organization that each year handles physical examinations for some 15,000 executives.

The study also showed that the majority of the businessmen, 78.5 per cent, are happy in their work and that they think they are not working too hard. However, one out of seven reported that he felt under constant tension.

The men who felt under tension while at work were also the ones who most frequently had personal problems, had trouble living on their incomes, worried about their health (although their report of their own health was not substantially different from that of the non-tense management men). The members of this tense minority typically drink more cocktails, smoke more cigarettes, take less exercise, and use sleeping pills and tranquilizers much more than the non-tense majority. This adds up, the report concluded, to the fact that it is a man's attitude toward his life and his work that makes him feel the pressure, not "age, occupation, or job demands." [20] As stated by Dr. Walter D. Woodward, full-time psychiatrist for the American Cyanimid Company: "The incidence of emotional illness is just about the same in every walk of human endeavor." [21]

One of the major implications for the prospective young executive from these and related studies is that the man who wants to become an executive may strive for mere extrinsic values in life, particularly status and money. If he strives for these, he is likely to be a tense person with many worries. He will worry about his security in the job, about what a rival associate hints concerning his faults, about whether he will get a hoped-for increase in salary, about whether he will or will not be promoted, about what intrigues are going on behind his back, about how his wife impresses the boss, about hidden meanings in apparently simple statements, and a host of other incidental daily experiences.

If, on the other hand, he disregards the usual achievement goals of status and money but seeks instead to attain goals of intrinsic value such as making a good product or providing employment, he will probably have few erosive tensions and, in the end, enjoy greater success. The man who seeks intrinsic values is deeply interested in the work as

---

[20] See *Business Week*, March 15, 1958, p. 21.
[21] See "Everybody Has Emotions," *Business Week*, April 22, 1950, p. 53.

SIGNPOSTS ON THE ROAD TO EXECUTIVE DECLINE

How do you tell when an executive is slipping? The retired president of a large steel company thinks these are the tell-tale signs that a manager has passed his peak of usefulness:

1. When he talks more about what he did in the past than what he plans to do in the future.

2. When he blames his failures on new competition, the weather, or "conditions."

3. When he begins to lose interest in statistics that pinpoint opportunities for improving company operations.

4. When he begins to think the company can't get along without him.

5. When he becomes adept at thinking of reasons why a new idea or method won't work.

6. When he begins to feel sorry for himself and tells friends that his boss does not appreciate the years he has "given" to the business.

7. When he begins to feel that his position rates a bigger office or a larger staff.

8. When he arrives at work later, lunches longer, and leaves the office earlier.

9. When he tries to convince people that the excessive time he spends on the golf course is good for the business.

10. When he loses the knack of talking *with* people and begins to talk *at* them.

SOURCE: Courtesy of *American Business,* July 1957.

work, in solid achievement, and sincerely thinks "to hell with the title and the pay—those will come of their own accord when I do a really good job."

Some young men start their careers with high ideals but fail to hold to their original intrinsic goals. They shift their thinking because of a disconcerting experience or two such as finding that a less able rival has successfully played politics to achieve his ends. When this happens, the impressionable or hasty young man may decide that "If that is what the business world wants, I'll play it smart and forget about my fine ideals of doing good work and letting my work speak for itself."

If such a disillusioned young man resorts to chicanery or even cleverness, he will probably fail to advance himself, especially if his basic life style is one of integrity rather than one of misdirected cleverness. The eventual reward for uncompromising integrity is confidence, the confidence of associates, subordinates, and of persons outside the company. When a man's word is as good as his bond and his motives are above suspicion, people conduct their relations with confidence. Confidence is so valuable an asset in business relations that it easily outweighs any temporary advantage that may be gained by sharp practice.

The Executive

Integrity and sincerity are closely related. They provide more powerful strength and influence than titles or wealth. Instead of succumbing to the temptation of using the questionable tactics of others, the young man ought to review his career objectives and techniques for attaining them. This is the time when he will benefit from a frank heart-to-heart talk with some wise oldtimer who himself has a record of solid achievement.

"The Organization Man"

William H. Whyte, Jr. has pointed out the dangers of having members of the young executive group become too organization-minded.[22] Presumably, as the young managerial men grow prosperous in the large corporation, they become content. They are assumed to lose their initiative and individuality. As a consequence, they are described as also losing their vigor and as relapsing into an uncreative way of life. Incidentally, Whyte conceives of this sapped vitality as possibly permeating other institutions: the medical clinic, the scientific laboratory, and the "law factory."

This kind of fear in regard to the effects of the institution is very old. Rousseau, the individualist, expressed the same kind of danger in pre-revolutionary France:

> So long as government and law provide for the security and well-being of men, . . . they stifle in men's breasts that sense of original liberty, for which they seem to have been born; and cause them to love their own slavery.[23]

Several writers have analyzed Whyte's contention in detail.[24] Inasmuch as the term, "Organization Man" has become a synonym for dutiful complacency in business, we should examine some of the reasons why the dangers are not as great as imagined.

First, we must admit that some young executives do succumb to the pattern of acquiescence encouraged by the bureaucratic organization. Those who become apathetic conformists are not, however, the executives who rise to the top in today's dynamic organizations. Few businesses could grow if their spirit were of this variety. Growth requires

---

[22] See his book, *The Organization Man* (New York: Simon and Schuster, Inc., 1956).

[23] J. J. Rousseau, *A Discourse on the Arts and Sciences,* tr. by G. D. H. Cole, (New York: Everyman's Library, E. P. Dutton & Co., Inc., 1950), p. 147.

[24] John H. Mueller, "Perspective on the Organization Man," *Business Horizons,* (School of Business, Bureau of Business Research, Indiana Univerity), Spring 1958, pp. 83-91.

men who have a drive to get ahead of the crowd, to compete, to do better this year than last, to reduce costs, to sell more, and to increase profit.

Second, one effect of success on superior men who have made some advancement is to seek more advancement. We see this occur in politics and labor unions as well as in business—those who achieve some power often want more power.

Third, modern corporations hire many men who have assignments that require creativeness: researchers, designers, inventors, methods men, advertising experts, specialists in sales promotion, consultants, and others.

Fourth, the rugged individualism in the business world of a century ago has not degenerated into nothingness in the big corporation of our time. Instead, it has been tempered by greater skill in a leadership that stimulates employees to cooperate in attaining new goals as stated in the objectives set up by management. Teamwork, not mechanical compliance, is sought. Leaders of today have profound respect for the individual—even the janitor is asked, not ordered. Certainly the young man of today should emulate the leaders rather than the conformists.

COLLATERAL READINGS

For All Students

"Does Big Business Breed Conformity?" *Dun's Review and Modern Industry*, March, 1959. Are we breeding a race of frightened men guided by their associates' approval? Company presidents, 160, give their views on pressures for conformity.

Warner, W. Lloyd, and James Abegglen, *Big Business Leaders in America*. New York: Harper & Brothers, 1955. A report of a research study of the characteristics of 8,000 business leaders. Summarizes qualities correlated with leadership.

For Advanced Students

Brady, Joseph V., "Ulcers in 'Executive' Monkeys," *Scientific American*, October 1958. A research study in which monkeys subjected to psychological stress develop gastrointestinal lesions. May have suggestions for overcoming executive stress.

Lipset, Seymour M., and Reinhard Bendix, *Social Mobility in Industrial Society*. Berkeley, Calif.: University of California Press, 1959. Treats mobility in the population and reports on social origins of business leaders in various countries.

For Men in Business

Cady, E. L., *Developing Executive Capacity*. Englewood Cliffs, N.J.: Prentice-Hall, Inc., 1958. A "How to" book, for self-development. Presented in an easy-reading style, it offers suggestions for executive growth and action.

The Executive

Conarroe, R. R., *The Decision Makers: Case Histories of Successful Management,* The Bureau of Business Practice, 100 Garfield Ave., New London, Conn. Fifteen top executives reveal management practices they applied to meet challenges.

QUESTIONS ON THE CHAPTER

1. The two chapters that precede this one also treat the executive. How does the treatment in this chapter differ from the others?
2. How does the educational level of top executives compare with that of the general public?
3. Compare the leisure time available to manual laborers and executives.
4. What is the most successful primary motivation which top managements use for their executives and supervisors and how does this affect middle management?
5. What factors are especially important in causing the effective executives to enjoy their jobs?
6. List four signs which indicate that a manager is on the road to executive decline.
7. Why is it impracticable to assume that every executive should acquire a standard pattern of behavior in dealing with people?
8. How does an executive who strives for goals with extrinsic values differ from the executive who seeks to attain goals of intrinsic values?
9. What is the eventual reward for the man whose basic life style is one of uncompromising integrity?
10. What factors seem to lessen the danger that White describes in *The Organization Man?*
11. List some of the factors which the effective executive considers or uses in his relations with higher management.
12. Describe some of the roles of an unconscious nature that the executive represents to other people.
13. Of the various ideas presented in the chapter, which ones are of special interest or value to you?
14. What did the chapter contribute toward your future relations with (a) the men who supervise your work, (b) the employees whom you may supervise?

PROBLEMS AND PROJECTS

For All Students

1. Look over some of the available literature, particularly the business journals, for articles on the executive, his personality, methods, etc. Write a summary of your main findings. Compare with the content of this text.
2. Interview several executives whom you know. Describe your image of each. How do your descriptions differ from those of the image often portrayed by the fiction writers? Are the men you interviewed hard workers?

For Advanced Students

3. Make study of reports of research studies on the executive personality. Here are two examples that should be considered: Ephraim Rosen, "The Executive Personality," *Personnel,* American Management Association, Inc., January-February 1959. Progress report of a clinical study, University of Minnesota, of some 200 executives who had been interviewed and tested. Findings are presented in terms of the typical executive in the production group. In the March-April issue, a follow-up by L. Huttner and others, amplifies the earlier report.

For Men in Business

4. Consider the individual executives whom you know. Describe one or more in terms of his (a) work habits and (b) psychological characteristics. How do you and other employees have to adapt yourselves to his strong and weak characteristics? To what extent do you identify yourself with each?

5. Compare some of the currently published business magazine articles on executive characteristics with an analysis of factors that make a man an executive as reported by a scientist such as Erwin K. Taylor in "The Unsolved Riddle of Executive Success," *Personnel,* American Management Association, Inc., March-April 1960.

MANY AMBITIOUS STUDENTS ASPIRE TO BECOME EXECUTIVES BUT few look forward to becoming foremen in a factory or supervisors in an office; yet that is the first stage in advancement through human relations skills to top management. As has often been said: "In business you have to show the people above you that you can capably handle the people below you if you want to get ahead of the people beside you."

The supervisory function is more than a stepping stone upward—it is a key role in human relations in industry. In a sense, the supervisors are management's employee-relations mirrors. Their attitudes reflect what the workers think of the company and its management. Top executives are aware of the important role of supervisors in management and in employee relations.

The supervisor is the immediate contact man with the employees. The solution of technical and methods problems can be delegated to specialists but the handling of people is an endless function for all supervisory members of the organization. The supervisor is the leader who deals with and directs the efforts of the individual employee. He is the one person who must get the work done by employees and he must deal with each individual employee who is careless, moody, hot-tempered, lazy, resentful, or anything else, good or bad, that a human being may be or do while at work. He is the front line of management.[1]

---

[1] The general term for a member in this front line of management is "supervisor." If he functions in the factory, he usually is called a "foreman." If he functions in an office, he is called a "supervisor" or head of a specific section or group of employees.

13

The Supervisor: Man in the Front Lines of Management

The foreman of today is expected to be both a production engineer and a human engineer.

Why many foremen are confused about their status

When the responsibilities of the present-day foreman are compared with those of the foreman a generation past, we note that his position today calls for a leadership quite different from that of the old-time "driver" who could do as he pleased. In many instances, today's foreman feels frustrated by the policies laid down by staff departments such as personnel, by collective bargaining contracts, and by a cultural setting that requires democratic consideration for the individual worker rather than obedience to arbitrary authority. His duties have increased while his authority has decreased. He must persuade rather than command employees. He thinks of his job as only slightly higher than that of the rank-and-file worker. An attitude survey in a plant with about 2,500 workers indicated that only 31 per cent of the workers were interested in a foreman's job.[2]

He is no longer in complete control of his department. He cannot hire, promote, demote, transfer, punish, or reward as he alone feels inclined. He cannot dominate by means of fear. Many of his disciplinary decisions are or can be overruled by management. Even methods of work and getting out the production are directed by a staff organization. The science of management has cast him in a more subservient role than he occupied in the old days. He is expected to motivate employees, be their friend and counselor.[3] Today's supervisor in industry is expected to get employees to *want* to do their best. He is the responsible front-line leader both to management and to his men.

The traditional role of the formal leader in times past involved an arm's-length relationship with his employees. In our present industrial world, aloofness on the part of the foreman is not effective. In the shift, however, from aloofness to our new form of leadership, the foreman has often become confused—he has thought of democratic leadership as the equivalent of letting people do as they please or as requiring him to be a "good fellow" to everybody.

The extent of foremen's confusion was indicated by an American Management Association survey of supervisory responsibility and author-

---

[2] See Alfred G. Larke, "How Foremen Get That Way," *Dun's Review and Modern Industry*, January 1955, p. 48.

[3] See Harry Seligson, "Re-Thinking the Foreman's Job," *Personnel Journal*, March 1957.

The Supervisor   **225**

ity as viewed by 187 first-line foremen and 53 of their superiors. The responses to the survey questionnaire showed that the foreman and his boss do not see eye-to-eye on what the foreman is supposed to be doing —what management *expects* him to do and what he *thinks* he is expected to do are often far apart.

In general, higher levels of managements are inclined to hold the foreman responsible for a wider range of activities than he recognizes. Of 108 functions listed on the questionnaire, all of which may fall within the foreman's jurisdiction, not one item was acknowledged by all foremen as their responsibility. Yet higher management men agreed on 15 items which they considered the responsibility of their subordinates.

The most marked discrepancy between foremen and their superiors concerned disciplinary layoffs. All the superiors held their foremen definitely responsible for this function in greater or less degree, but 14 per cent of the foremen recognized no responsibility in this area or were in doubt as to how much they were supposed to have.

As one management man stated: "Everywhere we hear that the foreman is a key man whose job must be built up, but we won't build it up if he has a fuzzy picture of his responsibilities that doesn't agree with his superior's picture of them." [4]

The typical foreman's insecurity is complicated by the procedures used in selecting new foremen. Some are chosen from the ranks by reason of proficiency and seniority. Some are made foremen because they have demonstrated leadership ability in elected union positions. Some are assigned to supervision because they are college graduates who are beginning their managerial training. The typical foreman who sees how men are selected for supervision is likely to wonder whether his position is really secure.

Why foremen "take sides"

Contacts with foremen of industry indicate that in too many cases the foreman feels somewhat forgotten. He sees himself as responsible to executives but he is not always recognized as a full-fledged member of the management team. He is in charge of production workers yet not fully accepted by the employee group. As one foreman stated: "You're really everybody's whipping boy."

The typical supervisor is an active member of two work groups. One group consists of his peers and his superior, the other is made up of

---

[4] Reported by Chester E. Evans, "Defining the Supervisor's Job: an AMA Survey," *Personnel,* American Management Association, Inc., January 1957, p. 314.

The Supervisor

his subordinates and himself. This dual role is often difficult to fulfill.

If he plays the role as a representative of his employees only, he loses effectiveness in helping management gain its objectives. If he acts as a representative of management only, he may lose effectiveness with his men. When he tries to integrate the two directions of his responsibilities, difficulties may arise. He therefore tends to take sides as a means of overcoming conflict. Some conflicts are bound to occur but investigation indicates that those supervisors whom management has regarded as most ready for advancement differ from other supervisors in their ability to deal effectively with employees on both the individual and on the group basis. The employees feel more free to discuss job and personal problems with them. They hold more group meetings where problems can be discussed. They create more opportunities for two-way communication between themselves and the employees under their supervision because they participate more with their superiors in decision making.[5]

Some supervisors do seem to achieve satisfactory integration in their management relations as shown in a survey by the National Council of Industrial Management Clubs. This organization is composed of more than 100 foremen's and supervisors' clubs which draw their membership from a widely diversified group of industries in 32 different states. The sample for the study was obtained from questionnaires administered to 1,602 industrial supervisors in 11 major labor market areas. Of this group, approximately 50 per cent were the foremen or first-line supervisors; the remainder was comprised chiefly of general foremen, assistant superintendents, and some persons in staff positions. The question and responses that dealt with job status in regard to the supervisor's feeling about being a part of management were the following:

The company's treatment toward me makes me feel that I am:

	Per Cent Answering [6]	
	All Supv.	*Foremen*
a. Just another one of the rank and file	5	7
b. Very little different from non-supervisory personnel	10	12
c. In a special category—neither management nor a non-supervisory employee	14	20
d. A part of management in most respects	44 ⎱ 81	42 ⎱ 61
e. Definitely a part of management	27 ⎰	19 ⎰

---

[5] See also Floyd C. Mann and James K. Dent, Human Relations Research Program, Survey Research Center, University of Michigan, "The Supervisor: Member of Two Organizational Families," *Harvard Business Review,* November-December 1954.

[6] James H. Mullen, "The Supervisor Assesses His Job in Management," *Personnel,* American Management Association, Inc., September 1954.

According to this survey, some 80 per cent of the supervisors and 60 per cent of the foremen felt that they are a part of management, wholly or in most respects. The remainder apparently had not achieved a satisfactory integration with management.

The supervisors' conflict as to goals

One of the most important problems facing the business leader of today is the choosing between, or balancing, or integrating, of two seemingly conflicting approaches to management. One approach emphasizes an immediate work or profit objective: high production and low costs. The other approach emphasizes morale and organizational maintenance as a means for reaching objectives.

The conflict between these emphases is felt at all levels of leadership as well as among supervisors. Top executives must strive for a balance between production and financial goals on the one hand and long-range effectiveness and stability of the organization on the other. The supervisor is torn between the goal of pushing for immediate productivity and that of trying to improve his workers' ability to produce in the future.

The problem of reaching the proper balance can be surmised, in part, from some of the research conducted by the Human Relations Program of the Survey Research Center, University of Michigan. Certain studies there indicate that leaders can be classified as primarily "employee-oriented" or as "production-oriented." The employee-oriented leader is one who sees his job mainly in terms of maintaining good human relations and a smoothly-running organization. The production-oriented leader is primarily concerned with the processes and techniques that contribute to high-level and efficient production.

Generally, the findings from research projects support one another on the principle that a supervisor's style of leadership is likely to be influenced considerably by the demands placed upon him by the organization and by his own superior. The studies fail to show the universal superiority of any one style of leadership. There may be no one style of leadership or set of leadership practices which is ideal for all situations. Just how a particular organization should decide on the proper balance for its needs is still a question for further research.[7]

---

[7] See Stanley E. Seashore, "Administrative Leadership and Organizational Effectiveness," in Rensis Likert and Samuel P. Hayes, Jr., eds., *Some Applications of Behavioural Research* (Paris and New York: Unesco, 1957), Chapter 2. The Foundation for Research on Human Behaviour conducted a two-year program of seminars dealing with administrative leadership and organizational effectiveness. The findings are too extensive for full condensation here.

One conclusion has emerged from several studies, namely, that *first-line foremen, far more than workers themselves, hold the key to both quantity and quality of production.* This conclusion is supported by several researches made by the Survey Research Center, University of Michigan, as well as by others. One investigation, for example, studied section gangs working for the Chesapeake & Ohio Railroad.

In the C. & O. studies, data were gathered from 72 section gangs— 36 of them rated by company officials as high producers, 36 as low producers. Three of the major findings were:

1. Foremen of the highest-producing section gangs considered themselves leaders—not just superior workmen. Their men also perceive the foreman as having good planning ability.

2. Foremen of the high-producing groups were more positive toward their men, and took a more personal approach to them. They tended to be employee-minded rather than job minded. They considered the employee's motivation. They were more "men-oriented."

3. High-production section foremen were found to evaluate their sections more highly than the low producers thought of theirs. They had more pride in their work groups.[8]

Supervisory techniques

Some training programs for supervisors give detailed instructions in the mechanics of supervision: how to say "Good Morning," how to give work assignments to employees, when to take sides with the employee rather than with management, and so on. Skill in the performance of the mechanics or incidental procedures involved in human relations is not, of course, the basis of effective supervision. The basis is the psychological strength and sensitivity of the supervisor. If he respects employees, genuinely likes them, and is sensitive to their feelings, he handles the daily procedures in ways that are natural for him. Employees learn to accept him as their leader because he is sincere and follows a consistent pattern of behavior which they understand.

Standard patterns of supervision which every foreman should follow are few. A pattern that is appropriate for one foreman may not be appropriate for another. The foreman of a construction gang may be able to cuss his men and they will respect and like him. To them, he is

[8] D. Katz, N. Maccoby, G. Gurin, and L. Floor, *Productivity, Supervision and Morale Among Railroad Workers* (Ann Arbor: Institute for Social Research, 1951). See also Richard L. Waddell, "Good Supervision: Key to Productivity," *Supervision,* February 1952 and *The Management Review,* American Management Association, Inc., December 1952, p. 785.

genuine. The same tactics used with a group of accountants in an office would frighten them into resigning their jobs.

Most employees size up the boss rather accurately. If, for example, he recommends employees for promotion or takes sides with them in a conflict with management, his espousal of the employees' interests will affect employee morale in the degree to which the supervisor is believed to be influential with management. If he is known as having considerable autonomy in his relations with management, the employee's satisfaction will be high. Employees usually know whether the foreman occupies a position of high or low influence.[9]

Employees also know whether the foreman is in a position where he must shield certain relatives or friends. They know which members of his group must be "carried." They know his entangling alliances. In many cases, they even know how well he gets along with his wife. Many do not resent his special situations—they may even cooperate in helping him to fulfill his difficult personal obligations.

The wise foreman, in turn, is sensitive to the employees' personal and work situation needs. If irregular overtime work must be done, he announces it as far in advance as possible. He does not tell them on Friday afternoon that they are expected to work the next day because he realizes that such requests disrupt many personal plans and cause resentment. He tries to arrange overtime hours that will be most convenient for each employee. He also allocates overtime assignments so that everyone gets equal opportunity to make extra money.

The socially skilled supervisor recognizes the mood of an employee before he explains a new task. He also emphasizes the value of the task before beginning instruction. If the employee to whom he is talking is tense or very slow in his comments, the supervisor helps him to relax by talking slowly himself.

The alert supervisor knows that variety is important to job satisfaction. He knows which job assignments offer variety and which employees need variety and which ones prefer monotonous tasks. He moves employees around accordingly. He also knows how to explain an assignment so that the worker feels that the task, however monotonous, is really important in its contribution to production.

Anyone who establishes rapport with workers and asks them to describe their supervisor is likely to hear many comments on his supervisory practices and his personality. Here are seven examples:

> 1. Yes, I like my supervisor. He's on a good basis with the workers—
> I feel at ease with him but yet he keeps a proper distance. He's always

---

[9] See Donald C. Pelz, "Influence: a Key to Leadership in First-Line Supervisor," *Personnel*, American Management Association, Inc., November 1952.

around when he should be and always knows what's going on. He has a lot of interest in us and you always feel free to talk to him any time. He wouldn't spread confidential information. He's very conscientious and pushes himself too much—he's always run ragged. There's nothing I can do to help him—I do my work and I'm harmonious with the others.

2. I like him as a person but he has no backbone—he's afraid of stepping on people's toes. He's very soft spoken and quiet but if he knows you'll take his screaming and yelling, he'll scream at you. If he knows you won't, he's passive. He should have more enthusiasm and work more closely with the management people in the office. I can't help him—it's not my place anyway.

3. Yes, I like her very much. She's understanding, patient, and has a good personality. She's very efficient and undemanding. If my work isn't done, she finishes it herself but I'd rather be made to do it—I do more when she isn't around. She's too sweet, too. You can't trust her—have to take her just on a friendly basis. She also tries to be motherly and that really gets me. She never talks of personal problems though, and that's good.

4. Yes, I like him. He's very understanding and patient. At first, my typing speed was down but he didn't say anything. He never asks me to do anything he can't do. He takes a lot of interest in my work and always praises me when I come up with a decent piece of work. He jokes around a lot and is real easy to talk to—I always take my problems to him. He's not overly-friendly and never gets fresh. Most of the men here are. He's a great guy!

5. Yes, she's wonderful. She trusts me to do things and is patient and very helpful. She can put her foot down and still be nice. She shows confidence in me which makes me feel good. She's a good organizer—everything's always done on time. She's so good herself that I want to do my best.

6. He's all right. He's kind of a mousy little guy. He isn't very pleasant—there's something wrong with his personality. He never kids around—always all business. He's also very moody—sometimes he doesn't talk at all. He's very fussy and exact too—everything has to be letter-perfect. I admire the work he does though, he has ability and does well in his field. He's just too quiet and reserved. I suppose I could try to draw him out more.

7. Yeah, I like him. He's very fair and understands the worker's point of view because he worked his way up. He distributes the work equally so that no one is overburdened. Actually though, he's a bit zany—he's always kidding around and acting nuts. If he would act more mature, he might get more accomplished. He could get more work from the workers if he were more forceful, I think. I take advantage of him myself and don't work up to capacity."

Fortunately, many employees can dislike or feel neutral toward the supervisor but enjoy their work. Dislike for the supervisor does not always cause the employee to dislike the company or the job. Generally, workers in the lower grade jobs are less likely than others "to obtain satisfactions directly from their work and are therefore more desirous

"He's a stickler when it comes to coffee breaks!" SOURCE: American Management Association, Inc., The Management Review (December 1958).

of obtaining satisfactions from close interpersonal relationships with supervisors as well as fellow workers." [10]

Disciplining employees

Many supervisors consider the disciplining of workers as their most difficult recurrent problem. Difficulties with work procedures clear up in time but problems with workers as persons tend to persist. Obviously, the employee who violates a safety rule or comes to work late habitually must be given some kind of special attention by the supervisor. The higher the level of the supervisor in management, the more likelihood that he will be willing to initiate disciplinary action. The lower-level supervisors usually identify more with their work groups and therefore hold a less critical attitude toward workers. Besides, they are not sure that top management will back them up in their disciplinary actions.

One of the most important aids in dealing with discipline problems is to revise shop rules to make them fair and reasonable, to change any plant conditions that create violations, and to agree on the enforcement of the rules.

Many companies have some obsolete rules. Rules must be rewritten, to make sure that the things expected of people are reasonable.

The plant areas where trouble is frequently encountered can be studied in order to remove the possible causes.

Instructions should be clear so that each employee knows exactly what is expected of him.

[10] See Howard M. Vollmer and Jack A. Kinney, "Informal Requirements for Supervisory Positions," *Personnel,* American Management Association, Inc., March 1957, p. 439.

The Supervisor

Reasons should be given for required standards of conduct and performance.

Most approaches to problems of discipline can be classified into two groups: the judicial and the educational. In the judicial approach an attempt is made to determine the rightness or wrongness of an employee's actions in a work situation that requires disciplinary attention. If investigation shows that the employee's conduct was wrong, he is reprimanded or punished in accordance with established rules or customs in the plant. In the considerate or educational approach the emphasis is placed on the re-education of the worker.

The trend in progressive managements is to think of discipline as mainly an effort to correct a worker's attitudes through training. One analogous situation is that when a machine gets out of order, the repairman does not punish the machine. Instead, he tries to find out the cause of the trouble. He then makes the necessary adjustments or repairs. In like manner, the human being who does not respond as expected is given similar constructive attention in an attempt to correct the cause of his trouble.

Some investigations have been made of the effectiveness of role-playing in getting supervisors to accept the educational human relations approach. The situation used in role-playing usually requires that disciplinary action be taken, as in violation of a no-smoking rule in a plant where flammable gases, if ignited, may cause death. One person plays the part of the supervisor, another the part of the union steward, and a third person identifies himself with the worker who is to be disciplined. The background of the case makes the violation of a no-smoking rule clear-cut so that a three-day layoff is in order. In the role-playing the steward intervenes, however, and tries to get the foreman to change his decision.

The results of one study of this kind of situation indicated:

> The human relations approach was more successful than the judicial approach in that (a) satisfaction for foremen, stewards, and workers was greater; (b) the interview was more of a problem-solving type discussion than an argument; (c) the worker was more inclined to be satisfied with the steward; (d) the worker was less inclined to reduce his future production; and (e) the steward was less inclined to file a grievance.[11]

Most managements believe that the supervisor tends to create his own disciplinary problems.

He is responsible for his own disciplinary atmosphere. The working relationships he has established with the more influential senior workers'

---

[11] See Norman R. F. Maier and Lee E. Danielson, "An Evaluation of Two Approaches to Discipline in Industry," *Journal of Applied Psychology,* October 1956.

"This will be your desk. We have a two-hour break for lunch: from twelve to one, when we go out, and from one to two, when the boss goes out."
SOURCE: *by Al Kaufman,* The Management Review *(December 1957). Courtesy American Management Association, Inc.*

group, and through his own example, set the tone for his employees' expectations and conduct. If he lets some offenders and offenses go without prompt attention, he encourages continued digressions. If he tries to solve his worst disciplinary cases by transferring or even promoting the offender, he incurs the disdain of all workers. The supervisor's own personal conduct is the most important influence for positive discipline. If he himself is well disciplined, his employees will tend to follow his example.

Fraternizing with subordinates

When a worker is promoted to a supervisory job, he is confronted with the question as to whether he should continue to pal with his old shop companions. If he gains his greatest social satisfaction from the continuance of old companionships, he fails to learn how to associate happily with members of management. His thinking is likely to remain on the leadman level. Also, he increases his difficulties in maintaining discipline.

On the other hand, he runs the risk of being labeled a snob when he abruptly discontinues pleasant old relationships. Some new supervisors try to solve the problem by explaining the requirements of the job to the old associates and asking for their help. Most employees appreciate the situation and assume that the new foreman will act like a foreman and will want to find satisfying companionship with those of

The Supervisor

his own or higher rank. They do, however, expect him to be friendly. They especially resent being ignored.

The new supervisor must learn to appreciate that to some employees, the supervisor is a father image, a person to be respected and obeyed. To others, he may be an authoritarian symbol, a person who should be avoided. The supervisor who becomes aware that such symbolisms apply to himself wants to have his employees avoid an unrealistic view of himself. He does not want them to see him as having either a halo or horns. To help them modify their image, he can explain his responsibilities to them in terms of the work. He must keep the requirements of the work situation in the forefront of his conversations with them. Above all, he cannot grant special privileges to some and withhold them from others.

A frequent question in the minds of many employees is "How am I doing?" or "Where do I stand?" The employees look for answers in the supervisor's manner. They interpret his smiles and frowns in terms of their psychological needs. If he is brusque or unresponsive, they are likely to feel that he dislikes them personally or that he is displeased with their work. Some will develop or accentuate anxieties about their status in the company. They will deduce a fear that the boss wants to get rid of them. No amount of assurance will overcome all these anxieties but the supervisor can follow the policy of thinking and acting in terms of the work requirements and, at the same time, seek to maintain an atmosphere of approval and respect for each employee as a person.

Coaching by superiors

The most common form of training supervisors is informal coaching by superiors. The disparity between the kind of supervision that supervisors want and the kind they are actually getting can be estimated from the replies of supervisors to this question in a questionnaire answered by 138 supervisors:

How many times during [the past year] did you and your boss get together to discuss how well you were doing your job or some particular part of it?

The number varied from 12 or more—reported by 26 per cent—to none at all—reported by 16 per cent. Yet 62 per cent of the supervisors said that they would like to have discussions with their superiors once a month and 88 per cent wanted sessions at least quarterly. Generally, supervisors had fewer discussions with their superiors than they feel they needed.

Asked whether they found the discussions helpful, 22 per cent of the respondents said, "not at all," or of "very little help." Thirty-nine per cent thought that the conferences were of "some help" and 36 per cent reported that they had helped "very much" enabling them "to do a much better job." This survey indicated that some management men are less effective than others in talking with their subordinates about improving job performance. Most companies should consider the need for educating top executives in working more closely, more frequently, and more effectively with their managerial subordinates.[12]

Formal training programs for supervisors

Anyone who conducts training programs of this nature soon discovers that there is a big difference between what supervisors know they should do and what they actually do in supervision. Indeed, one member of such a class who mouths the best answers as to how employees should be supervised may himself be the poorest supervisor in the class. Men do not change their ways of handling people simply by going to a few lectures or conferences; their motivating influences are too deep and strong to be changed easily.

A good example is the insecure foreman who is especially ingratiating toward members of management but exhibits other forms of defensiveness toward employees. They think of him as a domineering, egocentric, feather-my-nest type of person, and they will find many ways to impede the production of his department.

When a management man recognizes the motivations of a specific foreman who fails to develop sound working relations with colleagues and subordinates, he may try to help him overcome the influences of the unconscious motives. He may even tell him directly: "Don't be ingratiating to me—it only makes your men hate you." This may help the offender cease one variety of offensive behavior but to adopt another equally offensive to someone else. The deepseated needs within a man's psychic life are not easily throttled—they are merely redirected—most likely misdirected.

This means that the best way to retrain the inadequately adjusted supervisors and others is to have them become more aware, not only of themselves—their motives, prejudices, values, goals, and feelings—but also of how these influence their everyday behavior in the plant and the impacts they have upon their colleagues and subordinates.

---

[12] See Erwin K. Taylor, "Management Development Begins at Home," *Personnel*, American Management Association, Inc., January-Febrary 1958, p. 33.

Training courses should aim at self-awareness and a new tolerance for one's own make-up. If the individual can be helped to understand and tolerate himself, perhaps he can also achieve greater tolerance of others.[13]

The ideal method of training supervisors is not as yet available to most companies or colleges.[14] Its use requires a leader who has a clinical background and unusual skill in enabling members of a group to gain insight into the workings of their minds without inflicting psychological harm. Certainly, the temperament and unconscious motivations of a supervisor are more important in determining his success than his factual knowledge of supervisory practices. The need for this kind of specialized knowledge and skill is great. Eventually our behavioral scientists will develop the research and skills needed for removing mental blockings from supervisors who are emotionally incapable of learning new supervisory techniques.

Even though clinically-oriented training leaders are not yet available in sufficient numbers, certain other training procedures are available and helpful. The most promising at this time is role-playing.

Role-playing is a method of training that does not seek to rebuild the trainee psychologically or to remove deepseated emotional blockings in order that training may be effective. It does, however, contribute to the kind of training that is experienced without words. It does help to educate feelings and provide some benefits for personality growth.

In role-playing one trainee takes the part of a problem employee such as the always tardy worker or the incompetent who expects a promotion. Another trainee takes the role of the supervisor. The other trainees observe and make notes. The plays are unrehearsed. No script is used. All the characters act spontaneously. The method does afford some opportunity to see and to experience the emotions of people who deal with difficult situations.

Role-playing is to many persons an "unnatural" form of group training where the participants act parts in public. Many are shy. They do not think of themselves as "actors." Some even feel silly. Some fear that their performances may betray to others their personal anxieties. When skilled leadership directs the role-playing, it often becomes helpful in training men to become more skilled as supervisors.

The "play" gives the problem a "reality" which words alone cannot

[13] See F. J. Roethlisberger, "Training Supervisors in Human Relations," *Harvard Business Review*, September-October 1951, pp. 47-57.

[14] For evaluations of training programs, see Kenneth R. Andrews, "Is Management Training Effective?" *Harvard Business Review*, January-February and March-April 1957; and Edwin A. Fleishman, Edwin F. Harris, Harold E. Burtt, "Leadership and Supervision in Industry: An Evaluation of a Supervisory Training Program" (Columbus: Ohio State University, 1955).

provide. It is a reality that comes home to the work life of all the members. It provides the training of leaders with a practical tool.

The effective supervisor as viewed by practical management and research

When the man of extensive business experience combines his evaluations of supervisors with those of the researcher, the two can usually agree on certain basic characteristics of the typical successful supervisor. These are that the effective supervisor—

1. Takes seriously his job of supervision. He identifies with management and management's objectives but also recognizes the needs of his employees. He seeks to balance organizational objectives and human needs. He views his function as one of leadership. He respects his responsibilities and enjoys an inner pride in his achievements and in himself as a person.

2. Instills pride in the employees as members of a work group. He wants each person in his work group to be proud of the group and its members. Workers who have high group loyalty tend to show more teamwork and to cooperate with each other. The good supervisor finds it easy to say: "I am proud of you and our group." Good work groups have good interpersonal relationships among the members.

3. Gives general rather than close supervision. He tries to have each employee feel responsible for his work, to know the company's objectives, and to appreciate the results of his efforts as to whether they are good or poor. But he lets the worker do the work in the way that he thinks best.

4. Maintains his own morale at a high level. He realizes that he must feel friendly in order to be friendly. He knows that he must keep an optimistic confident manner in regard to his work standards and his own performance as well as the performance of his workers. He cannot succumb to the influence of the difficulties in the job or of his personal life but must view them in a constructive spirit in order that he may convey a constructive spirit to others.

5. Rises above his own negative motivations or urges toward hostility, self-pity, power, and revenge. Instead, he seeks to be of service to others. One of his most used answers when he senses that someone wants to make a request is, "How can I be of help to you?"

For All Students

Pfiffner, J. J., *The Supervision of Personnel.* Englewood Cliffs, N.J.: Prentice-Hall, Inc., 1958. Treats the main aspects of supervision. Incorporates recent research findings in the social sciences. Features selected study questions.

Steckle, L. C., *The Man in Management.* New York: Harper & Brothers, 1958. Presents a manual for the supervisor. Emphasizes the "why" rather than the "how to" aspects of supervision. Many interpersonal skills are treated in a perceptive manner.

For Advanced Students

Sayles, Leonard R., *Behavior of Industrial Work Groups: Prediction and Control.* New York: John Wiley & Sons, Inc., 1958. Presents insights on the basis of a study of the behavior of more than 300 work groups in 30 plants.

Zaleznik, A., *Foreman Training in a Growing Enterprise.* Boston: Division of Research, Harvard Business School, 1951. A case study of a supervisory training program in human relations in a manufacturing company.

For Men in Business

Bruce, M. M., and D. B. Learner, "A Supervisory Practices Test," *Personnel Psychology,* Summer 1958. The test may be obtained by writing to Martin M. Bruce, Dunlap and Associates, Inc., 71 Hanson Lane, New Rochelle, N. Y.

Cooper, A. M., *How To Supervise People.* New York: McGraw-Hill Book Company, Inc., 1958. About twenty-five pages are devoted to "Questions for Group Discussion."

QUESTIONS ON THE CHAPTER

1. Why is it said that supervisors are the employee-relations mirror for management?
2. Differentiate between the terms "supervisor" and "foreman."
3. Which areas are likely to have the most and the least restrictions on supervisory authority?
4. In what respects does a typical supervisor play a dual role in business?
5. Cite evidence to indicate the relation between foremen and production.
6. Define judicial and educational discipline, and explain why one is more effective than the other.
7. On the basis of survey figures, does it seem advisable or inadvisable for supervisors and their superiors to meet regularly for coaching by the superior?
8. Explain the aims that supervisor training courses should have and the needs for the aims.

9. Discuss the supervisors' conflict as to goals.
10. What problems must a skilled leader overcome when using the role-playing method of training?
11. Does an effective supervisor give general or close supervision?
12. Of the various ideas presented in the chapter, which ones are of special interest to you?
13. What did the chapter contribute toward your future relations with (a) the men who supervise your work, (b) the employees whom you may supervise?

PROBLEMS AND PROJECTS

For All Students

1. Here are four typical problems in the supervision of employees. The problems can be used for discussion or for role-playing:
   a. Assume that you, the supervisor, have done what you think is a good job in orienting a new employee. You have turned him over to an old employee for further guidance. The next day you check up on the new man and find him sitting down, doing nothing, in the midst of work that should be done. You are sure that he is loafing. What is the first thing you would do or say?
   b. Assume that you have just explained the work to a new employee: the rate of pay, hours of work, nature of the job, etc. You ask whether he has any questions and his first question is "The rate of pay on this job is ten cents an hour lower than it ought to be. How soon will I get the ten cents an hour more pay?" How would you answer him?
   c. After you have explained the job to a new employee who seems to be satisfied about the instructions, he says "One thing I didn't mention to anyone is that I have to ride to and from work with my brother. He will get here about a quarter hour before starting time and about a quarter hour before quitting time. Will it be all right for me to start a quarter hour ahead of time and quit a quarter hour sooner than the other employees on the same job in the plant?"
   d. An old company employee has been transferred from another department to your department. When you start to explain the work to him, he says "That's all right, young man. I've been around here for a good many years and I know all about this job." What would you say or do?

For Advanced Students

2. Make a study of the organizations and services available for the training of supervisors. Consider the American Management Association, Inc., New York; National Management Association, Dayton, Ohio; Bureau of National Affairs, Inc., Washington, D.C.; British Association for Commercial and Industrial Education, London; and others.
3. Collect additional information for the training of supervisors through cases for discussion and role-playing—add to the text treatment.

For Men in Business

4. Assume that you now have no supervisory responsibilities but that management has told you that you are to be designated the assistant head of the department. How would you prepare for it? In what ways would you change your behavior?

5. Do you have leadmen in your factory? Describe their functions. You might read George Strauss, "The Changing Role of the Working Supervisor," *The Journal of Business,* University of Chicago, July 1957, for more information.

0NE OF THE FIRST THINGS FOR THE STUDENT OF BUSINESS TO LEARN in this field is how to spell "personnel." Too many students irritate executives and teachers by spelling the title as "personal manager." ("Personal manager" applies to the personal business representative of a star of stage or screen, not to a corporation executive of the kind discussed here.) A personnel manager is an important executive whose functions are summarized in Table 14-1.

In some companies his title may be "director of industrial relations." This title is likely to be found in heavy industry and similar companies where labor unions loom large in management's thinking. In that case, his functions and training for them might be organized along the following lines:

Collective bargaining: multi-employer and industry-wide bargaining; union security; studies of collective bargaining in the industry and the company.

Management relations: executive training, managerial decision-making, and the role of supervision.

Employee relations: job satisfaction, productivity, and morale.

Labor disputes and their settlement: strikes, mediation, arbitration, grievance procedures.

Labor economics: wages, employment, unemployment.

Labor law and legislation: regulation of internal union affairs, labor injunctions, restraints on featherbedding.

Employment management: employing regular and other work-

14   Personnel Management

ers such as the seriously handicapped, merit or efficiency ratings, testing.

Trade unionism: policies and practices of American unions, union procedures for settling jurisdictional disputes.

Social security: health insurance, workmen's compensation, and others.

Table 14-1

THE PERSONNEL ADMINISTRATOR'S "MY DAY"

The American Society for Personnel Administration reported the results of a recent survey made in a midwestern city as to where and how the average personnel administrator spent his day. In theory, this is how his day should be spent:

60 per cent in his department.
35 per cent in the plant or other offices.
5 per cent away from his work area.

Here is how the work day averaged out:

18 per cent, hires, separations, transfers, etc.
11 per cent, personnel department operations (reports, correspondence, records, etc.).
12 per cent, union matters (formal or informal).
8 per cent, employee counseling.
6 per cent, employee activities (recreation, mutual benefit, social, etc.).
6 per cent, training.
4 per cent, matters pertaining to the Cafeteria, Plant Protection, Dispensary, etc.
4 per cent, wage and salary administration.
3 per cent, safety.
12 per cent, forward planning on personnel programs (reading, research, conferring with executives, etc.).
11 per cent, promoting and activating the personnel program (preparing material, meetings, selling supervision, etc.).
5 per cent, outside committee work, civic participation, etc.

SOURCE: *Personnel Panorama* (Pacific Northwest Personnel Management Association), June 1951. Reprinted by permission of the American Society for Personnel Administration.

The importance of the personnel director, whatever his title and specific functions may be, becomes evident when we recognize that a company's vitality and growth are determined by its manpower. A personnel man's responsibilities are likely to include any human relations function from management development to organizing the company glee club. We shall treat in separate chapters the managerial functions of interviewing, appraising employees (merit rating), and dealing with employee relations and with labor unions. This introductory chapter to the field will present some of the organization structural relations and typical human relations aspects of personnel management, particularly those aspects not usually treated in formal courses in personnel management.

The personnel executive does far more than hire new people and discharge incompetent employees. His functions are in the staff rather than the line. He thinks of himself as a colleague of both management and the employees of the company. He is also an analyst of employee relations affairs: he studies the company's current labor turnover figures, promotions and transfers per 100 employees, and other data that enable him to inform and counsel management in regard to management's responsibilities for its manpower.

In some companies, the personnel department is still looked upon as a "fire department, useful only in times of crisis." But in most cases it is considered a "definite asset which adds measurably to the company's productivity and success," or, at the very least, a "useful department which pays its own way." [1]

Of course the functions and objectives of the personnel manager vary with the man and the company. A few still think of their job as essentially paternalistic. Some think of it as specialization in the scientific techniques involved in testing applicants and rating employees. The more advanced men in the field think of themselves in a facilitating rather than an operating role. A survey of the personnel men in a typical industrial area is likely to indicate that the personnel worker sees his primary purpose as one of improving the working relationships between employees and supervisors so that the supervisors can perform their responsibilities effectively. Their objectives are those helpful in improving the work performances of the individual employee.

As a member of the managerial staff, the personnel director understands management's viewpoints and has perspectives that enable him to help others get work done. Ideally, he works with line executives to enable them to become creative leaders rather than operational supervisors only. He is a human relations catalyst for the line people. The present day personnel manager, regardless of whether he is an untrained traditional employment man under the production superintendent, or a vice-president in charge of industrial relations under the president, is still essentially a colleague of the line. He does not work *for* the line but *with* the line. His basic job is to help the line get work done.[2]

---

[1] See "Strictly Personnel," *Personnel*, American Management Association, Inc., May 1957, p. 510.

[2] See William M. Fox, "Personnel Administration: Past and Present," *Personnel Administration*, July-August 1956, p. 6.

In progressive managements, the personnel executive has a greater responsibility than that of facilitating production alone. His responsibility is often defined as "productivity plus."

The "plus" includes developing a real sense of affiliation with the company on the part of employees, providing a satisfying work atmosphere, establishing effective relationships in the organizational structure, and arranging for a framework of personnel regulations and practices "in which people understand what is expected, and firm, fair discipline is administered." [3] The personnel function is a permeating one that concentrates on the human values—the release of human values that tend to increase productivity.

The number of personnel officers who are full-fledged, major executives in their companies is increasing. Unfortunately, there are also many companies that have "personnel directors" in name rather than in function. In these instances, the man in charge of "personnel administration" may be a member of the third, fourth, or fifth echelons of management. [4] If he is a member of the lower echelons, the personnel man himself is likely to be someone grown old in company service whose performance in his better days was such as to justify "making a place" for him. Or he may be a promising young man who is being "brought along" until he can be given something to do that is considered more important.

"Frankly, Mr. Farrell, what I'm looking for in an efficiency expert is someone who'll leave the Personnel Department alone."
SOURCE: by Evan D. Diamond, Manage (August 1957). Courtesy The National Management Association.

Of course an effective personnel man, in practice, must be more than "purely advisory." Even though his authority is vested in his chief rather than in himself, he must accept some responsibility for carrying out his plans with line people. Basically, the status of the personnel man is dependent upon the way in which he perceives his functions.

---

[3] See R. L. Miller, "What Plant Managers Expect of Personnel Managers," *The Personnel Administrator*, Febraury 1958.

[4] See S. Avery Raube in "Holding Up a Mirror for Personnel Directors," *Personnel Journal*, November 1956.

Personnel Management

Observations indicate that most personnel directors have the status they deserve in the managerial line-up. As one analyst stated: "This is true of every executive whether a personnel director or a line operating manager. He is accorded the status he deserves by reason of his ability to contribute to the progress of the business. If his contributions are small, his status is low. If his contributions are great, his position is treated with respect. Those personnel directors who attain higher status than others do so because of their personal qualifications. Status must be earned." [5]

Relations with other executives

To be effective, the head of the personnel department must guard against accepting the tendency of those executives who want to rid themselves of what are really their responsibilities. This hazard becomes most evident when a medium size or small company has not had a personnel department and labor troubles arise. Members of management are apt to say: "Let's hire a personnel director. Then he can solve all our labor troubles." Smart personnel men do not accept a job of this kind until they change management's philosophy about the place of the personnel department in the company's corporate life. Most personnel work of the personal contact variety is part of day-to-day supervision and is the responsibility of the operating departments. Both supervisor and personnel man must realize that principle.

Some executives, particularly heads of the departments of finance and accounting, may fail to appreciate fully the need for or importance of the personnel department. "It's just another intangible," they say. When these men note the budgets of the personnel department they are likely to wonder what use has been made of the money to increase profits.

Of course what this kind of opinion signifies is that the personnel director has failed to give his critics a full appreciation of the department's objectives and programs. He should give them a part in attaining his objectives. People tend to accept ideas which they help to develop. For this reason, it is highly desirable to have the widest possible participation by all persons involved in a personnel program. Where that is not appropriate, either because the plan is already well established or because of the nature of the organization, the next best line of attack is to review periodically with members of management the various steps

[5] McCoy C. Campbell, "Personnel Man in Key Spot So Long As 'People Make Profits,'" *Personnel Journal*, February 1957.

that were taken in the development of the program. Criticisms and suggestions can be invited. Regular reviews and appraisals are essential in having a personnel program accepted by staff members.

Relations between foremen and the personnel department

The chain of command in any company is frequently modified by the informal organization as explained in Chapters 7 and 10.

One of the problems that often occurs is that employees fail to follow the chain of command. Certain employees have a tendency to come directly to the personnel department without first seeing their foreman. This, in some cases, gives the foreman the feeling that he is being left out.

Actually, the typical foreman knows a great deal about his workers and he resents the efforts of staff members who come between him and his employees. He frequently feels that management and staff members put tasks upon him and his workers without understanding the employees or the difficulties of the job. Many foremen feel that staff and management men understand so little about the employees and their problems, that they hate to take time off to go to meetings or classes which deal with personnel problems. Such meetings, to them, are just a waste of company money and time.

Foremen think that the personnel people are too willing to accept as fact every complaint from a worker. This is especially likely to occur when members of the personnel staff are young college graduates who have not worked their way up from the shop.

Some foremen also believe that personnel men are too willing to give their sympathies to the employee. Personnel men must, at times, disagree with the supervisor. When a foreman fails to consider the feelings of the employees or makes excessive demands on them, the personnel worker is likely to point to his failures in maintaining happy relations.

If the personnel man succumbs to the natural tendency to take over an employee relations responsibility that should remain with the foremen, he finds it very difficult to help foremen and other members of the line through training, coaching, and coordinating. The line man just "washes his hands" of the situation. Instead, the personnel man must avoid coming between a foreman and his worker except when genuine cooperation can be achieved. If the personnel man has or takes authority, and tries to correct the actions of a supervisor, he not only arouses resentment but also interferes with normal organization practices.

As one writer has stated:

> The relationship between staff and the line in *any* function may be improved if the staff man is guided by the following precepts:
>
> Help in every way you can in selecting, coaching, training, advising, and the like.
>
> Resist the temptation to take over any responsibility in the interest of expediting results. This takes infinite patience—but it will be rewarded in the end by a program that works more effectively. . . .

A typical example, which actually took place in a plant, points up work relationships that often occur:

Screw Machine Foreman to *Personnel Manager:* "Some of my men cannot reach their production quotas when the tolerances are close."

Personnel Manager: "Are you being fair about it—have you trained them as you should?—are the standards right?"

Foreman: "The standards are not right in every case but they are not 100% wrong. Some of the men shouldn't have been hired in the first place. They are not grade 'A' mechanics but they are drawing top rates. I haven't the time to wet nurse them."

Personnel Manager: "How did they get to the top of the range if they didn't deserve it?"

Foreman: "Through union pressure and seniority. They were raised before my results were being measured as they are now."

Personnel Manager: "According to the contract we can terminate anyone who consistently fails to earn his guaranteed rate. I'll check with Industrial Engineering and see that the tight standards are adjusted. Then if the fault lies entirely with the men, I'll transfer them to work they can do or I'll take some other action to relieve you of the loss." [6]

TYPICAL PERSONNEL PROBLEMS

Now let's look at some of the common situations which create problems the personnel manager must deal with in his work.

The "captive employees"

Almost every company has certain employees who cannot leave because they are "tied" to the company. Some are tied by inertia—it's easier to stay than to seek employment elsewhere.

Captives to "benefits." One large classification of captive employees are those who have worked for many years with a company and have

---

[6] Donald H. Sunderlin, "Each Supervisor a Manager," *Personnel Administration,* January-February 1957, pp. 27, 28.

acquired important "benefits," particularly seniority and pension rights. Under the provisions of union contracts or the company's benefit plan, they would have to sacrifice all these accruals if they left the company.

Captives to the community. Even though Americans are noted for their mobility, numerous individuals will remain with a company because the job enables them to enjoy old friendships, their relatives, and the community life to which they have become accustomed.

Captives of their special skills. The employee who has attained special skills which are useful only in the company where he acquired the skill finds it hard to find another who can use him. If he moves, he must start a new career at a lower salary and less job status.

Many captives of this kind hold positions whose salaries are not affected by competition from other employers. They realize that they have not gained increased incomes to the same extent as other workers. Their morale and efficiency are lowered. They feel defenseless. Many employees of educational and governmental institutions are likely to be members of this group. Some progressive personnel men make systematic surveys of the company's salary structure in order to discover these defenseless people.

Public utilities are likely to have many captive employees among their power plant operators. Theoretically, a power plant operator is free to leave one company and seek employment in another, but the market for his skills is limited. Very few vacancies of certain job classes in public utilities occur often enough to enable a worker to move. Turnover is limited. Anyone who takes a job with a public utility should ask himself: "Will ten years of employment in this company allow me to move with greater ease to another industry at a higher rate of pay or will I become another captive employee?" Few managements want any employees to become captive, but some "captivity" does occur. Progressive personnel men try to identify it and develop training programs which help to overcome the problem.

Alert managements do not want to have an atmosphere or work situation where employees can neither quit nor be fired. The employee who cannot take a job offer because of a bonus for length of service or a retirement benefit is not likely to be an energetic, enthusiastic employee—he may be merely frustrated by management's good intentions.

Privileged employees

Almost every large company has certain privileged employees. The research men, for example, do not abide by the same rules as the engineers. Research men like to have time to think. They wander around the company offices in a seemingly aimless manner. Some habitually come to work late and leave early.

In a publishing office, members of the editorial department are likely to come and go as they please. But the employees of the accounting department in the same publishing firm are expected to obey punctuality rules meticulously.

Of course the privileged individuals, whoever and wherever they are, tend to be a source of irritation to nonprivileged employees. Departmental frictions often arise from this kind of situation and the personnel man tries to placate the resentful ones without disturbing the work habits of the members of privileged groups.

Many blue collar workers look upon their white collar fellow employees of the company as having certain privileges which they do not hope to attain. The desks and offices of white collar employees are of better quality and higher cost than those of shop employees who do similar work. Furthermore, certain white collar members of the organization, particularly salesmen, have the privilege of spending the company's money to entertain customers and at the same time enjoy luxuries that are not available to shop people.

Salary payment plans during illness are likely to be more flexible for office than for shop workers. Even though the plan of payment during illness may be published as the same for all workers, the trend in actual practice is toward two sets of plans—one publicly proclaimed, the other practiced. And the latter is usually more flexible, but especially for the office workers.

For salaried and executive personnel, there is likely to be a base plan beyond which managers may grant extra benefits, depending on years of service, value, and rank. Executives are close to and friendly with the company heads and directors. Naturally they often get especially considerate treatment.

Most pay plans for absence from work are discretionary. An electronics manufacturer, for instance, will frankly admit, in private, that he coddles research personnel—good research men are hard for him to get and hold. Many companies have three sets of rules—one for hourly workers, one for salaried employees, and a third for executives. For hourly workers, the plan usually prescribes specific benefits hammered out in union negotiations and regarded as "rights" by workers.

Transferring employees

Every company finds it necessary to transfer employees at times. One department has a surplus of help and another needs help. Most employees involved in a transfer do not object if it is temporary. If it is to be permanent, many do object even though the pay may be as good or even better. The wise personnel man senses that the true causes for objection are likely to be in the social aspects involved in the change. Perhaps the new supervisor is less understanding or the workers are strange. Logical arguments are of little avail. The loss of old friends and the need for new habits of work loom too large in the mind of the worker to dislodge them by argument. Instead of trying to "sell" the new job to the worker, it is better to try to relieve anxieties by letting the employee try out the new job for a few days before making the transfer permanent. The personnel man therefore makes the transition on a tentative basis and allows the employee to alleviate his anxieties by giving him some time to make the adjustment through the gain of new friends and new job satisfactions.

Old employees vs. young college graduates—
pay differentials

Much rivalry occurs between senior employees and the new men recruited from colleges. Almost every company has a number of employees who are approaching retirement age. When the company grows, an active recruiting drive may expand the work force by hiring many young men. The older men feel greatly threatened especially when some of the young men advance rapidly to better positions. Naturally bitterness and resentment often develop on the part of the older men. They feel that with their experience and seniority they should have got promotions that have gone to the younger men. In the case of supervisors, it is especially difficult for an older supervisor having many years of experience to accept the authority of a young executive who has had little experience.

Starting salary rates sharpen the conflict. Competition between firms for new men with certain kinds of training has caused many companies to pay very high starting salary rates. For older employees, general wage increases have not always kept pace with the higher salaries paid the beginners. Hence, a company often finds itself paying a higher salary to a new man than to one who has worked there for years, even though both are holding the same job.

The executive who supervises the oldtimers and the newcomers is in a policy dilemma. If, on the one hand, he chooses to hire the bright young men at the high starting pay, he makes his older employees unhappy. The squeezing on pay differentials can make his department a hotbed of discontent and bring about an uncomfortably high turnover. On the other hand, if he does not hire any promising young men, he accepts the lesser talent that he can get at the old starting scales. Eventually, he may end up with a comparatively lethargic department that is staffed with mediocrities.

During an inflationary period starting salaries go up faster than the whole general range of salaries. In many cases, new employees, whether beginners or job hoppers, ask for and get salaries as high as, or higher than, employees who have had several years' experience with the company.

If the executive ignores the situation, efficiency drops and more people quit. Then he must replace those who quit with higher-paid new employees and train them. If he tries to solve the differential to keep his oldtimers happy, his direct labor costs for the department immediately jump so far that his budget is warped out of line with the forecasts for costs of the product.

Some salaried men take advantage of the situation by frequent job hopping. They know that the easiest way to increase take-home pay is to move to another company. Most salaried workers have less mobility —they prefer to remain in one company to build up their seniority rights and pension benefits. When the problem becomes too acute, the personnel manager, in conference with top management, usually sets up a course of action to be followed consistently. The policy chosen may include one or more of the following alternatives:

1. Hiring superior new employees at whatever rate must be paid. If old employees are not willing to accept the situation, some will leave.
2. Setting a rigid salary range for the job. If the personnel department cannot find a well qualified person who will accept that range, hire somebody of less ability who will.
3. Giving no general increases, but increasing the "merit" raises to those people whom management particularly wants to keep. Some companies have switched their entire pay system from one of periodic increases to a pure merit system. They have eliminated the seniority idea in relation to value. No employee is worth more merely because he has been there a long time. Of course this means that the personnel man must be especially alert to recognize

the superior employees who themselves will not request increases. To prevent the overlooking or neglect of competent employees management must systematically identify and reward them.

4. Telling the new employees to keep their higher salaries a secret. A few companies warn new employees to keep their salaries secret. One company goes so far as firing any employees who are caught discussing their salaries, but such a policy is antiquated and unrealistic.

5. Hiring "second-best" employees and training them. This, to some personnel managers, is better than trying to deal with morale of employees who feel that they are being treated unjustly. They set a rigid price for a job, then go to extra effort to fill it by locating someone who will take that salary, rather than hire a more qualified person who demands a higher price.

Managements are aware of hard feelings on the part of the older men, but most executives have assumed that the problem is of a temporary nature and that, in time, the differentials would be corrected. They have hoped that the effects of economic evolution would pull the wage structure back into line to take care of inequities. Unfortunately, this kind of evolution has not always occurred. Many managements have to live with some tensions and bitterness on the part of older employees until they are retired. Theoretically, the problem could be solved by raising the salaries of the older workers, but this would throw out of alignment too many other salary differentials. Also, inflationary pressures would be increased. Very few managements have been able to provide a completely satisfactory solution for the problem. If men are to be promoted on the basis of their merits and potentials for the future, then some younger men will continue to receive salaries above those of the "old guard." Of course each young man who is affected by this kind of conflict situation can accentuate or lessen the conflict by his manner toward the older men.

Some personnel men believe that when an employee resents the narrowing differentials between old and new employees, the best practical answer is to admit the squeeze and state frankly that management has decided that it cannot maintain the old differentials and still survive. The best policy for the employee is to keep faith in himself and his future—to earn by extra effort the highest raise he can achieve. Merit raises to those who make a superior contribution should, in time, correct some of the inequitable differences.

Personnel management (industrial relations) as a career

In terms of importance and scope, one of the fastest growing management jobs in recent years has been that of the industrial relations executive. A survey by *Industrial Relations News* indicated that the men in the personnel field are an educated group; nine out of ten respondents hold a college degree, and one out of three holds an advanced degree. Many are supplementing their education with further training, both inside and outside the company.

Of special interest to the college senior: only 15 per cent of the men surveyed entered the industrial relations field directly from college. One-quarter of the respondents were in the production field before they moved into industrial relations. The remainder came from a variety of other fields.

The survey indicates a growing trend toward moving men into personnel functions from other positions inside the company. An almost unanimous majority of the respondents believe that top management is cooperating with them in the areas of access to top management—development programs and budget allocations.

Most of the respondents perceive their biggest problems as internal rather than external: the most pressing being employee relations, communications, and morale. The single problems viewed as most important in the future were perceived, in order of rank given, as communications, collective bargaining, executive and supervisory development, automation, and employee development.

The majority of respondents believe that the industrial relations function will continue to grow in importance and value. One executive expressed it this way: "In an economy which is just discovering manpower as a capital asset, and with the increasing maturity of labor leaders, industrial relations will become a field on a par with sales and production." [7]

Young men and women in college and in industry who aim for the top jobs in industry find graduate professional training helpful. Legal training is especially valuable in handling labor relations problems that involve state and federal laws.

Personnel work in the government services usually requires a degree in one of the social sciences. College personnel work generally requires a master's or a doctorate, particularly when the job includes teaching

---

[7] Adapted from *"The Industrial Relations Executive,"* 1957, *Industrial Relations News.* See also *The Management Review,* American Management Association, Inc., July 1957.

on the graduate level. In secondary schools, a member of the personnel department is likely to teach as well as counsel; hence he must meet the requirements for teaching.

Personnel work cannot be learned from books alone. Knowledge acquired through experience in industry is as important as degrees.

One of the outstanding characteristics of the personnel man is his superior ability to remember faces, names of people, and facts in the history of each. Anyone who says that he can remember faces of people but not their names should improve this phase of his mental life before he enters the field. It is a "must" for effectiveness in personnel management. Fortunately, anyone who determines to improve this mental skill can do so through everyday practice in college, at work, and in his social life. (See page 487.)

An executive in this field must enjoy working with people of all types: the pleasant, the not-so-pleasant, and the downright unpleasant. He should have a personality that expresses friendliness and sincerity so that he will become the respected friend of both company officers and employees.

What are the main satisfactions that accrue to the member of a personnel department? The kind of answer given most often is similar to this statement by one personnel man: "A satisfaction that I have found through my work is a sort of compensation for my own personality shortcomings. My tendency toward introversion has decreased as a result of my work. The more I work with people, the more I have found a usefulness and confidence in myself. This is certainly more of a benefit or reward than any wage or security benefits that I receive. I now live more richly as well as more effectively as a person."

COLLATERAL READINGS

For All Students

New York Life Insurance Company, Dept. MM, 51 Madison Ave., New York, publishes career booklets as a public service. "Should Your Child Go into Personnel Work?" is an example of the kind of vocational information that is available for the asking.

Yoder, Dale, and Roberta J. Nelson, *Jobs in Employee Relations,* 1959 (New York: American Management Association, Inc., 1959). An example of the reports made by AMA on this topic from time to time. Ask for the latest report.

For Advanced Students

Industrial and Labor Relations Review, New York State School of Industrial and Labor Relations, Cornell University, Ithaca, N. Y. A publication.

Professional Standards for Personnel Work. A pamphlet by the Society for Personnel Administration, Washington, D.C. Prepared by a committee on professional standards. See also *Personnel Journal*, February 1957, p. 356.

Research in Industrial Relations. New York: Harper & Brothers, 1957. Thirteen contributors provide a good assessment of where we are and what is ahead.

For Men in Business

Black, James M., "Planning Ahead in Personnel," *Dun's Review and Modern Industry*, February 1958. Relates to planning in an organization which is installing automation in its production and office programs. Features fourteen key questions.

Strother, George B., "Personnel Management in Theory and Practice," *Personnel*, American Management Association, Inc., May-June 1959. Reports a survey of practices in 18 small, medium, and large companies in Wisconsin.

QUESTIONS ON THE CHAPTER

1. How does the typical personnel man see his primary purpose in the organization? What is his basic job?

2. What per cent of a typical personnel manager's time is spent outside of his department? What functions take up the largest percentages of an average work day of a personnel man?

3. Is a personnel administrator a colleague of management or of the employees? The personnel function concentrates on what values?

4. What is meant by the "plus" when it is said that the responsibility of the personnel executive is "productivity plus."

5. In what ways are many employees captives of their special skills or of the work situation?

6. What methods should personnel men use to alleviate many of the problems connected with transferring employees?

7. What problems do some salaried workers try to cope with by job hopping?

8. According to an *Industrial Relations News* survey, what per cent of the men questioned entered the personnel field directly from college? What does this signify for the student who plans to enter personnel work?

9. List the five most important internal company problems of personnel men.

10. What is a source of learning about personnel work that is as important as books?

11. Of all the ideas presented in the chapter, which ones were of special interest to you?

12. What did the chapter contribute toward your future relations with (a) the men who supervise your work, (b) Employees whom you may supervise?

For All Students

1. Ask several friends for their opinions as to whether you, if you were in personnel work, would tend to lean toward management or employees in a conflict between the two. How might your bias be corrected or utilized by yourself?

2. Assume that when you leave college and take a job, some of your work associates will think of you as privileged because of your extra education. What policies do you intend to follow to gain their good will?

For Advanced Students

3. Personnel men are seldom chosen for top management jobs such as president. Many think of themselves as professional aides to management, not as integrated management men. See J. M. Jenks, "Let's Stop Professionalizing," *Personnel Journal,* July-August 1958. How does this affect your planning for self-development?

4. Assume that you wish to remain in personnel work as your career. Note the functions in the list at the beginning of the chapter. Study sources for getting training in the functions. Suggest books and journals that would be helpful.

For Men in Business

5. Of all the employees whom you know, designate the "captive employees." What is the nature of their ties to the employer? Are these employees especially happy in their work? If not, how might they improve their morale?

6. Describe some of the "privileged employees" whom you know. How does their presence in the company affect other employees? If you were a privileged employee in a company, how might you try to gain the good will of other employees?

THE ONE OUTSTANDING PERSONALITY CHARACTERISTIC OF PER-
sonnel managers is, or at least ought to be, their *susceptibility
to stimulation by the behavior of people:* how they feel, think,
and live emotionally as well as how they work. The personnel
man's most important professional skills are those associated
with his keen sensitivity to people as persons. He makes his
special contributions to the company, its managers, and its employees through his "feel" as to the hidden meanings that underlie the overt actions of individual members of the organization.
At the same time, he respects the individual regardless of his
limitations or peculiarities.

He deals with real human beings in real situations. He not
only accepts people as they are but he also accepts the plant
or office situation as he finds it. He knows, for example, that
the company's work environment and equipment will be gradually improved, but in the meantime he works with the people
and the equipment that are there. He does not try to reform
or fire every employee or executive whose thinking is antiquated
nor does he insist that every machine and typewriter be perfect.
He works with what and with whom he has but he moves
toward the development of the better potentials in people and
their situations. He accentuates the positive. Weaknesses are
not emphasized as weaknesses but as opportunities for positive
action.

15

Personnel Management:
The Personnel Man's Sensitivity
to Employee Relations

Typical situations that exemplify the personnel manager's sensitivity and positive emphasis

The effective personnel manager is positive-minded. He looks for the strengths in people and the organization. He enables each executive to feel better about himself and his employees by calling to his attention the good qualities in his employees. Whenever possible, he brings to the attention of the head of the department any evidences of growth or accomplishment that one of his employees has demonstrated by taking evening courses, by leadership in the company's recreational program, by performance in community organizations, or by work suggestions made that may benefit the company or the employees. This does not mean that he is blind to weaknesses in certain individuals such as the clock-watcher, the malingerer, or the expense account padder. He notes them too and guards against their influence but he is more interested in the good than the bad that he finds in the personnel.

When he notes that one of the executives, perhaps the production vice president, is being adversely conditioned against the factory employees because he is being harassed by several ornery union officials, the personnel manager brings to the production executive's attention some of the more worthy union members.

If the plant manager is so deeply engrossed in paperwork and in carrying out his responsibilities that he is not becoming acquainted with the employees as persons, the personnel manager arranges for the executive to meet and become better acquainted with some of his own employees. He may, for example, arrange for the plant manager to greet and chat with each new employee.

When the personnel manager finds that unnecessary frictions exist between two groups such as those often found on the part of the engineering department versus the shop, he brings it to the attention of the heads of the two groups and helps them arrange situations where members of both groups can meet and work together—perhaps setting up a committee that deals with a problem common to the two classes of employees.

The sensitivity of the personnel man also sharpens his perception of the ways in which other people perceive their situations. When he assigns a new employee to a supervisor, he tries to place him with a supervisor whom the employee will respect. A new shop man's pride may be in his work, another's may be in his physical strength. The former will do his best work for a supervisor who is an expert in the work being performed. The latter will be happiest under a supervisor who is physically robust and somewhat gruff, the kind of man the new employee can

The Personnel Man's Sensitivity 259

brag about when he is chatting with his cronies at the local bar.

When a department head decides to assign an assistant to a specialist or expert worker for the first time in order that the specialist may be able to get more work done, the personnel man must think of how the older employee will look upon the new assistant. Will he view the assistant as a threat to him? Will he suspect that management is trying to take his job away from him? The personnel man must help to anticipate and prevent the development of such suspicions and anxieties before they arise.

When a foreman finds that an employee violates an important safety rule or policy, the foreman may be able to think only in terms of the penalty that is deserved. Members of management are less interested in punishment than in finding out why the problem arose and in preventing its recurrence. The foreman may perceive any leniency toward his errant employee as a threat to his foremanship prerogatives. It is the personnel man's function not merely to pass on to the foreman the decision made by management, but to help the foreman reinterpret the situation.

The personnel man's function of interpretation is especially important in such executive-employee relations as are found in committee meetings. If a major executive attends a meeting, some committee members will avoid getting openly involved in the issues under discussion. They will maintain a pleasant façade and show superficial interest in the problem, but they will not express their true feelings. Sometimes the personnel man can tactfully overcome a member's detachment by enabling him, through friendly questioning, to express his true feelings without embarrassing anyone present.

"*I think I'll give you to Mr. Willoughby. He's seemed a bit despondent lately.*" SOURCE: The Wall Street Journal (*Sept. 17, 1957*).

The Personnel Man's Sensitivity

His contributions through his sensitivity can be illustrated in the way that he deals with records of employee dispensary visits. Statistics about dispensary visits are kept in most companies but their meanings are not usually published. To publish the statistical analyses or their interpretations tends to cause employees to take care of their own minor cuts and bruises. The statistics are valuable, however, as possible indicators of sources of likely future accidents. If the figures are handed to the foremen without instruction, some foremen are likely to go to an individual worker and say: "Look here. You made eight trips to the company dispensary last month. The statistics show that you are going to have a serious accident within a year!" Instead, the personnel manager tactfully encourages every foreman to look for specific training problems with any of his employees who are having minor injuries. He can study the problem employee's work habits and teach him how to do his work safely. Furthermore, the personnel man should know which foremen are apt to misuse the information and be able to help them to use it constructively.

Another example of the personnel man's sensitivity occurs, or should occur, when the management considers the advisability of remodeling the company's cafeteria. Should a special dining room be built for the supervisors? Should it be designed to have supervisors and employees eat together? The answer depends upon the "tone" of the plant. If mixing comes naturally, supervisors and employees should be able to eat together with pleasure for both and with benefit for the company. The personnel man's feel for the situation should be a guide to management in planning the dining facilities.

The personnel manager should be able to convince management when employees need help in making adjustments to impending changes, such as moving the offices from a metropolitan center to the suburbs. One concern, for example, laid careful plans for three years to abandon the city for the suburbs. The company's officials and engineers pored over blueprints and plans for layouts of offices and placement of desks and equipment but failed to explain to employees the benefits they would gain from the move. As a result, many decided that they did not want to live in the country. Other companies in the same city were able to hire some of the firm's best secretaries, accountants, and experienced workers. When moving day was over, 40 per cent of the regular employees had decided to remain in the city. The personnel manager had given management ample warning and recommended a program of education, but management was too busy looking forward to fewer labor problems, lower taxes, and the delights of working in the country to give heed. Now the personnel manager is running expensive help wanted advertising in the metropolitan dailies in attempts to induce workers to move to the suburb.

Of course we might say that every man in a responsible job in business should have the kind of sensitivity and make the positive emphases mentioned in the above examples. True, but the personnel man has extra responsibilities in these human relationships. He is a specialist in human relations.

Noting the unvoiced grievances

Every personnel man deals constantly with grievances presented overtly by employees. Dealing with grievances, particularly in a unionized plant, may require a large share of the personnel manager's working time. Usually, rather definite procedures have been established for processing the formal grievances.

In addition to the formally-presented grievances, the personnel man must have alert antennae for the unvoiced grievances. These are commonly expressed in fairly subtle forms: noncooperation, chip-on-the-shoulder attitudes, insubordination, loafing, poor quality of work, and absenteeism. Investigators have pointed out the need for distinguishing

"You'll find we're just one big family here—intrigues, jealousies, fights. . . ." SOURCE: by Dale Mc-Featters, The Management Review (October 1957). Courtesy American Management Association, Inc.

between the manifest and the latent content of grievances. When, for example, the manner of a supervisor is so threatening that it cannot be consciously faced by the employee, he may give as the cause for dis-

The Personnel Man's Sensitivity

satisfaction anything from low pay to the location of the parking space assigned to him in the company parking lot. One woman employee expressed the correct interpretation of her grievance when she stated: "The company building is definitely too crowded. The employees, myself included, become annoyed at the implication of the 'cheapness' of the office. There is a need for better working conditions, for many times I have become tired and annoyed at physical conditions as an outlet for other annoyances. Any inadequate working condition tends to lessen efficiency."

A company that is known to be losing money is likely to have a high percentage of dissatisfied employees—their insecurity has grievance generating effects in regard to numerous aspects of the work situation. Such unvoiced grievances and their effects may not always be approached through direct questioning about them. Sometimes they have to be brought into the open through indirect discussion. Employees who work in a company that is losing money can be encouraged to enjoy their work for the time being. Employees who are happy in their jobs usually have relatively few grievances even though the future vitality of the company may be in doubt. The first requirement, however, for dealing with the unvoiced grievances is the sensitivity essential to their recognition. If they are recognized in their early stages, their causes can be dealt with before they snowball into big grievances.

EMPLOYEE ATTITUDE OR MORALE SURVEYS

The modern personnel man, however sensitive he may be personally to the feelings of others, realizes that he is not keeping in touch with all the feelings and emotional undertows in a large company. Also, he knows that his management needs an occasional comprehensive view of the morale situation in every department of the company. To give management such a picture, he convinces top management that a morale survey would be helpful.

To conduct a survey of this kind, questions are usually developed by committees of management and employees. Some companies also purchase standard questionnaire forms such as the one published by Science Research Associates, Chicago. The SRA *Employee Inventory* is the most widely used employee attitude survey instrument. It has been used to survey over 600,000 employees. The inventory is distinctive in that the percentage of favorable attitudes among any employee group toward various aspects of their employment can be compared with national norms. In addition, SRA has developed norms that are specific to particular industries and particular occupational groups. Specific norms are available for the following industries: Food industry, manufacturing, retailing, and utilities. Norms are also available for the following specific occupational groups: Administrative, office, sales, technical, supervisory, skilled production, unskilled production, and nonproduction hourly. This enables management to identify more accurately the specific areas of strengths and weaknesses within the company and within departments of the company.

If properly administered, tabulated, and interpreted, these anonymous responses gives a representative picture of what employees think about the areas covered by the survey questions. The survey responses present a comprehensive report of employee attitudes or morale. The survey is usually conducted for a company by an outside consultant such as an industrial relations consulting firm. In most cases, some technical know-how is required. Furthermore, outsiders are better able to keep the operation on a strictly confidential basis.[1]

Generally, the survey is conducted so that no information can be traced back to the person who answered the questionnaire. Employees must be assured that they can express criticisms without any possibility of being identified. Also, employees should be told why their answers are sought—that management is sincere in asking the questions, and what management intends to do with the tabulated answers.

Typical findings from surveys

Eugene J. Benge, consulting psychologist, has conducted employee attitude surveys over a period of several decades in many companies. The findings show roughly that 20 to 30 per cent of employees seem to be somewhat on the unhappy side—that is, they check more negative than positive responses. Additional findings are:

> We find that women have better morale than men as a group; that the lowest morale appears between the ages of twenty and twenty-four and that it is higher before and after this age period; that employees start in jobs with high morale and that morale falls for a period of about five or six years before it starts to rise again; that low paid and high paid employees have higher morale than the medium paid; that the closer an

---

[1] Louis A. Allen, "Action-Oriented Attitude Surveys," *Personnel*, American Management Association, Inc., September 1952, presents a good set of directions for making attitude surveys. For a description of various methods of attitude measurement, see Irving R. Weschler and Raymond E. Bernberg, "Indirect Methods of Attitude Measurement" (Institute of Industrial Relations, University of California, Los Angeles), 1949.

The SRA Employee Inventory uses easy-to-understand language. Since it requires only a few minutes to administer, it can be given during working hours with little disruption or loss of production time. The brief time required for answering the questions is equally important when the Inventory is given to employees on their own time. Because employees are asked not to sign their names, they are willing to answer frankly. Management can use the Employee Inventory to: (1) measure morale for a company as a whole; (2) compare morale between departments or plants in an organization; (3) compare morale between departments or plants in an organization; (4) compare morale in a company with the average of others, particularly in the same industry.

By using the Employee Inventory to find out what employees really think, companies can pinpoint weak departments, increase the effectiveness of supervision, learn if communication is adequate, discover training needs, improve employee relations, build community good will, and cut employee turnover.

The SRA Employee Inventory was prepared by the Employee Attitude Research Group in the Industrial Relations Center, University of Chicago. This group has members from both the University and industry.

The SRA Employee Inventory is published by Science Research Associates, Inc., 57 W. Grand Avenue, Chicago 10, Illinois; copyright 1951, by the Industrial Relations Center of the University of Chicago.

employee approaches in earning power to his immediate supervisor, the lower his morale is likely to be. We also found that small companies tend to have better morale levels than big companies and that night shifts tend to have better morale than day shifts, contrary to usual thinking. Usually the latter is associated with the fact that night shifts approach working teams much more than do day shifts. By indirect reasoning we are sure that those who have left or are about to leave a concern have much lower morale than the average of that concern.[2]

The above findings represent a composite for the employees of a large number of factories, commercial and financial institutions, offices, and sales forces. When the Industrial Relations Section, California Institute of Technology, had completed a total of 25 surveys in 18 different companies, covering over 50,000 employees, the Section formulated a number of conclusions based on all of its studies of employee opinion. One of these was that

> Morale is affected by length of service. Employees with less than a year of service have almost as high morale as employees with 25 years of service or more. The morale of employees declines with length of service, reaching its low point after 10 to 15 years of service. After this point, morale tends to increase.[3]

The findings are most important concerning what they reveal about factors that cause satisfaction and dissatisfaction of employees. In one survey of 1,000 persons, conducted by Robert L. Kahn of the University of Michigan Survey Research Center, 82 per cent said that, all things considered, they were satisfied with their jobs—yet only 28 per cent thought that they had a "fairly good" or "very good" chance of getting ahead. Of the others, 6 per cent said the opportunity was there if they wanted it, and 57 per cent saw little or no chance of advancing.

The biggest cause of job dissatisfaction was inadequate salaries (27 per cent), followed by work pressure (12 per cent), and "the hours" (9 per cent). Dissatisfaction with the boss was listed by 5 per cent.

Despite limited job satisfaction among respondents, 80 per cent of them said that they would continue to work, even if they didn't have to. Among the positive reasons given, 48 per cent wanted "to keep occupied"; 15 per cent said it "keeps the individual healthy," and 14 per cent said that their job was the best they had ever had. Among the negative reasons for continuing to work, 83 per cent gave such replies as "I'd feel lost," "Would go crazy," "Would feel bored," "Would feel useless." About half of the respondents said they would do the same kind of work; 5 per cent would prefer to be self-employed, and 20 per cent would change to a position of more prestige.

---

[2] Eugene J. Benge, Asheville, N.C.; from a letter dated April 3, 1956.

[3] Excerpt from *Annual Report 1953-1954*, Industrial Relations Section, California Institute of Technology, Project 5, "Surveys of Employee Opinion."

If they didn't work, said 40 per cent of the respondents, they'd miss social contacts more than anything else. Only 15 per cent would miss the kind of work they do; 9 per cent would miss the regular routine; 28 per cent would miss nothing specific—and 1 per cent "wouldn't miss a thing." [4]

A one-year attitude survey was conducted for a subsidiary of one of the major oil companies. Over 1,100 employees, the majority of whom were either professional or supervisory personnel, were interviewed. The workers were asked to rate morale within their own groups high, average, or low, and state what they felt was important to their "local" morale. Company policy stressed good employee relations, and the company was a leader in providing employee benefits. The study found most of the professional workers satisfied with the jobs in terms of type of work and salaries received.

During the study there was a change in top management, and company policy shifted from centralization to decentralization with authority being passed down during the entire year of the study. Results of the study indicated that in almost all sections with low morale the principal cause was faulty supervision. Good morale exists when management

> . . . avoids too close supervision of workers, delegates more authority and responsibility to employees, permits participation in deciding matters, and keeps workers fully informed about all matters pertinent to their unit, and their relationship with other units and the company.[5]

Putting morale survey results to work

Obviously, making an attitude or morale survey is only a first step in the improvement of communications within a company. Business concerns have been making surveys among their employees for several decades but the literature concerning their follow-through is sketchy. Generally, managements agree that at least two uses can be made: one, the findings can be reported to the employees and two, remedial actions can be taken to improve the situations that need it.

Some managements conduct meetings with supervisors and employees in order to clarify the reasons for negative findings. Shortcomings on the part of management are brought into open discussion and improvements in managerial practices and communications are developed. If

---

[4] See *Personnel*, American Management Association, Inc., January 1957, p. 326.

[5] Paul A. Brinker, "Morale Among Professional Workers: A Case Study," *Personnel Journal*, January 1957, adapted from *Personnel Management Abstracts,* Spring 1957.

such "feedback" sessions are conducted in a sincere and constructive spirit, later surveys of employee morale are likely to produce higher percentages of favorable reactions to conditions that were previously found to be "least liked" by the employees.

Some companies have found that morale surveys with feedback sessions have more beneficial and widespread effects than speeches by executives or formal educational conferences. The feedback sessions help employees develop a better adjusted view of their work situation.

Differentiating between griping on a questionnaire and productivity

Any person experienced in making morale surveys and in dealing with employees knows that some employees will complain constantly about their jobs yet, despite good employment opportunities in other plants of the area, they do not leave. These gripers may actually be loyal and hard-working employees. Morale may be high even though discontent is frequently expressed.[6]

Individual productivity, often defined as morale, is more significant than contentment in situations where employees can contribute through positive action as in exerting skill or effort, for example.

Current personnel research indicates that there is little or no proven relationship between morale, job satisfaction, and productivity. Studies conducted by the University of Michigan's Survey Research Center show that increases in production can be obtained with *either* favorable or unfavorable changes in employee attitudes. As far as job satisfaction is concerned, the all-important factors seem to be group cohesiveness, team spirit, and permissive, democratic supervision.[7]

Morale is a diffused or variable influence. It is the sum total of so many factors that it is difficult to measure. From the standpoint of personnel management, the important factor is productivity rather than contentment or the absence of griping.

Employees may remain with an employer and work hard for many reasons as indicated by this interview with an employee who had, on a morale survey questionnaire, criticized many aspects of his work situation:

---

[6] See Herbert E. Krugman, "Contentment or Morale? A Case Study," *Personnel*, American Management Association, Inc., March 1957.

[7] See Julius E. Eitington, "Bigness and Morale, A Look at the Record," *Personnel Administration,* January-February 1957.

The survey was likened to an examination of the company's health and general well-being.

Some of the employees complained, "When we have a problem to discuss, we don't know where to take it."

Others said, "Our equipment is old, it breaks down, and as a result we're not getting the production we should."

Or, "We have ideas, questions, and gripes but it's hard getting them to the attention of the top brass."

These cartoons were used by the management of one company as part of a series of "feedback" reports and sessions concerning the results of a morale survey. SOURCE: *The American Thermos Products Company, Norwich, Conn. See also* Management Record *(July-August 1958).*

Brazing department employee to interviewer: "What is my opinion of this company? Well, I feel indifferent toward the place. As you know, I have a wooden leg and and not every place will hire people like me. I am glad to have this job but I think I do my share of work so I don't owe the company a thing. Bill, the owner, is a friendly man. He knows almost all his employees by their first name. I wish he would do something in our department to clean the place up. I bet it hasn't been painted in over 40 years. The lighting is bad here. With these dark glasses we wear, we can hardly see what we are doing. We should have some type of hoist to lift our barrels of finished parts with. They weigh about 250 pounds and some of them haven't cooled off when we have to roll them out of the way as we haven't much room here to store our finished work till they cool off. This place is warm during the cold months and too hot during the summer months. Our holding vise isn't too good and we tell our foreman about it but he just laughs. You know, he was, at one time, the plant superintendent but he got moved down to be our foreman because he was charging the workers so much a month to keep their jobs. That was one of the first improvements Bill made when he took over as owner—he demoted the plant "super" to foreman.

The reason why I stay here is that it is the only place in town where I can work with a wooden leg.

Survey findings should be interpreted by someone who knows the individuals involved. As one psychologist has pointed out, management, looking at survey results, may conclude, for example, that the insurance plan is the real cause of irritation. It may be, or it may be only something for the employees' anxiety to attach to. Then the company might spend money on changes only to find that the anxiety had now attached itself to something else. Information may not be what is wanted. The needs of the group may be in their feelings and emotions rather than in their factual knowledge. In the follow-up, the employees may be less concerned with what is done with the results than with the supervisor's reaction toward them. It might even be that they do not really want the annoyance removed; it provides a convenient excuse for their attitudes.[8]

Giving meaning to work

The fact that the relationship between morale (depending upon how it is defined) and productivity is difficult to measure does not prove that morale is of no importance to management. Most executives feel better when they know that their employees are enthusiastic about their jobs and the company. To that end, they try to strengthen rather than ignore

---

[8] See G. M. Worbois, "Following Through on Morale Studies," *Personnel Psychology,* Spring 1958, pp. 89-94.

morale. One of the most effective procedures for improving morale is to explain, even glamorize the product made by the company. Here are two examples—the first is reported by F. J. Neary, Personnel Administrator with Don Baxter, Inc., Glendale, California.

> We believe the best way to make the employee's work interesting is to acquaint him thoroughly with the end uses of the products on which he is working. Our products, intravenous solutions and blood transfusion equipment, are "naturals" for this purpose because they have a long and well-known history of life-saving performance in hospitals and blood banks and on the battlefield.
>
> Not every company has so dramatic an opportunity to show end-use of its products. Yet regardless of the type of product, there is much that can be done to show how it is used, how it compares with competition, and what customers think about it. A considerable proportion of space in all employee newspapers and magazines is now being devoted to this purpose. . . .
>
> Morale exists when a man has pride in his company, and that pride can be fostered by effective communication. A sign that hangs in our Brooklyn plant reads: *Pfizer Terramycin Saves Human Lives.* The message is simple, but it is written in a language that cuts through the barriers erected in a man's mind by the humdrum events of a working day. That message reaches the worker, because it is true and because it is important. It lives proudly in some part of his consciousness, and he is a richer man for it.

John J. Hall, Director of Industrial Relations, Brown and Sharpe Manufacturing Company, Providence, R. I., reported:

> We have a showroom where our finished products are displayed, and we find that it is of value for the worker who normally sees only raw material or parts of finished products to visit this show area and see the finished products.[9]

Satisfaction with the job situation does not necessarily bring about productivity. An employee may be quite pleased to be a member of a company organization but have no strong desire to contribute to its production goals. To be stimulated by production goals, the employee needs to see those goals as worthy for him.

Most line executives are incapable of, or uninterested in, verbalizing the meanings and values inherent in the job. Executives who are engineers, in particular, are inarticulate in this respect. Hence, the personnel department must help provide the interpretation of the job to the workers. The effect on production of such interpretation was dramatically illustrated during World War II:

> Take the case of the atomic bomb plant at Oak Ridge, Tennessee. The workers there were above average. They had been meticulously screened

---

[9] From Fred H. Joiner, "Making Employees' Work More Interesting," *Personnel,* American Management Association, Inc., January 1953.

before they were selected—they had been chosen for their outstanding Americanism after a thorough check-up by the F.B.I. You would expect these people to give their best effort to war production, not only because of their general background but because they knew that "Manhattan Project" was considered an AAA1 priority operation. *But they did not know what they were doing,* for of necessity it was the policy of "Manhattan Project" not to let its "left hand know what its right hand did."

Taking the normal level of production as 100 per cent base, I am told on good authority that the first week after the A-Bomb fell on Hiroshima and they learned the full meaning of their efforts, production at Oak Ridge doubled! The week following when the second bomb fell on Nagasaki and they could begin to see that they could help bring the war to a quick close it went up to 300 per cent of the original level. *Here, dramatically, is demonstrated the stimulating effect of knowing what one is doing and why.*[10]

The personnel man should know how the supervisor feels about each of his employees

Strange as it may seem to the uninitiated in business, almost every supervisor has certain employees for whom he does not feel essentially responsible. True, he knows that he is technically responsible for each member of his group but his knowledge is on the intellectual level. Emotionally, or inwardly as he is likely to define it, he does not feel responsible for certain individuals. Perhaps he "inherited" them when he took over the supervision of the department. Perhaps he thinks of them as marginal employees whom he wants to transfer or discharge as soon as he can find a justifiable reason or an opportunity to get rid of them gracefully.

One of the most common causes for this feeling of nonresponsibility is the practice of letting the employment man interview and select the applicants to fill job vacancies without granting the supervisor the privilege of deciding which applicants he prefers. Naturally the supervisor feels that the personnel department "picked the guy." The foreman had to take him. Modern personnel managers recognize this hazard in hiring and try to increase the supervisor's feelings of responsibility for the new employee by giving the supervisor some participation in selection.

A few companies even carry this need for active participation in the

---

[10] "Worker Productivity, A Challenge to Management," a talk by Robert M. Creaghead, Employee Communication Specialist, Greenwich, Connecticut, before Industrial Marketers of Cleveland, Chapter of the National Industrial Advertisers Association, Inc., Hotel Carter, October 25, 1946.

hiring process by requiring each middle management executive to find and hire his own management trainee.

Executives and supervisors need this experience of participation so much that the astute applicant who is being considered for a high level job in management refuses to accept an offer unless the president interviews him in a rigorous manner. A casual meeting and handshake with the president is not enough—the president must himself go through enough thorough interviewing with the applicant to enable him to reach a firm decision: "This is *the* man I want on *my* team." Failure to carry through in this manner has caused many a potentially good applicant to be relegated, after having been hired, to the fringe of management by the president.

An important part of the personnel man's job is that of recognizing those situations where an executive or supervisor does not feel fully responsible for certain subordinates. These feeling-filled situations are not openly stated or expressed verbally to the personnel man. He must sense them from emotionally tinged statements and incidental comments. And then, if possible, he must try to correct them or at least contribute to their correction.

As one personnel man stated: "There are always some employees whom the boss would be glad to see leave. He won't fire 'em, but he hopes they'll quit. It's up to the personnel man to know who these employees are and to be as constructive as he can with both the supervisor and the employee."

OBJECTIVE FINDINGS CONCERNING EMPLOYEE RELATIONS

The personnel man need not depend entirely upon his sensitivity to the feelings of individuals nor to data obtained from a morale survey. He has many figures and other objective evidences of what is going on among the employees. He, for example, knows the data concerning absenteeism, tardiness, the numbers of employees who quit, the kinds of employees who quit, extent of moonlighting, and the reactions to fringe benefits. In the remainder of this chapter, we shall treat briefly only a few of these indicators.

The "personnel flow"

Employees who quit may offer the personnel man clues about influences that he should investigate. Few executives are so naïve as to imagine that the employee's first statement as to why he is leaving affords a wholly reliable guide to the real reason behind the terminating employee's decision to quit. If the real reason for his quitting would appear to criticize some other person or policy of the company, he is not likely to express it. To do so might bring about subsequent recrimination. (See "Exit Interviews," Chapter 17, page 310.)

In spite of the difficulties in learning the true reasons for quitting, the personnel manager wants to know the age and ability levels of employees who quit and of those who remain. To be healthy an organization needs a balanced structure in regard to factors such as age, technical training, and desire to advance. If a company has a disproportionally light or heavy concentration in any one bracket that is essential for the company's vitality, the equilibrium of the organization becomes unbalanced. Too many executives and employees of the same ability classifications may quit or retire in the same years. The personnel of a company contracts and expands in irregular manner. The turnover of employees and the composition of the organization must be watched constantly to spot and overcome imbalance. It is up to the personnel manager to note the "personnel flow," the types of men and women who come into and leave the organization.

Fringe benefits and their effect on cooperation

Modern industrial firms provide a wide variety of fringe benefits that range all the way from prenatal care to provision for burial expenses. These include legally required payments for social security, workmen's compensation; pension, insurance and other agreed-upon payments; paid rest periods, lunch periods, vacations, holidays, sick leave, and allowance for other time not worked; profit-sharing payments, bonuses, and so on. The costs of these benefits run to about one fourth of the total payroll. Some executives hope that employees will feel grateful for these benefits and put extra effort into their jobs to show their appreciation.

Experienced personnel men know that employees seldom act in the hoped-for manner. Employees rarely have any ego-involvement or participation in the granting of the benefits. Many managements decide to grant them because the competition is already giving them or the unions demand them. Enlightened managements tend to grant these benefits as one phase of their colleagueship with the community, employees, and stockholders. All are interdependent. The company should—

must as a matter of course—provide all the benefits it can for its workers, but enlightened managements do not expect to receive any special gratitude nor any obvious spurt in productivity as the result of granting fringe benefits or other "gifts."

The ultimate success or failure of personnel management will hinge on how people are valued as individuals—not by the gifts given them but by the attainment of values through participation in common goals. Personnel management cannot in itself give the highest values to the human beings in a company. It can, however, help to set goals and make its own unique contributions by working with management and employees.

The old authoritarian business structure in which management has power to demand and the workers are under obligation to comply is being displaced. In that kind of structure the management set up policies and procedures for the organized human relationships. Voluntary cooperation was excluded, the climate was dictatorial, and the full needs of the human personality were likely to be overlooked. Now the human personality is being taken into account to a greater extent in the attainment of corporate goals. We are learning that the corporate goal can be achieved and yet foster individual worth, health, security, and participation within the corporate venture.

Sensitivity training: group method for executive training

The personnel manager does not think of himself as the only person who should be sensitive to employee relations. He needs the help of every person in the company, particularly the executives. Sensitivity training is a type of human relations group training which aims to teach people to look more closely at themselves in order better to understand their own feelings and prejudices and to be more sensitive to the ways people relate to each other. This knowledge is essential for employees who must successfully adapt to change of any form. Further, the individual should have self-knowledge in order to recognize those aspects of his behavior which are used as defenses against real or imagined threats to his personal status, especially during these periods of change. Although this type of program is still in its infancy, the Human Relations Research Group at the University of California at Los Angeles is doing much to promote its development, through the

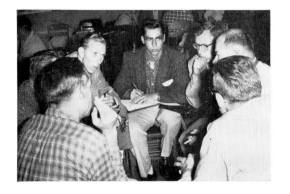

Other people have feelings, too. This is one of insights learned at UCLA's Sensitivity Training Program, participated in by such executives as Otis Brown, Syd Bash (hidden), Tom Alexander, Bob Groot, Willis Ware, Ward Baxter, and Don Warner from left.

The interdisciplinary origins of sensitivity training are highlighted by the background of three of its key practitioners. From left to right, Dr. Robert Tannenbaum, Professor of Personnel Management and Industrial Relations; Dr. Irving R. Weschler, Industrial Psychologist; and Dr. Marvin A. Klemes, Consulting Psychiatrist.

A sensitivity training group during one of its more pensive moments. Beginning at left: Willis Ware, Asst. for Engineering, Numerical Analysis—The Rand Corp.; Alfred M. Nelson, Head, Mechanical Development Department —Magnavox Research Laboratories; Robert Tannenbaum, Ph.D., Professor of Personnel Management and Industrial Relations—UCLA (trainer); Joseph Young, Coordinator—Automobile Club of Southern California; Richard Swanson, Supv., Engineering Training & Publications—Pacific Telephone & Telegraph; Charles Bahme, Director of Personnel—Los Angeles Fire Department.

intensive study of its nature and impact, using both student and executive groups.[11]

The group sessions, which usually follow a partially unstructured design where a permissive attitude dominates, deal not only with on-the-job problems, but also with situations that arise in the meetings themselves.[12] Because of this, the trainees are stimulated to become more aware of the attitudes and feelings of the other trainees and thus of the value of the group process as a whole.

Results of such studies indicating the changes that this type of training has incurred are still incomplete due to its newness. However, individual studies of student groups have shown that in the end, the trainees became more aware of the process of sensitization in interpersonal relations. Further, they became more aware of themselves and their role in these relations.

The effects on the executive trainees are especially enlightening in the application of their newly developed human relations know-how in their later work, as reported by themselves and their co-workers. This, in turn, most often leads to better morale, higher productivity, and lower turnover among workers.

Sensitivity training of both students and executives now promises to became a successful means of individual development. With the further refinements that are now in progress the method may eventually be applied to many persons in supervisory training and particularly to those who hope to improve their susceptibility to stimulation by the behavior of others as needed in personnel management.

COLLATERAL READINGS

For All Students

Hepner, Harry W., *Psychology Applied to Life and Work*, 3rd edition. Englewood Cliffs, N. J.: (Prentice-Hall, Inc., 1957), Chapter 22. Presents steps in making a morale survey, feedback sessions, limitations, and relations between morale and productivity.

"Just Looking, Thank You," *Personnel Journal*, May 1956. Treats certain criticisms of personnel management's lack of sensitivity to employee relations and offers acceptances and rejections of the criticisms.

For Advanced Students

Brown, J. A. C., *The Social Psychology of Industry*. Baltimore: Penguin Books, Inc., 1954. Written by a psychiatrist who has had experience

---

[11] Irving R. Weschler and Jerome Reisel, *Inside a Sensitivity Group* (Los Angeles: University of California, 1958).

[12] Irving R. Weschler, Marvin A. Klemes, and Clovis Shepard, "A New Focus in Executive Training," *Advanced Management*, May 1955.

in industry. Discusses morale and effects of industrial work on mental health.

Knudson, Harry R. Jr., "Enter the Personnel Generalist," *Personnel*, American Management Association, Inc., March-April 1960. A qualified personnel administrator is assigned to each significant group of employees for whom he has personnel responsibility. An experiment at Raytheon's Wayland, Massachusetts Laboratory.

For Men in Business

Marx, Herbert L., Jr., "Personnel's Place on the Management Team," *Dun's Review and Modern Industry*, August 1956. Suggests a program in which the personnel manager is used as an active member of management, not as an isolated specialist.

Sherman, E. L., "Turnover Cut One Third by 7-Step Program," *Personnel Journal*, January 1959. Gives typical examples of cost elements involved in turnover and a program that was successful in reducing turnover.

QUESTIONS ON THE CHAPTER

1. In what respects is an effective personnel manager positive minded?
2. What kinds of company conditions should an alert personnel man recognize as unvoiced grievances?
3. In making a morale survey, why do some companies use the questionnaire form from the Science Research Associates?
4. In which age group does the lowest morale usually occur? Describe other general findings from morale surveys.
5. Comment on the statement that expression of discontent is usually a sign of poor morale.
6. What important principle concerning workers and productivity was demonstrated in the Oak Ridge bomb plant during World War II?
7. Why are the age and ability levels of employees who quit and those who remain important to the personnel manager?
8. Discuss the relation between griping and productivity.
9. What is meant by the "personnel flow" of an organization?
10. What is the value of sensitivity training? In what ways does sensitivity training affect the work of executive trainees?
11. How can work be given meaning for the employees?
12. Of the ideas in the chapter, which ones are of special interest to you?
13. What did the chapter contribute toward your future relations with (a) the men who supervise you, (b) the employees whom you may supervise?

PROBLEMS AND PROJECTS

For All Students

1. Interview several students of an educational institution. Have them designate the positive and negative aspects of their situation. Are the

points of friction inherent in the institution or in the persons themselves?

2. Interview several employees of a company. Ask them about the things that affect their morale. Using your notes of the interviews, phrase questions that might be used in a morale survey of all the employees.

For Advanced Students

3. Interview several personnel men of your area. Find out what professional journals each reads. Does he attend seminars or workshops on personnel problems? Does he attend local professional organization meetings?

4. Make a list of sources that describe organizations and services that deal with personnel management and industrial relations. Examine available journals and textbooks for sources in this field. Describe them.

For Men in Business

5. Describe the fringe benefits available in a company of your area. To what extent do employees know about or understand them? Interview several employees to find out the accuracy of their knowledge.

6. "Moonlighting," the practice of an employee's holding two or more jobs at the same time, is high in periods of prosperity and low during depressions. Describe the extent to which it is practiced by employees whom you know.

THE PERSONNEL MANAGER IS LIKELY TO HAVE IMPORTANT DEALINGS with the company's labor union but he is seldom alone in making decisions that involve major company responsibilities to the union. The responsibilities are so serious that the several members on the highest management level, particularly the president, consider themselves responsible for union relations, especially during contract negotiations. The personnel department often represents the management in certain union relations, as in handling grievances, developing procedures for resolving controversial grievances, and in helping to interpret the contract. In some companies these relations are so numerous and involved that a special "labor relations" or "industrial relations" division deals with them.

Of course our major interest in labor unions is much broader than the functions of the personnel department in dealing with them. Unions have such varied aspects that any attempt to describe them in a comprehensive manner would have to be a description of human behavior plus much politics, psychology, economics, and sociology.

Any description of unionism is likely to arouse criticism or defense on the part of some readers, depending upon the psychological needs and identifications of the individual. Each reader is likely to be either an advocate or a critic of unionism even though he imagines that he is objective in his thinking. Thorough objectivity in this field is rare indeed. Management men find it

16

Personnel Management:
Relations with Unions

especially difficult to overcome bias in regard to unionism. One reason for their difficulty is that an executive likes to think of himself as the leader of his employees. Unions and union activities often interpose themselves between the executive and his employees. Some union leaders try to drive a wedge between the employee and his company. They may even go beyond the ". . . point of telling him that the union is a good thing, and far into the zone of trying to persuade him that his company is his natural enemy, never to be trusted or respected, actuated entirely by unworthy motives and managed exclusively by men who are stupid or dishonest or both." [1]

The psychological climate in companies whose employees are unionized may be peaceful and one of cooperation or it may be full of friction: bickering, arguments about trivialities, employees demanding rights rather than expressing a desire to do good work, arguing about what the contract calls for, or attempting to give the contract some new interpretation that will provide an advantage for some person or group of persons. Union leaders may be mature or they may be so disputatiously concerned about what they do not have to do and what management must do that a normal person would prefer to work elsewhere. Certainly, many supervisors of unionized employees must learn to take carping by union officers for granted—it's all a part of the day's work!

Managements realize that any union leader who is ambitious for advancement in union circles must measure his success by his ability to outdo what other union leaders achieve for their members. The aggressive tactics of union officers for more money and benefits are bound, in our type of economy, to contribute to wage inflation. Individual managements cannot long resist wage demands because long strikes can lead to business suicide. Usually, too, continued industry resistance brings government intervention and the public's verdict that it is better for wage costs to go up than for unemployment of strikers to go on indefinitely. Most leaders of organized labor are critical of advancing prices, but they also advocate cheap credit and bigger government spending, influences that create the market conditions in which industry can advance prices and finance higher labor costs.

In spite of the difficulties in maintaining peaceful relations with a union, many managements prefer to deal with a strong rather than a weak union. A strong union has the backing of most of the workers. Such a union can be of great assistance in smoothing out the frictions that take place during and after contract negotiations.

A strong union can help management in carrying down to the workers

---

[1] From an address by John L. McCaffrey before the Industrial Relations Association of Chicago, *The Management Review,* American Management Association, Inc., January 1955, p. 12.

the actions agreed upon in the contract. New contracts usually result in agreements that displease some workers. The union leaders can explain and justify the decisions to the displeased members. Management expects the workers' representatives to explain the agreements made and to induce any unwilling members to cooperate. Unfortunately, individual workers or groups sometimes refuse to accept the agreements. When workers refuse to accept the joint decisions, management is naturally disappointed and critical of the individual offenders and of the whole union relationship. The management then hopes that the next elected union officers will be strong enough as leaders to control the members.

Why workers join unions

Relatively few workers join unions because of coercion. If they do join for that reason, they are not likely to continue as members. Actually, most join because the union provides a business service: greater security in the job, higher wages, better working conditions, protection against arbitrary or unfair treatment by management, and other services. The worker who belongs to a union feels more secure—nobody in management can push him around unfairly. He cannot lose his job as easily as he might if he were dependent only upon his status as an individual.

Most employees have need for a business service organization that increases their feelings of job security. Even though the nonunion employee has a job that he likes and does well, he knows that he may be discharged because of arbitrary action by a superior. If he is discharged or laid off, his financial resources may not carry him over comfortably to the next job. As a family man, he probably is buying a home, a car, and one or more electrical appliances on an installment basis. As long as his regular income continues he can meet the payments and at the same time support his family adequately. As soon as his income stops for even one month, he and his family are likely to suffer and many of his savings in the form of equities in purchases may disappear. His financial reserves are so limited that he feels he should seek the protection and services that a union can provide. He also knows that the employer is not a completely free agent in the market—he must run the business to please the customers. Customers' wishes and the survival of the company take precedence over his welfare as an employee.

Workers naturally try to overcome this feeling of economic insecurity. The measures they and their union take are not always an unreasonable attempt to get "something for nothing." Managements should put themselves in the place of the worker confronted with this insecurity and seek to enable him to attain the maximum of security. If this is not possible, management should at least give the worker an appreciation of why the need cannot be answered by explaining the company's limitations and economic problems. Once the worker feels that his needs are understood and management wants to meet them, the worker can participate with management in dealing with the company's problems as a colleague, not as someone who must accept whatever management is willing to give.[2]

To the worker of the large corporation, members of management appear to be remote privileged persons who sit in luxurious offices. The union leaders, in contrast, are men like himself who cater to him and treat him as an equal. This is especially likely to be the feeling of people engaged in mechanized work. These are the employees who are more disposed to become union members.

To the worker, the labor union is an instrument for enhancing his dignity as an individual. When a worker's dignity is ignored and his human qualities are not recognized, his resentment is likely to be expressed by increased loyalty to the union. His incidental complaints and grievances are manifested, often irrationally, through wildcat strikes, slowdowns, and other forms of hostility.

Most employees who belong to unions are loyal to their union officials. They are not greatly concerned about newspaper reports of embezzlement and misuse of union funds by union leaders. After all, the members are getting a service from an organization that represents them and their interests.

Publicity and findings of union atrocities that are revealed in congressional and other hearings will not destroy overnight the faith of a union member whose leaders have accomplished something for him. He reviews his wage increases and his improved benefits and working conditions, and he believes—rightly or wrongly—that these improvements have been brought about by his union. He feels that if his union were to be destroyed or weakened at the top, he might once more be at the mercy of an arbitrary representative of management. His employer might be a kind person, or on the other hand, he might not be. To the worker, his union provides a set of effective brakes on management. He is not too confident about how well the business mechanism would operate if the brakes were removed.

---

[2] See Rensis Likert, "Motivation: The Core of Management," *Personnel Series*, No. 155, American Management Association, Inc., 1954.

Psychological characteristics of union leaders

The personnel man and other members of management who deal with union leaders tend, in time, to find that these men have certain typical characteristics. Of course these executives recognize that individual differences occur among labor union leaders as well as among executives and other occupational members. They do, however, become aware of patterns, or signs of behavioral patterns, in the make-up of union leaders. These patterns have not as yet been studied by social scientists to the same extent that behavior of business executives has been studied. The reason may be that union leaders are more defensive, less secure, and less confident about themselves. They therefore do not like to be analyzed even though the purpose of the analysis may be friendly. In contrast, the able, self-confident, secure executive does not, as a rule, care how much anyone studies him. This means that when we attempt to describe behavior patterns that characterize typical labor union leaders, we have to depend upon empirical judgment rather than statistically significant measurements. The approach must be qualitative, not quantitative. This limitation is, however, applicable to members of many groups in business and in society. Few evaluations of people are ever statistically proven—experience with the specific individual is our main guide.

Those who have had considerable experience in dealing with labor union leaders recognize that many of them are capable and ambitious but they never learned to feel at home in the presence of people in management or in the social groups frequented by executives. Many college students feel the same way but the ambitious student typically identifies himself with management. He looks forward to becoming an executive and associating with executives as an equal. The union leader does not. He does not identify himself with management and therefore has difficulty in understanding or trying to understand business problems and how to deal with them constructively. He identifies with the employees, whom he views as unappreciated, neglected, or exploited. He feels frustrated in his desire for advancement because he senses he does not fit into the group that is likely to advance into management.

Another type of leader is the one who is rebelling against authority. The man who has rebelled violently against authority is rarely found in management. He is, however, frequently found among those union leaders who are in power in the early history of unionism in a company— the fighting stage of union-management relations. He is elected to office because he has the characteristics that a new and insecure union requires if it is to achieve the things its new members desire of it at the time of organization. When such a union leader first appears across the table from management, he causes a good deal of consternation among the management men. Such a man is likely to be resentful toward management, and completely unwilling to bury the past in order to build a new relationship. Consequently the growth of peaceful industrial relations is checked so long as he is in power.

In the normal course of events, however, the union achieves some of its purposes, and with this achievement comes a measure of security. When this happens, there is likely to be a change in union leadership. Men who are motivated by rebellion to authority soon get tired of fighting for rights that have been recognized and granted by management. The fiery oratory of the aggressive rebel against authority is no longer appropriate. He does not get much response from members who cannot be whipped into a frenzy. He moves on to another company where his zeal fits the kind of situation that calls for inflammatory leadership. Of course a few of these leaders may remain for some years after management has accepted the union.

Mayo's Classic Illustration. Elton Mayo, one of the greatest students of the influence of feelings and emotions in industrial relationships, described the resistance to his search for union support for extending facilities for adult education in Australia as follows:

> Usually the more moderate and responsible union members sat in the front rows; the back rows were the haunt of those who represented the irreconcilable extreme left. Before long it became evident that six men were the nucleus of all the most savage opposition. In the course of many years, I came to know these six men well. The extreme party changed its name many times . . . but whatever the change of name or doctrine, it was always the same six who led the opposition at union meetings or spoke from soap boxes in the public parks. The fact that I came to know them personally made no difference to their platform attitude to me or to the university: but on other occasions they would talk freely to me in private. This enabled me to place on record many observations, the general tenor of which may be summarized as follows:
>
> 1. These men had no friends except at the propagandist level. They seemed incapable of easy relationship with other people; on the contrary, the need to achieve such relationship was for them an emergency demanding energetic effort.
>
> 2. They had no capacity for conversation. In talk with me they alternated between self-history and oratory which reproduced the compelling topic—revolution and the destruction of society.
>
> 3. All action, like social relationship, was for them emergency action. Any idea of routine participation in collaborate effort, or of the "ordinary" in living, was conspicuously absent from their thinking. Everything, no matter how insignificant, was treated as crisis, and was undertaken with immense and unreasoned "drive."
>
> 4. They regarded the world as a hostile place. Every belief and action

implied that society existed not to give but to deny them opportunity. Furthermore, they believed that hostility to be active, not merely inert; they regarded everyone, even their immediate associates, as potentially part of the enemy forces arrayed against them.

In every instance the personal history was one of social privation—a childhood devoid of normal and happy association in work and play with other children. This privation seemed to be the source of the inability to achieve "ordinary" human relationships, of the consequent conviction that the world was hostile, and of the reaction by attack upon the supposed enemy. One of the six drifted into the hands of a medical colleague with whom I was accustomed to work on problems of adaptation. Thus was established a clinical relation of confidence in his physician. He discovered that his medical adviser was not at all interested in his political theories but was very much interested in the intimate details of his personal history. He made a good recovery and discovered, to his astonishment, that his former political views had vanished. He had been a mechanic, unable to keep his job although a good workman. After recovery he took a clerical job and held it; his attitude was no longer revolutionary.[3]

Imberman's study of labor leaders

The purpose of Imberman's study was to facilitate labor relations by an analysis of the leaders' characteristics. Over a two-year period, he worked for a public relations firm having two large unions as clients. His work brought him into friendly contact with 249 labor leaders of 42 unions.

He found that most of the labor leaders come from a laboring class family, do not have much schooling above grade school, and have found the union the most feasible means of attaining financial success and power. But the labor leader finds that neither he nor his family is accepted socially, because polite society thinks of him as on the occupational level of the members of the union, and as a dishonest power-grabber. Even political office, which many of the successful union leaders seek, does not protect him from social rebuff. The resulting frustration breeds bitterness.

The bitterness over being unaccepted socially works itself out by: (1) antagonism toward the employer, resulting in unreasonable union rulings and demands; (2) accepting bribes for favorable decisions. The bribe may not be in the form of immediate cash but in an "arrangement" whereby the company agrees to buy products in accordance with a special contract that benefits the labor leader's private business on the outside. Bribes are a common practice with certain types of union leaders

---

[3] Elton Mayo, *The Social Problems of an Industrial Civilization* (Boston: Graduate School of Business Administration, Division of Research, Harvard University, 1945), pp. 25-27.

only and when a bribe is refused by them it may be because of the insulting manner in which it is offered.

Imberman also found that a high proportion of these leaders found some solace in the company of women who were "of better social graces and elegancies than the original wife, seeming to indicate that even here the drive for acceptance and higher social status may be operating."

Imberman concluded that the difficulties that exist between labor and management exist not so much over issues but over the fact that management as a group snubs or appears to snub the labor leader socially. He suggested that the remedy is for management people to accept the labor leader, make him an important member of the community, and have him join exclusive clubs. This, he thinks, would tend to cause the antagonism expressed across the bargaining table to dissipate itself.[4]

This recommended remedy, unfortunately, is not feasible. Any union executive who would hob-nob with management would provide suspicion on the part of his own rank and file members. They would assume that he was taking the points of view of management and would not fight for the members' rights. Such a union leader would be in office until the next election only. Few labor leaders would care to adapt themselves to a new social environment that would lead to identification with management. The main contribution of Imberman's study is its implication that management men in all their relations with union leaders should be relaxed, respectful, and friendly toward him as an individual even though he may be an embittered unreasonable person.

In many companies, the psychological patterns of the union leaders differ markedly from those of the majority of members. Management men note this and often ask the question: "Why do our friendly well-balanced employees usually vote into union office the most cussed candidate rather than the typical normal cooperative type of employee?" The answer becomes simple when we appreciate that most employees think of the union as a business service—the contentious officer is more likely to get higher wage rates and better working conditions than the easy-to-get-along-with union official. The union leader must watch the wage increases being secured in other plants and be sufficiently aggressive to make his members feel that he is achieving the best wage arrangements that can be obtained. Union leaders do, of course, find causes of grievances and correct them but these are extra services between contract negotiations rather than the main service to the members.

Characteristics in the pattern of typical union leaders, as noted from contacts with them, are:

---

[4] A. A. Imberman, "Labor Leaders and Society," *Harvard Business Review*, January 1950, pp. 50-60.

1. Little education
2. High intelligence
3. Laboring class family
4. Leadership ability
5. Feeling of rejection by members of social classes who are on same income level as the union leader—management symbolizes a social rank unattainable by labor leaders
6. Usually functions in a situation that does not permit close associations with management as a colleague of management for fear of being accused of "selling out"

Member participation in union affairs

Leonard R. Sayles and George Strauss have reported findings from a series of unstructured interviews with union members. They found that the members' participation in day-to-day union activities contrasted sharply with their loyalty to the union in strikes. Also, even though members exhibit strong loyalty toward their union as an institution they frequently criticise the union's officials.

The interviews revealed that the typical member is convinced he needs his union for protection against arbitrary management action and for obtaining economic security. Members expressed their need for the union: "Without a union we would be lost; the company could really take advantage of us." Members will endure privations to belong to the union and to win strikes. The typical member will remain loyal during a strike even though he is subjected to tremendous pressures such as those from seeing his children hungry, lack of his wife's sympathy, and putting up with an openly hostile community.

At the same time that the union member demonstrates firm loyalty in regard to the union's economic functions, he is apathetic toward the union's internal activities. For example, attendance at regular meetings of large industrial unions averages 2 per cent to 8 per cent of the total membership. Attendance at meetings for a strike vote or contract negotiation averages from 40 per cent to 80 per cent.

Many workers do not seek or accept union offices. Reasons given are "All those meetings to go to," "No time with the family," "Always some guy after something he doesn't deserve," and so forth. An important conclusion was:

> For a small group, the union is a way of life; for the majority, it is but a method of representation, although a very important one. For the lead-

ers, the union has become an end in itself; for the rank and file, it is but a means to an end, a way of gaining greater security on the job, *not* a great social movement.[5]

Management's insistence on management rights

Managements of unionized plants accept the principle that the company should delegate certain duties to its employees and that it is the proper function of the union to secure for its members the performance of these obligations. Decisions that lie beyond these areas are the function of management, not the union. And when the union wants to invade management's areas, management becomes adamant. Management must have the flexibility necessary to run the business efficiently and to maintain the vitality of the company as an enterprise. The areas of management's discretion include such matters as the unlimited right to decide upon the number and location of plants, the products to be manufactured, the schedules of production, the hours to be worked, the methods of manufacture, the purchase of equipment, and financing. They include the right to select employees for promotion within the bargaining unit and to select individuals for promotion to supervisory positions or other jobs outside the bargaining unit. Management wants responsibility for enforcing rules and regulations, imposing discipline, assigning work, and the enforcement of work standards. Management wants the right to introduce more efficient tools and methods of manufacture and to adopt whatever technological advancements may be vital to growth.

Perhaps the most common subject of conflict in regard to union-management relations is the union's rigidity in that portion of the contract which governs adjustments in the workforce to meet changes in production schedules and unplanned interruptions, usually referred to as seniority provisions.

Many unions prefer to insist that all layoffs and transfers be made on the basis of lowest seniority. Managements prefer a more flexible procedure because of the evils of "bumping." "Bumping" is a common expression for the procedure of an employee of greater seniority employed in one department forcing, during layoff periods, an employee of lesser seniority in another department to be laid off so that the former may

---

[5] Leonard R. Sayles and George Strauss, "What the Worker Really Thinks of His Union," *Harvard Business Review,* May-June 1953. See also book by same authors *The Local Union: Its Place in the Industrial Plant* (New York: Harper & Brothers, 1953), pp. 3, 4.

have his job. In many cases, the "bumped" employee is more efficient and cooperative than the one who takes his place.

In principle the unions want to participate in certain kinds of protection of rights of the personnel only, not in production. Changes in personnel as caused by bumping and other marginal areas of control may have marked impact on production. When a management feels threatened in regard to what it believes to be its rights in regard to production, management becomes as resistant as the union.

Featherbedding

One of the most frequent encroachments by unions on management's areas of operation takes place in featherbedding. This term is supposed to have originated many years ago when the local representative for the men on the Rock Island Railroad complained about mattresses that had been placed in cabooses for the train crews' use. The mattresses were composed of corncobs, shucks and cotton seed hulls. The trainmaster's answer to the complaint was, "What do you damned brakemen want—feather beds?" [6]

The story may be apocryphal, but the term "featherbedding" has come to stand for rules or practices that require the employment of unneeded workmen or the slowing up of work under a featherbed rule. A common definition is getting pay for work not done. It also applies to those union contracts which compel management to put extra men on a job where they are not needed in order to spread the available work. An example is the successful insistence of railroad workers' unions that Diesel engines be run by three men when impartial observers agree that two can easily do the job. The third man is a leftover from coal-burning steam engine days when three men were necessary.

In some cases, featherbedding provisions have increased an employer's costs to such an extent that he could not increase wages.

Traditionally, featherbedding is associated with the printing, building, amusement, and railroad industries, all of which have been organized for many years by craft unions. In these industries it includes such practices as the employment of unnecessary personnel such as paying for standby musicians, doing unnecessary work as in cutting off factory-threaded pipe ends and rethreading on the job, insisting on use of time-consuming work methods as in using handtools instead of power tools, and compelling the employer to hire skilled men to perform unskilled labor.

---

[6] See "They Call It Featherbedding," *Financial World*, September 25, 1957.

The craft unions have been most successful in imposing such uneconomic regulations because their members usually provide a service of skill or they produce against a time deadline. The companies are therefore vulnerable to strike action and to union power. Restrictions and requirements of the featherbedding variety increase gradually year by year. Eventually they affect the competitive position of the industry and bring about decreased opportunity for employment of members of the craft. Printers have been forced out of work because of newspaper consolidations and the shift to competitive reproduction methods. No one knows how much decline has taken place in the railroad industry as an effect of featherbedding, but the demand that requires a company to give two railroad men 24-hours' pay for one man's eight hours of work has taken place during an era when railroad jobs are only one-third of what they were in the preceding generation. One reason for the rise of the do-it-yourself movement among American consumers has been the arbitrary rulings of building craft unions.

Certainly featherbedding rules have not eliminated intermittent employment in the building and amusement industries, nor halted the secular decline in railway employment. There is some evidence that they have aggravated the problems in these industries.[7]

Thus far, legislation to prevent featherbedding has not been especially effective. One hope for its gradual decline is that big unions are beginning to realize that they are an integral part of big business. They share some of the problems of management. As unions accumulate pension funds and other cash assets, they must invest in revenue-providing securities, including common stocks. The profits on their common stocks depend on good management and a high level of productivity. More and more union officers who are entrusted with investment responsibilities are finding it necessary to consider the costs of featherbedding and production restricted by the unions.

Collective bargaining—contract negotiations

The negotiation of the contract in collective bargaining calls for high degrees of skill in human relations on the part of both the representatives of the company and of the union. To some, it is a process of "haggling," comparable to the bargaining in an oriental bazar. The best price offered by the dealer at the outset is not his best price at the end of the last bargaining session.

---

[7] See Herbert R. Northrup, "Plain Facts About Featherbedding," *Personnel*, American Management Association, Inc., July-August 1958, pp. 54, 55.

In modern collective bargaining between the larger unions and companies, the business agent of the national or international organization negotiates the contract. He works full time at this, negotiates day in and day out, and is usually of an alert aggressive character. Business agents of this caliber receive salaries that compare very favorably with or exceed the salaries of company executives.[8]

Negotiating is no longer for the man who comes off a machine to sit at a bargaining table once every few years. In big union negotiations as in the automotive industry, economic and other specialists back up the teams of both sides. Experts are hired as consultants.

In some cases the dealings between the company and the union are approached in a legalistic manner. More often, they become similar to the last days of a hot political campaign.

Pitfalls that an experienced company negotiator avoids are:

1. *Smugness.* Representatives of labor unions are typically quick to resent any implications of their social or other inadequacies.

2. *A show of undue concern.* If management is scared at the start, the opposition can capitalize their defensiveness.

3. *Personality conflict at the bargaining table.* If two or more persons there hate each other before the sessions begin, the negotiations will tend to accentuate the hostility. One or both parties should withdraw tactfully by claiming that his presence is needed elsewhere.[9]

The negative aspects are, of course, less significant than the positive as summarized in the following recommendations:

> Collective bargaining is not an isolated event to be treated like a David Harum horse trade. It is a way of life—a way of living with the employees upon whose services you rely and with the union of their choice . . . resign yourself to the idea that you will have nothing better than a cold war, with only the hope of intermittent peaceful coexistence, if your labor relations are not well managed.
>
> And since dealing with unions is a continuing job for management, I'd like to make some suggestions that may be useful in establishing sound labor relations.
>
> 1. Earn a good reputation with your employees so that you may bring it with you to the bargaining table. . . . I am speaking of a reputation for firmness, a demonstrated willingness to fight for your rights, together with a reputation for open-mindedness, reasonableness, truthfulness, trustworthiness and a decent respect for your fellow man at every level. . . .
>
> 2. Your representatives should be able to take advantage of your good reputation without soiling it. Be sure that they understand human nature.

---

[8] For further information, see *The Management Review,* American Management Association, Inc., January 1955, p. 61.

[9] See Andrew J. Dalton, Jr., "Learn How To Deal with Organized Workers," *The Office,* November 1956, pp. 140, 224-26.

Brilliant men who quickly step on the toes of anyone who steps on theirs are not necessarily helpful in the long run. . . .

3. Never let your bargaining team forget that the union bargaining team has its own internal political problems.[10]

Employees respect firm leadership

Unions are constantly arguing for and demanding more privileges. There is no end to what they ask for when they know that they have a management that thinks in defensive terms only. Conversely, they will respect firm management.

This firmness does not imply that management may use the same verbal tactics that are used by a union. A union representative or editor of a union journal may call a company president various vile names. The president, however, may not retaliate in kind. If he were to use the same language, no matter how great the provocation, he would lose the respect of the employees. He is in the same position as the lady shopper who is reviled by a fishwife—the fishwife can use that kind of language and remain a fishwife but the lady cannot use the fishwife's language and remain a lady! Similarly, union leaders may use language and tactics that are "out-of-bounds" for management. This limitation does not, however, mean that management cannot be firm in holding to those principles in which management believes.

Positive approaches to union relations

Most managements of unionized plants try to develop and maintain constructive relations with their unions. They realize that labor peace in the sense of absolute freedom from conflict is not possible. They do try to keep the conflict within reasonable bounds. Thus far, their best hope for doing so lies in maintaining a balance of power between management and the union. Theoretically, this calls for men of mature leadership on both sides. Practically, that cannot be expected. It is up to management therefore to achieve on its own part the highest level of participative leadership it is capable of bringing about. Certainly, dealings with labor problems require the same executive strength and com-

---

[10] Walter Gordon Merritt, from an address before the National Industrial Conference Board. Reported in *Management Record*, August 1955. See also *The Management Review*, American Management Association, Inc., April 1955, p. 257.

petence as do all other aspects of managerial responsibility. There are no solutions of the "quick tricks" or "gimmick" variety.[11]

The employer who is experienced in union relations tends to develop certain helpful policies and procedures such as the following:

He gives full recognition to the union collective bargaining status. He wants the union to know that he fully accepts the union as the spokesman and voice of the employees on matters of wages, hours, and working conditions.

He does not compete with the union for the loyalty of its employees. Employees can be loyal to both the employer and the union for certain relationships.

He works with rather than around the union in the field of employee communications. He does not try to out-maneuver the union in getting a message across to employees. He works out with the union an agreement on channels of communication.

He recognizes that the union is a political organization and that at times union officials will do certain things simply because it is politically expedient for them.

The wise employer separates the areas of conflict from the many non-conflicting interests between management and labor. In some relationships such as contract negotiations, grievance procedures, and arbitration, the interests of the union and the company are frequently at cross purposes. In others, there is little or no conflict of interests, as in dealing with production problems, office methods, and marketing. Certain union leaders may be fanatical about the union but most employees are mature, reasonable people who want to participate in the company's growth. Management should concentrate on earning their good will.

COLLATERAL READINGS

For All Students

Dubin, Robert, *Working Union-Management Relations: The Sociology of Industrial Relations.* Englewood Cliffs, N. J.: Prentice-Hall, Inc., 1958. Emphasizes organization theory and decision-making in companies and unions.

Steiber, Jack, editor, *U. S. Industrial Relations: The Next Twenty Years.* East Lansing, Mich.: Michigan State University Press, 1958. Presents six forecasts by leaders. Evaluations, interpretations, and analyses are given.

---

[11] See Robert N. McMurry, "War and Peace in Labor Relations," *Harvard Business Review,* November-December 1955.

For Advanced Students

Arensberg, Conrad M., *et al.*, *Research in Industrial Human Relations: A Critical Appraisal.* New York: Harper & Brothers, 1957. Treats some changes taking place.

Chalmers, W. Ellison, *et al.*, *Labor-Management Relations in Illini City: I, The Case Studies; II, Explorations in Comparative Analysis.* Champaign: Institute of Labor and Industrial Relations, University of Illinois, 1954. For the social scientist who is interested in research in labor and management relations.

For Men in Business

Emmons, Russell J., "Union Contract Negotiations without Fireworks," *Personnel Journal*, June 1956.

Labor and Management Face the Future, Personnel Series No. 172, American Management Association, Inc., 1957, is an example of the kind of report on current problems that is available. Ask for copies of the latest reports.

QUESTIONS ON THE CHAPTER

1. Why is it often difficult for management men to view unions objectively?

2. In what ways may a strong union rather than a weak union be preferred by management?

3. List some of the reasons why workers join unions. What are the main functions of unions to the workers as they see them?

4. Describe the role of the union leader who is rebelling against authority.

5. In labor-management relations what problem and remedy did Imberman suggest? What problem would his remedy involve for union leaders?

6. Who are the most ardent and the least ardent supporters of unions among the membership?

7. What is the implication of the statement that unions are *not* a great social movement?

8. What is the relation between the seniority provisions of union contracts and "bumping?"

9. Define the term "featherbedding." Give examples.

10. What positive aspects of collective bargaining are experienced company negotiators concerned with?

11. What is meant by management rights in employer-union relations?

12. Describe managements' positive approaches to union relations.

13. Of all the ideas in the chapter, which ones were of special interest to you?

14. What did the chapter contribute toward your future relations with (a) the men who supervise you, (b) the employees whom you may supervise?

For All Students

1. Review some of the available literature on unions. Try to evaluate each writer as to his bias or objectivity. Which statements in the text, in the light of other published information, would you modify?

2. Interview several persons who belong to unions. Ask each as to why he belongs, the amount of the dues and fees, the extent of his activity at meetings, the quality of the leadership, the union's problems with management, and so on.

For Advanced Students

3. Make a study of arbitration, state and federal mediators, and related topics. Study arbitrators' actions in conflict situations. Consider the fact that arbitrators leave the situation when it has been resolved.

4. Make a study of the kinds of economic data published by unions. Do the economists who are not in the trade union circles tend to pay much attention to the data put out by unions? To what extent is it likely to be biased or objective?

For Men in Business

5. Describe some of the union activities that you have experienced. Did the experiences increase or decrease your respect for the unions or unionism? Why?

6. If you were offered a job that required your joining a union, would you take it? Give reasons for your answer. If you were offered a job as a supervisor in a union or in a nonunion plant, which would you take? Why?

7. When a foremanship is given to a union steward, how does the company gain or lose by the typical selection of a union leader? What are possible effects on the union?

THE INTERVIEW MAY BE DEFINED AS A PURPOSEFUL CONVERSA-
tional exchange of ideas between two or more persons. It is,
however, more than a social conversation; it is a conversation
having a serious purpose. In business, its typical purposes are
for hiring an employee, for obtaining information as in credit
arrangements, for learning unconscious motives as in motivation
research, for counseling the employee as in the post-appraisal or
merit rating of an employee, and for discovering the reasons
why an employee quits his job.

The interview is an important tool in the daily work of the
personnel man and of the professional member in the fields of
journalism, psychiatry, and diplomacy. Almost everyone conducts and participates in numerous varieties of interviews. In
business and management, the interview is so essential to effective human relations that many of its frequent users realize that
they do not conduct it as effectively as they would like. One of
the characteristics of the good interviewer is humility. Many
people who do interviewing erroneously imagine that they are
competent interviewers. As has been well stated:

Many reasons can be advanced for humility among interviewers—just
one should be sufficient. The interviewer in 20 to 60 minutes is trying to
obtain an accurate understanding of a lifetime of many years, a lifetime of
thousands of experiences producing attitudes, motivations, and behavior
which in many cases are unknown to the applicant himself and which he
can and does modify, either slightly or substantially, at different times and
in different places. Humility will help motivate the interviewer to avoid
hasty judgments, to obtain the evaluations of others in order to check his
own conclusions, to improve his skill and knowledge as much as possible,
to use effectively other selection devices to the extent that they can contribute to the accuracy of selection, to limit the interview to those factors
which can be appraised adequately, and to omit from it those factors
which should be measured by other methods.[1]

---

[1] *Personnel Methods Series No. 5,* U. S. Civil Service Commission, June 1956;
prepared by Milton M. Mandell, Standards Division, Bureau of Programs and
Standards, with the assistance of Joseph Brooks and Sally H. Greenberg.

17   The Interview, with Examples of Good Interviewing

The man who does the hiring in a company contributes to the strength or weakness of the organization. If he hires strong applicants, the organization will tend to be strong. Conversely, if he hires weak people, the organization will be weak.

The employment interviewer must do far more than estimate abilities of applicants. He must also do a lot of screening to keep out persons who are drifters, troublemakers, seriously maladjusted mentally, epileptics, sexual deviates, and others who would be liabilities rather than assets. He must also know what kinds of persons mesh with the personality of each supervisor and his employees.

In the hiring interview, the main purpose is to evaluate the applicant's potentials for the vacant job but an additional purpose is to forecast his behavior in relations with the other people who are involved in the job. The interviewer must forecast how they will react to him as a person. For this reason, the interview may be called a test of acceptability in human relations. It provides a basis for judging not only job skills but also how well the two persons, the employer (or his representatives) and the applicant, will get along with each other.

The incompetent interviewer often fails to get correct information and to make sound estimates of abilities and social characteristics because he is too easily influenced by an impressive personal appearance and glibness in oral expression. More basic facts about the applicant go unobserved or are overlooked.

The halo error

The halo effect to which all interviewers are to some extent subject is the tendency to accept an overall impression, either favorable or unfavorable. If we like a person, that liking casts its light over all his qualities. If we dislike him, that shadow envelops all his traits. Friends are viewed as superior in many characteristics and enemies as inferior to a greater extent than they deserve. The interviewee frequently does or says something that causes us to see every other fact about him in accordance with the one outstanding impression. If he has some unusual ability as in art, music, mathematics, even crossword puzzle solving, we tend to overestimate his intelligence and probable competence for activities that are unrelated to the special skill.

Usually the interviewer gets scanty information and he naturally fills in the gaps from the halo effect. He tends to assume that the applicant who is neat in appearance will also do neat work and come to work on time. The applicant who is good-looking, well-dressed, and talks glibly is often overrated. The homely person is likely to be underestimated as to his abilities. Instead of letting the halo effect influence us, each factor should be interpreted in terms of its specific value for the job under consideration. The interviewer should keep in mind the old saying: "You can't judge a book by its cover." Actually, good employees vary in appearance, size, age, education, and racial background. Generalizations to many factors cannot be made safely from one.

The mechanic who is reserved in manner during the interview may or may not be non-aggressive in performing mechanical work in the factory. Indeed, many skilled craftsmen are not socially aggressive during the hiring interview. The main value of knowing one's natural tendency toward generalization is to stimulate us to do further questioning. Research studies of interviewing indicate that many people tend to judge from key words or actions, inferring, for instance, superior traits about those labeled as "warm" as compared with those labeled as "cold." [2]

Personal bias

Almost every person has certain likes, dislikes, and preferences which he in his better moments recognizes as unjustified. No one can escape all prejudices. Any distinctive feature of a good or poor applicant is likely to carry over to later applicants. This applies to such features as having a mustache, wearing a bow tie, having red hair, wearing a pink shirt, or any personal characteristic.

Investigations indicate that college students as well as interviewers have some tendency to be influenced in their estimates by incidental physical factors of appearance, such as the wearing of glasses. Wearing glasses tends to cause students to rate the wearer as more intelligent and more industrious, but not more honest.[3] The applicant who fails to get a job because of a simple personal characteristic should not lose faith in human beings. Instead, he should recognize that we are all "human," and that the same feature that caused one employer to turn him down may be the very feature that causes another employer to hire him.

---

[2] See Herbert H. Hyman, *Interviewing in Social Research* (Chicago: University of Chicago, 1954), Chapter III.

[3] G. R. Thornton, "Effects of Wearing Glasses upon Judgments of Traits," *Journal of Applied Psychology* (American Psychological Association, Inc.), June 1944, p. 207.

One variety of bias, usually more important than simple personal characteristics, is directed toward the applicant's previous experience. If he has worked for a certain competitor, that may be a definite plus or minus for him. On the positive side, many employers like to hire men who have worked on certain jobs in companies which are known for the excellent training they give their employees. Some forward-looking college seniors know this. They take their first jobs with companies that offer relatively low pay but give especially good training in order that they may later move to other firms at an extra high rate of pay because of their training.

Requiring applicants for salesmen's jobs to bring the wife along for the interview has been burlesqued by the cartoonist of a London newspaper. Note the applicant who gets the job! Reproduced by permission of the Daily Express, *London, England.*

Some interviewers prefer college graduates who have been out of college for several years. They have done enough floundering by that time to be willing to work. Besides they may have learned how to work. Of course if an applicant is a recent college graduate and the last one hired from his college was a success or a failure, the applicant is likely to be evaluated in terms of the predecessor.

Some interviewers believe that young single men succeed better than young married men on the assumption that the young married man is either too greatly interested in his wife to study his job or he is overly anxious to buy his young wife gadgets which they can't afford.

Beliefs such as these are the results of a few dramatic instances. Many are without sound statistical basis.

Prejudices creep into interviews that are supposed to be so systematic as to overcome subjective influences. In one famous study, the research man made an analysis of the findings of twelve trained interviewers as to the cause of the downfall of 2,000 vagrants who had applied for free lodging. The interviews were standardized, but different investigators obtained different results. One interviewer who believed in socialism reported that 39 per cent of the vagrants were down and out because of industrial conditions, and 22 per cent because of excessive use of alcohol. Another interviewer, an ardent opponent of alcohol, attributed but 7 per cent of the failures to industrial and economic conditions and 62 per cent to drink. Prejudices were even more significantly revealed when we note that, according to the socialist, the *vagrants themselves* gave as the cause of their downfall: industrial conditions, 60 per cent; drink 11 per cent. But according to the prohibitionist, the *vagrants themselves* blamed industrial conditions in 42.5 per cent and drink in 34 per cent of the cases. Obviously, each interviewer influenced the interviewees to give answers in line with his own biases.[4]

The illusion of previous experience. Most employment men tend to assume that the applicant who has had previous experience on a similar job is bound to be a better employee than another applicant who may have superior potentialities but lacks experience. When a secretary is desired, the interviewer usually chooses the applicant who claims secretarial experience in preference to the stenographer, who may actually be brighter and more competent.

> Actually, previous experience when taken in conjunction with other pertinent factors is an extremely valuable indicator of future performance, *but it is not, of itself, a guarantee of ability to do a job well.* Mediocrity is tolerated in much of the world's work, and *experience* too often cloaks such mediocrity. There is danger, therefore, in making a criterion of the fact that an applicant has done similar work in the past. The applicant who is willing to accept a job on the same level as his previous one is as likely to be below average in performance as above average. The tendency to *over-value* previous experience in weighing qualifications should be discouraged, for it may be costly to a company in terms of valuable talent lost and of commonplace or inferior performance perpetuated.[5]

Insisting on a duplication of ourselves is often called "projection." The interviewer has a tendency to put his own value system into the rating situation, to assume that only a duplicate of the interviewer can be successful. He prefers applicants who match his own age, appearance, manner, voice and background. The applicant who deviates from his patterns is labeled as undesirable. As one writer stated: "This error can cause more harm to an organization than almost any other error; it tends to produce a homogeneity which often leads to mediocrity."[6]

---

[4] See S. A. Rice, "Contagious Bias in the Interview," *American Journal of Sociology,* Vol. 35, 1929, pp. 420-423.

[5] *Manual of Employment Interviewing,* Research Report No. 9, American Management Association, Inc., 1946.

[6] See Hyman, *Interviewing in Social Research,* Chapter III.

"I like your looks Gillis . . . you're hired!" SOURCE: by Homer. Reprinted from Commerce Magazine, published by the Chicago Association of Commerce and Industry.

There is, however, an old saying among personnel men: "Each interviewer has a tendency to choose persons who are either similar to or the opposite of himself." Certainly, an interviewer's selections are greatly influenced by his images of himself and by his own psychological needs. (see Chapter 24)

Practices that improve the interview

Any person who wants to become a trained interviewer can do so by means of special college courses, special institute courses for interviewers, and books. The material presented here has been chosen to show the need for training, not to provide that training. Practices that improve interviewing are known and can be acquired by the intelligent practitioner.

The good interviewer has a plan in his mind, a basic framework for his thinking before he talks to an applicant. He knows the kind of information he wants and the techniques he intends to use to obtain it. This framework is developed from systematic training in the social sciences, particularly psychology. He has a background for interpreting the information that he obtains. He is a pattern-minded interpreter of what he hears, sees, and knows. He looks for patterns in the educational and occupational history that indicate growth rather than a series of erratic changes in courses and jobs. Also, he develops his skill in stimulating an applicant to talk freely. He tends to follow practices such as the following:

1. He puts the applicant at ease. He himself has a relaxed, cheerful manner. If the applicant is obviously tense, the interviewer may give

him time to pull himself together by picking up the application blank and saying: "Do you mind if I look at this so that I need not ask you questions that you have answered on the application form?" He reduces the tension by purposely asking a question that makes the applicant feel a bit better informed than the interviewer. The question may deal with some fact about the applicant's home town, college attended, or previous employer.

2. He asks many open-end questions, especially in the early stages of the interview. Direct questions are avoided. Instead of saying, "Did you like college?" he may phrase his question in a less directive manner as, "Tell me about your college and the courses you took there." After the applicant has answered the inquiry, the interviewer can elicit further revealing responses by saying, "Tell me, how do you now feel about your college education?"

When open-end questions do not elicit all the information that appears to be pertinent, the interviewer asks questions of a specific nature, such as, "In the last job you held, what did you do? Please describe a typical day's work."

3. The effective interviewer listens. He gives the impression that he is interested and unhurried. He pauses for at least a few seconds after the applicant has seemingly finished his answer before he asks any more questions. He gives the applicant a chance to talk further. When the applicant stops talking, the interviewer asks questions about the last statements made, but he tries to keep the conversation moving in the direction of more complete information. He may also ask questions that reveal the applicant's level of aspiration such as "What kind of job do you think you should have to give you chances to develop your abilities?" "Tell me some of the things you liked better about your last job than about the one before the last;" and "In what ways do you think that you improved your opportunities when you changed from the second last to the last job?"

4. The good interviewer avoids or asks few questions of the following kinds:

(a) Questions that can be answered "Yes" or "No."

(b) Questions that invariably elicit the same answer from all applicants. *Example:* "Do you usually come to work on time?"

(c) Embarrassing questions that compel the applicant to defend a statement or admit an error in an earlier statement.

(d) Leading questions, such as: "You finished high school, did you?" "Would you be willing to work in an office where most employees are much older than you are?" "Were you a stenographer or a secretary on your last job?" and, "Don't you agree that this is a good company to work for?"

5. The good interviewer carries on a conversation that enables the applicant to state his job preferences and to express his feelings. He does not dominate the interview but encourages the applicant to describe his preferences, abilities, and inabilities. This kind of two-way conversation with a purpose means that the interviewer's statements consume less than 50 per cent of the interviewing time, preferably less than 25 per cent.

6. A great deal of the information obtained is in the nature of clues rather than facts. Clues are in the form of gestures, voice inflections, and avoidance of certain topics.

Every alert interviewer notices the applicant's appearances and gestures. These behavioral signs may or may not be significant. If, for example, a young man wears a beard, does it indicate that he has deep-seated need to feel recognized as an individual? It may or it may not, but it certainly suggests that the known facts in his development should be reviewed in order to note whether that hypothesis is confirmed. At any rate, the interviewer has a right to wonder why he chose a sign of individuality such as the growing of a beard rather than the development in himself of some ability having intrinsic value.

Does the careless appearance of the woman who obviously "tosses on" her clothes signify that she has given up the hope of making herself attractive, does she suffer from an emotional problem that is too great for her to solve, or does it mean that she is so deeply interested in her professional work that her appearance is incidental to her? Only further review of her developmental history is likely to indicate the significance of the lack of normal grooming.

When a person folds his arms firmly and quickly, is he outwardly expressing his inner hostility to the interviewer as a person or to what the interviewer symbolizes?

When the applicant is asked a question and he passes his hand over his face or covers his eyes, is he trying to avoid giving the answer which he feels is correct? Or is he trying to give a better phrasing of the correct answer?

When the applicant leans forward toward the interviewer, does it mean that he is doing so spontaneously or is he doing it consciously in a studied manner to make a favorable impression?

What do such clues or hypotheses really mean? What is the context of the clues? Little research has been done to answer these questions. However, one noteworthy study of the validity of specific clues was made of interviews conducted for the purpose of distinguishing between successful foremen and workers of equal technical skill who had been judged incapable of successfully supervising others. The relatively few significant conditions that occurred more frequently among the capable men were:

Good attitude toward early associates.

More than 20 years' experience in the company.

In contrast, items found more frequently among those believed to be incapable of supervising others were:

Restless movements in the interview.
Repetition of one or more subjects in school.
Self-conscious manner in the interview.
Tense or strained facial expression in interview.
Low intensity of voice during interview.[7]

Obviously, interviewers need the benefit of more research studies essential to improvement of interview validity. We know that *expressions of emotion are dictated by the culture* and clues to feelings vary with the cultural background of the individual. To us, the clenched fist indicates anger but it has a friendly meaning to some peoples of the world.

When a Chinese fiction character sticks out his tongue it means surprise—not what the small American boy means by the same gesture.

However, expressions of emotion that depend upon involuntary action of the body mechanisms are likely to be interpreted alike in East and West.

"Every one of his hairs stood on end," "A cold sweat broke forth," and "His face was red and he went creeping alone outside the village" are understood in any land.

The good interviewer asks for facts and records that improve his interpretations of clues whenever possible. Then he tries to note relationships between clues and verifiable facts. He asks himself "What kind of pattern of growth or decline in ability is evident from the facts?"; "When and why did the applicant change the direction of his growth or decline?"; and "Does he have the kinds of potentials needed for the job?"

NONDIRECTIVE INTERVIEWING

This kind of employment interview stems from the nondirective counseling interview developed by Carl R. Rogers and his disciples.[8]

The nondirective technique is well known to psychotherapists but is not as yet widely used in industry. The interviewer says little but concentrates his efforts on encouraging the interviewee to tell his own story

---

[7] Carroll Leonard Shartle, "A Clinical Approach to Foremanship," *Personnel Journal,* Vol. 13, No. 3, 1934, p. 137. See also Ralph F. Berdie, "Psychological Processes in the Interview," *The Journal of Social Psychology,* Vol. 18, 1943, p. 28.

[8] Carl R. Rogers, *Counseling and Psychotherapy* (Boston: Houghton Mifflin, 1942).

in his own words. The interviewer listens closely and analyzes the interviewee's words, gestures, expressions, and meanings, both as to content and as to implication. The nondirective interviewer tries to keep the applicant talking by giving his entire attention to the applicant; by not interrupting or changing the subject abruptly; by using few questions, and by allowing pauses in the conversation.

One goal of a job applicant is to find out as much as he can about the job, and then to present himself in the most favorable light for the job. The nondirective interviewer tells the candidate only as much about the job as is necessary. Only after the applicant's history has been thoroughly covered, is job information given. A typical indirect interview usually begins with a generalized question such as, "Tell me, Mr. Blank, how did you happen to get interested in coming in here to see us?" This kind of question is so general that each person has a tendency to talk about the things and feelings important to him such as a desire to get away from a certain supervisor, to work where transportation to and from the place of employment is easier, a chance to advance, and so on. If the applicant is merely shopping, that fact too is likely to be expressed.

The nondirective interview does require special training and preparation. It must be conducted with care. If the interviewer knows a great deal about an applicant beforehand, he can alert himself to listen for the things he needs to know.

> Responses should be brief and should refer to the applicant's interests or feelings. It is often helpful to repeat the last few words of the applicant's statement, make a short comment, or ask a brief question, such as:
> "Tell me more."
> "That's interesting."
> "What were the circumstances?"
> "What happened then?"
> "Exciting wasn't it?"
> ". . . until 11:00 P.M.?"
> "You say, 'It's not worth the effort'?"
> "H-hm." [9]

Even though the nondirective interviewer appears to function in a completely unguided manner, he actually structures the interview to some extent. Furthermore, his final evaluation of the applicant is usually modified by findings from home visits and investigations of school and employer references.

---

[9] N. A. Moyer, "Non-Directive Employment Interviewing," *Personnel,* American Management Association, Inc., March 1948, and "Using the Non-Directive Interview," *Supervisory Management,* June 1957, pp. 28-29. Also *Personnel Management Abstracts,* Autumn Issue, Vol. 3, 1957.

Of course the interviewer must be a good listener and sincerely interested in what the other person is saying.

He keeps his own emotions out of the interview.

He does not question the factual accuracy, inaccuracy, "rightness" or "wrongness" of statements, but looks beyond the surface of expression, for what the interviewee does not or cannot tell, as well as what he tells.[10]

EXECUTIVE INTERVIEWS

The good executive delegates responsibilities but must also keep himself informed about the progress being made. To get correct information from subordinates, he must be able to talk with them in a manner that does not cause feelings of threat. If the subordinate feels threatened by his superior's questions, he will not give complete answers. Too often the executive says to himself: "Everybody covered himself, and I learned very little. I know it's always tough to talk to the boss, but I've got to know what the problems really are before I can help my men solve them." The skilled executive learns to use the permissive or nondirective type of interviewing technique in order to get all the facts necessary for his effective guidance of operations. He needs accurate information to do his decision-making.

Robert L. Kahn and Charles F. Cannell, Survey Research Center, University of Michigan, have given some examples of the benefits to the executive of the indirect technique as applied to a vice president's inquiry of the production manager as to why a good customer has not been getting deliveries on schedule:

> Suppose, after the introductory statement by the vice president, the production manager replies by saying: "Well, I think the main problem is that new die-casting procedure of ours hasn't really shaken down yet. You know conversion from sand-molding to die-casting really calls for a lot of changes and adjustments all along the line." What should the executive-interviewer do next in order to increase the respondent's intrinsic motivation to communicate? Below are three possible rejoinders by the executive, along with the subordinate's probable reaction to each.
>
> 1. *Interviewer:* Well, let's not blame all our problems on a technical change, Bill. Changes like that one have been made successfully in thousands of plants.
>
>   *Subordinate:* (to himself) The boss won't believe the truth when he hears it. O.K., I'll give him the kind of story he's looking for. Better watch out, though. Sounds as if he's trying to pin this one on me.

---

[10] See William M. Fox, "For Non-Directive Interviewing You Must Know Yourself," *Personnel Journal,* July-August 1956, p. 99.

What are the rules for conducting a successful executive interview? Test yourself by answering the following true-or-false questions, then check the answer panel on page 316.

	True	False
1. Wording questions in advance interferes with the spontaneity needed for successful executive interviewing.	—	—
2. Thinking about what you should have said after an interview is over is probably a neurotic waste of time.	—	—
3. If you are doing a good job of supervision, you have no need for special information-getting techniques.	—	—
4. A subordinate will give only information that he thinks will please the boss.	—	—
5. A subordinate never gets much satisfaction out of being interviewed by the boss.	—	—
6. The best way for the boss to get good information from an employee is to talk to him outside the office.	—	—
7. An executive learns the most when the employee does not even realize that he is being interviewed.	—	—
8. The good interviewer listens well and avoids directing the conversation.	—	—
9. The interviewer learns most by sometimes putting the respondent on the defensive.	—	—
10. The best way to get information from an employee is to convince him that you are meeting on an equal basis—that you are both just employees of the same firm.	—	—

SOURCE: Robert L. Kahn and Charles F. Cannell, "Nobody Tells Me Anything!" *Dun's Review and Modern Industry*, November 1957, p. 37. Copyright © 1957 by Dun & Bradstreet Publications Corporation.

Another possible rejoinder by the executive is less threatening, but has its own problems:

2. *Interviewer:* Bill, I'm only surprised that you're not in more trouble in the manufacturing department. You've been doing a marvelous job down there. I think your approach to this conversion is just terrific, and I want you to know I appreciate it.

Subordinate: (to himself) Gosh, if everything's going so doggone great, what am I doing here? Things aren't as good as the boss seems to think. Does he really believe what he's saying, or is he stringing me along? Either way, he's making it awfully tough for me to tell him what some of the real problems are.

For a more constructive alternative, consider the following:

3. *Interviewer:* Well, I can understand those die-casting problems. Changing manufacturing procedures always causes some difficulties. Can you fill me in a little more on the kind of troubles you're having?

Subordinate: (to himself) I guess he's not going to put me on the spot, anyway. He seems to have some idea how tough these conversions can be. Maybe I can even get some help.

How do these three alternative approaches by the executive-interviewer measure up in the light of our criteria for developing intrinsic motivation? The first approach is openly threatening. It subjects the subordinate to immediate pressure, strongly implying inadequate performance on his part. The second approach appears to be more satisfactory: It meets the superficial "human relations" requirements. But as a method of getting information it isn't likely to work. The subordinate will evaluate his burst of praise in one of two ways. If it is insincere, the boss is merely trying to make him feel good. If it is sincere, he must live up to the image of impossible perfection the boss has painted. Far from stimulating frank communication, the boss has only made it more difficult for the subordinate to confess to problems or inadequacies.

Contrast these two approaches with the last alternative. Here the executive makes no evaluative judgment, either good or bad. Instead, his statement implies that he can understand the subordinate's difficulties and that he is interested in learning more about the nature of the problem. His subordinate concludes that the boss is genuinely interested and can accept the existence of problems without looking for a scapegoat. Because the subordinate does not need to be defensive or prove himself, he can communicate more freely and accurately. As the vice president continues to develop this type of relationship, barriers are removed and positive motivation to communicate is increased.[11]

---

[11] Robert L. Kahn and Charles F. Cannell, "Nobody Tells Me Anything!" *Dun's Review and Modern Industry,* November 1957, pp. 99-101. Copyright © 1957 by Dun & Bradstreet Publications Corporation. These two authors have written a very helpful volume: *The Dynamics of Interviewing* (New York: John Wiley & Sons, Inc., 1957). As in most communications processes, we have in the interview two people, each trying to influence the other and each actively accepting or rejecting influence attempts.

Some personnel managers conduct an interview with each employee who leaves or wishes to leave the company. Purposes of exit interviews are to keep good employees from resigning, build better public relations with former employees, clear up petty misunderstandings, spot faulty administration or supervision, and discover and overcome morale problems. Even though they are one-sided because they reflect only the feelings of an employee when he is leaving a job, they still help to indicate the attitudes of many workers who are staying with the company.

One investigator made a study of 125 employees who resigned during one year from a research laboratory. It was found that 90 per cent of the professional workers who were quitting already had other positions. Only 50 per cent of the nonprofessional workers had another job waiting for them.

"You can't quit! You're the only one who knows how to shut this thing off." SOURCE: by Porges. Courtesy Today's Health.

Both professional and nonprofessionals were concerned about "Opportunities for advancement," but many more nonprofessionals expressed it as a cause for leaving. "Pay not commensurate with work" was listed as the second major cause for quitting by nonprofessionals. The professional men, on the other hand, were more concerned with the "Accomplishments of your work unit" and the "Importance of your work."

Neither group felt that their abilities were being utilized enough, but almost twice as many professionals felt this as others. They were also three times more critical of the supervision they received than the nonprofessional workers.[12]

When a supervisor is asked, "Do your workers have enough to do?" the usual answer is, "Of course they have." Yet a study of University of Illinois researchers indicated that one of the reasons for quitting is that some employees do not have enough work to keep them busy. Out of 2,713 persons who quit their jobs, 415 answered a questionnaire that included questions about the climate in which they worked and reasons for quitting. Answers to questions about the work load indicated that 19 per cent felt that the load was too heavy and 9 per cent felt that it was too light. "It will be no surprise to most employers that 19 per cent of his employees feel that the work load is too heavy, but it will be a surprise to many to learn that one out of 10 who quits feels that he is not kept busy enough." [13]

The exit interview is a very difficult interview for both the interviewer and the interviewee. An employee who quits is likely to be under some emotional stress. He is leaving old friends and has many uncertainties about the future even though he has been hired for another job. The causes for his decision to quit have been the result of several cumulative influences: resentment of the pay, treatment by supervisors, limited chances for advancement, and so on. As a result, the quitting employee does not always state the true reasons for his leaving—he still wants the old employer to speak favorably of him when a future prospective employer investigates his record.

Obviously, the exit interview must be conducted with considerable skill if it is to elicit valid and truly useful information. One of the most effective techniques for the purpose is the nondirective approach.

Two examples of the nondirective approach, as contrasted with the directive method, are shown below.

Traditional Directive Approach

I–1 Well, Mary, you're leaving today, I hear.
E–1 Yes, I am. My mother is sick and I have to take care of her.
I–2 I'm sorry to learn that. I hope she'll be better soon.

---

[12] See Robert D. Melcher, "Getting the Facts on Employee Resignations: An Exit Interview Program," *Personnel*, American Management Association, Inc., May 1955.

[13] Robert D. Loken, "Why They Quit" (University of Illinois, Bureau of Business Management, 1951). See also *News Letter* (The Dartnell Corporation, Chicago), September 20, 1952.

E–2   Thank you. I do, too.

I–3   But don't you think you could have given us a little more notice? I understand your mother has been ailing for some time. It's not as though she had been taken ill all of a sudden.

E–3   I would have liked to, but it just didn't work out that way.

I–4   Well, you know the company expects you to give adequate notice when you leave. I don't think you're acting properly at all.

E–4   Well, I'm sorry, but I couldn't work it out any other way.

I–5   All right, then. Good-bye and good luck.

E–5   Good-bye and thank you.

Non-Directive Approach

I–1   Come right in, Mary. This is your last day with the company, I see.

E–1   That's right. This is my last day here.

I–2   I understand from your supervisor that your mother is ill. I'm certainly sorry to hear that.

E–2   Yes, she's not feeling too well and I sure have my hands full these days.

I–3   Of course, with your mother ill there must be many more burdens on your shoulders.

E–3   You don't know the half of it. With mother out sick now, I've got to take care of the whole household—shopping, washing, ironing, cleaning— just about everything. I'm worn out, what with working here in the office until five and all the things I have to do at home.

I–4   That certainly doesn't leave you much time for anything else.

E–4   I would have given you a couple of days' notice if I weren't needed so badly at home.

I–5   Yes, I can see that as things are you weren't able to give much advance notice.

E–5   No. And besides you don't need me, anyway.

I–6   Oh, really?

E–6   Yes. If you ask me, I don't think anybody cares whether I stay here or not.

I–7   You feel you are not going to be missed at all.

E–7   That's just it. In my department, the supervisor leaves everything up to the assistant supervisor. And she's a part of the gang. They eat lunch together and since they all live in the same part of town, all they ever talk about is their boy friends.

I –8   That sort of leaves you out of things.

E–8   Yes, just because I live in a different neighborhood, they don't seem to care about me at all. They never ask me to come along for lunch, so I have to eat alone.

I–9   Eating all by yourself isn't much fun.

E–9   I'll say. After mother gets better, I'm going to find a job where the girls aren't so standoffish. I want to work with a bunch of friendly girls and not like it is here.

Traditional Directive Approach

I–1   So Bill, you've resigned, I hear.

E–1   Yes, I got a better job closer to home.

I–2   Better than your job here? What kind of a job is it?

E–2 Well, for one thing, there's more money.

I–3 More money than you're getting with us?

E–3 I'll say. You don't pay the going rate here.

I–4 I don't know how you can say that. Didn't you know that in the last wage survey of all the firms in this area our pay scale compared favorably with all the others?

E–4 Is that so? Well, I've got a friend with the Dalton Company doing the same kind of work as I'm doing and he gets twenty-three cents an hour more.

Non-Directive Approach

I–1 Hello Bill, I hear you've resigned your job.

E–1 Yes, I've found a better job closer to home.

I–2 That's interesting. Can you tell me a little more about it?

E–2 There's not much to say about it except that you pay such low wages here and I think I can get more pay elsewhere.

I–3 You feel that the pay scale here is not as high as it should be.

E–3 You're darn right. I've been doing work that's usually done by the boys in Grade 6, but I was just paid my old Grade 7 rate.

I–4 If a person does Grade 6 work, he should get Grade 6 pay.

E–4 That's what I told the foreman, but he said he couldn't do anything about it at that time. I spoke to him again a few weeks later and he said he would take care of it, but I guess he never got around to it.

I–5 You think the foreman should have taken the time to adjust your job grade.

E–5 Oh, he takes care of those boys that belong to his car pool, but the others he doesn't care about.[14]

The superiority of the nondirective approach in certain interviewing situations is self-evident, but the technique requires training and practice. Any management that plans to use it should enlist the aid of specialists to instruct its interviewers and conduct the necessary practice sessions. A firm of management consultants who specialize in the training of interviewers may be used. The psychology or management department of a nearby college or university would also, in many cases, be able to render helpful advisory assistance.

Interviewing college seniors

One company in a recent year screened some 1,200 students at 22 colleges, and hired six. This suggests that college students should become acquainted with the procedures used by employment interviewers.

Each recruiter conducts his private meeting with seniors in different ways, but in general there are two main approaches. Some like to get

---

[14] Erwin Schoenfeld, "The Non-Directive Exit Interview," *Personnel*, American Management Association, Inc., November-December 1957, pp. 49, 50.

right down to business, while others prefer a "bull session" first and business afterward. The reactions of the seniors showed that 57 per cent prefer the "bull-session"-business formula, and 33 per cent favor the "brass tacks" approach.[15]

When the seniors of one college were asked to rate the relative importance of certain factors in influencing their final decisions, they listed "promotion possibilities" and the "nature of the firm" as their first two considerations. "Starting salary" was third and "extra benefits" was a poor fourth.

One of the most striking findings from the study was the prospects' impressions of the role played by the company representative, the interviewer. In answer to the question, "Did the appearance and manner of the interviewers convey to you any immediate impressions of their firms?" 81 per cent of the applicants says "yes." A frequent kind of comment was "The company was generalized by the interviewer."

One student felt that the recruiters were looking for stereotypes. "I took a look at the interviewer," he said, "and thought, 'Am I like him, or could I be like him? Could I fit into the mold?'" In many cases, it was obvious to them that they couldn't, or didn't care to "fit into the mold." In fairness to the regular interviewers, it must be recognized that company men are pulled from their regular departments to fill in during the recruiting drive. When these are drawn from the higher echelons, students are likely to gain good impressions. Those drawn from the lower ranks of superfluous staff men and long-service failures are not so likely to know enough about the overall operations of the company to interview effectively.[16] Of all applicants, 94 per cent rated the interviewer's style of presentation as important.

COLLATERAL READINGS

For All Students

Fear, Richard A., *The Evaluation Interview*. New York: McGraw-Hill Book Company, Inc., 1958. A "how-to-do-it" book. Treats selection, evaluation and placement.

Yonge, K. A., "The Value of the Interview: An Orientation and Pilot Study," *Journal of Applied Psychology*, February 1956.

For Advanced Students

Hepner, Harry W., *Psychology Applied to Life and Work*, 3rd edition.

---

[15] "Agencies' Baffling Personnel Problems," *Tide*, August 23, 1957, p. 33, and Stanley E. Smith, "What Companies Get the College Boys—And How Do They Do It?" *Sales Management*, June 7, 1957, pp. 38-40.

[16] See Robert N. McMurry, "What's Wrong with College Recruiting?" *American Business* (The Dartnell Corporation), September 1958.

Englewood Cliffs, N.J.: Prentice-Hall, Inc., 1957. Chapter 15 treats the hiring interview, and Chapter 16 deals with the use of tests in hiring.

McMurry, Robert N., "Validating the Patterned Interview," *Personnel*, American Management Association, Inc., January 1947.

For Men in Business

Balinsky, Benjamin, and Ruth Burger, *The Executive Interview: A Bridge to People*. New York: Harper & Brothers, 1959. A handbook for the executive who is called upon to talk informally and formally with people. Reviews the best techniques.

Employment Interviewing: Personnel Methods Series No. 5, U. S. Civil Service Commission. Washington: Superintendent of Documents, 1956. A helpful pamphlet.

Recruiting the College Graduate, American Management Association, Inc. A guide for company interviewers. Includes an interview procedure chart and scales for interview recording.

QUESTIONS ON THE CHAPTER

1. What is an interview and what are its purposes in business?
2. Name the several kinds of interviews treated in the chapter.
3. Explain the halo error.
4. Describe the Rice study of vagrants and what it signifies for interviewing.
5. List practices that improve the hiring interview.
6. What are the values of nondirective interviews? Describe principles or rules for its effective use.
7. What are the purposes of the exit interview? Why is it difficult to use effectively?
8. Under what conditions in a nondirective interview should the interviewer talk or ask questions?
9. What are two approaches which recruiters use when interviewing college seniors and which do the students prefer?
10. Of the several ideas presented in the chapter, which ones were of special interest or value to you?
11. What did the chapter contribute toward your future relations with (a) the men who supervise you, (b) the employees whom you may supervise?

PROBLEMS AND PROJECTS

For All Students

1. Answer the questions on page 308, "How Good an Interviewer Are You?" Explain reasons for your answers. Also make a list of your bias tendencies and ask several friends to modify your list.
2. Do some role playing as an interviewer who is hiring college stu-

dents on completion of their studies. Have the other students observe your procedures and make suggestions.

For Advanced Students

3. Get acquainted with the wide range of published material on the interview. Look for different varieties and purposes of the interview. Try to identify some of the patterns of thinking used by certain interviewers.

4. Make a special study of the nondirective interview and do some role playing with it. Note the extent to which you slip into directive procedures. Also try to make records, immediately after the interview, of what happened.

For Men in Business

5. Describe an executive whom you know and his characteristics that should be considered when applicants are hired to work under his direct supervision. What kinds of employees does he like? What kinds "get under his skin"?

6. Ask several persons in business to tell you about some failures in their interviewing. What did the interviewer fail to discover that was learned later and might have been caught in the interview?

Score yourself on the interviewing test, page 308, by counting one point for each "true" response. The perfect score is zero. In the opinion of the authors, every one of these ten statements is, in fact, incorrect.

Good Interviewing

THE TYPICAL EXECUTIVE USUALLY KNOWS EACH EMPLOYEE UNDER his direction more accurately and comprehensively than the employee realizes. The executive, however, does not usually tell the employee what he knows. At the same time, almost every employee asks himself the question: "How am I doing? In what respects is my work good, in what respects is it poor?" Management, too, must seek answers to the same kinds of questions about the employee when decisions must be made regarding a request for an increase in pay, selecting an employee for promotion, and deciding whether a problem employee should be retained or discharged. Management also likes to know the strengths and weaknesses of the individual members of its personnel in order that training and selection programs may be organized to improve the strengths. These and other needs on the part of the individual and the company have stimulated many managements to develop some kind of employee appraisal system.

Early appraisal systems utilized a merit rating form that dealt with various personality and other employee characteristics such as cooperativeness, dependability, emotional stability, ability to get along with others, and literally hundreds of other traits of people. The great majority of these forms used graphic rating or check-list techniques. See page 514 for an example. Most companies still use this kind of form; it has become accepted mainly for its administrative advantages.

18

Appraising the Employee –
Merit Ratings and
Job Performance Coaching

In recent years, however, the earlier merit rating plan in some companies has evolved into a variation called, "Appraisals for Coaching Purposes." Both types of plans are currently in use and are treated in this chapter.

MERIT RATING FOR ADMINISTRATIVE PURPOSES

Rating is a term used to refer to the process of judging people and things. A *rating scale* is a standardized device for recording personal judgments. The use of a scale provides a method whereby judgments may be secured in a uniform manner and treated quantitatively. Personal estimates and subjective opinions can be dealt with in much the same way as test scores and other psychological measurements. However, a rating scale is *not* a test and a rating scale should never be referred to as a test. It is a subjective estimate used because tests to measure certain personal characteristics are not as yet available.

The term "rating" applies to areas of judgment which are not susceptible to the testing process. A rating is a personal judgment, but a test is or ought to be an objective measure. If a characteristic of a person such as intelligence can be tested, it should not be rated.

Merit rating should also be differentiated from job evaluation. Merit rating attempts to measure some trait or characteristic of the employee, whereas *job evaluation* measures the job and usually includes a description of the ideal personal characteristics of the kind of person who should be hired to fill the job. A merit rating estimates the characteristics of the specific person who is actually holding the job—not the ideal person, in the abstract, who theoretically might be found to fill the job.

Ratings do *not measure* "merit"—they *portray* the pattern of perceptions which someone has about the individual. They present what certain acquaintances *think* they know or are willing to say about the person. Obviously what executives think they know about an employee is very important. They will treat the employee as they perceive him.

Purposes of employee evaluations

A rating system has the purposes which we would expect, such as giving each employee some information about his accomplishments, abilities, limitations, and potentials. Employees like to know where they stand in the opinion of the supervisor, particularly in regard to complimentary characteristics. They seek reassurance about themselves.

From the standpoint of management, the primary objectives of most merit-rating programs are to improve job performance, select individuals for promotion, and determine wage increases. Of these, improving job performance is cited most often as a primary aim. Secondary objectives include guiding supervisors in systematic appraisal, bringing about better communications, facilitating transfers, and determining fitness for continued employment. In most companies, ratings are made annually or semi-annually.

One of the indirect benefits of ratings of employees by executives is that detailed attention is given to the person on the job. Raters are forced to analyze their men in a more or less systematic manner. This process often brings into the open potentials that might otherwise be overlooked. A good man is likely to get lost in the shuffle unless each employee's qualities are reviewed periodically.

Many employees who fail to meet normal work standards need extra attention to develop properly. Most managements prefer to develop rather than dismiss the marginal employee. Dismissal hurts the employee and costs the company money to train the person who takes the place of the one dismissed. Ratings are especially helpful in finding promotable employees. One of the critical needs of management is to identify and select those employees who are capable of advancing to executive positions. Managements conduct unceasing search for management talent, talent that will improve upon and eventually replace the existing management.

Executives as well as lower echelons of employees must be analyzed regarding promotability. In one analysis of 3,000 executives,[1] the research project indicated that only slightly more than one-third qualified for any advancement and fewer had potentials for development into top management jobs. This, in some companies, might become a serious problem because approximately 40 per cent of all top management personnel are in the age bracket from 55 to 65. Many of these will retire in the course of their next 10 years. Death, disability, and turnover are continuous.

Every company of course inspects management performance by examining performance against budget figures. Budget figure comparisons are not, however, sufficient for evaluating executive performance. Every executive knows that cost and production figures can be made to look especially favorable for a specific executive by postponing some costs to a later calendar period and by taking early credit for production or

---

[1] Data from an unpublished survey by the Management Research Department of Booz, Allen & Hamilton. See "How to Identify Promotable Executives," by C. Wilson Randle, *Harvard Business Review*, May-June 1956, p. 122.

Appraising the Employee   **319**

sales figures. Furthermore, for some service departments there is no way of measuring accomplishment in monetary terms.

In spite of the many arguments for and benefits of merit rating, a few managements refuse to use them. They believe that a personnel function of this kind should not be formalized. They dislike the idea of cataloging any person's qualities and limitations. People, they say, deserve to be accepted and treated as members of a team, not as machines whose features can be listed on a sheet of paper. Those who cannot be fully accepted should be dismissed in a respectful manner.

Most managements believe that the use of an appraisal system does not detract from the dignity of the individual. They remind the critics that anyone who attends school is rated throughout the years of his formal education.

Recent college graduates take to merit reviews quite easily. They are accustomed to having their work graded and their characteristics listed. They look upon such devices as means of getting tips that will be of value in their growth. Rising young men are usually confident of their records. Those who dread the reviews are usually men who suspect or know they are doing poorly.

Employee reactions to a merit rating plan

Surveys of employee opinions of rating plans are made by many companies but many of the findings are of questionable validity. When employees know that management is enthusiastic about merit rating, they are less likely to express their true attitudes. Some ingenuity in making such a survey is necessary.

One of the writer's graduate students [2] was a regular employee in a local metal working plant where management was enthusiastic about their rating plan. The student arranged to interview the employees as a fellow worker, not as a consultant or a personnel man. This particular plant was one of several operated by a large corporation whose personnel men had developed and installed an elaborate employee merit rating system, known as the "Job Performance Record." Each foreman was instructed to maintain a "Red-Blue Book," a record of each employee's poor and good job performances. The records were used as the basis for making the merit ratings. The foreman was required to rate each employee on a standardized form once every six months. He was also instructed to conduct a post-appraisal interview concerning the

[2] Gerald H. Shaw, now in personnel management and teaching.

rating with each employee. The plan had been in operation several years before Shaw's survey was made.

The employees who were interviewed for this survey were approached while on the job by this graduate student, a fellow worker to them, who stated, "I am taking a course at the University. We're studying Job Performance Records like the one this company uses. The books tell us a lot on what they're for and what they're supposed to do, but they don't tell us how the workers feel about them. My instructor wants me to ask a number of fellows in each department how they feel about it. So I was wondering. . . ." He proceeded to ask each fellow worker the following four questions:

1. "What do you think about the Job Performance Record?" If the interviewee did not seem to understand, he continued, "That is, do you think it's a good idea or a waste of time or what?" If the interviewee did not voice an opinion, he then asked, "Do you think it helps the company or the workers or what?"
2. "Has it benefited you or been helpful to you?"
3. "How does the company use your Job Performance Record or for what?"
4. (a) "Do you think you know where you stand with your foreman?" If the employee was puzzled, he was then asked, "That is, do you know how you're doing?" Toward the end of the survey, another question, a (b) part, was added: "Do you know where you stand because of the Job Performance Record?"

In order to promote free responses by the employees no answers were recorded in the employee's presence. The interviewer memorized the answers of each employee to the four questions, and, after thanking him, proceeded to record the answers in a place removed from his presence. This procedure was followed after each interview.

The total number of men working on the first and second shifts in this company under study was 271. Of these, 105 randomly selected employees were interviewed. All employees were either semiskilled or skilled machinists.

Of the 82 employees who indicated they knew where they stood or how they were doing, 47 were asked the question: (b) "Because of the Job Performance Record?"

Answer	Per cent
Yes	60
No	36
No reply	4

Table 18-1

FACTORY EMPLOYEES' OPINIONS OF THE EMPLOYER'S RATING PLAN

QUESTION 1. "What do you think about the Job Performance Record?"

QUESTION 2. "Has it benefited or helped you?"

Answers indicated:	Per cent	Answer	Per cent
Approval	46	Yes	29
Disapproval	18	No	63
Mixed	17	No reply	8
Neutral	19		

QUESTION 3. "How or what does the company use these records for?" (*more than one answer permitted*)

Answers	Per cent	Answers	Per cent
Promotions: for filling vacancies	44	Incentive: gives the employees something to work for or to stimulate increased production	16
Tell how you're doing: a good or poor job	36		
		References: record for future employer	13
Discharges or layoffs: those with the poorest records may be discharged or laid off first	25		
		Not used: they do not affect promotions, discharges, etc.	6
Don't know:	23		
		Transfers: provide record of performance for new foreman	3

QUESTION 4. "Do you know where you stand with foreman or how you're doing?"

Answer	Per cent
Yes	78
No	17
No reply	5

The employee's attitude toward the Job Performance Record in terms of the entire interview given each was:

Answers indicated	Per cent
Approval	44
Disapproval	15
Mixed	30
Neutral	10

Table 18-1 presents the findings but the percentages of the responses to some of the questions should be examined for their significance. Example: answers to question 2, "Has the Job Performance Record benefited you or helped you?" indicated that 63 per cent of the employees interviewed felt that it had not. Yet a great many of them in answer to other questions said that they felt that it helped them to know how they were doing or that it would be used for promotions or references, and so on. They did not seem to perceive the Job Performance Record as being beneficial to them. This suggested that management had not made them aware that they were benefiting from the plan.

Another interesting finding occurred with question 4. "Do you know where you stand or how you're doing?" Approximately 78 per cent said they did, but many of these same employees did not feel that it was because of the Job Performance Record. The reasons given were many but the most frequently stated was that they had been given too few or no interviews by their foreman or that many of the entries made by the foreman were given unjustly so that such a record had little meaning.

The interviewer made other observations at the time which might be mentioned:

1. There is considerable variation in the way each foreman uses the Job Performance Record. Some foremen give only the minimum number of interviews (one every 6 months). Their employees do not seem to be as appreciative or interested in the program as the employees under a foreman who spends more time keeping the records and discussing them with the workers. His employees are more aware that they benefit from it.

2. Those employees who show the most disapproval have usually been with the company many years. In most cases they have progressed little in their jobs. Newcomers, in contrast, tend to think it is a good idea and are interested in it.

3. Almost all the employees show a lack of knowledge about its application, uses, etc. A great many of them would like to know more about it.

4. Many employees feel that the only items the company is really interested in are production and absenteeism. Others feel that they are

on jobs which do not permit much chance for their development or for the use of the Job Performance Record.

5. All employees were familiar with the foreman's "Red-Blue Book," the one in which he noted facts about each employee's work record. These facts were used by the foreman in determining his ratings and in conducting the interviews with his workers.

Of course the results of a survey such as this would vary with the specific company but it does give emphasis to certain universal findings for management:

1. The management that installs an employee appraisal system must spend much time and effort in educating employees about the purposes and benefits of the plan.

2. Foremen need a great deal of training in order to have the plan used as management wishes.

3. Any survey for the evaluation of employees' opinions of an employee appraisal system should be made by persons in whom the employees have enough confidence to give their honest answers.

Experience indicates that the employees' reactions to and values of a rating program vary with the type of plan, its purposes, the way it is explained, and how it is used or misused.

When foremen conduct the post-rating interview

Most foremen find it difficult to discuss an employee's rating or appraisal with him. It is embarrassing to tell a subordinate to his face that he lacks personality or a sense of humor. The foreman realizes that when a man is informed that he lacks "vision" or a "dynamic personality," he is likely to feel baffled rather than enlightened.

When one foreman was told that he should conduct post-appraisal interviews with his employees, he answered: "I'll be darned if I'll do that. I'll take the time to sit down and rate each one of my men, but I won't discuss the ratings with the man. When I tried to do the reviews last year, it took me several months to get back to normal with each man." Many foremen feel that it is useless to talk to a man about his personality and shortcomings unless it is possible to give each deserving employee a raise in pay right after the interview. As one foreman stated: "If he does not deserve a raise in pay, you can't convince him without a long argument." Some foremen feel silly when they sit down and try to talk to a worker as though the interview were a special occasion. They believe that if the worker deserves coaching, he should have it given to him as soon as the need arises—not once or twice a year on a special occasion.

The list of excuses given by foremen for procrastination in conducting a post-appraisal interview are many:

The employee who is counseled may react badly, he may argue, he may be upset emotionally, he may be made to feel insecure, or he may become conceited about his own importance.

Some employees will tell others the complimentary content of the merit rating interview and thus provoke jealousy on the part of fellow workers.

Foremen and lower level executives are not sufficiently skillful to counsel their subordinates.

These objections are justified. Few supervisors know how to cope with an employee's resistance when it is shown by tense silence, obviously emotionalized but with resentment repressed rather than expressed openly. Nor do they like to deal with counter arguments.

The personal relationship between a supervisor and a subordinate is similar to that between two good friends—neither mentions to the other certain touchy subjects. Most foremen do not know how to conduct an effective interview of this kind. Some companies find it easier to spend money necessary to hire specialists such as psychologists and consultants to do it for the foremen. And yet few hired specialists are in so strong a position for counseling as the man's own boss.

The hired specialists, in time, discover that an employee's behavior will not be changed until he is involved in action—in the performance of a real task whose outcome will be significant to him. The most meaningful action plan to an employee is one set up under the guidance or direction of a senior who is responsible for the work being performed.

Why personality trait rating plans are of limited value

The one type of merit rating found most deficient even though it is still widely used is the kind that rates traits such as personality, initiative, honesty, and so on. Experience of executives who have used this kind of rating device shows rather definitely that it is impractical to try to measure a man's character and personality traits on a numerical scale.

Trait-rating has a number of serious shortcomings. There is little or no scientific basis for deciding that certain personality traits are essential for good performance on a given job. The traits chosen for rating are selected by "common sense" reasoning, not by statistical validation. Extended experience in life situations often controverts the common sense variety of reasoning. Common sense, for example, may cause one to assume that a top executive needs a high degree of tact and skill in public relations. Much evidence to the contrary is available. Some of the most successful corporation presidents are low in this trait.

The best evidence available concerning the weaknesses of trait rating was developed by a committee of executives, researchers, and consultants in a four-year research program for the General Electric Company. The main conclusion from the research in regard to this question was the following:

> *You cannot base your development activity on "personality traits."*
>
> We have no idea what "personality traits" are needed to make a good manager. Men of widely divergent personalities are successful managers. Therefore, we are wrong when we appraise people and select people on the basis of "traits" which we cannot define or measure.
>
> Furthermore, if we did establish a "prototype" ideal manager, saying "We want only managers of this personality pattern," we would be in danger of pressing toward uniformity and conformity which are not only undesirable but dangerous.
>
> We must, therefore, focus on the *work* that a man does, and do all of our appraising, development, selection on the basis of observed work methods and performance.[3]

The main positive conclusion from the failure of systems of ratings that purport to measure personality traits is that employee appraisals should stress work performance.

APPRAISALS FOR COACHING PURPOSES

Merit rating systems that involve the use of an elaborate printed scale for evaluating personality do not encourage the "judge" to examine the factors that are most important to the employer—getting the work done. After all, if management finds that the employee is not getting his work done, the employee needs coaching about the work and his procedures rather than an evaluation of his personality traits. Generally, merit rating plans of the trait variety have been used mostly by personnel workers. Appraisal plans for coaching purposes are used mainly by executives above the average supervisory level.

The trend toward the use of formal appraisal systems for coaching purposes has increased. Executives do some informal coaching of their subordinates every day. The main value of a formal appraisal system

---

[3] Moorhead Wright, "Development of Men," in Papers from the 38th Annual Meeting, American Association of Advertising Agencies, New York.

Executive Appraisals

(Reaction to a conference discussion of executive rating)

I listed all his qualities,
I measured them both fore and aft—
His prayers and his frivolities,
His immaturities, his craft.

I put them down upon a form
Replete with every latest symbol,
Reduced the angles to a norm
And hid a pea beneath each thimble;

Then plied the statistician's art,
His concepts, ratios and weightings.
But he spoke warmly from the heart,
"A fig for all your pompous ratings!

"A twinkle in my father's eye,
A moon in May, a moment's passion,
A woman's pain—and there was I,
A unique creature in my fashion.

"All your psychologist's analysis
Tells nothing of my dreams last night.
It's just an infantile paralysis,
A play-pen. Learn to stand upright,

"To know me, use me, man to man,
To judge me wholly. In your eyes
I'll soon discover if you can,
For all your knowledge, still be wise."
—Anon.

SOURCE: *The Management Review* (American Management Association, Inc.), December, 1952, p. 776.

is that the executive is encouraged to think more systematically about each subordinate and to review with him all those factors that might enable him to do a better job.[4]

Several investigators of appraisal systems have pointed out the difficulties in trying to be judicial in appraising people and advocated the use of a plan that gauges "management by objectives" rather than by judgment of the personal worth of a subordinate. Certain large com-

---

[4] See Virgil K. Rowland, "From the Thoughtful Businessman," *Harvard Business Review*, September-October 1957, p. 140.

Appraising the Employee

panies such as General Mills and General Electric are experimenting with different methods that implement this concept.

The first stage in the procedure used in this new approach is a simple statement, conversational, of employee work responsibilities rather than a formal job description. From this the boss and the subordinate establish the subordinate's "targets" or short-term (about six months) performance goals. At the conclusion of the six-month period, the subordinate makes *his own* appraisal of what he has accomplished relative to the target which he had set. The boss and subordinate then hold an "interview" to discuss the record, evaluate the weaknesses and strengths in what has been done, and set new targets for the next six months. In this procedure the subordinate is an *active* figure in the system, and the major difference between this approach and the conventional trait-rating technique is that it "shifts the emphasis from *appraisal* to *analysis*." There is also a shift of emphasis from the past to *performance in relation to work goals* in the future, and this serves a more constructive end than judicial evaluations of the person. The personality of the subordinate is not a central issue, but the prospects for self-development through work are greatly enhanced.[5]

Coaching by the executive provides a meaningful method for letting a subordinate know where he stands in the company and for discussing specific ways in which he can become more effective in his job.

Many executives who believe in coaching would like to improve their skill in doing it. The intensity of interest on the part of executives is indicated by the experience of the American Management Association. The AMA reports that whenever it announces a seminar on appraisal reviews, it is flooded with applicants. Another barometer of management interest on the subject is the increase of management consulting firms who have entered the field.[6]

In an appraisal review session for coaching purposes the boss and the subordinate conduct a comprehensive give-and-take discussion of the subordinate's performance on the job, relations with fellow workers, standing with his superiors, and all strengths and weaknesses in regard to the work. The session ends with a summary of what the junior manager or subordinate can do to improve his performance. Great skill is needed by the executive who conducts a soul-searching discussion of the subordinate's performance and how he can improve it. Yet the practice is spreading as more top management men see it as a help in coaching junior executives. Before this interview takes place, the boss

---

[5] See Douglas McGregor, "An Uneasy Look at Performance Appraisal," *Harvard Business Review*, May-June 1957. See also *Personnel Management Abstracts*, Summer Issue 1957.

[6] See "Executive Coaching Catches On," *Business Week*, March 9, 1957.

Appraising the Employee

usually talks with and gets suggestions from other executives to improve his appraisal and recommendations.

The committee or group approach to appraisal review systems is gaining. The typical executive does not want to be the only person to evaluate a man. In the committee approach, the group consists of personnel specialists and senior executives, including the man's immediate supervisor. They hold an appraising session, essentially constructive in spirit. Later, the immediate supervisor sits down with his subordinate and presents the group's findings and suggestions. The two men then discuss ways in which improvements can be made in the performance. The committee approach eliminates tendencies toward personal prejudice. It also takes a great load off the supervisor. Instead of saying "I think . . . ," he can say, "We believe. . . ."

What goes on in a coaching interview varies with the individuals involved. The typical executive usually starts the interview with a review of the subordinate's strong points.

Then he gradually moves into areas where the ratee could stand improvement. The executive will, if he is skilled, let the subordinate do most of the talking, let him tell what is wrong with himself. The executive adds comments of approval or disapproval, or makes recommendations.

Skilled interviewers use the "turnback." When the ratee asks a question, the rater turns the question back to the ratee before he tries to give an answer.

Here are four examples of turnback:

1. Ratee: *But how does my rating stack up with the other employees in the department?*
   Rater: *How do you feel you compare with the others?*
2. Ratee: *But I try hard all the time. What can I do to improve?*
   Rater: *What do you think you might do to improve?*
3. Ratee: *Have I been doing any better lately? Do you think my work is improving?*
   Rater: *Do you feel you have been improving?*
4. Ratee: *I would like some time to get to be a secretary. How should I go about it?*
   Rater: *Do you have any ideas as to what you might do?*

When the person rated responds with strong feeling, the interviewer does not give a logical explanation. Instead, he encourages the ratee to talk out his feelings and thereby clarify his thinking so that he can develop his own solution. If pent-up feelings have been released, he may become more receptive to a logical explanation.

These permissive techniques do not mean that an employee should

Appraising the Employee

not become aware of his weaknesses and needed improvements. On the contrary, the processes of making him aware are achieved by different techniques. The permissive procedure of the kind that uses the turnback is designed to enable the ratee to discover and to accept the criticism rather than hear it given but refuse its acceptance.[7]

Some executives can or at least think they can do effective coaching. When they do, the executive and his subordinate try to agree on what areas of performance are poor and what the subordinate will do to bring about improvement. At the next appraisal, or perhaps sooner, they will meet to see how the improvement program is progressing.

Recommendations for effective post-appraisal interviews

Experience of management men and researchers indicates that the effectiveness of interviews can be increased by means of the following procedures:

1. Do not tell a man how or in what respects he should change himself. Instead, ask him questions about his work responsibilities, his objectives, and his methods of work. Use the job-centered rather than a man-centered approach.

2. Interviews should not begin with a review of what is wrong with a man or his work. Let him suggest the first topics for discussion so that he may feel that his interests are being recognized. Always preserve a man's dignity.

3. Stress the team approach. Discuss the relationships with other members of the company and procedures for getting work done by bringing those people into the program who are or should be participants.

4. Some executives and others who do post-appraisal interviews find that going through an interview themselves with their own chiefs helps them improve their interviews with others. To be effective with others, it is necessary to be relaxed and self confident. The man who has experienced an appraisal interview himself usually improves his manner with his subordinates.

5. The coaching type of interview should not involve a review of the advisee's present salary or promises of reward for the future. The focus of discussion is the employee's job, not his pay. This procedure is the

---

[7] Bernard J. Covner, "The Communication of Merit Ratings: A Philosophy and a Method," *Personnel*, American Management Association, Inc., September 1953.

Appraising the Employee

opposite of that used in merit ratings for administrative purposes. In many merit rating programs, salary is discussed. Some companies use merit ratings in deciding whether to grant or withhold raises. In many companies the rating system has this meaning for the employees. When all appraisals are made in the same month of the year, the appraisal date becomes the time when every employee expects a raise. Hence, some managements conduct their appraisal of each employee about two months prior to the anniversary date of his employment. This spreads the administrative task throughout the year and prevents the expectation of an increase being given to most employees at the same time.

Even though a merit rating system is well planned, it often raises extra difficulties as in the case of the worker who must be discharged. Too often, a poor employee is given a raise in the hope that the raise will improve his work. Quality and output in work frequently do not agree with the salary increases given an employee under a so-called merit rating plan.

6. When an employee raises the question of pay during the coaching interview, the coach should point out that that subject must be treated in another type of interview. An appointment for the purpose can be made. During the coaching interview, the coach should stress satisfactions from the work in the "professional" sense. Doctors, teachers, and other professional workers are likely to continue to improve their work and abilities even though financial rewards do not follow immediately. Rewards are by-products of good work. As in the professions, most intelligent workers in business improve their abilities because they increase their respect for themselves, not for money alone.

7. To be effective as a coach or counselor, the executive must be held in high esteem by the subordinate. If the subordinate merely acts in a respectful manner because the superior holds a higher rank, the coaching benefits will be negligible.

8. Executives who do systematic coaching as in post-appraisal interviews realize that much skill is essential. This kind of interview cannot attain its full benefits when the executive acts in his usual authoritarian manner. If he is to learn to respect the special contributions that can be made through permissive techniques, he may have to develop a new kind of respect for himself as a skilled counselor, diagnostician, and teacher. The executive coach can get self-appraisal values out of the interview, too. He does this when he asks, "What can I do to help you make your job go better?" He reports that few hesitate to tell him frankly.

9. Use "playback." Ask him to state his ideas as to the conclusions and plans that were developed during the interview. If he wants to make promises that he cannot or is not likely to fulfill by the time of

the next coaching session, it is necessary to help him set goals that are attainable.

10. Whatever appraisal and coaching program may be used, let all employees know about its nature and its purposes. Employees should be given the information *before* the plan is put into effect. One bank management made the mistake of hiring an interviewing organization that had its interviewers "shop" each teller in the bank in order to rate the teller. When management presented the "shoppers'" reports to the tellers, they felt resentful. Management had failed to be aboveboard with them. Cleverness cannot be justified when it also implies insincerity.

Summary

Any rating or appraisal system is of little practical benefit if the results are buried in company files and employees never find out how their performance is measuring up against management's expectations. The communication of evaluations after they are made is, however, a more difficult process than is generally recognized. Currently, merit rating without emphasis on post-appraisal is most commonly used for administrative purposes: to allocate wage and salary increases and to determine fitness for promotion and transfer. The appraisal procedure so used remains one of contributing to judgment rather than to stimulation of the employee.

Thus far, the focus of attention in merit rating has been on evaluation of the individual, but progressive managements are learning how to communicate the appraisals to the employee in terms of job performance coaching.

Companies vary in their use of appraisal systems. Some companies make appraisal reviews for clerical employees and executives but not for engineers and research staff members. Some have a program for getting the ratings but give interviews about them only to employees who ask for them.

In a few concerns, the junior executive may not only see the appraisal on himself but he also helps to write it. In one branch of our armed services, officers are appraised but the officer sees the report only when it is bad.[8]

Many executives do not write out any appraisal but conduct an interview in which the individual being appraised is asked how he himself thinks he is doing. The employee, in some cases, makes a written appraisal of himself in advance of the interview as the basis for the discus-

---

[8] See "Executive Coaching Catches On," *Business Week*, March 9, 1957.

sion. People who are given such a wide-open opportunity might be expected to overrate themselves. Actually, the majority underrate their own performance and usually mention, besides flaws in themselves and their work that the boss sees, others that have not occurred to him. This method of interviewing gives the superior ample opportunity to point out to the man where he is doing a better job than he himself imagines. The executive also gets helpful suggestions for himself when he asks: "What can I do to help you do your job better?" Employees frequently give frank and helpful suggestions to the executive who is so mature that employees know he can take them without resentment. Fortunately, the percentage of mature executives in America is on the increase. The novice who enters business today is likely to be surprised and pleased by the number of executives who are openminded about themselves as well as sincerely interested in helping the man with growth potential get ahead.

COLLATERAL READINGS

For All Students

Mahoney, Thomas A., *et al.*, "Applying Yardsticks to Management," *Personnel*, American Management Association, Inc., May 1957. Reports findings from a St. Paul study that dealt with management appraisal.

Soik, Nile, "Employee Performance Review," *Journal of the American Society of Training Directors*, November 1958. Describes difficulties in conducting the performance review and offers suggestions for improving procedures.

For Advanced Students

Maier, N. R. F., *The Appraisal Interview*. New York: John Wiley & Sons, 1958. Discusses three kinds of appraisal interviews and offers valuable suggestions.

Zander, Alvin, and John Gyr, "Changing Attitudes Toward a Merit Rating System," *Personnel Psychology*, Winter, 1955. This study deals with the effects of supervisors' attempts to change negative attitudes of subordinates to positive ones.

For Men in Business

Blake, R. R., "Re-examination of Performance Appraisal," *Advanced Management*, July 1958. Recommends telling the employee not only where he stands but also how to alter his situation; appraisal is a two-way street.

Grela, J. J., and F. B. Martin, "The Counseling Interview—Crux of a Man's Development," *Personnel Journal*, November 1958. Communication of the findings and gaining the employee's acceptance of the evaluation are regarded as the real keys to motivation through counseling.

1. Why should the term "test" not be applied to a rating scale?
2. Differentiate between merit rating and job evaluation.
3. What are the primary objectives of rating systems from the standpoint of management?
4. Do employees feel that it is more effective to have their own superiors do the counseling interviews, or hired specialists?
5. Describe the Gerald H. Shaw study of factory employees' reactions to an employee rating plan.
6. What was the main conclusion in the General Electric Company study concerning the weaknesses of trait rating?
7. Why is it difficult for foremen to conduct a post-rating interview?
8. What is the main value for the executive of an appraisal system used for coaching purposes?
9. Differentiate between the trait rating technique and the newer appraisal method.
10. Why is a group approach to appraisal review systems more effective than an individual approach?
11. Why do skilled interviewers use the turnback when talking with ratees?
12. What should be the focus of the post-appraisal interview for job performance coaching in contrast to merit rating interviews for administrative purposes?
13. How should "playback" be used for an effective post-appraisal interview?"
14. How should the question of pay be handled during a coaching interview?
15. Of all the ideas presented in the chapter, which ones were of interest or value to you?
16. What did the chapter contribute toward your future relations with (a) the men who supervise you, (b) the employees whom you may supervise?

PROBLEMS AND PROJECTS

For All Students

1. To appreciate the difficulties in conducting the post-appraisal interview, rate a friend on a rating form. Try to conduct an appropriate post-appraisal interview. Let some observers evaluate your skills and suggest improvements.
2. Have several persons rate themselves. Have acquaintances rate them on the same traits. How do the two kinds of ratings differ? On what kinds of traits do individuals seem to overrate or underrate themselves?

For Advanced Students

3. Examine several rating scales for traits such as initiative and personality. Classify the traits as to whether they are objective or refer to reactions to persons. Which kind seems to be the more useful in evaluating an employee?

4. Write anecdotal descriptions of a person, descriptions that seem to to be characteristic of the individual. Show your descriptions to someone who knows the individual. Are your anecdotes truly descriptive in their opinion?

For Men in Business

5. Think of several executives whom you know. Describe the manner that is natural for each when he coaches a subordinate. Do you want the coach to adopt a special manner or to be natural in the counseling interview? Why?

6. Industrial Psychology, Inc., 515 Madison Ave., New York 22, N. Y., publishes a rating scale which has "bias" statements to show whether the rater is overly lenient and consistent in his estimates. National norms are available for the scale. Compare this type of scale with the one used in some company whose rating system you know.

M OST STUDENTS OF BUSINESS AND YOUNG PEOPLE WHO PLAN TO enter the business world think in terms of an office job. This is in line with the trend in the distribution changes of our working population. Back in 1945, there were 21.6 million blue collar workers and only 17.5 million in white collar jobs, but in 1955–56, white collar workers in the United States displaced production workers as the biggest single group in the working population. Some firms such as insurance companies and banks have 90 to 100 per cent of their employees in the office work classification.

As a result, the number of people in office management has increased greatly even though some office managers do not function under that exact title. Many firms are so small that they do not need the full-time services of an office manager—his duties may be performed under the title of vice president, secretary, auditor, chief clerk, personnel manager, or something else. In spite of the importance of the job, many who earn their living as office managers dislike the title. They associate it with the old "chief clerk" concept and the "green eye-shade." They prefer to be called a "Director of Administration," "Auditor," "Assistant to the President," or some title of recognized prestige. Every office must provide itself with the functions of the office manager. Even though he may not do detailed office methods study work or have major executive responsibilities, the company management must observe, carry out, and provide for efficient ways of filing, billing, and checking of records. Someone must

19   Office Management

be responsible for taking care of all the numerous operations performed in an office. The office manager, whatever his title, is in charge of clerical and related services.

Office management responsibilities that must be performed in every company are the following:

1. Planning and supervising of office services such as filing, typing, and stenographic services
2. Preparing and submitting reports to management and governmental bureaus
3. Hiring office workers
4. Training office workers
5. Promotion and transfer of office workers
6. The control of office costs, the budget for office expenses
7. Purchase of adequate office equipment
8. Development of efficient supervision in the office
9. Carrying out the personnel policies of the company as they affect the office staff.

Many of these functions involve personnel management. If the company has an organized personnel program, some of these responsibilities will be shared with the personnel manager or carried out in cooperation with him.

Obviously, a system of records, reports, controls, and forecasts must be directed by an office executive in order that the business can be transacted in an orderly manner. The office manager's job involves two types of responsibilities. As a *line manager*, he hires and discharges, gets production out, and worries about the thousands of details necessary to keep the office going. He is also a *staff man* whose reports and forecasts affect, directly or indirectly, the decisions of top management. His office is both an operations and an information center.

In many companies, the office manager is likely to be an important contact man to the community. He, to many people, represents the company because he is the executive whom many people call on when they apply for a job, want to sell a product, or get a donation for a local charity. His personality contributes to and, in some cases, represents the company's personality.

The "red tape" mind

"Red tape" is usually defined as the excessive making of records in operating a business—too much paper. It means making extra copies of letters and reports and storing them where they may be available in future years. It includes the unnecessary use of date stamps and the initialing of papers and reports by every member of the organization who might have a direct or a remote interest in the content. It may even bog down a business because of its costs.

According to one study, the average company maintains at least 2,000 pieces of paper for every person on its payroll. Processing these records at a conservative estimate of 20 cents each creates an overhead cost of $400 per year for paperwork alone for every man on the payroll.[1]

Fundamentally, red tape is a state of mind, a kind of mentality that insists on self-protection rather than an emphasis on constructive action. The alert office manager must fight it in himself and in others.

Much of it develops from special or one-time needs. A vice president, for example, asks for a special report on the date when the warehouse windows were washed and the amount of washing detergent used. The

Executive in a Blizzard

SOURCE: *Bank Building and Equipment Corporation. Courtesy Krupnick & Associates, Inc.*

---

[1] See *Super Market Merchandising,* September 1958, p. 131.

clerk who writes the report asks him whether he would like to have monthly and quarterly reports on the subject and the typical vice president says "Yes." The reports continue to be prepared and sent to the executive for years, in many cases long after they have any usefulness for anyone. It is too easy for clerical workers and executives to continue making records simply because "We've always done it that way."

One cause for red tape is the new executive. He usually wants to inform himself about every aspect of his job. He asks for special reports. He may even have consultants come in to tell him about accounting controls that are needed. Soon a flood of facts washes over his desk and leaves him gasping for air. But the reports keep coming. Eventually he must decide whether he should become an absorber of information or an active, effective executive. Some corporation presidents are expected to read and understand hundreds of reports every month, many dealing with trivialities. A review and housecleaning of all reports is necessary more than once a year. Even though the making of hundreds of reports may be eliminated in a large company during an annual housecleaning, the overload may be evident six months later. Daily supervision is essential. One man, usually the office manager, should have authority for records control.

The office memorandum

The office memorandum is universally used as a medium of communication. When used intelligently, it serves its purposes well but it may also hinder true communication by management. As one management leader has stated:

> Recently I was discussing with an executive a number of things that should have been done several months before, some of which had now developed into crises. In great agitation he called for his general manager and asked for an explanation. The general manager went to his own office and quickly returned with a handful of memoranda.
>
> These memoranda, addressed to various members of the organization, contained instructions to take care of the items in question. Almost smugly the general manager put the memoranda on the chief executive's desk with an expression suggesting, "There, I have taken care of them." His attitude seemed to be that the writing of a memorandum had disposed of the matter.
>
> That is the great danger of memoranda. There is some kind of feeling that when you have dictated instructions to somebody the job is done. Unfortunately people do not always do what they are instructed to do in memoranda, and frequently they are not able to without further clarification and assistance.

There is another aspect to memoranda that is a rather interesting commentary on human nature. We are inclined to speak much more harshly and dictatorially in a memorandum than face to face.

It is virtually impossible to cover all aspects of a problem in a memorandum. Almost invariably the memorandum is written to the wrong person, and others affected are not adequately informed. The result is friction, misunderstanding, and, many times, hard feelings.[2]

Typewritten reports to executives

Every college graduate who enters business is likely to find it necessary to write reports for executives. Executives are deluged by letters, reports, and other typed and printed materials that bear on their work.

Unfortunately for them, it is probable that more than half of that time spent in reading is wasted because the material the executive is required to read is of little value to him in carrying out his executive responsibilities. He realizes this and therefore skims and skips as a means toward getting his work done.

This means that a key problem in office communication is getting executives to read things. In one company, for example, the research department sends a detailed monthly report of work done to its members. The director tested the report's readership by sandwiching a fake report, decidedly offbeat, in the volume. It was meant to be quite funny but he got not a single comment about it.

In another firm a rather complicated letter on a company matter was sent to some 40 members of the company's management men. In it was buried the statement, "If you have read this, wire collect and we'll send you $5." Fewer than half a dozen readers cashed in.[3]

These incidents mean that anyone who wants to communicate with busy executives should put forth extra effort to make reports inviting and readable.

The first page of most multipage reports is given over to "background material." This usually is well known to the reader. To save the reader's time, the purposes of the reports should be itemized.

In the body of the report, long paragraphs should be broken into keyed paragraphs of a few lines. Important paragraphs should be indented and underscored. Sections and paragraphs should be numbered for easy reference. Headings should be numbered in order. Underscoring should be used for a few key ideas only.

A report that is well written invites reading. To invite reading, solid

---

[2] Lawrence A. Appley, "Management Enemy Number One," *Management News,* American Management Association, Inc., May 1957.

[3] See Harwood F. Merrill, "The Listening Post," *Management News,* American Management Association, Inc., October 1957.

pages of typed material can be broken into paragraphs of different lengths of lines. Pages should have a varied rather than a monotonous appearance.

At the end, a brief summary of points covered and recommendations for the action should be stated. Executives like concise reports that recommend action.

"*Didn't they teach you to make decisions at business school, Hobart?*" SOURCE: *by Joseph Serrano,* The Management Review *(July 1956). Courtesy American Management Association, Inc.*

In writing, it is important to realize that management men are not interested in what someone thinks. They want to read what the writer knows. Executives also like reports which present both sides of a problem rather than a onesided statement of a preconceived theory or opinion. Extravagant statements, unsupported by facts, and designed to "prove" a preconceived idea are anathema.

If the report quotes published authorities or sources of data, it should be documented by means of footnotes. Exhibits of tables, copies of questionnaires, and similar supporting material should be placed in an appendix or in a separate binder.

Few college students have developed their potentials for writing attractive, meaty reports. They still present term reports in pages of solid typewritten material. Worst of all, too many have not acquired the habit of reading and correcting every page before it is submitted. At least the misspelled words might be corrected!

The office manager deals with people

A description of an office manager's job usually fails to stress sufficiently his human relations functions. However, anyone who works in an office soon becomes aware of the importance of its people. He must, for example, sense the bad feelings that often exist between the girls who work in the office and those who work in the shop. The ones who work in the shop probably have less social prestige and make more money. The office girls may show the friction between members of the two groups by means of evidence such as a handmade sign placed on a washroom door: "WOMEN—OFFICE ONLY."

Status symbols are tremendously important in the office world. Secretaries play a key role. Some companies call the secretaries of department heads "executive assistants." Women employees who perform identical chores for lesser executives or employees are merely "stenographers." Equipment may also be significant. Members of the executive stratum are likely to be the only persons who have electric model typewriters. And the executive who has two secretaries is a VIPI, a "Very Important Person, Indeed." That, of course, means that the fortunate executive has the problem of supervising two women so that they get along amicably. One executive solved the problem by inducing his company to construct a wall between the work spaces of his warring secretaries!

The selection of stenographers for secretarial positions is fraught with many hazards for the office manager as reported in this example:

> The secretary of one of our executives left rather suddenly. I needed someone to fill in quickly so assigned Grace, one of the general office stenographers. I specified that it would be temporary as she did not have the required qualifications in shorthand and statistical typing. When I was able to hire a qualified person, Grace stirred up quite a fuss and complained that she should have the job. She even told some of the girls that I told her the assignment would be permanent. So she quit. Unfortunately some of her friends here believed her and the situation has caused a lot of dissension among the other girls.

Typical grievances of office workers

When one office manager was asked to state his biggest problem, he answered: "I'd say my biggest problem is to get people to work together. The girls seem to squabble a lot over trivial things. You can get them to work individually all right, but for some reason they don't want to work together. They get ideas that one girl is getting a bit more pay or recognition and then they get miffed. There isn't as much trouble with the men in this respect."

The alert office supervisor recognizes that, regardless of the seriousness of an employee's grievance, the way the employee feels about the grievance should dictate the amount of consideration he must give to it. If he gives an employee the brushoff or makes light of a grievance, he may intensify other dissatisfactions.

He cannot express indifference, but neither can he remove all the causes for grievance. There will always be, in most companies, certain salary differences which some employees will consider unfair.

There will always be some human relations situations that certain employees will construe as favoritism.

Temperatures in the office cannot be adjusted to the satisfaction of everyone.

Office surroundings are likely to be drab to a few employees.

And somebody will always want to take his vacation at the same time that somebody else wants to take his.

The most common grievance is the pay. The office manager is constantly besieged by employees who believe that they are underpaid. Surprisingly, however, a survey of turnover among office workers in 25 companies in the Philadelphia area showed that of the 1,186 employees who had left the employing company, only 129 had succumbed to the lure of higher salaries.[4]

One office worker summed up the problem of grievances as follows:

> During the past four summers I have been employed by Office Temporaries Incorporated, a New York firm that supplies temporary office help to New York business firms. While in their employ, I worked for three days to three months in the offices of approximately fifteen different companies.
>
> One of the very first and, I feel, the most basic lesson I learned from these experiences is that *every* office has problems. I have yet to work in an office in which everyone was in perfect harmony. There was always at least one employee with a complaint, a petty jealousy, or some frustration. If all employees could understand this basic fact, most offices would operate more pleasantly. I learned, through observation, to weigh in proper perspective the various advantages and disadvantages encountered in any working situation.

The office neurotic

For supervisors in American offices, neuroticism among female workers is likely to be an especially difficult problem. Dr. Sylvia A. Sorkin in an

---

[4] See *Office Executive* (National Office Management Association), July 1957, p. 38.

address before a national conference of the National Office Management Association gave results of a questionnaire sent to office managers. Approximately 900 responded. She told the conference delegates that from a listing of nine common office management "headaches" mentioned in the survey, the problem of dealing with neurotic female workers was rated second only in importance to the problem of securing well-trained clerical workers.

Although a third of the executives who gave their opinions said that securing trained help was their biggest problem, nearly a quarter of them ranked the neurotic female as their most difficult problem. Neurotic male workers, on the other hand, got top billing as a problem by only 3 per cent of the executives.[5]

The neurotic (see Chapter 25) is found in the factory and the classroom as well as in the office. Somehow he seems to stand out more in the office than in the factory. Perhaps it is because most office workers can talk with their associates more easily in the office than in a typical noisy factory. At any rate, the office neurotic is a prominent member of most offices. He appears in many styles.

He (she) may be the chronic griper who interprets every incident as a threat to himself. He is unhappy with the world because he is unhappy about himself. He sees evil or danger in every happening. He is not sufficiently mature to view his work situation, the company, or his fellow employees in objective manner. He (she) may be a hypochondriac who constantly talks about his health. His desk drawers have bottles and boxes of medicines and pills. The weather outside and the air in the office are so unhealthy that he has numerous colds, ailments, and oncoming ills. He can't do his work because he doesn't feel well. Another headache and so on and on.

He (she) may be a projectionist, one who ascribes to others or the external world repressed mental processes which are not recognized as being of personal origin. A common example is the office worker who borrows money from a friend, fails to pay it back, and then subconsciously discovers that he really need not pay it because the person who loaned it to him is too despicable to deserve repayment! Some women employees also accuse the boss of immoral conduct because of their own repressed impulses toward him.

The *office wolf* is not usually classified as a neurotic but he is a similar nuisance. If he is not too aggressive, the girls in the office may enjoy his threats—at least he relieves the monotony! If he is a persistent threat, he disturbs the work atmosphere and must be transferred to an all-male

---

[5] Condensed from a release from the National Office Management Association, 1954.

group or put into his proper place by an executive who calls him into his office and bluntly lays down the customs expected in a productive work environment. Of course the executive may also have to tell certain girls in the office that their attire seems chosen "to bring out the beast in the male," and that they must reduce their efforts to show off their physical charms.

Generally, the office neurotic utilizes his maladjustments to gain certain personal ends, to obtain answers to psychological needs such as recognition and attention. Sometimes the behavior also indicates that the office neurotic is trying to get other employees to do his work for him. Most normal employees recognize this subterfuge and simply say: "Sorry Mabel, I haven't time to do your work too. You just go ahead and do as I do when I have a headache—work harder and the headache will disappear."

Office customs and cliques

Each office has its own customs about matters such as attire, coffee breaks, extra time off from work without loss of pay, participation in the grapevine, and the amount of work to be done. The employees may have one title for the supervisor when speaking in his presence and another, less conventional but more humorous, when not in his presence.

As in all groups, cliques develop. Here are comments from three office supervisors:

1. Most of the workers under my supervision are women. I have relatively little trouble because they get to know each other intimately and eat and take coffee breaks together. This causes some problems because they stick together against me when they want something. Also, if they get into any of their silly women's fights, they stab each other at their weak points. This isn't good and is hard to control. However, they usually work together pretty well, but sometimes fight over who is doing more work, or trying to take authority.

2. I really have quite a bit of trouble with the thirty girls who work on the bookkeeping machines in our bank. They don't want to do any more work than they have to. They want to get done so they can leave as near three o'clock as possible. If they're held up by the check sorters, they get all upset. And if a check has been mis-filed and is out of order, they are ready to quit. The working quarters aren't as good as they could be, but with the space we have the layout is as good as possible. They all have new machines and all the latest equipment. Only about half of them come to me if they have a problem. The rest just complain to other girls and spend their time griping in the restroom. I guess the low rate of pay has a lot to do with it, but I assumed that they understood the pay situation when they took the job.

Office Management

3. There's a clique going on right now that's really a headache. It's that switchboard. It's the smallest work area in the office but it gives me the most trouble. Mrs. McF. works it full time, and she gets two coffee breaks and lunch time like every one else. The girls have their own groups that they like to go out with, and since there are two shifts going out at different times we have trouble getting girls to take over for Mrs. McF. Two girls, Edith and Laura, have been assigned to take over for her, but when one of them is out or wants a different lunch hour, things get all balled up. We've tried all sorts of plans to smooth out the problem without success. One of the causes for the problem is the fact that the girls are so anxious to be with their own clique members during lunch that they refuse to take over for Mrs. McF.

Office managers take these customs and cliques as a normal part of business life. People work together as human beings, not as mechanical robots. The function of the office manager is not that of trying to make perfect persons out of typical people. He simply does his best to direct the efforts of the typical employees and to encourage the development of the potentially superior few. He prefers that work gets done in a reasonably pleasant atmosphere. Of course, if the work relations become a means for the office politician to gain his ends, management is anxious to correct the influence of undesirable cliques.

Office politics

This term is applied to the intrigues, spying, and tale-bearing of individuals or cliques who seek illicitly to gain privilege, control or advancement for themselves. Every management must be alert in regard to this kind of chicanery. It may appear in hostility toward certain employees, partiality by a supervisor, or inequitable salary schedules. Sometimes the office manager becomes a target of the individuals or factions that seek to control him. They may spread rumors about his personal life or seek to undermine his authority. If he merely goes to lunch with a certain clerk or drives to and from work with him, the office politicians will spread the rumor that his companion is the fair-haired boy of the boss.

Differences in pay often furnish grist for the mill of the office politician. Many office workers know the pay rates of their associates. No sensible management today assumes that salaries of employees below the supervisory level are kept confidential. When a department head tells a new employee that she should keep her rate of pay confidential, it usually remains confidential until her first lunch hour.

Sometimes a new employee is an innocent victim of office politics. If, for example, a girl is discharged for incompetence but is well liked by

Advice on how to succeed in office politics is virtually taboo. The personnel officer never explains the political setup when he gives you the orientation spiel. You will find no guidance in the employee's manual. You may get clandestine tips from your associates, but they are so inextricably entangled themselves that their counsel hardly can be unbiased.

There just is no mentor who can say, "Play your office politics according to my simple rules, and you are bound to succeed."

Yet there are some useful warnings that can steer you away from common errors and thus indirectly help you become a succesful, even if unwilling, office politician.

According to experienced hands who are willing to talk, these six admonitions are sound in principle:

Don't let politics get you down. Angry frustration simply makes you look querulous and ineffective. Try to detect the political realities around you, and then accept them as you do the climate. You are not required to condone the climate, but you must live with it.

Don't blame politics for all your troubles. Politics has a bad name because it frequently is a scapegoat. Every bungler, misfit and incompetent is quick to excuse his shortcomings by blaming "politics." Remember that in most organizations politics is less a hostile cabal than the normal mode of getting things done. All your troubles may boil down to just one basic difficulty—your failure to catch on to the local rules of the game.

Don't be an angler or a fixer. This may look profitable. For the long haul, though, it isn't. Angle players and fixers usually are suspected of making their gains by back stabbing and hence are thought untrustworthy. You can't afford such a reputation, especially if you don't deserve it.

Don't lose sight of the ball. Good workmanship and good politics have the same objective: success of the business. Any maneuvers directed at other goals are dirty politics, likely to hurt the business and you, too.

Don't buy a raw deal. A few organizations have no politics but dirty politics. In such a situation, if you are sure you are appraising it fairly, you face a practical and ethical decision. You can refuse to play and go under. Or you can bow to the ground rules, get into the game and play rough. Since neither alternative is satisfactory, your best answer to a messy political setup is to get out.

SOURCE: "How to Play Office Politics," *Changing Times,* The Kiplinger Magazine, December 1955, p. 18.

the other girls, the girls may decide that no one should be allowed to take her place. They may ostracize the replacement.

Similarly, when one employee is given a promotion over another who is better liked by the employees, they may carry on intrigues against the chosen person. Bitterness over situations such as these may start office politics going—it may even rankle in the minds of individual employees for years.

Of course factional groups can be broken by means of transfers, but the main solution for the control of office politics is that of keeping in touch with the attitudes of the employees and applying the principles of good supervision. When workers are treated fairly as individuals by impartial, competent supervisors, they are less likely to engage in office politics to a pernicious extent. But it must be admitted that some politically-inclined workers are likely to appear in even those offices having excellent supervision.

"Clerical bandits"

Even though the typical office manager does not often mention it, one of his major responsibilities is working with the accounting department and management to prevent thefts, embezzlement, and fraud. Office employees are constantly handling the company's or the customer's money, the company's merchandise and equipment. It is easy for them to appropriate postage stamps, help themselves to expensive articles in the stockrooms, filch from the petty cash box, manipulate payrolls, or share in profits from inflated expense accounts. The dishonesty may be on the small change level or in the form of a complex scheme of embezzlement. The employees involved may be cashiers, salesmen, janitors, or even executives. Some just "borrow" from the company in order to clear financial emergencies or to overcome gambling losses.

The big offenses are likely to come to the attention of executives of higher management rather than of the office manager alone. One of his greatest concerns is payroll padding by clerical workers. "Some of these cases have stretched out over the course of years to mount the stolen proceeds into substantial sums. A typical case concerned a bookkeeper for a contracting firm who added one name to each of four weekly payrolls and then cashed the checks (for himself) after endorsing the names of the payees. He used the names of former employees, thus keeping his employer from suspecting any irregularity. Within about six months an accountant who regularly checked the books and records discovered the losses by comparing the time sheets from various jobs against the payrolls. The figures did not jibe and a loss of slightly more than $6,000 was uncovered." [6]

In many companies it is fairly easy for clerks and salesmen who receive payments from customers to pocket some of the company money.

[6] Sidney Feldman, "Clerical Bandits," *The Office,* November 1952, p. 63.

False receipts can be given to customers. Eventually, some of these shortages are detected when customers complain of not having their previous payments credited on their accounts.

Many stockroom and shipping clerks handle thousands of dollars worth of company goods. A case often cited is that of a large television maintenance and repair firm that went bankrupt because its employees individually were doing better business than the employer. These employees just helped themselves to spare parts and materials which they either sold to dealers or used in their own television businesses.

Bank deposits provide easy opportunities for a dishonest office worker. A good example is that of a Cleveland man who was responsible for a motion picture house popcorn concession from which he dutifully collected income for one month:

> Each day he gathered up receipts, supposedly deposited them in a bank, then sent the concession owner a duplicate bank deposit receipt which showed how much money had been banked each time. By the end of that month the concession owner no longer heard from his representative. He learned why when he received the genuine monthly bank statement which did not show a single penny having been deposited to the popcorn account. The representative had collected all profitable popcorn proceeds, pocketed them entirely, then wrote out bank deposit slips for amounts which he stamped with a phoney rubber stamp he had had made-to-order, simulated a bank teller's scribble over each slip, and mailed to the concession owner. He even set aside a traveling fund out of the several thousand dollars with which he skipped town.[7]

Research studies of office supervisors

The study cited most often is the initial project in a long range research program in human relations in group organization conducted by the Survey Research Center, Institute for Social Research, University of Michigan. The setting for the study was the home office of the Prudential Insurance Company. The persons studied were clerical workers and their supervisors.

The members of the clerical staff were divided into sections or work groups of ten to twenty-five people. The researchers evaluated the productivity of the various sections and chose for analysis twelve high-producing and twelve low-producing sections.

As one would expect, statistically significant relationships between the productivity and the supervision of the work groups was found to be very complex. The investigators were unable to find evidence for some of the usual assumptions about the nature of effective supervision such

---

[7] *Ibid.*, p. 67.

as the effects on production of different attitudes of employees. Certain findings, however, as reported by the investigators at the time followed consistent patterns:

> The supervisors of the high producing sections seem to think and act differently with respect to their supervisory functions than do the supervisors of the low producing sections. They regard supervision as the most important part of their work and spend most of their time on it. Their method of supervision appears to be one of setting up certain general conditions for their employees and then permitting their employees to work out the details of when and how the work will be handled. They do not seem to feel the need to get into the production process at every point to check on how things are going, to make changes, to reassign the work and, in other ways, to keep a close check on operations. Their attitudes toward the employees are consistent with this approach. They appear to look at the employees as people not essentially different from themselves, people capable of taking some responsibility, people with many different interests and needs.
>
> Most of the differences found between high and low work groups appear to be related to the differing nature of the supervision of these groups. This is revealed to a limited extent from the analysis of the non-supervisory employee interviews, but primarily from the interviews with the supervisors themselves. Some of the most important findings indicate that the heads of the high-producing sections are significantly more likely:
>
> (1) to receive general rather than close supervision from their supervisors.
> (2) to like the amount of authority and responsibility they have in their jobs.
> (3) to spend more time in supervision.
> (4) to give general rather than close supervision to their employees.
> (5) to be employee-oriented rather than production-oriented.[8]

One outstanding finding was the greater degree of pride in his work group revealed among employees in the higher producing sections. A second finding indicated that, in one department of the company, the higher producers were more critical of certain aspects of company policy, such as the rating system and the placement system. Interestingly, too, the employees in the low productivity sections participated more in company recreational and athletic programs.

The introduction of automation in the office

The office manager's responsibilities for providing management with the basic data of the business mean that he must familiarize himself

---

[8] Daniel Katz, Nathan Maccoby, and Nancy C. Morse, *Productivity, Supervision and Morale in an Office Situation*, Part I (Ann Arbor: Research Center, Institute for Social Research, University of Michigan, 1950).

with the modern equipment and changes wrought by automation. The new concepts of integration of data that involve factory and office operations are as revolutionary as the invention of factory machinery. They require changes in the organizational structure of the company and the office staff, in the scope of decision-making, and in business operations.

The increased use of automation means that every person who intends to become an executive should read about its benefits and limitations. He should, at least, be acquainted with the name of the science that is basic to its origin. That science is cybernetics.

Cybernetics is the scientific study of those methods of control and communication which are common to living organisms and machines, especially as applied to the analysis of operations of machines such as digital and other computers, the so-called "brain machines." Cybernetics is derived from a Greek work meaning "steersman."

We have read about guided missiles that automatically make adjustments for variations in the speed of the projectile, wind direction, wind resistance, temperature and, most important of all, *select* the target that is to be hit! These feats would be impossible without cybernetic devices.

Cybernetics as a science is likely to have a greater effect on our lives during the next thirty years than will the physics that may eventually give us ample and cheap atomic energy. Thus far, cybernetics has had its most prominent applications to the development of computing machines that reel off in 4 hours a 7-day job of preparing a payroll, or do a 3-week production-planning chore in 20 minutes. Everyone who reads newspapers and magazines has learned of machines that can multiply 42 or more nineteen-digit numbers per second. Computations such as these, useful as they may be for office work, inventory control, production, and marketing, have a significance far greater than computational only. When a computing machine, capable of making lightning calculations, is teamed up with a feedback system that monitors an automatic process, the potentials for future production and our living standards become vast indeed. They bring about a new kind of automation in industry.

Automation in industry means automatic handling of materials and parts as they go through the production process. To some extent, automation has been used in industry for many years. The current development of this trend, however, which makes use of feedback or self-correcting controls, is a new kind of technology for production.

The electronic devices that are coming into modern offices gather data much faster than ever before and almost instantly interpret its meaning.

The office manager and his colleagues must acquire special knowledge and judgment to gain the potential benefits in the use of automation for obtaining, recording, and interpreting data but their biggest problems will not be technical. The most difficult problems will be the selecting and training of people who will provide the benefits on a practicable level. When automation is installed in an office, management must expect more grievances about unfair work assignments, noise, the condition of machines, and fatigue. Even though such grievances usually have a more deepseated origin, they are projected against the mechanical device because it is a tangible symbol against which the employee can direct his dissatisfaction. "The office manager must help employees to become more conscious of what they can do with the machine than with what the machine does to them." [9]

COLLATERAL READINGS

For All Students

Niles, Henry E., *et al.*, *The Office Supervisor: His Relations to Persons and to Work*. New York: John Wiley & Sons, Inc., 1959. Emphases are given to major management developments and to relationships between group and individual values.

Suojanen, Waino, and G. C. Hoyt, "Differences in Motivation Among White Collar Workers," *Personnel*, American Management Association, Inc., September-October 1957. Discusses differences in career orientations of women as compared with men and presents findings of several research studies in the field.

For Advanced Students

Hoos, Ida Russakoff, "When the Computer Takes Over the Office," *Harvard Business Review*, July-August, 1960. Discusses the view that all classes of jobs, from office clerk to vice-president, are affected, quantitatively and qualitatively.

Katz, Daniel, *et al.*, *Productivity, Supervision and Morale in an Office Situation*. Ann Arbor: University of Michigan, Institute for Social Research, 1950. A leading study, still a classic, on the subjects listed in the title.

For Men in Business

Keelan, C. I., "How the Office Manager Can Improve His Status," *The Office*, March 1959. Recommends that office managers should produce fewer reports and discover how to operate office functions at lower cost.

Men, Machines, and Methods in the Modern Office. New York: American Management Association, Inc., 1958 and later. The Office Manage-

---

[9] See E. R. Becker and E. F. Murphy, "Human Problems of Office Mechanization," *Supervisory Management,* American Management Association, Inc., July 1957. See also *Personnel Management Abstracts,* Autumn Issue 1957.

ment Division of the AMA currently produces a timely series of contributions to provide a better perspective on the revolution in office management and how to meet it effectively.

Smith, Robert M., "Problems of the Computer Age," *Office Management*, July 1959. Discusses some of the sociological and business implications of automatic control and processing devices.

QUESTIONS ON THE CHAPTER

1. Why do some "office managers" dislike the title?
2. Why is it said that an office manager is both a line manager and a staff man?
3. Comment on two major reasons why red tape develops.
4. In what ways may written reports be made inviting and readable?
5. What is the most common problem that the office manager must cope with?
6. Explain some of the behavior patterns characteristic of the office neurotic.
7. Why is the presence of cliques considered a normal part of business life?
8. What methods in dealing with employees did the supervisors of the high-producing section employ in the Survey Research Center study?
9. What is one of the office manager's biggest problems involving dishonesty among employees?
10. Define the term "cybernetics."
11. Define the term "automation."
12. Why must management expect grievances from workers when automation is introduced into an office? How can some of the grievances be prevented?
13. Of all the ideas presented in the chapter, which ones are of special interest to you?
14. What did the chapter contribute toward your future relations with (a) office managers, (b) office employees whom you may supervise?

PROBLEMS AND PROJECTS

For All Students

1. One of the criticisms made by some office managers is that college graduates do not learn, while in college, how to write a good business letter or a technical report. Discuss the criticism and the facilities available to you for overcoming this kind of criticism before you enter business.
2. One of the significant findings from studies of the factors influencing the productivity of office workers is the pride of the high producing worker in his work group. Pride in the group, or lack of it, is often evident in college groups. Discuss factors that seem to bring it about in college groups with which you are acquainted.

For Advanced Students

3. Examine some of the available books and business journal articles on office management. To what extent and in what ways does each stress the human relations aspects rather than procedures or equipment?

4. Interview several office managers of your area. Ask each to cite some of the human relations problems he has experienced. What are his policies in the supervision of office employees? How does he try to raise the importance of his own job in the estimation of top management?

For Men in Business

5. Describe the functions and status of the office manager in a company where you have worked. What are his relations with other executives? What are his influences on the supervisors in regard to their relations with the employees whom they supervise?

6. One of the big human relations problems in some offices is the office or Christmas party. Describe some of the parties you have attended. Suggest some rules or policies you would follow in planning a Christmas party for the office employees.

An old story about the importance of using the right appeal with women has been told concerning a well-dressed woman who was threatening to jump off the Brooklyn Bridge. The passersby and a policeman were yelling to her: "Don't jump. Please!" She continued her threat. One man who supposedly understood women shouted: "That's awfully dirty water down there—it's sewage!" She didn't jump.

When women are asked what their major desires are for themselves, they give idealistic answers. One researcher, for example, found that when 150 women were asked to characterize themselves in terms of a number of descriptive phrases, the five types most often selected for self-identification were a sensible woman, a motherly woman, a modest woman, an all-American girl, and an efficient woman.

Strangely, none of the women chose to identify herself publicly as a very beautiful or glamorous woman! [1]

The need for skill in supervising women who are employees in business has increased rapidly in recent decades. Anyone who successfully supervises women employees must do more than ask the women what they want—he must use insight and ingenuity of the kind that develops from extensive experience.

---

[1] See data reported by John Kishler, "Men Aren't Sexy; Women Are Glad, Says Consultant," *Advertising Age,* August 19, 1957.

20 Women as Office Employees and as Participants in Business

Psychological characteristics of women

Psychologists and consumer researchers have made many studies of feminine traits and compared the behavior of women with that of men. The findings indicate that most of the sex differences found are caused by environmental rather than by hereditary influences.

Investigations of psychological sex differences show that the individual differences within one sex so enormously outweigh the differences between the sexes in *intellectual* and *semi-intellectual* traits that such sex differences in practical affairs may be disregarded. When men and women show equal ability in an aptitude test, it is because they are equally gifted; not because women are less talented than men and have to work harder to get equal results.

In *non-intellectual* traits, the sex differences are more pronounced. Women exceed men in interest in persons rather than in things, in emotionality, impulsiveness, religiousness, sympathy, vanity, and shyness. Men exceed women in traits such as pugnacity, humor, and independence.

Several studies of conversations of men and of women suggest that women are more likely than men to talk about clothes, about what to do in social situations, and about the opposite sex; men are more likely to talk about sports, business, and things having money value.

Almost every woman, of course, is keenly interested in her personal appearance. The salesman who barges in on a woman at home when her hair is in curlers and her face lacks make-up is likely to find her irritable. If she can get her glamour on, she is more likely to be in a receptive mood. She feels better when she knows that she looks all right. The responsiveness of women to offers of information about improvement of personal appearance has been demonstrated again and again by publishers and advertisers.

A woman is deeply interested in people. She wants to be liked, admired, respected. Generally, she lives for others: the members of her family, friends, and those with whom she identifies herself. Because the good will of others is so important to her, she needs more encouragement than men. She responds to praise and admiration.

Her sense of humor differs from a man's. She does not care for practical jokes nor does she like to be kidded or teased. Contests do not challenge her, especially when the contest involves women whom she knows. And yet she will consider other women personal rivals for the admiration of those people who are important to her, particularly the boy friend or husband.

Women identify with other women whom they admire. One reason for the use of advertising that depicts beautiful women is that those who see the illustration wish hopefully that they will look like the model.

No man can understand women fully but some of their ways of behaving can be recognized for their importance in supervision. A woman, in some circumstances, as in opening a window, will ask a man to help her in order to stimulate interest in her. Under other conditions, as in moving a typewriter to another desk or in carrying a heavy bag of groceries into the house, she may not ask for help—a man ought to see that she needs help and offer it without being asked!

The woman who is learning a new job such as operating a machine will hesitate to ask for help even though she needs it. She does not like to admit ignorance. As a learner, she feels insecure, anxious and friendless. If she must compare her bumbling efforts as a learner with those of a skilled worker, she will feel unduly discouraged and quit. Quit rates of beginners in machine operation are high. Some training directors follow the policy of training women only in groups of learners so that each woman will compare her output with that of other learners, not with experienced operators.

Women feel less secure than men in regard to their work abilities. They have less knowledge of the business as a whole. Hence, they learn and follow rules. If rules are not available to guide them, they will look for symbols of status to guide them. In hiring and evaluating people, they are more likely than men to depend upon academic degrees and other symbols as indications of ability. Men, on the other hand, are more likely to evaluate ability regardless of degrees or symbols of status.

Women are especially observant regarding details of appearance. If, for example, the supervisor wears the same shirt or tie to the office two successive days, the women employees will notice it. The men, as a rule, will have no recollection as to what the boss wore yesterday. Also in television commercials, the housewife usually pays more attention to the dress worn by the demonstrator of the refrigerator advertised than to the refrigerator itself. They even note whether the demonstrator is wearing a wedding ring. When a television station used a commercial showing a baby being bathed by a mother who was not wearing a wedding ring, the station received numerous letters of protest.

Women are supposed to be less business minded than men in regard to such details of business as getting their fare ready in a taxi before the destination is reached. The typical woman seldom has the fare ready. She will not start to fumble in her purse for the money until after the destination has been reached.

Women will take low-paying jobs in a city center because the place of work is convenient for side activities such as shopping. Industrial concerns on the outskirts of a city often have to pay higher salaries to hold women employees than firms near the city center. Some companies that have moved out of congested metropolitan centers into the suburbs have had much difficulty in getting women to come to the new office even though the working conditions, once the worker is there, are excellent.

The emotionality of women

Few situations in business disturb a man as much as a woman who weeps, especially when the situation is one that either arouses his sympathy or disagrees with his point of view. And when a woman cries simply because she finds that a friend bought a hat like hers for a dollar less, a man can't understand "why a woman should carry on so." Most men wish that women were less emotional. Actually, their emotional sprees probably have a great deal of therapeutic value.

Dr. Wilson T. Sowder, U. S. Public Health Service, has stated that women escape the consequences of woe and worry in our complex civilization "by being more vocal about these conditions through tears or, occasionally, hysterics." Men shun such feminine actions, but women outlive men. Their emotionality seems to contribute toward survival. And as one writer has stated "Nothing succeeds like survival." [2]

Women deal with many of life's catastrophes by means of good crying spells, but men tend to let the emotional back pressure accumulate. Women are more susceptible to troubles of an emotional sort, but three times as many men as women commit suicide. However, many more women than men make an unsuccessful attempt to commit suicide!

Of course men as well as women suffer emotional upsets but men have been taught to show only certain kinds of emotion, while women have been taught to show other kinds. The fact that men swear at a recalcitrant golf ball may be just as emotional as a woman's crying when her roast burns to charcoal. [3]

Women who work

Women not only work to a greater extent than in previous generations but a sizable portion of the gain is from older and married women.

[2] See Sidney Feldman, "Physiology of Women in Business," *The Office,* November 1956, p. 103.

[3] See Donald A. Laird and Eleanor C. Laird, *Sizing Up People* (New York: McGraw-Hill Book Company, Inc., 1951), p. 165.

The increase in the number of married women who work is not caused solely by the middle-aged matrons returning to the labor force. Many working women are mothers of dependent children; currently about 2½ million of them have children under 6 years of age.[4] Nor are most of the working women widows who must work. Most come from homes that have husbands, thus increasing the number of families that have two incomes. In years of normal business activity, about one third of the families in the United States have a husband and wife who hold outside jobs.

A high percentage of women work for a while after getting married and then retire to start their families. As soon as it is practical, many of them return to take their place in the working world. This additional income adds to the disposable-income status of the family. They can buy more clothes and grooming aids, as well as contribute to paying the mortgage on the home, meeting installments on the new car, and paying for the children's education.

The lower the husband's income, the greater the likelihood of the wife working. In a recent Census Bureau study it was found that one in every three wives worked when the husband's income was under $5,000 yearly; one in every five worked when it was between $7,000 and $10,000; and only one in every nine when the husband made over $10,000 a year.

The woman who works increases the sales not only of semiluxuries but also of certain necessities. She is likely to shop for "convenience foods" and thereby help to stimulate the food industries to improve their product and process research. New convenience items have gained sales much faster than standard products. According to one expert, by spending $1.80 on convenience foods, a housewife can save four hours of work for herself.[5] Of course she can earn more than that in the four hours saved.

Individual women work for many different reasons. Some enjoy work. Many have to work in order to maintain the family. As one stated: "I have to work to support myself and the children because my husband is so lazy that he wouldn't put his hand out to keep from falling out of bed!" Anyone who knows the personal and family life of women employees will find numerous examples of heroism on the part of women in their effort to keep the family together.

The reasons for and importance of working can be surmised to some

---

[4] Many of these mothers have a feeling of guilt about working while they have children at home. Advertisers who appeal to working mothers recognize this guilt feeling. See "What Puts Women in a Buying Frame of Mind," *Printers' Ink,* June 20, 1958.

[5] See *Industrial Marketing,* December 1957, p. 86.

extent from the reasons for leaving a job. One survey of reasons for termination of employment of 498 single girls and 499 married women indicated that about 16 per cent of the single girls were discharged for incompetence. Less than four per cent of the married women had to be discharged for the same reason. Generally, single girls seem to be a somewhat uncertain bet until they have been on the job several years. Like the men, they are frequently tempted by higher money, more opportunity, and more congenial work. Married women, on the other hand, seldom seem to leave for these reasons, though they are much more likely to give up work on account of family obligations.[6]

Employer considerations in hiring women

Employers do not expect most women to be seeking a career in the job. The quest for a mate is primary. When a single woman takes a job, one of her first thoughts in looking over the place is the number and kinds of males eligible for marriage. Young girls who seek short-term jobs want regular hours, little overtime, and no other conditions that might hinder their leading a normal social life.

"I can take 70 words a minute, if you can spell that fast." SOURCE: Modern Office Procedures.

Generally, women have less physical strength than males, and less interest in gaining advancement or earning more responsibility, but they do have certain abilities such as greater manual dexterity and usually more tolerance of routine. As a rule, women employees have better morale than male employees.

Physically, most women are chunkier than men. The trunk is rela-

---

[6] See *Office Executive*, National Office Management Association, July 1957, p. 38. See also *Personnel*, American Management Association, Inc., September-October 1957, p. 4.

tively longer than that of the typical male but the arms and legs are shorter. She cannot reach far or often without strain. Hence, her work equipment should be designed for about 10 per cent less reach than for male use. However, a woman's arms and muscles are structured so that she can fasten a dress that buttons down the back—a man imagines that he is breaking his arm when he tries to reach an itchy spot on his back.

Women tire easily when they must perform a rotary action as required in turning knobs or dials. Machines with foot pedals should be built so that little pressure is required to operate or control the machine. Seating for female workers requires special consideration.

Women tend to tire more quickly than do men when the job requires physical stamina. Their lungs are not as well adapted as those of the male to eliminate waste products by means of oxygen supplied through the lungs.[7]

Generally, the influence of physiological and structural differences varies with the culture and with the attitude toward the work.

Women who work differ from males in that their absence record is worse at *all* ages and the difference is even greater after age 45 than before. Their absence frequency rate, already somewhat higher than males under 45, does drop with advancing years, but the severity rate (duration of absence) goes up so much faster than the males' that their over-all disability rate (frequency rate × severity rate) is actually higher after 45 whereas the males' is lower. Physicians' diagnoses, however, indicate that so-called female disorders are *not* what makes the rate so high. Attitude toward the job and responsibilities in the home are more significant as causal factors.[8]

The experience of some companies indicates that the problem of excessive female absenteeism can be dealt with effectively by intelligent management. A number of companies have found that the women in jobs which afford them little recognition are the ones most likely to be absent and that when women are upgraded or given more recognition as workers, they are more regular in attendance.

Supervising women employees

Managements often have difficulty in persuading a man to take over the supervision of an all-female or largely female work group. Some

---

[7] See Sidney Feldman, "Physiology of Women in Business," *The Office,* November 1956.

[8] See Hilda R. Kahne, Claire F. Ryder, Leonid S. Snegireff, and Grace Wyshak, "Don't Take Older Workers for Granted," *Harvard Business Review,* November-December 1957, p. 92.

men feel that they do not want to cope with all the special difficulties.

Women as employees have somewhat different attitudes toward their work than do men.

The findings of one survey [9] indicated women tend to be less interested than men in the work itself. They place more emphasis on "human relations" in supervision, as contrasted with the "work" orientation of most men. When men are offered a transfer to another job, they usually ask questions about the work, the rate of pay, and chances for advancement. Women want to know about the friendliness of the new group.

Women want to know how to get along with the boss. When one woman, for example, resigned from her job, she was asked to break in her successor. She started by showing the new girl the files, how to handle routine work, and where the supplies were kept. Before she had gone very far, the newcomer interrupted her: "I can learn the systems without much trouble, I think, but you can help me most by telling me about the boss. What is he like? What jobs are most important to him? What upsets him most easily? Does he have moods? What puts him into a good mood? When is the best time to ask him questions?"

Most women employees want the supervisor to show his friendliness by pleasant greetings and conversation, but they do not desire close friendship. They prefer to maintain a slight social distinction between the supervisor and themselves. They define the supervisor's human relations skills in terms of impartiality, respect, and courtesy.

Women as employees deeply resent favoritism. The supervisor must be extra careful to avoid giving the impression that he has any "pets" in making his assignments of work. He cannot even smile more cordially or use a more friendly tone of voice in greeting one woman employee than another. If he wants to talk to one of three women employees, he must also recognize the presence of the other two. He should at least show that he knows they are there!

Women like to be with other women. Office executives whose desks happen to be located where they can see the entrances to the men's and women's washrooms are amused to see so many women workers go to the washroom by two's and three's. Women are gregarious but they are poor team workers. Note the differences in athletic interests of the team variety. Girls have almost no team interests such as those of boys' team sports.

Women are especially aware of the moods of those with whom they work. They take comments and simple questions as personal matters. As one supervisor stated: "Ask a man where he got a new suit and he'll

---

[9] See Howard M. Vollmer and Jack A. Kinney, "Supervising Women Is Different," *Personnel Journal*, December 1955.

"Why is it that a girl has to show a man she's smart to get a job—and act dumb to get a raise?" SOURCE: Advertising Age (*November 12, 1956*).

name the store; ask a woman the same about a new dress and she'll likely respond, 'Do you like it?' "

Women as executives

The rarity of women as executives or as holders of the higher salaried jobs is indicated by the fact that only one-half of one per cent of employed women, compared with 12 per cent of men, attain this level. When male executives are asked for the reasons, their answer is usually that women are a poor investment for training—by the time they are trained they get married and leave. To a woman, her family, not her job, is her first responsibility and interest. Men cannot talk to women or associate with them in the same ways that men can with men. Keeping the sex urge under control requires rigid adherence to established custom.

Women have difficulty in making tough decisions, especially when the decisions involve people whom they like. Most important of all, very few women are willing to study and work as hard for advancement as are ambitious men.

The ambitious man has an upward career orientation. He has a long-range point of view toward job rewards and satisfactions. He is willing to make sacrifices of time, money, and energy to earn future rewards. He will tolerate poor supervision and unpleasant working conditions on a job because the experience gained there leads to another higher objective. He identifies himself with top management men and is willing to earn their approval. The typical female worker, even though she may like her job, usually has a different image of herself, different goals for her ambitions. Even though she has high intelligence, vocational training, and some ambition, she still sees her greatest career as one of getting married, taking care of a home, and rearing children.

The ambitious-to-succeed-in-business type of woman senses the differences in attitudes toward women and men executives. Most men who work under the supervision of a woman, particularly older men, have difficulty in tolerating her. They get enough of that kind of supervision at home! And they resent the kidding of other men in regard to having a woman supervisor. Men are quite willing to employ women in the office and in certain kinds of factory jobs but they do not want to accept women as their equals in directing a business. To be successful as an executive, a woman must be better than a man. To accomplish this, some women adopt male personality characteristics but these are disliked by both women and men. The woman who wants to advance in business must not act too much like a man, nor too much like a woman. As one woman stated: "The woman who wants to advance in business must look like a girl, think like a man, act like a lady, and work like a horse."

In many instances, a woman's greatest difficulty, if she advances, is not in overcoming the prejudices of men, but of women. They are apt to rationalize her success by attributing it to the unscrupulous use of sex.

Women have achieved recognition in certain fields. One is personnel work in department stores, hospitals, banks, and insurance offices. The fact that the New York Personnel Club, membership of several hundred, is exclusively female, indicates their achievements in this area of business. The positions of members range all the way from interviewer to industrial relations director and officer of the company. Job titles they hold are job analyst, training director, company communications editor, and assistant manager of compensation and benefits programs. Their functions include hiring, testing, employee relations, training, counseling, handling welfare programs, writing employee magazines, preparing cases for arbitration, exit interviewing, and handling grievances.

Few women are in the top personnel jobs in heavy industry or in collective bargaining positions.

Women are especially fitted for work where extreme patience is required, where individual personnel problems arise, and where details are extremely important. As one man puts it, "She doesn't lose patience when the details would drive a man crazy." [10]

Executives' wives

Many managements realize that the wife often plays a controlling influence in a man's upward movement in a company. When a junior executive is being considered for advancement to a senior job, the wife's possible influence may be reviewed. In a few cases, she may be invited to a social affair for the purpose of giving her a "once-over" evaluation. This kind of special examination is, however, exceptional. It usually is not necessary. If her husband has been in the company for several years, she probably has met his associates and superiors on numerous social occasions. Her major characteristics are likely to be well known long before her husband's abilities, qualities, and limitations are considered in relation to a higher executive opening. Certainly, wives are not subjected to any rigid corporate pattern to which they are expected to hold in regard to conduct or personality.

If her antennae for social situations are sensitive, the wife has learned that she can help or hinder her husband's chances in many ways. On the negative side, she has learned certain "Don'ts" such as

1. Do not visit him at the job. Do not drop in on him just to pass the time of day or to tell him that one of the children has a cold.

2. Do not gossip with the wives of other employees about what is going on in the company. Avoid hearing or passing on information about company policies with which you disagree. This applies particularly to conversations at bridge parties of wives where most of the gossip deals with real or imaginary scandals of executives, who is going to be promoted or demoted, and exaggerated reports on salary increases of lucky employees.

3. Do not "high hat" any other employee's wife, no matter how low her husband's position in the organizational hierarchy. Be a congenial mixer with wives of low, middle, and high position employees. If they like you, they will also tend to like your husband.

4. Do not expect your husband's secretary to defer to you or perform errands for you. Be friendly but not suspicious of her. Limit most of your contacts with her to necessary telephone conversations.

---

[10] See Edith M. Lynch, "Women at Work in Personnel," *Personnel Journal*, January 1956.

5. Do not tell your husband how to run his job or the company. You should take a sincere interest in your husband's job and company but not a meddling one. Do not tell him whom to hire, fire, or promote. When a wife tries to call the shots at home, others will soon learn it and management will consider the husband less likely to succeed as a responsible executive. (As one humorist said: "The woman who insists on wearing the pants frequently finds that some other woman is wearing the mink!")

6. Do not complain to other members of the company about your husband's job. Above all, never tell the president that your husband is not appreciated and that he could handle a much better job if the company management were less stupid. And do not complain to your husband about his lack of promotion.

> One of the vexing questions is as personal as it is emotional: "Why were you passed by on the promotion list? How come Jack got the branch management job when you were in line for it?" Other questions she doesn't ask may often be on the tip of her tongue: "Are you losing interest in your work? Are you developing bad working habits? Are you getting in an emotional rut?" Here is where nagging is sandpaper on the sensitive tissues of a disturbed mind. A little praise and comfort would serve better.[11]

To obtain suggestions on the positive side, John A. Patton, Chicago management engineer, decided to ask the women themselves. He polled 230 wives of executives. His findings indicated that for all the talk about the allegedly domineering attitude of women of the United States, the wives he polled took an essentially traditional view of themselves and their influence on their husbands.

The women did not think that office politicking was the best way to help their husbands. Instead, a clear majority said they could be most helpful by sending their man on his way in the morning in a good mood, feeling that he was tops so far as his family was concerned.

In the light of his survey, Patton listed these five ways in which a wife can best advance her husband's career:

1. Supplement his abilities by encouraging him and supporting him morally.
2. Be his sounding board. Be genuinely interested in letting him unburden himself.
3. Act as a publicity agent, though a wise, discreet, and modest one, for the man of the house.

---

[11] See "Executive Staff and Distaff. A Wives'-eye View," *Dun's Review and Modern Industry,* February 1957, p. 73. Copyright © 1957 by Dun & Bradstreet Publications Corporation.

4. Be friendly, but not intimate, with other wives in the corporation. Be gracious both to peers and subordinates.
5. Realize that the rewards of higher income and prestige demand the sacrifice of certain other privileges. A strictly nine-to-five job usually means a strictly nine-to-five income.

When Patton asked the 230 wives whether they considered *money* or *standing in the community* more important, 90 per cent said they would prefer their husbands to take a job with more prestige and a lower salary rather than to sacrifice social standing to money.

Most wives of executives do not resent the amount of extra time the husband's business consumes nor do they resent the intrusions of business entertaining. Most executives' wives seem well satisfied with their lot. When asked how they felt about the term "business widow," most of the wives were philosophical. Some of the answers Patton received were "No differently than about golf widows;" "It's the price you pay for your husband's success;" and "If you want the advantages of being an executive's wife, you have to go along with the disadvantages—and there is no other way to look at it." [12]

Wives of executives also realize that American business requires executives to change their location at short notice. An advancement or a transfer often means severing pleasant social connections, taking children out of school, selling one's home and buying another. Pulling up roots and moving is to some a painful procedure, especially to women. This means that wives of ambitious men have to learn how to look with hope for new satisfactions in a new home, a strange community, and with new neighbors. Some company personnel departments are careful to explain this job requirement to the ambitious men on hiring so that the man may either refuse the job or try to educate his wife about her need for adaptation to company transfer requirements. Many Army and Navy men usually make these adjustments with pleasure.

Employees' wives

Companies that wish to do a comprehensive job of communications include the employee's family members, particularly the wife, in their program. The majority of wives have a vital interest in their husband's job, its social status, and the dependability as well as the amount of the income. Her main interest is in the steadiness of the income.

---

[12] See Malcolm S. Forbes, "Fact and Comment." Reprinted by permission of *Forbes Magazine,* September 1, 1957, p. 12.

Tell the Wife that She Can Go
And then Watch Hubby Hustle

The hand that rocks the cradle can pack a mighty wallop when properly "caressed."

Women folk—bless 'em!—can do more to push your incentive travel program than almost any other element that can go into your campaign. Tell a wife she can go on a glamorous trip if her husband works hard, and you have a motivated salesman. It is not just theory. More and more users of incentive travel are including wives because it pays off in a campaign's results.

Basic formula for inclusion of wives in an incentive program is to set two quotas for salesmen or dealers. First quota provides a trip for the husband. When the husband reaches the second and higher quota, his wife goes along.

If wives are to be included on your trip, these are some of the things you should do:

1. Address all promotional literature to the home.

2. Have a few mailings directly to wives.

3. Play up shopping attractions of your site as well as glamor.

4. Explain to the wife how she can help her husband reach quota.

5. Keep both husband and wife advised of progress toward quota.

Many clever approaches have been developed to stimulate favorable reaction from wives. One company uses a telephone campaign to wives. After the contest is underway for awhile, a call is made to several wives each day. If the wife can answer correctly—"How many points does your husband have in the trip contest?"—she receives a small gift.

Another approach by an incentive user is to send a set of dinner place mats to each wife. Campaign promotion is printed on each mat and wives are instructed to use one each time she serves a meal to her husband. Still another technique is to send a check list to each wife on what her husband should be doing. She is to make sure he has planned a certain number of calls each day; carries all his samples and catalog; has shoes shined before leaving home; reads all home-office mail carefully; makes out call reports promptly, etc.

You can make an interesting bulletin for wives as a result of a little contest. Offer wives a free gift in a contest to tell how they help their husbands reach quota. Best answers earn gifts, and these answers can be incorporated into a bulletin to all wives.

This technique has several advantages: It gets wives to think about helping; it creates a little excitement

with possibility of a gift; it provides an exchange of information for use by all wives; it establishes a pattern of interest by wives which carries over past the contest period.

Some incentive packages include a personal-expense check for winners. One manufacturer, instead of providing a personal-expense check (most popular seems to be $50 for husband and wife) offered a $50 check toward baby sitter fees. This little twist had special appeal for wives who sometimes have great concern about leaving the kids behind.

A novel mailing to wives is a baby-sitter check list. This list covers all the instructions the wife wants to leave with the baby sitter for each day she will be away from home. The check list, with blanks to fill in, covers such things as feeding, clothes, bedtime, what to do in case of illness and other special instructions.

While wives are an invaluable source of assistance in a salesman's effort to win a trip and a prime mover, they contribute greatly to smooth functioning during a trip. It is easier to plan activities for husband and wife than for stag groups, say incentive planners.

During a tour, wives make activities dignified, show a marked degree of appreciation and create an especial friendly atmosphere. It helps to keep a group under control to have wives along. They are responsive to group activity plans. **The End**

What to Tell the Wife
When She Can't Go on Trip

Problem for any incentive travel planner may be the wives that are left behind when a campaign is for travel by men only.

While the wife can't go, she can still help her husband—if she is told how and is rewarded for her efforts. First, point out the importance of her husband's reaching the trip quota—the prestige, economic benefits, deserved rest.

She can be made a member of the "team" by giving her instructions to help her husband's progress. A small gift midway in the contest to the wife for her help always is well received.

Many companies make it a point to send a gift to wives to arrive the day before or on the day the husband leaves on the trip. This kind of thoughtfulness engenders goodwill for the company and makes the wife more receptive to a husband's travel without her.

SOURCE: Sales Management (*March 1, 1957*).

Investigations indicate that when the company sends literature to the home such as an employee publication, a letter, or an annual report, the wife's interest in the company is increased. She must depend on the company and friends rather than the husband for information. Most husbands do not tell their wives very much about their jobs or the company. The wife would like to know more. Usually, a wife wants to feel that the company is interested in giving her understandable information. After all, the union communicates with her by sending her information and asking for her good will. She'd like to hear the company's story as well as the union's. Most wives are against strikes of any kind at any time and therefore have a tendency to advocate agreements that will prevent a strike.

HOW TO DEAL WITH THE MAN

As every woman knows, the way to a man's heart is through his ego. It's also the way to prime him for success. Nothing will put so much steam into your husband's ambition as his faith in himself; and no one can bolster that faith as well as you can.

So build him up: praise and encourage him. Show that you're proud of him, and teach the kids to show their pride, too. Give him credit, when you possibly can—for his good looks, good taste, wit. When he falters, remind him of past successes and spur him on.

But—and as a woman you know this by instinct—while you boost him, also guide him. As unobtrusively as you can, help him to improve himself. Perhaps an evening a week at school would strengthen his technical background, or would help him speak better before large groups.

Above all, help him to set a goal. Are you both chiefly interested in money, prestige, security, power, job satisfaction, early retirement? Choose your priorities. Talk over your aims together. Help find direction for his ambition and you find it for your marriage, too.

Be certain, though, that you do not dominate him or push him beyond his capacities. He must be able to make decisions on his own. And there's no point in setting a goal that he cannot possibly attain.

SOURCE: "Help Your Husband Get Ahead," *Changing Times,* The Kiplinger Magazine, November 1957, p. 41.

Most wives of industrial workers are ambitious for their husband in regard to getting more money but they are not especially concerned about advancement opportunities in the company. They do not visualize their husbands as future executives. They want a steady income more than prestige.

Of course actions that are helpful to her count greatly. One company that had been active in communicating with the home had a business slump. To help the employees, the company set up an employment

"It's a fringe benefit that goes along with being a wife." SOURCE:
by Lepper. Courtesy Banking (December 1957).

bureau to get other jobs for laid-off employees. One wife said that the
first job they got for her husband went sour, but they took the trouble
to get him another. She was deeply appreciative.[13]

Some managements aim at the personal touch: a potted plant for the
employee's wife when she enters a hospital or a gold brooch for her
when her husband receives the 25-year service watch. One company
gives a party for workers and their wives when a plant passes the one
million mark in man-hours without a lost-time accident.

Programs for workers' wives are especially important for those families
who are transferred to new locations. They give attention to housing
problems, loneliness experienced by the wives in the new community,
and the school facilities for children. The stage is set for making new
friends and getting oriented in the new community. Tours are arranged
to points of interest. Old employees welcome the newcomers.

COLLATERAL READINGS

For All Students

Heal, Edith, *The Young Executive's Wife; You and Your Husband's Job.*
New York: Dodd, Mead & Co., 1958. Designed to show the wife of
the young executive how she can be a positive force in furthering her
husband's career.

Stessin, Lawrence, "Managing Your Manpower," *Dun's Review and Mod-*

---

[13] See *Modern Industry*, May 15, 1951, p. 47.

ern Industry, October 1959. Discusses a survey of several thousand office secretaries.

For Advanced Students

Pressey, Sidney L., and Raymond G. Kuhlen, *Psychological Development Through the Life Span.* New York: Harper & Brothers, 1957. Summarizes much of the best data that deal with the title, including many topics that involve sex differences.

Smith, R. M., "Graduate Business School Trains Women for Executive Roles," *Office Management,* February 1957. The Radcliffe College (for women) management program has joined with the Harvard Business School program to handle instruction. Aimed to prepare women for executive or other upper level positions in business.

For Men in Business

Newcomb, Robert, and Marg Sammons, "Easy Life for the Office Worker," *Advertising Age,* May 30, 1960. Presents a summary of a survey of office workers of 2000 American and Canadian industries, made by The National Office Management Association.

Slote, Clair Trieb, "Women Executives: Fact and Fancy," *Dun's Review and Modern Industry,* December 1958. Discusses possible effects on the character of management of having an increasing number of women executives in industry.

QUESTIONS ON THE CHAPTER

1. In what ways do men and women differ in nonintellectual traits?
2. What does it mean when it is said that a woman lives for others, and what is the importance of realizing this?
3. Why is a new woman employee often trained in a group with other learners?
4. Why are the weeping sprees of women therapeutically valuable?
5. In what per cent of American families do both the husband and wife work?
6. Compare the per cent of male and female executives.
7. What types of work are women especially fitted for?
8. List three ways that a wife can hinder her husband's chances for success on the job. How do wives contribute to his success?
9. Which factor do wives rate as more important—money or standing in the community?
10. What methods should a woman use to reach her husband's heart and also prime him for success?
11. Give suggestions for the supervision of women workers.
12. Of all the ideas presented in the chapter, which ones are of value or interest to you?
13. What did the chapter contribute to your future relations with (a) women executives, (b) women employees whom you may supervise?

For All Students

1. Interview a woman who has worked about a year and another who has worked for about twenty years. Ask them to describe their problems with supervisors and fellow workers. What studies on your part might deal with the problems they present?

2. Summarize some of the articles in current journals that treat problems of women who work. Does the material modify or amplify contents of this chapter?

For Advanced Students

3. Study available published material concerning courses or meetings for executives' wives. List the suggestions made for the wives. Show the list to a college girl. How does she react to the suggestions?

4. Interview several mothers who are working about their special problems. Study the literature on the measured effects on children of the mother's working. Compare the popular assumptions about the effects with scientifically made studies.

For Men in Business

5. Interview several women employees where you work regarding their suggestions as to what management might do to enable them to do better work in better spirit. Are any of the top secretaries working in an "isolated island" social situation?

6. To what extent are the career-minded women employees of your company encouraged to develop their career potentials? Can secretaries become executives?

PART 4

Interpersonal Relations of
Typical Departments

M ANY STUDENTS AND BUSINESSMEN THINK OF ACCOUNTING AS AN impersonal part of business. The student who takes an accounting course is likely to have so much trouble in learning the logic and the mechanics that he fails to appreciate its interpersonal relationships. Actually, if he enriches his perspective by means of the human relations approach, the logic and the mechanics often become more understandable and stimulating.

Accounting is the nerve center of a business. The department members collect, sort, classify, record, analyze, and distribute the data essential to directing the business intelligently. Many of the data are necessary for the *control* of operations: to keep score on the number of units produced in the factory, to determine the costs of producing them, to check the number sold and the costs of selling them, as well as to obtain numerous other data to tell management whether things are going as desired.

The term "control" can be defined as a system or procedure that provides standards of comparison and means of verification or a check on operations. A typical example might be that of a company that manufactures five product lines. The president may organize the company into five semi-autonomous divisions, each charged with a specific share of the total invested capital. Each division is held accountable for earning a stipulated return on that investment. The accounting department sets up a system of internal records and reports which enable the president to

21   ## Human Relations in Accounting

see regularly how each division is meeting or failing to meet the designated standards or objectives.

The control process involves three ingredients: the *goal*, which states what is to be done; the *procedure*, which specifies (1) how and when something is to be done, (2) who is to do it, and (3) what makes up satisfactory performance; and finally, the *checkup*, which indicates how well the job was carried out.

Obviously, many people feel resentful toward being controlled and judged. They think of the accounting reports as "report cards" to management. Supervisors, for example, feel that the reports put pressure on them and the employees. The figures do not, for example, show when standards were not met because of factors beyond the responsibility of the supervisors or the employees. The accounting controls usually cause supervisors to believe that they are constantly being goaded into greater efficiency. This kind of reaction is, of course, one result of inadequate communication.

In a sense, accounting is or should be a tool of *communication*. It collects and organizes facts and communicates to management the financially-significant facts of the business. The accountant is far more than a calculating machine. He not only records and reports data but he also communicates with others about the data that are necessary for conducting the business. In his informative relations with others, he:

(1) communicates to management the data necessary for decision-making.
(2) communicates by means of internal reports with other people inside the company, particularly department heads.
(3) communicates with many employees about the necessary instructions for making records and gathering data.
(4) communicates with people outside the company, usually in the form of financial reports to stockholders.[1]

The accountant's first responsibility is to do accurate recording and reporting. A correlative responsibility is to convey understanding. When he writes a report, for example, he should write in terms of the person who is supposed to read and understand it. Major points must be properly highlighted. Even the bias of the recipient should be recognized.

When he gives instructions to employees outside of the accounting department, extra difficulties arise. Most employees know nothing about accounting and care less. They may even be antagonistic to accountants' requests. A natural reason for the antagonism on the part of some employees is that they have been required to make and send to the accounting department certain records that require a lot of bother and

---

[1] See George R. White, "Accounting Is a Communications Tool," *National Association of Cost Accountants Bulletin*, September 1956.

extra labor on the part of the employee. The records go to the accounting department where the employee suspects that they really are put to little or no use. No one in the typical accounting department has ever made an effort to explain to him the need for or the uses of the records. As a result, some employees who record figures for the benefit of the accounting department consider the figures unimportant. This lack of respect for the need for certain data may affect the accuracy of the reports the accountant will compile. The human-relations-minded accountant will follow up his requests to employees in other departments to make sure that they appreciate the importance and uses of the records that they are asked to provide. He shows the employees that their reports are put to good use. He may also ask them to suggest suitable procedures for getting the information from them.[2]

Accountants are technical men

Generally, accountants have been technically trained in the handling of figures rather than in the human relations skills involved in the figures. The personnel in the accounting areas are likely to be more intensively educated than their colleagues in sales or manufacturing. As one consultant stated, the relatively concentrated training of accounting people, coupled with the technical demands of the job, raise these questions:

"Does the well-trained accountant use his personal ability as efficiently as he uses his technical ability? Does he tend to rest his case primarily on the facts and figures? Is he careful to convey a personal message when he is communicating his conclusions? Does he lead the horse to water and try to make him drink—when he should first make him thirsty?"

The problem is one faced by all trained specialists. It is no small task for these men to learn to think in different ways than they have previously. It is not simple to shift from a tightly analytical approach to a broader outlook. It is quite difficult to change from dealing with tangible, quantitative, and specific matters to broad, vague, and intangible ones.

I would like to urge industrial accountants to make the most of their technical training, but also to master it. In reports, remember that you are communicating to another person and that the extent to which you get through is in many ways directly proportionate to the keenness with which you appraise the receptivity of your listener.[3]

---

[2] For additional suggestions, see Edward L. Anthony, "Effective Control for Better Management," *Management Aids for Small Manufacturers* (Small Business Administration, Washington), January 1957.

[3] James W. Rohrer, "To Technical Competence, Add the Human Touch," Letters to the Editor, *N.A.C.A. Bulletin,* September 1956.

The accountant who senses the importance of human relations will have many opportunities to apply his insight into the way people feel about his activities. Let us assume, for example, that the management sets up a suggestion system for cost reduction. The plan is to be designed to have each employee receive a definite percentage of the savings that accrue from his suggestion. The logically-minded accountant may argue that a 25 per cent share of typical gross saving on a suggestion that reduces production costs $1,000 is just exactly the same as a 50 per cent share of a net reduction (after deduction for costs of extra equipment) of $500. Actually, the typical employee would, however, prefer 50 per cent of $500 to 25 per cent of $1,000! To the employee, the division seems more fair even though the number of dollars he receives is exactly the same. To the logically-minded accountant this kind of reasoning does not make sense—to the person-centered accountant it does.

Compliance with the mechanics of accounting tends to modify the thinking of non-accounting employees

The accounting department may have need for so much data from so many employees outside the department that the mechanics of figure-gathering tend to divert the employees' thinking from the productive and the creative aspects of business to the purely routine and mathematical. When a foreman, for example, is required to fill in ten copies of each of several forms every working day, plus numerous other periodic reports, he gradually learns to think in terms of the mechanics rather than the spirit of the business. Consider also the salesman who must spend hours each evening and weekend in writing up reports for the home office. His attention is directed away from his own functions to the performance of clerical work.

Peter F. Drucker has described this influence on executives and others, in part, as follows: "The things he is asked about or required to do for control purposes, come to appear to him as reflections of what the company wants of him, become to him the essence of his job; while resenting them, he tends to put effort into these things rather than into his own job. Eventually, his boss, too, is misdirected, if not hypnotized, by the procedure." [4]

---

[4] Peter F. Drucker, *The Practice of Management* (New York: Harper & Brothers, 1954), p. 134.

The industrial accountant as a "go-giver"

In addition to his usual property and legal control functions, the industrial accountant has certain management service functions.[5] These services assist management in formulating policies, planning long range and short term programs of business activities, and controlling operations. The services include reports that provide a picture of current business operations plus those required for decision making. When the reports deal with the setting of budgets or standards and the making of forecasts, the accountant can think of his function in either of two ways:

1. He can set the standards entirely independently of the operating men who are responsible for meeting the standards. He can set up checks and balances that provide the control, or
2. He and the management can follow the policy that the operating executives should determine the standards for their own activities. The accountant, in this case, supplies information, and makes reviews and evaluations of the standards.

Typically, accountants tend to lean to the side of thinking of control as a matter of mechanical checks and balances. Those who have this tendency may try to "sell" their ideas to management and the operating employees but they hold to the idea of control as a force that is imposed upon the members of the operating organization. This kind of auditing often results in an implied or even a direct evaluation of the competence of executives and other employees in meeting the standards. This means that the accountant becomes in essence the authority who rates the performances of the operating executives in all major areas of the business. No accountant is adequately equipped to assume such broad responsibilities even though he may carry the title of controller and be a member of the board of directors.

Since the industrial accountant is not equipped to control operations by mechanical checks and balances, he can meet the needs of the situation by putting the emphasis of his thinking on cooperative effort. He should learn all he can about the operating men's problems and establish a basis for working with them toward common objectives.[6]

---

[5] See David R. Anderson, "The Industrial Accountant as a 'Go-Giver,'" *N.A.C.A. Bulletin*, June 1955.
[6] Cf. *op. cit.*

Audits

In most large companies, a control section or accountant examines and verifies the records of each one of the managerial units of the company. The results of the audit go to the president or executive vice president. He then requests each manager or department head to come to his office where he is in many cases, "put on the carpet" on the basis of the audit of his operations. The effects of this procedure are likely to be just what one would expect. The control section is referred to by numerous disdainful terms and the members of the control group are looked upon as stooges. One of the most common criticisms of auditors, for example, is that they seldom read or understand contracts with the labor unions. As a result, the managerial head of a production unit may be criticised unfairly. The department heads after such a session then run their units to make a good showing on the control-section audits. Instead of trying to reduce costs and make profits in the most practicable manner, the goal becomes one of operating in terms of the factors that happen to be measured by the audit.

Fortunately, some managements recognize this hazard and require the auditors to make their reports directly to the head of the managerial unit studied. Here the stimulation becomes one of self-administered control rather than control by a distant authority whose evaluation is dependent upon the figures obtained in an audit.

In some companies, a Cost Control Council is organized to meet at regular intervals in order to review cost figures and search for means to keep them down. The accounting department's cost forms are carefully studied. If any members of the council such as supervisors do not know how to read the forms, accountants are invited to attend the sessions in order to explain the figures.

Such a procedure trains the members to cut down delays due to mechanical failures, to reduce training time by giving more personal attention to learners, and to encourage employees to perform economically. The effects are better control of work flow, superior quality, less absenteeism, and closer communication between all departments from designing to shipping.

Budgets

Most well-managed companies use a budget system that consists of estimates of the financial needs of each department. Usually, budgets are accounting techniques that are designed to control costs for a given period in the future. Over-all estimates are made of the future needs of the business, the funds available, and the amounts to be spent by the various managerial units. Estimates of expenditures are set up for certain purposes: materials, equipment, maintenance, direct labor, and administrative expenses. Each managerial unit operates or attempts to operate within the framework of predicted expenditures. The budget has so much importance in some companies that virtually every member of the organization feels its impact.

Budgets are frequently used as a basis for rewarding and penalizing the members of the organization, particularly executives and supervisors. Failure to meet the budget in many plants invites a reprimand or even "punishment." Success in meeting it brings rewards or at least smiles from management.

Budgets affect people so directly that special consideration should be given to their human relationships.

In some companies, department heads set up an excessively tight budget. Some executives have a fetish for making up a budget lower than any other department of the company, and then trying to have expenses run far below estimated expenditures. Since cutting costs frequently means holding the line on wages and salaries, ill feeling is often created between the employee deserving a raise and his immediate boss, whose hands are tied by the budget.

Budgets have a very common influence on the morale of employees who deserve increases in pay. Raises and promotions are supposedly given on the basis of merit. The immediate boss or supervisor initiates the request for an increase, but the recommendation must be approved by a department head or other member of management who is budget conscious. He protects his budget figures by means of rules and procedures. A great deal of red tape must be unravelled before a raise is approved.

Chris Argyris [7] made investigations of the impact of budgets upon front-line supervisors. This was a field study of three small plants, each with less than 1,500 employees. The plants manufactured both "custom made" products and products "for stock." All three were unionized and the work covered the full range from highly-skilled to nonskilled workers.

Argyris pointed out that some negative reactions to budgets are perhaps inevitable:

> (1) Budgets are, first of all, evaluation instruments. Because they tend to set goals against which to measure people, they naturally are complained about.

---

[7] Chris Argyris, "Human Problems with Budgets," *Harvard Business Review,* January-February 1953.

(2) Budgets are one of the few evaluation processes that are always in writing and therefore concrete. Thus, some of the supervisors tend to use budgets as "whipping posts" in order to release their feelings about many other (often totally unrelated) problems.

(3) Budgets are thought of as pressure devices. As such they produce the same kind of unfavorable reactions as do other kinds of pressure regardless of origin . . . the effects of management pressure upon supervisors is not necessarily limited to budgets. For example, a company "saddled" with a domineering executive but which has no budget may well be affected by the same factors as those reported.

Argyris found that one of the most common of the factory supervisors' assumptions about budgets is that they can be used as a pressure device to increase production efficiency. The need for pressure is based on the assumption that most workers are inherently lazy. Many employees also believe that top management thinks the workers do not have enough motivation of their own to do the best possible job. Such feelings, even if never openly expressed to the employees, filter through to them in very subtle ways. Once they sense that feelings of this kind exist in top management, they may become very resentful.

The pressure, while increasing efficiency, may also release forces that pull in the opposite direction. Employees try to keep production at the new level and to prevent it from rising again. Tensions begin to mount. People become uneasy and suspicious. They increase the informal pressure to keep production at the new level.[8] The employee can release some of his tensions by joining a group against management. The supervisor cannot because he at least partially identifies himself with management. Certainly, he would not help his chances for advancement by joining an anti-management group.

Of course, relatively few supervisors get ulcers or experience a nervous breakdown because of pressure from budgets. Managements must, however, use intelligent approaches to the problem of pressure. One of the approaches invariably recommended is to gain acceptance by having supervisors participate in the making of the budgets that affect them. Controllers usually emphasize the need for participation of all key people in instituting any changes in budgets, plus the willingness on the controllers' own part to revise their budgets whenever experience indicates it is necessary. Argyris' observations indicated, however, that some controllers find it easier to follow the form than the spirit of participation:

> The typical controller's insistence on other's participation sounded good to us when we first heard it in our interviews. But after a few minutes of discussion it began to look as if the word "participation" had a rather

---

[8] See Kurt Lewin, "Group Decision and Social Change," in Theodore Newcomb and Eugene L. Hartley, eds., *Readings in Social Psychology* (New York: Henry Holt and Co., 1947), especially p. 342.

strange meaning for the controller. One thing in particular happened in *every* interview which led us to believe that we were not thinking of the same thing. After the controller had told us that he insisted on participation, he would then continue by describing his difficulty in getting the supervisors to speak freely. For example:

"We bring them in, we tell them that we want their frank opinion, but most of them just sit there and nod their heads. We know they're not coming out with exactly how they feel. I guess budgets scare them; some of them don't have too much education. . . . Then we request the line supervisor to sign the new budget, so he can't tell us he didn't accept it. We've found a signature helps an awful lot. If anything goes wrong, they can't come to us, as they often do, and complain. We just show them their signature and remind them they were shown exactly what the budget was made up of. . . ."

Such statements seem to indicate that only pseudo-participation is desired by the controller. True participation means that the people can be spontaneous and free in their discussion. Participation, in the real sense of the word, also involves a group decision which leads the group to accept or reject something new. Of course, organizations need to have their supervisors accept the new goals, not reject them; however, if the supervisors do not really accept the new changes but only say they do, then trouble is inevitable. Such halfhearted acceptance makes it necessary for the person who initiated the budget or induced the change, not only to request signatures of the "acceptors" so that they cannot later on deny they "accepted," but to be always on the lookout and apply pressure constantly upon the "acceptors" (through informal talks, meetings, and "educational discussions of accounting").

In other words, if top-management executives are going to use participation, then they should use it in the real sense of the word. Any dilution of the real thing "will taste funny," and people will not like it.[9]

Of course budget installations should not be made to appear as edicts of accounting department experts nor as dragnets for substandard performance. Budgets should be looked upon as aids in achieving objectives. Lack of understanding of these objectives can lead to suspicion of the budget—even to its rejection. Top management should therefore state the objectives in a manner that causes employees to desire a budget that is reasonable and challenging.

Generally, one reason for hostility towards existing budgets is the typical accountant's tendency in reporting budgeted performance to show, and even to emphasize disproportionately, what is wrong, without considering why variances occurred. The budget reporter should note first where actual performance has been significantly better than estimates and then mention what has fallen short of expectations. Analysis of the latter should be cautious because the origin of shortcomings may be in factors not evident to the financial analyst.

---

[9] Argyris, "Human Problems with Budgets," p. 108.

Human Relations in Accounting

383

Department heads, for example, should not be held accountable for machine down-time, unavoidable re-runs, and faulty material unless normal allowances for these are made in the departmental budgets. Also, if budgets are based on standards of maximum possible efficiency at full production, it is likely that actual costs can never approximate budgeted goals.

As a teacher of accounting has stated:

> Because of the complexities of budget preparation, especially at first, perhaps the best policy is to make the program frankly experimental. By doing so, management is saying, "Here is a plan based on the best judgment of all of us and on certain available past-performance data. Let's try it out and use it for what it is worth. After this first tryout, we shall be in a position to have more insight when we prepare our next budget." Such an approach puts operating department heads on their mettle. If the experiment is even partly successful, it will be because junior echelons of the management team have helped to make it so. And, in the right kind of business enterprise, foremen and other leaders should welcome the opportunity to take a greater part in management through further development of the budget as a useful means of planning and controlling business operations.[10]

A controller may control so rigidly that management cannot discover its competent men

Most executives should, of course, know how to interpret financial records. All find it helpful to be aware of the effects of accounting controls on the spirit of the organization. The controller's primary function is to gather and interpret data which will assist other executives in the determination of sound policies and their successful execution. In some cases controllership is performed by the financial vice president; more often it is the chief accountant who is responsible for this function.

Anyone who notes the influence of the controller in a number of companies is likely to find that some managements follow so rigid a policy of accounting controls that top management has difficulty in discovering its competent self-initiating employees. Advocates of rigid executive controls insist they are guarding against broad delegation of authority to employees who do not have the capacity to exercise it efficiently.

Some accountants think that it is more important to set up controls that will assure right behavior than to find out which individuals are men of initiative.

---

[10] See Colin Park, "Giving Budgeting Appeal for the Foreman," *N.A.C.A. Bulletin,* October 1951.

Management men who are more interested in discovering their men of initiative than in having the benefits of obedience may resent the rigidities imposed by the controller type of mind. The senior vice president of a large corporation, for example, voiced his objection to the tight mechanical controls set up by the company's controller by defining a controller as "An accountant who thinks slowly!" [11] Such an executive would say that it is usually more important for a supervisor to find out which one of his employees is capable of exercising initiative and good judgment than to control the actions of all the employees in accordance with the policies laid down by the supervisor himself.

The term "controller" in itself implies a firmness that calls for obedient rather than creative thinking.

Obviously, different philosophies of management are followed by different managements. Some have developed the practice of very rigid controls; others set up controls in a manner that still allows ample breathing and working space for the men of initiative. This suggests that the student of accounting, or perhaps better, the practicing accountant, should note whether the internal controls set up by the accounting department or controller tend to inhibit or release the creative potentials of the people in the organization.

Typically, the technically-minded accountant is trained in the importance of standard procedures and good business practice. A system, once it has been set up, should be obeyed. It is perfectly natural for him to check the work records of others. However, we should also bear in mind that not all rigidities are discretionary. A lot of record keeping must also be attributed to the nature of the business, not to the zeal of the controller.

Usually, the personnel man and the other alert members of an organization recognize this kind of influence in the company. When, for example, an applicant applies for a job, the human-relations-minded interviewer tries to estimate the extent to which the applicant would fit into the company's rigidities. Consultants who make incisive observations in many different companies note that employees who like a rigidly-controlled working environment tend to find that kind of employment. Employees who like the opposite work situation tend also, in time, to find it. The student who is aware of company and individual personality similarities and conflicts should, when choosing an employer, consider the influence exerted by the accountants—would he be happier in a rigidly controlled working situation or in another company where controls are more flexible? To make his decision, he should discuss with

---

[11] This kind of humorous definition of an occupational member is found in many groups and mature members do not resent it—they accept it as humor. Consider the many definitions of statisticians you have heard.

the prospective employer the kinds of controls that are made on operations by the accounting department.

Cost controls should be checked to find out their actual rather than their imagined effects on costs

One of the stories often told to illustrate the effects of absurd rigidities in controls is that of the "railroad washroom doors." According to the story, the new president of a railroad was surprised to find that some twenty thousand dollars was being spent each year to replace the damaged outer doors of washrooms in small stations on the line. Upon investigation, he learned that the doors had been damaged and had been replaced in accordance with the company's accounting rules. Doors to washrooms were kept locked except just before and after trains were at the depot. Quite frequently a traveler who had come to wait for a train would request the key and thoughtlessly not return it before boarding the train. Station agents were allowed to spend only 25 cents a year to buy new keys for the washrooms. The station agent reasoned that if he sent through a requisition for a new key, it would be six weeks before his request was approved. Furthermore he also had to file a detailed explanation. If, however, he should break open or otherwise damage the door, he could purchase a new door, because according to the controller this was a capital improvement, whereas a new key was an "expense item." The simple practice of breaking the door was followed by all the station agents and was costing the railroad a considerable sum of money a year! If the controller had allowed the station agent to buy a new 25-cent key whenever one was needed, this unnecessary expenditure could have been saved—and the dignity of the agent preserved.[12]

Retrenchment periods—cost-cutting drives

When profit margins are being pinched, managements know why. The usual causes for the pinch—higher labor and material costs plus sharpened competition—are evident. To bring profit margins back to normal often necessitates the cutting of costs.

This kind of situation is so common in American business that the sophisticated oldtimers look upon a retrenchment period as the expected phase of a familiar cycle. When business is good, no one worries very

---

[12] For further details, see Peter F. Drucker, *The Practice of Management* (New York: Harper & Brothers, 1954), p. 125.

much about extra expenses and minor added costs. When profit margins dip, the cost-cutting programs multiply. The drive usually starts in the manufacturing operations and then moves into the offices where expense accounts, telephone bills, paperwork, and added personnel are coldly scrutinized. Departments are often merged to reduce supervisory costs.

The effects on the morale of many employees is, of course, terrific. To most employees, the terms "economy program," "cost reduction," and "retrenchment" are frightening, particularly to recently-hired employees. They fear that their jobs will be the first to be eliminated. Older employees, too, particularly those who feel insecure about their positions, begin to fear the possibility of dismissal. This fear has special portent for the old employee who suspects that the boss thinks of him as being out-of-date in his methods. Perhaps, he thinks, he's only deadwood in the organization to his superiors?

Doubts and worries accumulate during these periods and managements wonder how the unnecessary fears may be prevented. Should management tell the employees that expenses have to be reduced? Or should the economy program be put into effect quietly and unobtrusively?

Progressive managements know that there is no alternative—employees *must* be told. They must be told because expenses cannot be reduced without the cooperation of the people down the line. But they need not be scared if the accounting department is human-relations minded and works with management and men to show where costs are out of line or might be reduced.

Transal Engineering Corporation, a relatively small producer of electronic equipment and radio gear, found one way. With ten separate assembly lines for different products, relatively long runs, and a simple assembly task, management improved the profit rate from 4 per cent or less to 12 per cent by means of daily cost reports to the ten foremen. Each day each foreman was given a statement telling him in dollars and cents whether his operation was in the red or black, whether it was on schedule the previous day, and what his current standing was on his contract. These daily statements replaced previously used month-end reports that usually came too late for action. Under the old system, by the time a foreman realized something was wrong the damage was already done.

In a larger company with a more complex production setup, this daily type of control is next to impossible. Such companies turn instead to standard costing and the targeting of specific savings goals for divisions and departments.[13]

---

[13] See "It's Cost-Shearing Season Again," *Business Week*, September 7, 1957, p. 84.

Regardless of whether the company is large or small, when employees are told about the need for the economy drive and their participation is sought in a sincere spirit, the drive does not arouse unnecessary fears. A favorable human relations climate is basic to make the program effective.

> One company president launched an expense-reduction drive with a memorandum to all department heads stating that the economies must be realized "without hurting any of our people."
> This phrase got around via the grapevine, and was probably more responsible for the success of the program than any other factor. Some jobs were eliminated, as was inevitable, but other jobs were found—some of them much better—for those affected. The organization was tightened up and made much more efficient because of the cooperation of the whole working force.
> The cooperation was insured in advance by the simple phrase—"without hurting any of our people." [14]

Property control and auditing functions of the accountant

One important function of the accountant and auditor is to keep an accurate check on the property and assets of the company, not only for management's use but also for the protection of the stockholders who own the business.

The fact that some large and small losses are sustained by companies and are allowed to continue undiscovered over long periods of years brings blushes to the faces of the accountants who are expected to devise proper systems of control. Accountants are supposed to prevent dishonesty losses and to make an early discovery in the event of any serious breakdown in operational procedure.

Two things are essential in preventing dishonesty losses and assuring early discovery when they do occur:

1. A good system of internal control. Poor internal controls are an invitation to the dishonest employee.
2. Continual vigilance. The success of the system of internal controls depends entirely on the human beings responsible for its administration.

> The system may break down through an officer or employee allowing someone else to reconcile his bank accounts for him; though his failure

---

[14] "Keeping Morale UP and costs DOWN," *Modern Management*, March 11, 1957. Copyright © 1957 by The Bureau of National Affairs, Inc., Washington 7, D.C.

to maintain proper control over customers' accounts: or through relinquishing any part of his assigned duties (no matter how small) to another employee who volunteers to perform them. Large scale embezzlers are generally the most willing and hardest workers in an organization and often when a loss is discovered the management or executive officer is surprised to find the scope of the defaulter's activities. . . .

Employees may be divided into two groups. There is the larger group which is thoroughly honest and trustworthy. They are morally honest and just could not be dishonest under any circumstances. We do not have to worry about them. On the other hand, there is a second group of employees—I'm glad to say in the minority—who consider themselves honest and actually do not think they will ever be dishonest. But, let them have domestic trouble, sickness or become involved in gambling or women, and then expose them to a loose system of internal audit and to a good system which has sprung a leak, and they have an open invitation to steal, or, as they feel, "borrow," their employers' funds. In my opinion, management is largely responsible for the casualties in this second group. It is necessary to protect these employees from themselves by keeping temptation out of their way. Practically all large dishonesty losses are caused by persons who were never found guilty of prior dishonest acts. Occasionally we have repeaters, but these are very much the exception rather than the rule.

All officers and employees should be required to take a vacation. A successful embezzler cannot afford to take a vacation or even get sick. For that matter, he cannot afford to die. Beware of the person who voluntarily assumes to take care of part of another employee's duties or operations.[15]

Typically, embezzlers are trusted employees. They are believed to steal more than all the nation's professional criminals.[16]

The typical embezzler usually has no previous police record. He earns enough to live comfortably. The employer usually has a high regard for his work. He is usually considered a desirable employee with a secure future. Sometimes he is even looked upon as a pillar of society. To his friends he is quite normal mentally. Actually inside his head he is fighting battles with himself. The origin of the conflicts is not so much in the opportunity to steal as in his early childhood history. His thievery may be a maladjusted attempt to gain the affection of others. When caught, he usually feels better because the element of self-punishment is mixed in with his crooked motives.

Some thieves of company property have a vengeful motive, like the employee who justified helping himself by saying he was underpaid. Hotel patrons steal towels partly because they feel they are overcharged.

When the accountant sets up safeguards to prevent defalcations or

---

[15] George A. Conner, "Management's Responsibility for Dishonesty Losses," *The Office*, November 1952, pp. 69, 140, 157.

[16] See "Embezzlers, the Trusted Thieves," *Fortune*, November 1957, p. 142.

thievery, he does not remove the embezzler's motives. That is a psychiatric function but the accountant can help detect these badly motivated individuals as soon as possible and help place them in positions where their conflicts do not damage themselves, the employer, or their friends. Sometimes he may even be able to get them to seek psychiatric treatment. Certainly the usually designated motives of "high living, slow horses, and fast women" only tell us where the money went. Removing the opportunities to gamble does not change the urge to gamble. Only psychiatric treatment can do that.[17]

"*Methods may be different from the old days, Perkins, but we still check expense accounts in the same old way.*" SOURCE: *by Charles D. Saxon. Reprinted from Sales Management.*

When you study or practice accounting

Accounting to many students and employees in business is viewed as a mechanical, mathematically precise operation only. Actually, it is the center of a communications system for management and employees. All the accountant's figures and reports involve people. This means that when you study or practice accounting, you should do more than record

---

[17] See Donald A. Laird and Eleanor C. Laird, *Sizing Up People* (New York: McGraw-Hill Book Company, Inc., 1951), p. 194.

figures accurately—you should also think of them as a means of conveying understanding.

This kind of attitude should make the subject and the people in accounting more interesting to you. Bear in mind, also, that accountants are intelligent. Most are receptive in regard to the effects of their work on others. They want to do their work in ways that develop good will toward them as well as toward other members of the business team.

COLLATERAL READINGS

For All Students

Carey, John L., *Should You Be an Accountant?* New York Life Insurance Company, 51 Madison Ave., New York 10, N. Y. Pamphlet prepared for young people who seek vocational information on the subject.

White, George R., "Accounting Is a Communications Tool," *N.A.C.A. Bulletin*, September 1956. Aimed at bringing certain phases of the communications problem into focus, insofar as the accountant is concerned.

For Advanced Students

Reporting Financial Data to Top Management, American Management Association, Inc., Special Report No. 25. Financial executives discuss how to organize and administer financial reporting programs, and how to present financial reports on *specific* areas of management planning.

Walton, C. W., *et al.*, "How We Report to Various Levels of Management," *N.A.C.A. Bulletin*, Section 3, October 1956. In this panel session, five executives of the Minnesota Mining and Manufacturing Company gave a composite picture of financial planning and controls in their organization.

For Men in Business

Hennessy, John R., and E. I. Roberson, "Budget Preparation from the Bottom Up," *N.A.C.A. Bulletin*, Section I, December 1956.

Jaspan, Norman, President Investigations Inc., "Thieves in White Collars," *Sales Management*, February 20, 1959. Internal thefts—most of them by "honest, trusted" employees—cost $1 billion a year. Are your salesmen falsifying orders, giving or taking bribes, stealing parts? Here are the steps to take.

Willson, James D., "Dynamic Budgeting—Getting the Most from Your Program," *Dun's Review and Modern Industry*, June 1957, p. 62.

QUESTIONS ON THE CHAPTER

1. Name several ways that enable an accounting department to be a tool of communication.
2. Why and how should an industrial accountant become a "go-giver," instead of a "go-getter"?

3. What is the value of having auditors report directly to the head of the managerial unit they are studying?

4. According to Chris Argyris' field study, what is the most common negative reaction to budgets by factory supervisors, and what effect may this have on the employees?

5. In what ways do supervisors ease the pressure applied to them by top management and how do these differ from the employees' reactions to the same pressure?

6. Explain the functions of a controller. Name some of the ways in which he can help or hinder the effectiveness and spirit of management and employees.

7. What principle of cost controls is suggested by the story of the "railroad washroom doors?"

8. What action should management take toward employees in order to prevent unnecessary doubts and fears from accumulating during a retrenchment period?

9. Discuss ways to prevent dishonesty losses in a company. Should the main objective in the prevention be that of catching the thieves or giving honest employees more emotional security? How do you personally look upon the purposes of the cash register where you buy merchandise?

10. Cite from your own experience any instance of thievery from a business concern. Could a better accounting system have prevented that kind of theft?

11. Now that you have read about ways in which accounting may dominate the spirit in a company, would you prefer to work in a company that has many or few accounting controls? Explain your reasons for your choice.

PROBLEMS AND PROJECTS

For All Students

1. The student who has majored in accounting may find his first jobs dull, routine. His supervisors may know little theoretical accounting. How can the well-trained young accountant make his first jobs challenging and enjoyable?

2. Some persons think that accountants are likely to be introverted and impersonal. Study the question. If available, read Stanley J. Segal, "The Role of Personality Factors in Vocational Choice," *The American Psychologist,* August 1955.

For Advanced Students

3. Make a study of economy programs that have been made stimulating to the employees. For suggestions, read E. Lee Tallman, "Top Management and Cost Reduction," *The Management Review,* American Management Association, Inc., October 1957.

4. Examine recent issues of the *Harvard Business Review.* Read articles that deal with accounting. To what extent do they treat human relations?

For Men in Business

5. Discuss the advantages and disadvantages of having the foreman hand each employee's pay to him rather than have the payroll department perform the chore.

6. Describe some of the human relations problems of members of accounting departments of companies with which you are well acquainted. To what extent does the content of this chapter treat or fail to treat the problems observed?

F INANCE CAN BE DEFINED AS AN APPLICATION OF ACCOUNTING, business economics, business law, and statistical inference, plus human relations, to the acquiring, administering, and distributing of business funds. Money is so basic as a resource of a business firm that the head of the firm usually retains control of its finances. He may be an owner or chief executive officer. In some corporations major responsibility for financial matters is vested in a committee of the board of directors. In most corporations a treasurer or a financial vice president functions as a center of financial matters.

The financial executive of a company provides services for the administrative units in many of their functions that involve people. Some of these are providing data and making recommendations in connection with wage policies and union negotiations, determining the services to be rendered to customers, and deciding whether the company should meet competitors' prices or ignore them. He is also vitally concerned with stockholder relations, and to a considerable extent with public relations since he is the authority on questions relating to any aspect of finance in which the public is interested.

The chief financial officer has work relations with almost all executives of the company. When the board of directors and the chief executive officer are considering any program for expansion such as the building of a new plant or the purchase of a costly machine, the inevitable question is "Do we have (or

22 Human Relations in Finance

will we have) the money to pay for it?" When the production manager, research director, or sales manager wish to set up expansion programs, the counsel of the chief finance executive is essential. He must have money available whenever it is needed. His responsibilities usually involve the development of contacts with sources of money such as banks and other financial institutions. The effective financial officer sounds out bankers long before the company actually needs money. He finds out which ones would like to participate in serving the company's financial needs. When he is ready to borrow money, he knows which banks are favorably disposed toward making the loan. Before making the final approach for a substantial amount, he has informed the bank's officers of his company's financial status and the plans for the use of the money. A well-formulated plan for the use of the money is basic to the getting of a loan or raising capital.

The one important function that affects the security of the employees is obtaining working capital for the company. The finance officer must decide whether the company's working capital shall be obtained through borrowing, through retaining profits, or through selling securities in the stock market. He must be acquainted with the profit possibilities and the risk factors in the business.

The finance officer has major responsibilities in regard to the financial health of the company and he must guide the management in its use of the company's funds. He must help to keep the members of financial circles, the public, and the employees properly informed in regard to the company's financial status and needs. Much of his work is informative and educational.

Need for educating employees in regard to the employer's finances

We can appreciate the need for informative services when we review the opinions and attitudes of employees toward the finances of employers. Employees are likely to have warped opinions about wealth and how it is acquired. Many individuals are likely to be defensively envious toward persons of wealth rather than objective about the economic benefits of saving. This attitude toward wealth is very old as indicated by one of Socrates' statements made more than two thousand years ago, approximately 354 B.C.

> "When I was a boy, wealth was regarded as a thing so secure as well as admirable that almost everyone affected to own more property than he actually possessed. . . . Now a man has to be ready to defend him-

self against being rich as if it were the worst of crimes. For it has become far more dangerous to be suspected of being well off than to be detected in crime."

Worker bitterness toward company and profits is frequently found today. Surveys of employees' opinions have brought up statements such as the following:

"This company has lots of dough! They could pay us more wages out of their big profits if they wanted to."

"Let business pay all the taxes. They can stand it better than we can."

"Wage increases don't need to raise prices to the customers."

"All profits ought to go to the workers. The stockholders are all rich people who have too much money now."

"'Capitalism' means that my employment is insecure and that my opportunity for advancement or self-employment is reduced."

"'Capitalism' means that the world's wealth is unfairly distributed."

"Profits are idle dollars in the bank."

"All profits go to stockholders."

"Profits are something in the nature of a gift to the owners, something obtained without work."

"Most stockholders are rich men, and chief among them are the officers of the company."

The errors in some of these opinions are indicated by surveys of stock ownership in America. Of all adults, about one in eight owns some stock. The number of shareholders in the United States is greater than the number of factory workers. Most shareholders need their dividends. They are not persons of great wealth. In United States Steel, for example, the owners of the business outnumber the employees by a considerable margin. No one person holds as much as three-tenths of one per cent of the outstanding stock. A survey showed that more than half of the shareowners had incomes that were less than the average wage the company was paying to its steelworkers.[1] Similar findings have been obtained from analyses of stockholders of many of our largest corporations.

Companies that have tried to teach workers the economic facts of

---

[1] Roger M. Blough, *Learning To Multiply and Divide* (United States Steel Corporation, 71 Broadway, New York, 1957).

In Exhibit Hall and Visitors' Center at New York Stock Exchange, guests find glimpses of industrial wonders planned for the world of tomorrow.

Do-it-yourself demonstration of B. F. Goodrich tire (above) is mounted so the visitor himself may puncture it to observe its self-sealing quality. The tire will take well over 2,200 punctures before a replacement is needed.

An atomic power plant in miniature (below) is displayed by Consolidated Edison Company of New York—a working model, demonstrating how nuclear energy is to be harnessed in Con Ed's Indian Point generating plant. Catherine Whittemore, Chief Receptionist, explains exhibit to a visitor.

Exhibits in the financial district showplace bring out the close link between the increase in shareownership and the capabilities of publicly owned companies to work ahead in the exciting industrial future. Photos courtesy New York Stock Exchange.

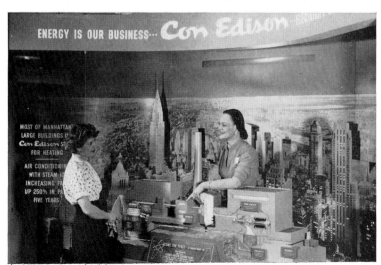

life find the task very difficult.[2] The management of a large manufacturing company, for example, planned and conducted a campaign of economic education among its workers in order to explain the benefits of profits, the need for adequate returns for investors, and the values of our system of free enterprise. The campaign failed to make any change in the workers' attitudes. As a result, the company officials concluded that the workers were short-sighted and stubborn.

This particular management did not realize that the employees were as interested as management in what affects the security of their jobs. The problem had not been presented to the employees as one which was related to the workers' bread and butter. Logical reasoning and economic abstractions about the need for a more adequate return on the investment of somebody who, in the opinion of the employees, had a good deal more money than they did, aroused no interest on their part. Instead of recognizing the contribution of stockholders to the employees, the effect was to cause the workers to think that people who had enough money to invest in the corporation were avidly arguing for even more.[3]

Very few employees think of the need for adequate financing, yet the problem, illustrated in the Thompson Products' story of the "The Solid Gold Turret Lathe" is a very serious one to management.

> The story starts back in 1942 when the company bought a lathe for $12,000. Under federal tax laws, the company was permitted to depreciate the cost of the lathe over a 14-year period. So, last year, when the lathe became obsolete, there was $12,000 to buy a new one, plus $1,000, which was the resale value of the old one.
>
> But the replacement cost in 1956 was $35,000 for a lathe that would perform the same functions as the old model, or $67,000 for a new one with attachments to meet today's more exacting needs.
>
> The company had only $13,000 to do a $67,000 job. The difference of $54,000 had to come out of profits, and in order to get that amount in 1956 the company had to earn a profit of more than $112,500 before taxes, because $54,000 was all there was left after taxes. The corporate profit tax is 52%.
>
> And to earn that amount of profit, the company had to sell more than $1,250,000 worth of products to replace one lathe which originally cost just $12,000!

---

[2] For a more complete treatment of false ideas about profits and efforts of companies to give employees economic facts, see *Telling Employees about Business Operations: Profits* (Policyholders Service Bureau, Metropolitan Life Insurance Company, New York). For helpful descriptions of books on finance for college students, see "Looking Ahead," *Harvard Business Review*, January-February 1960, pp. 33f.

[3] See also William C. Menninger and Harry Levinson, *Human Understanding in Industry* (Chicago, Ill.: Science Research Associates, 1956), p. 49.

Sounds like a lot of profit—$112,500. BUT: The stockholders got none of it. The government took more than half of it. The rest went to replace a machine so three Thompson people—one per shift—could continue working.

Sounds fantastic? Sure. But it's true. It's fantastic *because* it is true! This tale of the million-dollar lathe was part of Thompson Products' annual report to its stockholders which gives details on how much money the company took in and what happened to it.

Only a relatively small amount of profit a company makes is paid to stockholders in dividends. A large portion must be retained and plowed back into the company to finance expansion and replacement costs so the company can continue operating and employees can continue working.[4]

Annual financial reports

The key medium of the typical employee educational program when sponsored by a financial officer is likely to be the annual report. The extent to which these annual reports are read by employees of a typical industrial company is indicated by the answers to four questions used as part of an employee morale survey:

1. A 24-page copy of the Company's "Annual Report for the Past Year" presented to employees for the first time the financial facts, balance sheets, dividends paid, average weekly earnings, etc. Did you see a copy of the report?

	Men	Women
Yes	87%	73%
No	12	20
Not Sure	1	7

2. If you saw a copy of the report, about how much of it did you read?

	Per Cent of Men Who Saw Report	Per Cent of Women Who Saw Report
a. All of it	60%	16%
b. Most or about ¾ of it	17	14
c. About half	12	16
d. About one-fourth	3	8
e. Glanced at a few pages	8	42
f. None	1	5

3. If you gave a copy of the report to any other members of your family or friends to read, about how many persons read parts of the report?

---

[4] "To Members of the Thompson Organization," annual report of Thompson Products, Inc. (Cleveland, Ohio, March 5, 1957).

	Men	Women	Total
a. No one	20%	22%	21%
b. One or two persons	52	47	50
c. Three to five persons	17	9	13
d. Six to nine persons	3	0	1
e. Ten or more persons	2	0	1

The response to this question indicated that for every employee who saw the report there were 1.3 other people who saw it.

4. After seeing the report, what is your impression about the division of the income of the Company in the last five years?

	Men	Women
a. The payments to *stockholders*, in comparison with payments to or for the benefit of employees, went up and payments to the employees went down (wrong answer)	3%	4%
b. The payments to *employees* went up and those to stockholders went down (correct answer)..	64	20
c. Don't remember	33	77

One of the basic ways in which reports may be improved is in their tone or spirit. Too many reports still have a protestation-of-virtue tone. Information is usually presented in a manner that is decidedly favorable to management's interests. A low-paid manual worker, for example, is not likely to be impressed by a chart which shows that the compensation paid to executives is only a tiny slice of the sales dollar pie while the portion that went to labor is represented by the biggest piece of all. The employee thinks in terms of the relative number of individuals involved and the average per capita income of the persons represented by the two cuts of the pie.

Some reports present figures to show that if executives worked for nothing and their salaries were divided equally among all the other employees, the increase for each employee would amount to only a few cents per week. The employees know that the salaries of executives on an individual basis are much higher than the wages of the worker. Why try to kid the worker? Why not simply state that good executives, like good workers, cost money?

Some reports present the stockholder's financial investment in the company as one of benevolence—he puts his money into the company in order to give employees good jobs at a high rate of pay! To the typical employee, the stockholder's risks are meaningless. The stockholder to the typical employee is a rich person who doesn't have to work while the worker is investing all his "capital"—his skill and energy —in the business.

The evolution of accounting and financial reporting has been influenced by the needs of those whose interests are affected—the proprietor

ARE YOU A "MISSING" SHAREHOLDER?

ARE YOU ONE OF THE NEARLY 3,000 Sunray Mid-Continent Oil Company stockholders whose current mailing address is missing from the Company records? If you are you may share in a fund composed of past dividends that were mailed, and returned for lack of proper address.

Lewis Lacy checks on the whereabouts of one of Sunray's "lost" shareholders with Murva Renfrow, stockholder relations supervisor. Sunray mails 98,000 dividend checks quarterly.

EVERY THREE MONTHS some 98,000 dividend checks are mailed to holders of Sunray Mid-Continent common stock. Invariably some of the checks are returned by the Post Office with the notation . . . Moved, Left no Forwarding Address, Unknown, etc.

THE SECRETARY of the Company starts his detective work at once in an attempt to locate "missing" stockholders. Despite the fact that no stone is left unturned to deliver dividends to rightful owners a great many stockholders have not yet been found.

MOST OF THE CHECKS ARE SMALL but one missing stockholder has to his credit over $1,400 in dividends, accumulated during the last 20-odd years.

SUNRAY'S "MISSING STOCKHOLDER" FILES are worked daily in an attempt to locate wandering stockholders. As the corporate secretary says, "Chances are that the missing stockholder file will never be empty. If it is, the secretary's department will have completed a remarkable task of hide-and-go-seek."

Beverly Howell cross-checks the "missing" file with outstanding check numbers on list of Sunray shareholders.

The clerical problem of keeping in accurate touch with stockholders can be appreciated when we realize that many companies have more than 100,000 stockholders, some as many as 500,000. Most of these shareholders depend upon receiving regular dividends as needed income.

of the business, the creditors, stockholders, the investing public, the tax gatherer, the regulatory agency. In many companies, labor is recognized as having a legitimate interest in the over-all results of business operations and it has become a new addition to the list. As a result new accounting and reporting methods are being devised to serve this purpose.

The writing of financial statements for employees, as well as for stockholders or anyone else, is a very difficult task. One of the main difficulties is the commonly-held belief that all corporate income is in liquid form, that it is all available for distribution to the employees and stockholders, and that it is annually distributed by the management. To most people, corporate income and corporate cash are the same. To them, all the corporate income can be distributed without impairing the business. Actually, income may be in the form of land, plant, machinery, patent licenses, or contractual benefits as well as money. The distribution of all income would in most cases require the liquidation of assets necessary to the continued operation of the business.

Most people do not understand the nature or dynamics of business. Many persons, college educated as well as not, imagine that business organizations are deliberately designed to extract unfair profits from the public and the employees. To them, corporations constitute a system of power which will be exploited for selfish benefit only. Those corporations which are owned by absentees, they feel, bleed the communities where they manufacture or sell goods. Presumably, the only cause of unemployment is greed.

Financially alert men try to overcome these and other false notions. They realize that a corporation is the legal name for a group of persons who own certain facilities or tools of production and exchange that are used in a business. Improved tools enable man to change raw materials into products that contribute to better living. Such tools can come only from the savings of individuals who exchange some of their income, in the form of stock purchase, for eventual hope of getting some pay—dividends—for the loan.

Few people realize that the public interest is served through the mutuality of interests of manager, stockholder, worker, and customer of the business. All depend for their livelihoods upon the manner in which a company serves the public.

Stockholders' meetings

During recent years many companies have stepped up their efforts to lure stockholders to annual meetings. As a result, former poorly attended annual meetings are now attended by hundreds, even thousands of stockholders.

A cross-country survey showed that annual meetings are planned to be both entertaining and informative. Some companies arrange plant tours and provide attractive product displays. Management-shareowner discussions are becoming increasingly frank. In a few cases management hospitality has even become lavish. The reason for the attempt to increase attendance is the growing awareness that dissatisfied stockholders can make life rather uncomfortable for a complacent management.

When earnings drop, some shareholders place all blame indiscriminately on management. A marked downturn in profit margins causes the top executive in some companies to wince at the thought of the heat of stockholder wrath that he is likely to feel at the next annual meeting. Naturally management circles are anxious to keep stockholders off their backs. Small wonder that annual meetings are being planned more and more to please the shareholders. The good will that may be engendered toward management may be more important than the displays and plant tours organized to sell stockholders on company products. The development of respect for the competence of the management often dominates the program. The stockholder who has personally met or seen the top management in action is more likely to invest additional money in the company, especially when he has been impressed by the forthrightness and competence of the executives who conducted the meeting.

Many of the individuals at stockholder turnouts are likely to be employee-stockholders. In the case of one oil company, half the stockholders are employees and they are allowed time off their jobs to attend the annual meeting.

A question often asked is "What role does the annual meeting play in attracting—and keeping—investment dollars?"

The answer is difficult to ascertain. Finance officers, however, know that when the company needs additional financing, most of the new money will have to come from present stockholders. They will have to risk more dollars.

Success in getting new investor dollars is governed, to a large extent, by how well the investing public knows the company. Most finance officers therefore prefer to see the number of stockholders grow rather than shrink.

Each meeting has its share of "professional kibitzers"—men and women who own as little as one share in a large number of companies. These individuals make it a practice to attend every possible annual affair. The question period offers the kibitzers and the serious intelligent shareholders an opportunity to ask for information which otherwise might remain shut up in executive briefcases. Today's annual meetings in many companies are a step in the direction of shareholder democracy.

The best and most incisive questions are often those of the security analysts who attend annual meetings. For example, Merrill Lynch, Pierce, Fenner & Smith has fourteen specialists and ten assistants who make it their business to attend 400 or more annual meetings a year. They ask questions and jot down notes. It is generally believed that the professional security analysts and counsellors influence as much as 75 per cent of all stock purchases and sales. They are equivalent, in a sense, to the dealers and distributors of a company's consumer product. Their sphere of operation is finance. Their analysis usually determines whether a company's stock is described as a "dog," a "blue chip," or something between.

Top management and financial men who preside at these meetings know that they may face tough and informed questioning. They come as thoroughly prepared as a British cabinet minister who must face questioning in Parliament. The presiding executive must prime himself so well with facts and figures that he can answer many who intend to ask questions before they have time to take the floor. More and more annual meeting audiences are showing a reluctance to allow themselves to be sidetracked.

The evidence indicates that annual meetings can be a valuable institution, one that an alert management does not ignore. If the meetings have not yet become the socially useful forum that they are capable of being, it is as much the fault of the stockholder as of management. As one writer stated: "It is not enough for stockholders simply to flock to annual meetings to prove that they are not acting like sheep. In the last resort, the annual meeting, and stockholder participation in general, can be no better than stockholders make them."

The need for the continued wooing of stockholders is indicated by the forecast of financially astute men who believe that if we are to find the private funds necessary for our anticipated economic expansion there must, down the years, be 40 to 50 million stockholders in this country.[5] Keith Funston, President of the New York Stock Exchange, thinks that "everybody's capitalism" will provide the funds: "The spread of corporate ownership among additional millions of people willing to undertake the risks of stock investments—in return for the rewards, is not only a measure of the country's economic vitality. It is an indication that the goals of the future, which will require enormous quantities of risk capital, can be achieved." Certainly the healthiest condition for

---

[5] Prediction made by Philip Reed, Chairman, General Electric Company. See "Who Owns Industrial America?" *The Management Review,* American Management Association, Inc., September 1956, p. 748.

a capitalist economy to seek is one in which an increasingly greater number of people share in its fruits by becoming capitalists.

The term "capitalism" is still disturbing to some people. As a result, some spokesmen for business have dropped that phrase and taken up "free enterprise" instead. Of late the more fashionable terms in the executive suites are "people's capitalism" or "everybody's capitalism."

Profit-sharing

Some managements try to improve the employee's understanding of the business through profit-sharing. Profit-sharing is an agreement between the employer and the employees under which the profits allocated to the workers rise or fall in proportion to the increase or decrease in the profits realized by the employer. Plans of this kind are very old in the history of business. They were used in England as early as the thirteenth century. The earliest recorded plan in the United States began in 1784 in Albert Gallatin's glassworks at New Geneva, Pennsylvania. Hundreds of companies now have a profit-sharing plan of some kind. The numbers fluctuate over the years in accordance with influences such as the business cycle, long-term trends in stock prices, and inflationary tendencies.

A few plans were started by wealthy employers who wished to share their success with the employees. Most plans, however, have come about as the result of the employer's belief that both the employer and the employee share responsibility for the success or failure of the business and that profit-sharing would stimulate the employees to appreciate more fully the problems of management, especially when the employees imagine that the business is more profitable than it actually is.

Companies that adopt profit-sharing usually hope that the plan will encourage employees to take the management viewpoint and develop a more helpful interest in management's problems. It is assumed that the employee will increase his efficiency because he will share in the rewards of greater productivity. Some plans, too, are designed to promote thrift among the employees and to help them provide for their retirement.

In general, profit-sharing has not become the one simple hoped-for solution to employer-employee relations problems. One reason for the lack of complete success is that when profits shared are relatively stable over a number of years, the employees confuse them with or consider them a part of their regular wages. If the company suddenly finds that its profits are less than in the several preceding years, the typical employee feels that he has been given a cut in his wages.

And when a company makes more profits than usual, the employees tend to assume that the same or greater profits will be distributed in the years that follow. Profits are usually distributed at the end of the year, a time when employees have extra expenses for the holidays. Many do extra spending on the assumption that the profits distributed will be the same as before, or greater. The disappointment of the overly optimistic employee can be imagined when he discovers that the profits to be shared in the current year are less than he had anticipated!

When the profits of the company do not allow the employer to distribute the expected amount of money to the individual employees, some question the honesty of the management. The integrity of the management is especially likely to be questioned when it is noticed that the president happened to buy a bigger house at the same time that the decreased profits were announced.

Many employees would rather have a definite wage than a basic wage plus an uncertain share in the profits. Furthermore, the profits to be shared in most companies are not especially exciting when we realize that the amount distributed to the individual in most companies is less than 6 per cent of the employee's annual wages.

Dissatisfaction over the amount received occurs more often with the good than with the poor employees. The reason is that when a profit-sharing plan is first inaugurated in a company, the good employee wants to work harder so that he may have more money at the end of the year. At the end of the year, however, the lazy employee by his side receives a check just as large as his own. As a result of this finding, he may decide during the following year to work as slowly and as carelessly as the poorest worker in his group. Thus, profit-sharing under some conditions tends to bring the efficiency of the best workers down to the level of the poorest rather than raise the productivity of the poorest up to that of the highest. Profit-sharing benefits the undeserving as much as the deserving.

Actually, the making of profits in many firms is largely beyond the control of the wage earners of the factory and the office. Profits usually depend upon the managers' abilities to organize the whole scheme of production efficiently, to sell the product at a satisfactory profit, to purchase economically, and to find new products to take the place of those that have become obsolescent. The key executives such as the production manager, the sales manager, the purchasing agent, and the treasurer can see direct relations between their individual efforts and the profits made. They, rather than the wage earners, usually influence profits perceptibly. They can be stimulated by profit-sharing more easily than can the workers.

Employers who adopt a profit-sharing program for the workers on the lower levels of responsibility do so, not to increase profits but to improve the psychological climate in the company and to express management's sense of colleagueship with the employees. If a management does decide to install a profit-sharing plan, the following recommendations are helpful:

1. Conduct a sound compensation program before the profit-sharing plan is adopted. Equitable base pay schedules should be in operation and well established before profit-sharing begins. If the pay structure is inequitable, a supplementary form of compensation such as profit-sharing is more likely to accentuate the inequities than to correct them.

2. Provide a good psychological climate before setting up the plan. Management and workers must have confidence in each other, otherwise the sharing of profits is more likely to fail than to succeed. To succeed, a profit-sharing program must be consistent with the way the business has been managed in the past. Companies that succeed with profit-sharing would, in most cases, also succeed without it.

3. Be willing to give employees the important facts about the business. Under profit-sharing, management must be willing to share with employees many essential facts that otherwise might not be communicated to them. If certain kinds of financial information and sales records are withheld from the employees, they are apt to view the fluctuations in profits with suspicion, thus defeating the aims of the plan.

4. Have everyone share alike, percentagewise. Each employee expects to receive the same percentage of his annual wages as that of an employee in a different wage or salary bracket. The number of dollars received need not be the same but the percentage must be. When the percentage varies with the wage or salary bracket, those in the lower brackets object to the differentials.

In general, the difficulties involved in the use of profit-sharing are so serious that the adoption of this kind of plan should be approached with considerable previous investigation into the experiences of other companies, particularly those who have had plans and dropped them. Certainly, when a management hesitates to adopt profit-sharing after several employees request it, the employees should not immediately assume that all the members of top management are benighted tightwads who want to keep all the profits for themselves. Perhaps the management simply wants to be reasonably certain of the values of the plan for the employees as well as for the company before profit-sharing is adopted.

Stock purchase plans for employees

Stock ownership by employees, rather than profit-sharing, has been advocated by some executives. One argument for the stock purchase plan is the increased number of shareholders in our population. The number of stockholders in many companies is greater than the number of employees. Of all U. S. households, about one of every four gets one or more dividend checks each year. The popularity of stock purchase plans for employees is indicated by the fact that more than 150 companies listed on the New York Stock Exchange adopted a stock purchase plan for their employees during a recent ten-year period. Of all companies listed on the New York Stock Exchange, more than 50 per cent have a stock purchase plan for their employees. This trend is in line with the belief that increased participation in the "people's capitalism" is beneficial to the public, the employees, and the employers.

When an employee owns stock, he is a financial partner in the business, though a small one. Advocates of the plan believe that it promotes loyalty to the employer, rewards the employee for faithful service, encourages thrift, and helps to educate the worker in regard to some of the basic principles in our economic life.

The extent of employees' ownership of stock in the companies where they work varies with the industry. Generally, stock ownership by employees is relatively greater in public utilities than in manufacturing or transportation companies. The percentage of employees who buy stock in the employing company when it is offered to them varies greatly —it may be as low as one per cent and as high as 90.

When employees who do buy are asked their reasons for purchasing, they are likely to answer in one or more of four categories: as a speculative venture, as a hedge against inflation, as a means of attracting the good will of management and thereby increasing the chance of promotion, and as a nest egg for old age.

Of course employers do not want to encourage their employees to speculate in stocks of their own or other companies. Employers know that those who buy in the expectation of making a quick profit are more likely to be interested in watching the stock market reports than in studying their jobs and trying to improve their work. Eventually, too, any paper profits made by the employee will rise and fall with the normal fluctuations in the prices of stocks. And whenever an employee's paper profits are lessened or even wiped out, he is apt to blame the employer for the loss and decrease interest in his work.

The older employers of today are likely to be especially conscious of the hazards in the owning of stocks by employees. They remember some of the tragic incidents that occurred after the crash of 1929. One railroad, for example, had sold stock to employees in 1925 at $115 a share. In 1932, the same stock sold for less than $9 a share! Even though the crash that began in 1929 may not be repeated, we do know that some severe fluctuations in stock prices are bound to occur from time to time.

The misgivings about the value of stock purchase plans become acute whenever the employer sees the market price for his company's stock fall below the price paid by employees. When it occurs, some employees become disenchanted. Their morale suffers. To maintain morale and help employees overcome disenchantment about the company's financial progress, managements find it necessary to provide employees with educational programs that help them understand why some fluctuations in stock prices are an inevitable aspect of stock ownership. Special brochures and financial reports must be prepared and given the employees. Foremen must be trained to answer their employees' questions about the reasons for the price of the company's stock. Meetings must be held to give employees correct answers. Some managements have discovered that these difficulties and the costs of dealing with them are so great that the benefits of stock ownership are questionable.

In spite of the hazards and difficulties in operating a stock purchase plan for employees, the number of plans has increased in recent years. Stock ownership by employees fits into the American way of economic life. Our middle income class has increased to the extent where many people can afford to assume some minor risks in making investments. More and more people are buying stocks as indicated by the growing number of investment clubs which are now found in all sections of the country. Articles about finance and investments are constantly appearing in our mass publications because many people are interested in the possibility of buying new stocks or more of their presently owned stocks.

Many managements think of their stock purchase plans as educational services to the employees. The ownership of an employer's stock tends to encourage many an employee to direct some of his speculative tendencies into the study and proper evaluation of all stocks and the economic influences behind the prices. Managements are, of course, aware of the many unintelligent reasons for buying stocks and the hazards involved in their ownership, but they hope to set up their own company plans in ways that prevent disaster and, at the same time, increase good judgment in financial matters. Some companies do this by requiring regular savings, augmented with contributions from the company, and investing the funds in the stocks of several companies as well as in the equities of the employing company.

Most managements realize that they cannot hope to develop a stock ownership plan that will do everything that is desirable for the company and the employees. They also realize that the adoption of a stock ownership plan will not increase production or lower costs. Instead, they seek to plan and conduct a program that develops a more favorable psychological climate in which management and employees can share responsibilities and work together to mutual understanding and economic advantage. This is the main purpose of a well-designed stock ownership plan in many of our most intelligently managed companies.

Various meanings of money

Money itself has many unique meanings and the people who have or deal in money also have special terms applied to them. "Wall Street's half-affectionate, half-mocking term for the average stockholder is 'Aunt Jane.'" [6] "The old lady of Broad and Wall" is the term used by the common stock dealers when they refer disparagingly to the quiet, orderly corner occupied by the bond traders on the floor of the New York Stock Exchange.[7]

Of course money has the important meaning of purchasing power to everyone. In addition, it also has many deeper meanings of a subconscious nature.

One of the most common meanings is *power* as exemplified by the expression "The Almighty Dollar." Many employees who resent employer wealth think of money as a form of control, a kind of control which they feel they cannot combat.

Money has had an *unclean* connotation for centuries. We often hear expressions such as "filthy lucre" and "the love of money is the root of all evil." The question as to whether a certain person's money is "tainted" also implies that the money itself rather than the means of its getting may be evil.

To some people, money stands for *security*. People who have suffered from financial difficulties during childhood are likely to become painfully thrifty in later years and remain parsimonious even though they have acquired ample income for their needs. Our best savers in this country, as a group, are the foreign-born poor who have suffered poverty in the country of their birth and still feel insecure in the adopted country. Money in the bank spells security.

---

[6] See *Forbes*, July 15, 1958, p. 18.
[7] *Ibid.*, p. 27.

To the young person who has just become fully self-supporting, the first paychecks signify *adulthood*. Some of these "new adults" spend money foolishly by buying items that they do not need, probably representing escape from parental restraint. They are one of several varieties of the easily-recognized "compulsive spender," the person who has a strong impulsion to spend money.

Another variety of the compulsive spender is the extravagant buyer whose income, however large or small, is frittered away through the purchase of unnecessarily high-priced items. This kind of customer rationalizes his purchase of expensive clothing by claiming that the label from "Snob Shoppe" will help him get a better job or associate with the "right people." Such extravagance may really have its roots in an unappreciated desire for companionship, a feeling that no one really cares for him. This kind of motivation may also cause the individual to lavish costly gifts on friends. The adolescent boy who buys an expensive wrist watch for a new girl friend is an example.

Both reckless spending and unnecessary hoarding often have their roots in disappointment and discouragement. The miser is likely to be a lonely person who does not know how to gain satisfying companionships and then takes recourse in the security and superiority that money symbolizes.

Young couples who bicker over money matters imagine that the lack of sufficient money for their needs is the crux of their marital difficulties. One writer has given a more significant explanation:

> Many young couples will tell you, "Our fights are mostly over money. If we weren't broke all the time, we'd get along fine together." This is putting the cart before the horse. Those who get along reasonably well in other respects, may still have differences over managing their money, but they tend to work out these disagreements without deep or persistent bitterness. Certainly a large proportion of marital troubles do focus on finances, but their roots often lie in entirely different situations. Disputes over spending or saving frequently provoke quarrels whose real cause may be resentment at a husband because he never hangs up his clothes or because he paid too much attention to that pretty girl at the party last week. If a man is annoyed at his wife because she sleeps late and leaves him to get his own breakfast, or because she has invited her sister to come for a long visit, a discussion over whether they can afford to go to the movies this week can flare into a nasty quarrel.
>
> It is easier to accept the fact that you are angry at your husband or your wife for being stingy or careless with money than to admit to being disappointed in him or in her for a reason harder to put into words.
>
> Nancy and Don Bryant, a highly competitive couple, each used money as a way of getting the best of the other. When she bought a blouse or a bedspread she didn't need, Nancy would say, "If I don't spend what we have, it's a sure thing Don will."
>
> Don, in his turn, took the stand, "If I let my wife get away with wast-

Coffee Break...

And they can really use it. They're part of Class 44 currently taking the toughest course we know about in the securities business — the eight-month training program to become an account executive at Merrill Lynch.

To graduate—they've *got* to work.

First, they spend three months in any one of 125 Merrill Lynch offices finding out just how a brokerage firm operates—all the basic mechanics of the business.

Then it's back to New York for nearly four months of classes—9 to 5, five days a week, with at least two hours of homework every night. Four months of intensive study—accounting and corporate finance, business

law and taxes, investment management and security analysis. Course after course, test after test in something like 26 subjects—all taught by Merrill Lynch managers and department heads, plus the best outside teachers we can find.

To get through it all, you've got to be good—and they are.

The 47 members of Class 44 were originally screened from almost 500 applicants. On average, they're married, about 30 years old, and can all point to outstanding records in school, college, the service.

If they match the marks set by 1282 other graduates since the school first started in 1945, they'll hit the New

York Stock Exchange examination for a solid 97% average at the end of the term.

But that's not their final exam by a long shot.

The big test doesn't begin till a month or so later in some Merrill Lynch office when we think they're finally qualified to work as full-fledged account executives.

That's when we expect them to justify the eight or ten thousand dollars apiece it cost us to train them.

That's when they'll start to provide the kind of investment service and help that will make the whole thing really worthwhile—*to you.*

MERRILL LYNCH, PIERCE, FENNER & SMITH

Members New York Stock Exchange and all other Principal Exchanges
70 Pine Street, New York 5, N. Y.   •   *Offices in 112 Cities*

ing money, we'd never have a cent. She's got to learn who's boss. Best way to teach her is to keep the cash right in my own hands." [8]

If you study or work in finance

The various meanings of money indicate how easy it is for anyone to react too strongly away from or toward money as a possession and finance as a subject of study or as a function of business. Objective thinking in regard to all aspects of finance is greatly needed. The more you study or work in finance, the more you will find that adequate knowledge of the subject becomes beneficial to you as a citizen, as an employee, and as an executive.

Regardless of the phase of business that you enter, you can add zest to your work when you appreciate the functions of money in our economy and its meanings to you as a person. If you will increase your acquaintance with the people who are active in finance, you will find that most do not think of it as a symbol of power but as an instrument of service to mankind. Many are also keenly conscious of the human relations aspects of finance and are trying to inform employees and the public about it. Much remains to be done. Perhaps your study will stimulate you to see the human relations aspects of finance as a challenging interest in your business career.

COLLATERAL READINGS

For All Students

Forbes, Financial World, Barron's, The Wall Street Journal, and other financial magazines are available in many business libraries. They offer many articles on human relations aspects of finance.

"Security Analysts Get Industry Primer," *Business Week*, February 1, 1958. Describes how some companies are offering analysts quick courses in the fundamentals of their industry. One purpose is to help the analysts evaluate the company's financial potentials.

For Advanced Students

Hettinger, Herman S., "Getting Across to Your Financial Public," *Dun's Review and Modern Industry*, January 1958. As "people's capitalism" spreads throughout grass-roots America, companies with publicly traded stock need to win and hold the confidence of Main Street. Public opinion remains a key to many corporate futures.

Rothschild, V. Henry, "Financing Stock Purchases by the Executive," *Har-*

---

[8] Edith G. Neisser, *The Many Faces of Money* (Human Relations Aids, 104 E. 25th Street, New York 10, N. Y., 1958).

vard Business Review, March-April 1957. Presents some of the purposes and problems in the use of stock options as a means of providing extra incentives to management men.

For Men in Business

"Using Your Banker's Advisory Services," Small Business Administration, Washington, D.C., No. 68. The bankers' interest is strongly in favor of helping small firms to prosper and grow. For this reason they offer a good deal of practical management assistance to their customers, on a free basis.

Burck, Gilbert, "Singer: Hardening of the Assets," *Fortune,* January 1959. This article describes certain adverse effects on management when the company has had a hundred years of success and has accumulated an extra large amount of cash.

QUESTIONS ON THE CHAPTER

1. Describe the chief financial executive's work relations with other members of management.
2. In what ways do the surveys of stock ownership in America invalidate the opinions of many workers toward company profits?
3. In the morale survey concerning one company's Annual Report, what per cent of the employees who saw the report read all of it? Half of it? None of it?
4. Describe several common errors made in the presentation of financial reports.
5. Explain a method of preparing financial reports so that they are understandable both on the level of the employee or general public, and on the professional level of the investment men or security analysts.
6. State reasons for management's attempts to increase attendance at stockholders' meetings.
7. List several reasons why it is a difficult task to try to educate people to buy common stocks wisely.
8. Why should the student of finance also develop his insight into human relations, especially in respect to buying stock?
9. Describe some of the deeper meanings that money may have for various people.
10. Is an adequate knowledge of finance of importance solely to the prospective financier? Explain your answer.
11. Of all the ideas presented in the chapter, which one is of most interest or value to you?

PROBLEMS AND PROJECTS

For All Students

1. Visit several brokers' offices in your community. Note the information that is available. Look particularly for booklets that warn the

unwary about unethical salesmen or companies that exploit rather than serve investors.

2. Assume that you will have to borrow money to finance your education. Do you have a well-formulated plan for how you will use the money, repay it, and give evidence of good character in deserving the loan?

For Advanced Students

3. Make a study of the "psychology of the stock market." You might start by asking Arthur Wiesenberger & Co., 61 Broadway, New York, for published material on "The Wiesenberger Senti-Graph." A local broker's office may also have the material.

4. The most dramatic conflicts in the financial world are the corporate raids in a proxy battle. Study such raids. A good source is James P. Selvage, *The Management Review*, American Management Association, Inc., December 1957.

For Men in Business

5. Collect several financial reports to stockholders. How could they be improved for reading by employees? Interview several employees who own stocks in any company. What do they read in the reports?

6. Look through several business journals for reports of meetings for stockholders. Consult the "Industrial Arts Index" for current articles. What kinds of stockholders attend the meetings and what do they contribute?

Any person who works in or studies business is bound to become acquainted with modern research. Its spirit and benefits permeate all phases of business.

To the man in the street, research is often synonymous with progress. To the typical consumer, it means such things as more or better food, clothing, housing, health, life, and leisure. Also, these benefits are obtained with less physical effort than was needed in previous generations.

Research courses are found in almost every department of the large university. Research is defined and interpreted in many ways. The academic scientist sees it from the standpoint of exploring the unknown. He is looking for information for its own sake rather than for its use in the solution of a particular problem of immediate concern.

The tangible aspects of progress—new products and processes that produce a higher standard of living—very clearly derive from discoveries in pure science. Between pure research and the manufacture of new products, a wide middle ground is found. In this area, we have applied research, process development, and product development.

The term "research" is widely misused. A student, for example, goes to the library to investigate materials for writing a term report and blandly states: "I conducted a lot of research in order to write this report!" A more accurate statement would be "I did some reading on the subject in the library."

23   Research and the Development of New Products

Many companies, too, kid themselves when they tag routine product testing as research. They should say that they have a product testing lab to provide certain limited services for the customers who use the company's products.

Pure research is generally carried out in an environment that allows the investigator freedom to follow the lead of his curiosity. In the words of Glen T. Seaborg of the University of California, the scientist in basic research is not concerned with "utilitarian goals, but a search for deeper understanding of the universe and the living and inorganic phenomena within it." In its initial purpose, basic research may be an essential prerequisite to applied research and product development. Some of the greatest technical advances of recent years have come from basic research projects that had no immediate practical objective. Examples are radar, transistors, neoprene, and nylon.[1]

Billions of dollars are spent annually for new plants and equipment as the result of research made in a previous decade, or even a year earlier. More than one-half of our jobholders in the United States are in industries that owe their birth to research laboratories. This means that industry is compelled to spend more and more for research each year.[2]

Research is becoming an industry in itself. The percentage of a modern company's gross income allotted for research ranges from 2 per cent to 10 per cent or even more. The tremendous amount of effort that goes into intensive research is exemplified by the statement of a pharmaceutical manufacturer who described his company's experience in antibiotics in a recent year: "We screened approximately 40,000 substances for activity in this field. Out of that 40,000 we found about 200 which showed promise enough to justify further study. Out of that 200 we had 30 that we actually manufactured for trial. Out of that 30, six wound up in the Department of Clinical Investigation. So you start with 40,000 and you wind up with six; this makes quite an interesting study in that particular field." [3]

Companies engaged primarily in producing products or services rather than research find it necessary to organize their research program systematically. Usually this requires the careful selection of people who are competent to do sound research.

---

[1] See "Basic Research More Practical Than You Think," an editorial that appeared in November and December, 1957 issue of McGraw-Hill publications, (McGraw-Hill Publishing Company, Inc., 330 West 42nd Street, New York 36).

[2] See Milton Pauley, " 'Research-Rich' Companies Are Not All Giants," *Investor,* August 15, 1957, p. 1.

[3] Stated by Harry Loynd, President of Parke, Davis & Co. as reported by William Bloeth, "Stock Movement," *New York World-Telegram and Sun,* January 26, 1959.

THE BASIC LIFE CYCLE OF NEW PRODUCTS

SALES VOLUME

ADDITIONAL NEW PRODUCT
PROFIT NEEDED TO SUSTAIN
GROWTH OF COMPANIES

PROFIT MARGINS

INTRODUCTION   GROWTH   MATURITY   SATURATION   DECLINE

New products have a characteristic pattern to their sales volume and profit margin curves. The time scale varies by product and industry, but every product must expect to be pre-empted eventually by another product. And long before this occurs, production will catch up even with growing demand and the product degenerates into profitless price competition, as the typical profit margin curve shows.

This means that as a business strategy, a company must plan to run ahead of price competition by differentiating its products and introducing new products that can command better margins.

Business success is governed not only by what you do, but by what others do. Therefore, throughout history, the underlying secret of business success has been to be in the right business at the right time—and this strategy is expressed by the selection and development of company products. Over-all profit margins can be sustained only by a continuing flow of new products—not only to replace sales volume but also to bolster shrinking profit margins.

The company plans must begin with the product plans. To project sales, costs, capital, facility, and personnel needs without clear product plans is indeed a hollow activity. The growth plans of a company are at the core of management interests. New products are a major factor in the growth plans of companies today (Reproduced by permission from C. Wilson Randle, "Weighing the Success of New Product Ideas," Industrial Marketing, *July 1957).*

540 IDEAS PROPOSED

MORTALITY OF
NEW PRODUCT IDEAS

20 CHEMICAL COMPANIES - 1955

92 PERTINENT IDEAS

8 APPROVED IDEAS   **1 APPROVED PRODUCT**

EXPLORATION ◄ SCREENING ► ◄ SPECIFICATIONS ► ◄ DEVELOPMENT ► ◄ TESTING ► ◄ COMMERCIALIZATION

♦ ♦ ♦ ♦ ♦ 6 YEARS, 2 MONTHS   AVERAGE ELAPSED TIME ♦ ♦ ♦ ♦ ♦

SOURCE: COMMERCIAL CHEMICAL DEVELOPMENT ASSOCIATION

Companies should seek literally those rare ideas that are both low-risk and high-payout. They can measure their effectiveness in product selection by examining the degree to which their projects cluster in the lower right-hand corner of the chart.

A characteristic of the new product selection game is the progressive rejection of ideas by stage. The chart above shows the survival rate curve for industrial chemical ideas. You might say, as in a poker game, you ante a lot of times before you develop a hand you're willing to play clear through to a final showdown.

As good a screening job as is represented here, we still see seven out of eight development projects—which run $150,000 to $500,000 or more each in this business—never reach the full commercial stage. This gives us a clue on what might be happening to some of our scientific manpower. A large share, by definition in commercial terms, is being wasted.

Another characteristic of this game is that each stage is progressively more expensive; like in a poker game, each card drawn costs more than the one before it (Reproduced by permission from C. Wilson Randle, "Weighing the Success of New Product Ideas," Industrial Marketing, *July 1957).*

Personality characteristics of research men

If you were to visit a number of companies and ask executives about the personality characteristics of their research men, you might get comments such as the following:

1. "Good research men cannot be expected to conform to the behavior patterns typical of most other employees. The researchers are likely to be seclusive thinkers, deeply engrossed in their problems, somewhat unconcerned about problems that bother most executives, poor coordinators of their own work, and likely to go off on any tangent that interests them."

2. "The feelings of research men are easily hurt. Many are pronounced introverts. The introverted person, who wants to keep to himself and to avoid social contacts, finds that laboratory work offers an opportunity to do so. He can bury himself in the lab and then build a shell around himself so that he can easily avoid social affairs, meeting people, and other situations unpleasant to him. A good research employee can lose all awareness of the people around him because he buries himself in his work. Although this form of adjustment may give us great scientists, many of them are not able to communicate their ideas to someone else. They have so little facility of expression that their good ideas fail to be modified by other thinkers and, as a result, they often fail to accomplish as much as they might."

3. "In our company's research lab a person at one desk will notice that his colleague at the next desk is going about something in a completely wrong manner, but will not say anything to him. Oftentimes management finds that a research chemist or other type of lab worker hates to be questioned about his work. He feels that any questioning or checking proves that his boss doesn't trust him and won't give him a chance to prove what he is worth. In our research laboratories we have men and women who refuse to speak to their colleagues because of a difference of opinion that occurred years ago."

Admittedly, some unusual personalities are found in laboratories, but we should realize that research men and women exhibit all the individual differences found in any group. They are not personality freaks. In regard to a few traits, however, there is sufficient similarity to warrant generalization. In matters of judgment, most of them are careful and precise. They accept nothing on hearsay—every theory or claim must be tested and tested rigorously before it is accepted. They are intellectually curious. They respond to the challenges presented by the unknown. They are scientists and they realize that a science is only as sound as its research. They enjoy their work and often disregard hours of the working day as they respond to challenge. Many are unorthodox in their working habits. They are not awed by management because they are guided by the criteria of science—not the criteria of men.

They themselves can apply the appropriate criteria to their work and they take inner pleasure from achievement that stands the examination of sound scientific testing. Many have an air of assurance because of undeniable accomplishment. Each achievement leads to new search into the unknown. They have individual and group pride because they often know that they are spearheading some phase of technical progress of the nation and the age.

Great scientists have "respect for the power and beauty, not just the utility, of unrestricted human thought." Poincaré expressed the idea when he wrote, "The scientist does not study nature because it is useful; he studies it because he delights in it, and he delights in it because it is beautiful." [4]

Some persons think that creativity is one aspect of cleverness or great learning. Experience indicates, however, that many men who are very clever never originate anything. The true originator is usually a trained and alert observer. His chief asset is the ability to recognize analogies and appreciate the significance of apparently accidental happenings. Curiosity, alert observation, and the ability to recognize the importance of a finding are necessary qualities of a researcher.

Organizing the personnel for effective research

About two-thirds of the total personnel in a typical research organization are nontechnical: stenographers, mechanics, operators, laboratory assistants, clerks, and so on. Two-thirds of those classed as technical personnel are usually engaged in development and engineering work, work that requires a great deal of planning and organization. This leaves only about 10 per cent of the total personnel who are actually engaged in truly creative research.

To gain the benefits of what these men can do, managements have found it necessary to implement their talents and those of their associates by means of special organizations. "Research is people" as has often been stated but the fruits of the labors of research people can be reduced or increased by means of the organization and environment where they work. Integration of their efforts through teamwork and good leadership by management is essential to their success.

In many companies, the research function began with a testing lab, and in time was gradually elevated to a subdivision reporting directly to the president. As a result, it is still very much in the process of evolution in many companies.

---

[4] See J. H. Hildebrand, "Motivation of the Top Level Students Who Enter the Research Field," *Research Is People* (New York: New York University Press for the Industrial Research Institute, Inc., 1956), p. 19.

Research men realize that they need direction as well as stimulation. Without the proper supervision, many a researcher will waste his potentials through unproductive efforts such as the following:

1. Working on a problem that interests him instead of the problem that has been assigned to him. An effective researcher will pursue the main problem without allowing his personal interests to sidetrack him.

2. Working in a sullen manner because the work of others is not coordinated with his efforts in the exact way he wants. The productive researcher is a member of a team and he adapts his efforts to those of the team program.

3. Failing to maintain his own morale and that of subordinates and associates when difficulties arise.

Professional recognition is very important to the able research man. This may be granted by the company by means of a title such as "Senior Research Associate" but this has more significance within than without the company where he works. He wants something more substantial than a title—he wants to be recognized as an outstanding scientist by those persons whose opinions he respects.

Some managements have found it necessary to give a certain amount of freedom to the research man who likes to work on projects that interest him personally. They let him experiment during working hours with pet projects of his own. A few companies give the research man free rein but most put a limit on the time to be spent in this way. About ten per cent of working time is the maximum usually allowed by research administrators. This privilege keeps researchers happy and stimulates their creative ability.

Organizational structures and communication

Scientists, who think and talk among themselves primarily in a mathematical language, often have difficulty in putting their ideas on paper in ways that laymen can understand. When ideas are passed through many echelons of management, they lose so much in the interpretation that management is unable to see their implications. Also, when separated from other sections of the plant, researchers themselves can fail to appreciate what a discovery means in terms of a company's sales needs and capabilities.

The communications problem in research has prompted a great deal of analysis of organizational structure. Experts in management believe that research is likely to be more effective and researchers less disgruntled when they are organized on a project basis around their particular talents rather than on the typical functional basis usually found in the sales and production departments. Generally, an organization of some sort has to be built around the most able research men. This is better than trying to fit each man in some way into a job-described slot.

Research is problem solving, technical achievement by professionally trained men. Hence, relatively few levels of organizational structure are necessary even in large research staffs. The research worker should be close to his supervisor in order to prevent ideas generated "at the bench" from being lost or misinterpreted on their way to the top.[5] Instead of increasing the number of levels of supervision, the number of subdepartments or laboratories may be increased.

When a research department is small, say 15 people or less, all members of the staff can have enough personal contact with each other to understand each member's projects and problems. When the department has hundreds of employees, the group leader or head of the specific project functions as a director to the members of his small group.

Experience with research workers indicates that practices such as the following are dangerous: a strictly enforced chain of command or communications, strict office hours, requirement of frequent formal progress reports, strict scheduling or restriction of researcher attendance at seminars and meetings. When the personnel turnover is as high or higher than that of the regular work force this discovery should be a warning signal to the management.

Managements have found that a researcher can go stale if he continues year after year in the same narrow fields. He can become too satisfied with the way things are done. He loses his curiosity. Sometimes he can be rehabilitated by shifting him to another area of research where his powers of observation can be used afresh.[6]

The research director

The research director is the focal point of the research problem. He must be able to act as a liaison between research and management as well as supervise research. He must understand and be understood by both sides.

One principle is clear: research cannot be integrated into a company simply by putting a scientist on the board of directors. In most com-

---

[5] See Robert K. Stolz, "Organizing for Effective R/D," *Research & Engineering*, February 1957.

[6] See "The New World of Research," *Business Week*, May 28, 1955, pp. 126, 128.

panies where research has succeeded, however, a scientist is on the board. The research director should be a competent scientist, a qualified administrator, informed of company policies, and firmly grounded in economics and industrial technology. He should have a keen appreciation of the qualities of each individual researcher and sufficient flexibility to adapt his department organization so as to make best use of their unique talents.

Past practice has been to take technical men who are believed to have potentials for administration and make them directors of research departments. Most of those chosen are untrained in administration and have to learn from experience. Some become effective administrators, others never do. Sometimes a "business manager" is appointed to aid the director. He relieves the technical director of some administrative details. In small scale operations, this is not practical because of the expense.

The research director is likely to be a scientist because one of his principal tasks is the design of experiments. A carefully and creatively conceived design is the crux in research. Well planned, it can save money and time as well as increase the chances of success. An effective director must be a person who can ask the right questions, foresee the implications of the study, and can stimulate others to develop new approaches to old problems.

Directors trained in science often fail to realize that human relations problems cannot be solved in the same way as problems in physics or chemistry. As a result, some of these directors fail as administrators.

If an administrator is appointed from the sales department on the assumption that he knows how to handle people and can direct research toward solution of the company's sales problems, little basic research is done. Instead of directing research to meet future needs, he is likely to have the department work only on the service needs of customers. A customer's complaints become more important than the search for new products that will enable the company to survive against competition five years later.

If the director has been trained by the comptroller, only beautiful reports are likely to be produced. If he has come from the production department, the research department will be busy on equipment and layouts.

It is easy to understand why scientists near the top of the research-administration ladder invariably insist that their own scientific backgrounds are the most appropriate for their jobs. They perceive the needs of the job in terms of their own experience. They assume that anyone else could not understand the technical aspects of the situation. In actual practice, any director who has earned his position on the basis of scientific merit usually gains the respect of research workers. If his short-

More than in most occupations, the education of a scientist is continuous and intensive. Today's methods may be obsolete tomorrow . . . and long-accepted theories may be disproved. It is one task of research to assemble, evaluate and share new knowledge.

Modern research is generally a well-organized teamwork job . . . and cooperation is the key to success. Confronted by a problem, nobody in this laboratory hesitates to draw on the experience of a fellow worker.

Sometimes, of course, the problem is more than a little complex, and that is the time for putting heads together, perhaps with a learned book for reference. Usually there are several ways to approach a difficult undertaking . . . but only one choice may be best.

There is fascination, even for men familiar with them, in every laboratory experiment . . . especially when a microscope is being used.

It is a rare visitor who spends much of his time in this room! Unless he happens to be a scientist himself, he is likely to be puzzled by the instructor's "technical" terms . . . and those drawings will have less meaning for him than the abstractions of a cubist.

Nelson Morris photos.
Courtesy Cities Service Company.

comings as an administrator are corrected by means of an assistant who can handle people, the research department can produce good results.

Attitudes of management men toward research

Most forward looking members of top management appreciate the importance of research as a competitive weapon in the company's future, but we must not assume that all management men are enthusiastic about research. Only a few are antagonistic toward research, but many are impatient. We can understand the reason for such impatience when we realize that a high percentage of management men reach the top through production and sales. The production and sales executives need answers quickly. Results in these fields are attainable more quickly than in research. The immediacy of management's need for a new product in order to meet the competition of the moment is inconceivable to the research man who is developing new concepts for space travel or some equally great dream for the future. Management's urging toward specific dates in attaining cost reduction and product development elicits disdain and some pity from the research man. The two do not think or act according to the same time scale.

Management and research men often talk on different levels. One company president expressed the problem in a typical manner when he said "I ask for a 'Yes or No' answer and I get back a forty-page report that I cannot understand." [7]

The research man realizes that he is misunderstood. He wants to be helpful and sensible but he is often inarticulate, unable to communicate with members of management. Here is where a research director skilled in human relations can often integrate the thinking of the researchers with the needs of the company. He can help plan a committee control in which members of management from sales, production, and finance work more happily and effectively with research. The wise research director knows that he needs the counsel of men in production and sales —without it research may lead the company into fields where sales and production are not as yet ready to operate profitably.

Case histories of manufacturing companies that have been directed by a research man who was not intelligently guided by colleagues from the production and sales departments show that this situation can be disastrous. In one case, for example, a new president, called in to save an ailing company, found that under the administration of a research man the company's costs were excessively high and delivery dates on

---

[7] See "The New World of Research," pp. 108-110.

major contracts were running three to four years late.[8] Management as well as research men benefit from an integration of the company's needs through mutual respect on the part of all members of management. As Robert S. Ingersoll, President of Borg-Warner Corporation, indicated:

> Executives who think and speak of their research people as long hairs and ivory tower dwellers, are actually locking themselves in a tower and tossing away the key.
>
> Many executives tend to insulate themselves from those strange people and projects "over at the lab," and thereby lose out.
>
> Research is costly business and badly handled it will bleed away precious cash, time, and talent. Management should lay out clearly what it wants longterm. With this well established it mustn't hesitate to ride herd on its researchers.
>
> What's more, it pays to keep researchers constantly rubbing shoulders with the production, sales, engineering, and management people.[9]

Management men have to learn how to guide research into productive channels through the use of the company's financial resources. One of management's fundamental roles is decision-making. Management must perform its role in deciding what to research even though it cannot decide the date when the research is to be completed. Sound planning is a first requirement for success in industrial research. Planning is a top management responsibility.

One investigator who has studied the needs for and benefits of planning research reported that when a company analyzed the results of project work for a five-year period, it found that close to 35 per cent of research and development time had been spent on projects that had proved useless to the company and whose uselessness *could have been anticipated before the project was undertaken.*[10]

Evaluating the individual researcher

Most companies that have research departments find it very difficult to evaluate the efforts of their research men. A research program is a long-term speculation. If management has confidence in the research man and in his objectives, management usually accepts his reports at their face value.

---

[8] See "Putting Arma Back on Its Feet," *Business Week*, February 1, 1958, p. 84.

[9] "Executives Told To Rid Themselves of Ivory Tower Research Notion," *Business Week*, May 18, 1957, p. 107. This quotation from *Business Week* is a paraphrase summary of Mr. Ingersoll's talk before the National Industrial Research Conference, Chicago, April 24, 1957.

[10] See Robert K. Stolz, "Planning—Key to Research Success," *Harvard Business Review*, May-June 1957.

Several years ago a leading manufacturer of fireplace equipment hired designers to develop a prefabricated fireplace that could be *completely* factory-built, eliminate the need for costly masonry, and blend with any style of home architecture or room decoration.

Naturally, the first step was to get some indication of the market potential. Assuming that the product would be sold primarily to home builders, the market research men showed the product to the building trade at several trade conventions. The reactions were so favorable that further market studies were not deemed necessary and the fireplace was put into production. A complete marketing and promotional plan was developed, and distributors and dealers were appointed to concentrate on builder sales.

Unfortunately, the expected sales volume failed to materialize. The market research men had jumped to their conclusions too quickly. They had failed to uncover the fact that few builders would accept the new product until there was a recognizable consumer demand for it. As a result, the original enthusiasm for the product faded quickly when it was actually placed on the market. The manufacturer then had to completely revise his entire marketing approach, which entailed a substantial loss in both time and money.

Sooner or later, almost every large manufacturer goes through this kind of learning experience. That is one reason why preparation for marketing research requires good training plus astute insight into what the market research data really signify for the manufacturer. SOURCE: *Vega Industries, Inc., Syracuse, New York.*

Naturally, management men would like to feel certain that the money spent for research is well spent. Some top level executives realize that they are not sufficiently trained technically to evaluate what goes on in the research laboratories. They do realize that success in research usually requires a disregard for time and ordinary accounting of costs. Research men are dedicated in their effort to persist beyond hope. They pursue the chosen objective patiently, persistently. These virtues, however, do not guarantee results.

Some attempts are being made to measure results. One study made by University of Chicago scientists of an oil company showed that the scientists who produce the most new ideas are not "hunch players" but are long-range thinkers willing to "delay immediate success for eventual solution of problems." Also, they are individuals who do not seek the approval of either their associates or society, but are intent upon their own goals and willing to achieve them. One surprising finding from the study: "The higher creative scientists rise with a company, the less individual—and the less creative—they become. Pressures for conformity to a success pattern are blamed for this." Success appears to diminish creativity.[11]

The *climate* for research is especially important for its growth. If the climate is inadequate, a research program does not contribute to the vitality of an organization. If, however, management's philosophy promotes the application of science and technology to current problems, the employees in the research department will know it and produce all that it is humanly possible for them to accomplish.

This suggests that the student of human relations who expects to deal effectively with research workers should learn about the principles that guide them. If he can appreciate their objectives and their characteristics as individuals, he will merit their good will and gain their personal cooperation.

COLLATERAL READINGS

For All Students

"New Appraisals of Engineers," *Dun's Review and Modern Industry,* September 1957. Reports of three projects conducted by research groups on the self-perceptions and career satisfactions of engineers. Many of the findings are also applicable to research men.

Randle, C. Wilson, "Problems of R & D Management," *Harvard Business Review,* January-February 1959. Reports a survey by Booz, Allen, and Hamilton on "R & D" activities of 100 companies and the views of 3,500 individual scientists and engineers.

For Advanced Students

Bush, George P., and L. W. Hattery, editors, *Teamwork in Research.* Washington, D.C.: The American University Press, 1953. Problems posed by team research are discussed by members of several national research groups and their representatives.

Livingston, R. T., and S. M. Milberg, editors, *Human Relations in Industrial Research Management.* New York: Columbia University Press, 1957. These 27 essays explore human aspects of organized research and possible managerial frameworks.

For Men in Business

These reference sources list contract research organizations and the kind of work they specialize in:

Directory of the American Council of Independent Laboratories, Inc.

---

[11] See *Business Week,* October 19, 1957, p. 199.

Available from the ACIL, 4302 East-West Highway, Washington 14, D.C.

Directory of Industrial Research Laboratories in New York State, 1954. Available from the New York State Department of Commerce, Albany, N. Y.

Directory of Member Institutions, Engineering College Research Council. Available from Renato Contini, secretary, ECRC, New York University, New York 53.

Industrial Research Laboratories of the United States, annual editions. National Academy of Sciences, Washington, D.C.

QUESTIONS ON THE CHAPTER

1. Differentiate between "pure research" and two commonly misused meanings of the term, "research."
2. What are some noticeable traits which can be attributed to many research men?
3. What per cent of the total personnel in a typical research organization are actually engaged in creative research?
4. Comment on the statement that many a researcher will waste his potentials through unproductive efforts.
5. Why is it important for adequate communications to be established by research directors in their departments?
6. Describe some of the qualities required of a competent research director.
7. Give arguments for and against having a scientist in the position of research director.
8. What does the statement, "Success appears to diminish creativity," mean?
9. What are some of the problems of members of management who deal with research men?
10. Of all the ideas presented in the chapter, which ones had special interest for you?
11. How did the chapter contribute to your relations with (a) your future supervisors, (b) employees whom you may supervise?

PROBLEMS AND PROJECTS

1. As a student, if you are sincere and intelligent in your approach, you can have access to and interview many executives. You can call on the head of a research laboratory or a member of management who deals with researchers and introduce yourself with a statement such as "I am a student in _____ and am taking a course in _____. I'd like to learn more about human relations problems involved in dealing with research workers. Would you kindly tell me about some of yours?" You may wish to utilize this procedure.
   (a) What limitations can you recognize in this approach?
   (b) What courtesies are expected by management from the student?

2. A survey of 252 companies made by the American Management Association revealed that the responsibility for the creation of new products rests with marketing management in 43 per cent, with general management in 41 per cent, and with directors of research and development or engineering in only 11 per cent of the surveyed concerns. Some companies use product planning committees. The best sources for new product ideas are the company's salesmen. Next are the research and engineering staffs, followed by suggestions from customers.

   (a) Examine current journals of marketing to find articles that explain ways in which marketing departments function in new product planning.

   (b) How can salesmen be stimulated to bring new product ideas to the attention of management? See *Sales Management*, October 18, 1957, p. 94.

3. Utilize the facilities of your library to make a study of the importance of research in our growth as a nation. You might begin your project by reading "A New Way to Grow," *Business Week*, Jan. 23, 1960.

Improving Your Relations
with Individuals

Ｏne of the most difficult lessons to learn about people is that they often react quite differently from what might logically be expected. To the obtuse observer, their behavior is unexpected, even senseless. A supervisor, for example, does a favor for an employee who becomes angry and berates the supervisor. The supervisor who is unaware of the employee's psychological needs is nonplussed. The more insightful person, however, realizes that people do not always act logically. Quite often they react psychologically, in accordance with their deepseated needs.

We learn to become aware of the influence of needs when we deal with a person with whom we cannot discuss certain subjects. We discover that with regard to those topics, he will react in accordance with an unconscious motive. We do not, as a rule, know the exact nature or origin of the drive but we recognize its influence as shown in his conversation or when it appears again and again as a dominating influence in his daily behavior. Every individual's life has certain patterns of behavior that indicate the motivating influence of continuing deepseated needs on his part. The observer who studies and works with people is constantly improving his awareness of such motivations as expressed by the individuals whom he observes.

Most college students become acquainted with some aspects of motivation by their studies in literature. They read the biographies of famous men. An example is that of William Cullen

24 Motivation – Increasing Your Sensitivity to the Individual's Needs

Bryant (1794–1878), whose father was so strong a physical giant that he could "take a barrel of cider and lift it into a cart over the wheel." To toughen his son and make him manly, he dunked him in a cold spring each morning. To please his father, the son became a lawyer, but spent more time writing poems than in doing legal briefs. His poems "Thanatopsis" and "To a Waterfowl" show the tender side of his nature, which the dunking in ice water could not eradicate. After the father's death, William quit law entirely and became a quarrelsome editor who fought for the underdog. Journalism enabled him to fight the kind of tyranny that reminded him of his father's domination and cruelties. At heart, Bryant was a feminine sentimentalist. His father's "hardening" made him hate hard things, but fortunately it did not destroy his creativity. Instead, it caused him to have needs which he released through literary potentials.

Other examples in literature and art of how needs develop and their later influence in adult life can be perceived when we study the behavior pattern of a child who is physically weak, sickly, or deformed such as Henri De Toulouse-Lautrec (1864–1901). At the age of fourteen, he had an accident that broke both his weak legs. The legs did not mend well. Walking was a torment. His short stumpy legs and appearance made him an ugly cripple who was repulsive to most people. He was rejected by others but hungry for acceptance. He found acceptance in the cafés and brothels where he could practice his art making posters of café scenes and disreputable women. He used color and design to portray the life and the people whom he knew in the places where he was accepted. His art reflected his deep emotional needs.

The intelligent student of literature, philosophy, and the other humanities wants to know more than what the writer or speaker said—he also wants to know the early influences and the resultant needs that motivated him to choose and express the specific ideas which he chose and expressed.

Every man's points of view are colored by his inner needs. We can easily note the influence of needs on a person's thinking when we study people in stress situations as in war. A former prisoner of war described the outward changes in behavior of prisoners as their hardships changed. He wrote the following letter to Dr. Ernest Dichter, head of the Institute for Motivational Research, in regard to his concept of four basic drives in human motivation:

"When we were starving and freezing (one bowl of watery soup per day for over a month), we talked and dreamed only of food; when rations were increased to the point where hunger pangs were less severe, we talked about women; when the food situation improved still more, we became concerned for our safety; and when, on the two occasions we were privileged to eat all we wanted (Christmas 1944 and May 1945), we got ambitious and philosophical and began to talk about our stations in life and those to which we aspired." [1]

Unfortunately, too many college students who enjoy biographical reading assume that the motivating influences in the lives of great men apply only to the men of bygone days. They fail to realize that the same influences and patterns evident in the lives of great men of literature are also evident among the everyday people whom we meet in business.

Numerous approaches to the "why" in the lives of people whom we see every day have been made by psychologists. They have developed special concepts such as "motive," "drive," and "need." The terms apply to predisposing influences in behavior of a psychogenic nature. Currently, the term "need" is receiving considerable emphasis in certain behavioral researches.[2]

The inner or unconscious needs of the individual are fundamental to understanding what he does and why. These are given much study by the psychologist, but the business man is more concerned with the manner of expression than the origin or the exact nature of the underlying influence. A good example is the need for personal recognition, which may be expressed either in selfish behavior that has a ruinous influence on an organization, or, on the other hand, in outstanding work. Even though our main interest is in the outward expression rather than the origin of the drive, we can understand and, at times, direct the manifest behavior more intelligently if we can sense the motivating influences, the needs, that give the behavior impetus and continuity.

Even though he is not a trained psychologist, every socially alert person daily recognizes the special needs of friends. A supervisor, for example, receives a suggestion from a new employee. The suggestion, let us assume, has very little or no practical value. The socially alert supervisor does not immediately express his frank opinion of its value because he notes that the employee has a deepseated need for recognition. He therefore expresses appreciation for the presentation of the suggestion and promises to have its value investigated. Furthermore, the supervisor realizes that complete lack of interest in the first idea submitted by an employee will cause him to submit few or no ideas in the future. The hope of eventually getting a few good ideas causes the supervisor to

---

[1] Letter from Forrest W. Howell, Jacksonville, Florida; published in *Memo from Dr. Dichter and Staff* (Institute for Motivational Research, Inc., Croton-on-Hudson, New York), May 1956.

[2] See Sidney L. Pressey and Raymond G. Kuhlen, *Psychological Development Through the Life Span* (New York: Harper and Brothers, 1957), Chapter 7.

welcome the many poor ones, particularly from the employee who has a need for recognition.

Another example of insight into an employee's needs often occurs in the typical salaried worker's request for a pay increase. This request may represent a desire for recognition rather than an exigency for relieving financial pressure. An excellent study of this kind of want as applied to industrial research scientists has been reported, in part, as follows:

> It is often said that people work mainly to get paid, and that the prospect of getting a raise is the main spur to hard work. Similarly, it is widely accepted that employees drag their feet if they think they are being paid under the prevailing rates. Salary is also generally regarded as an important status symbol. . . .
>
> In order to find out what industrial research scientists think about pay and other incentives the authors recently conducted a survey among two representative groups. Group A consisted of 102 non-supervisory scientists and technicians selected by random sampling techniques at a large research and development organization. Group B was made up of 70 research and development scientists enrolled in graduate evening courses in industrial engineering and physical sciences at Stevens Institute of Technology. Since the scientists in this group were employed by a variety of industrial concerns, they may be considered a heterogeneous sample.
>
> Asked how they felt about their current salaries, 74.5 per cent of Group A and 49.9 per cent of Group B expressed the opinion that these were lower than they should be. . . .
>
> . . . it must be remembered that complaints about salary are often symptoms of other dissatisfactions.
>
> How would these scientists feel about their jobs if their salaries were raised? In response to this question, 53.5 per cent of those in Group A and 64.5 per cent of those in Group B said that they would feel they were being adequately rewarded for the work they were doing. Yet, only a handful (6.6 per cent and 1.6 per cent respectively) admitted that they needed the money to relieve financial pressures so that they could give more attention to their work; and only about 15 per cent of the respondents in both groups felt they would perform their work with more enthusiasm.[3]

Every individual, regardless of whether he has had much or little formal education, has some inner needs. The need may give rise to demands for more pay or some other expression such as criticism of educated persons. Certainly, many a college student who has worked in factories during summer vacations has met a certain type of foreman who has had little formal education. The lack has made him both proud and resentful—proud because he has achieved a good position despite his lack of formal education and resentful because in the company where

---

[3] George A. Peters and Max Lees, "Better Incentives for Scientific Personnel," *Personnel*, American Management Association, Inc., January-February 1958, pp. 59, 60.

he works special recognition is given to "college men." A foreman of this kind is apt to divide industrial employees into two groups: the "practical" and the "theoretical" men. Whenever he deals with a college-educated man such as an engineer, he enjoys finding evidence of the theoretical man's stupidity. Such a foreman may treat members of management with great respect but he likes to bawl out subordinates, particularly "dumb college men."

If the college man is aware of the influence of such a foreman's needs, he is not disturbed by the bawlings-out. Instead, he accepts them as of incidental note with a comment to himself such as "Aw, the boss just has to bawl me out occasionally—it makes him feel better!" The smart college man recognizes the probable origin of the foreman's behavior, overlooks it, and concentrates on learning worthwhile matters from the foreman's practical experience.

We must not assume that sensitivity to individual needs is limited to educated persons. On the contrary, many industrial workers are quite sensitive to the psychological needs of their fellow workers. A. Zaleznik has described an instance that occurred in a machine shop where he studied the workers. The occasion was a birthday party in the shop for an employee named Larry.

> One incident in relation to Larry's birthday party that we thought revealed a great deal about the group's sensitivity toward its members was described by Hal. Not only did the group sing "Happy Birthday" to Larry, but they also sang to Nick. It was not Nick's birthday, but the group, as we were told about the incident, sang to him as a joke. This is a matter of interpretation, and we do not have proof, but we believe the group had, intuitively, a serious intention behind their recognition of Nick. He was a sensitive person who seemed to need support and reassurance. He made cleanliness almost a fetish, and the men respected his feelings by keeping clean the soldering work area if they had occasion to work there. He seemed also to be more bothered by assignments outside the machine shop than any other worker. We believe that the birthday song to Nick, even though done in jest, was nonetheless to support Nick and to reassure him that he had standing in the group.[4]

Each researcher uses a classification of needs that he finds appropriate for the specific project which he investigates.[5] The terminology in regard to the designation and definitions of needs is unstandardized. A reading

---

[4] A. Zaleznik, *Worker Satisfaction and Development* (Boston: Harvard Business School, Division of Research, 1956), p. 48.

[5] One of the oft-quoted lists of needs as developed by a psychologist is that of H. A. Murray, *Explorations in Personality* (New York: Oxford University Press, 1938). See also, Calvin S. Hall and Gardner Lindzey, *Theories in Personality* (New York: John Wiley & Sons, Inc., 1957), Chapter 5.

of the current literature on the subject would, however, probably cause the reader to accept the list used in this chapter.[6]

Need for achievement

We can define this as the need to do useful work well. It is a salient influence characteristic of those who need little supervision. Their desire for accomplishment is a stronger motivation than any stimulation the supervisor can provide. Individuals who function in terms of this drive would not "bluff" to get a job in which they would not do well.

As everyone knows, some employees have a strong drive for success in their work; others are satisfied when they make a living. Those who want to feel that they are successes have high levels of aspiration for themselves. This drive is especially prominent in the evaluations made by the typical employment interviewer who interviews college seniors. He wants to find out whether the senior has a drive to get ahead or merely to hold a job. Too, some want to get ahead; but have a stronger drive to avoid failure.[7] Most employers who seek future executives try to avoid hiring the seniors who are satisfied to become the passable performers. They look for those who aspire to the highest vocational levels which they might possibly attain. Generally, college men have stronger achievement needs, to dominate, to be aggressive, and to be autonomously self-directing than college women. The college women have stronger needs to defer to others, to have close affiliations with others, to introspect regarding their personality, to help others, and to be dependent on others.[8]

Of course these differences in achievement needs between men and women often cause frictions in the marital state. The typical wife who is married to a man of high achievement needs cannot understand why he should neglect her and the children in order to give full attention to his job. She may feel neglected, treated unfairly. Her needs differ so decidedly from his.

---

[6] The fact that specialists do not agree in the labels that are applied to needs does not prevent researchers from obtaining valuable data. Chris Argyris, for example, was able to obtain high predictive validity scores from an apparently inconsistent list. See his *Diagnosing Human Relations in Organizations, A Case Study of a Hospital* (Research Project, Division of Labor and Management Center, Yale University, 1956), p. 32.

[7] See D. C. McClelland, "Measuring Motivation in Phantasy: the Achievement Motive," in McClelland, D. C., ed., *Studies in Motivation* (New York: Appleton-Century-Crofts, 1955), pp. 401-413. McClelland is one of the leading investigators in this field of motivation.

[8] See A. L. Edwards, *Manual of the Edwards Personal Preference Schedule*, New York: The Psychological Corporation, 1953.

If she accepts the situation but does nothing to lift her career or intellectual achievements, she may, in time, feel that her husband has risen to a high level but she has remained on a low level. This feeling on her part is likely to develop special needs which she may satisfy by positive or by negative value activities. Her special needs may cause her to become keenly devoted to children or friends. These are positive value tendencies. Of course she might instead acquire negative value adjustments such as neurosis and faultfinding toward those who appear to be on a higher career level.

Also, to satisfy this need, some women try to make themselves *indispensable* to others. The woman who makes this kind of adjustment wants others to be dependent upon her. Many college students have the kind of home situation where the father is a vocational success and the mother feels she has been left behind in the race. Hence, the mother tries to make herself indispensable to her children—she supervises and fusses over them to a degree that causes the children to rebel. Typical expressions on their part are "Oh, mother, I do wish you'd stop worrying about me and just let me alone."

Young men of high achievement needs are likely to have certain intense emotional problems not experienced by the low achievers. The *volunteer problem solver* in business is typically a high achievement-need person. He spends weeks or even months struggling with a company problem; and, in the flush of success, submits his solution to a superior in a written report. He then waits. And waits some more. He is expecting something. His daydreams at this point would reveal that he expects anything from a friendly telephone call, on up to a new office with a bigger title on the door!

One writer suggested that the most acceptable approach for an ambitious employee to use when answers start popping into his head, is usually the opposite of what he is naturally inclined to do. Instead of providing the answers on a volunteer basis, he should think in terms of questions that may stimulate management to give him a boss-requested assignment.[9]

When the person of strong achievement needs finds himself in a work situation where he cannot make progress he feels frustrated. Tensions develop. It is the frustration of wanting promotion and perceiving no possibility of getting it that often contributes to the nervous tension of certain employees.[10]

Occupational frustrations build up in him as a result of his gradually

---

[9] See Robert Sessions, "Is Gravel Grating Emotions in Your Company?" *American Business*, June 1958, pp. 16-19.

[10] See Robert G. Neel, "Nervous Stress in the Industrial Situation," *Personnel Psychology*, Winter 1955.

"I'm glad to see that your sales equal your blood pressure."
SOURCE: Arnett, caption by D. Phillips, Tide (July 30, 1955).

recognizing that his vocational progress is not reaching the level set in his earlier aspirations. Some develop an urgency that causes them to change jobs. Several investigators have concluded, as the result of analyses of life histories, that at age forty or thereabouts, a certain stock-taking of progress with respect to goals is likely to take place. An upsurge of new effort occurs when the results of this evaluation are not satisfactory.[11]

Achievement needs do not usually decline steadily with increased age. Instead, there is a likelihood that frustrations tend to accentuate the need for achievement at certain ages as compared with the earlier years. We also know that some people who have achieved success are thereby stimulated by that success toward continued striving. For those persons, achievement needs may not decline at all with age; the drive toward more successes becomes increasingly stronger. A recent investigation, for example, indicated that a group of older "high-achievers" of average age 56 reported greater willingness to move their homes and accept various other inconveniences if this move meant greater opportunity, than younger men of average age 36, who had also achieved success. Older, as well as younger men need outlets for satisfying strong achievement needs.[12]

Of course many persons seek satisfaction for their achievement needs through status symbols: a respected title, a distinctively furnished office,

[11] Sidney L. Pressey and Raymond G. Kuhlen, *Psychological Development Through the Life Span* (New York: Harper & Brothers, 1957), pp. 290-292.
[12] See L. Reissman, "Levels of Aspiration and Social Class," *American Sociological Review*, June 1953, pp. 233-242.

Motivation—Increasing Your Sensitivity

a home in a high income area, or ownership of a car that elicits social recognition. Many achievers are motivated by an urge to acquire status symbols. (See Chapter 6.) To some persons, however, status symbols are of little value. The lonely single girl who lives by herself in an apartment may, for example, decline an offer of a better job that includes a prestige title because she has a stronger need to work with old friends who are congenial.

Aggression needs

Almost every student has experienced the need for aggression. He has expressed some of his antagonisms toward unpleasant educational-institution frustrations by criticism of a teacher's marking methods or even by derogatory comments about the college's food service. A wise administrator learns to differentiate between objective comments and griping. Generally, griping is only partially justified, but it frequently makes the griper feel better because it satisfies some of his aggression needs.

The aggression drive, in its simplest form, expresses itself in destructive thoughts. When the individual fails to grow up emotionally, the drive continues to express itself in acts of faultfinding, selfishness, procrastination, jealousy, and hostility. The aggression drive is a force that makes us want to hit out when we are frustrated or angry or hurt. It helps us defend ourselves against attack. However, when it is coordinated and balanced with a constructive purpose, the aggression drive can lead to or become transformed into a constructive drive. It will conquer obstacles that stand in the way of reaching a difficult but worthwhile goal. A constructive drive makes us want to build rather than tear down, to create rather than destroy. In infancy, the constructive drive is self-centered and pleasure-seeking. Its primary aim is self-preservation as exemplified by the baby's efforts to obtain food, warmth, and affection from those around him. These things are essential to the baby's survival. In later stages, the earlier self-centered drives normally become constructive—they are expressed in thoughts and actions that are kind and creative. That is why we do not admire the adult who functions mainly in terms of aggression. We recognize that he has not as yet attained the maturity of control and direction of his aggression tendencies.

Sometimes the individual turns his aggressive drives against himself in self-punishment or, in extreme cases, suicide. In industry, this is seen most often in the form of accidental injury. Of course, many accidents are not a form of self-punishment, but close study of accidents has shown that the people involved often "forgot" or disregarded safety precautions in a manner that is difficult to understand on a conscious or logical basis. Unconsciously these individuals created a situation in which they could be and were injured.

Many of our aggressive drives go around our conscious guard to find expression in activities which we perceive as commendable. An example is the supremely honest man who must give his frank opinion to his friends on everything that they say or do. He not only believes that honesty is the best policy in all cases, but he practices it even though it sometimes harms those whom he likes. These are the self-righteous persons whom we avoid because they go out of their way to find fault in order to make themselves feel better.

An example of unconscious hostility is the not-too-well-disguised joke aimed at other people. We can temper aggressive feelings by humor that is enjoyed at the expense of the other person. True humor is enjoyed by all the persons involved in the joke. Humor, however, is one of the more subtle ways in which we can express our aggressions. We should all examine the forms of our humor and the people against whom it is directed.

The need for outlets of aggression tendencies is frequently exemplified in the history of nations. The demagogue has had great influence in the evolution of world affairs. He can always find some people who seek a new or better outlet for their hostilities. Scapegoats are universal in the history of nations. These destructive aggressors do not follow ordinary codes of ethical conduct—they have a deepseated need to be cruel to even those people who treat them kindly and justly.

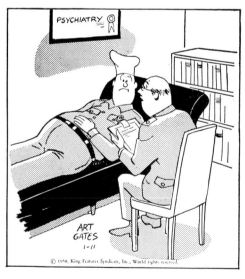

"Subconsciously you hate your grandmother, but you transfer this hostility to the troops by over-seasoning the chow!" SOURCE: by Art Gates. Reproduced by special permission of King Features Syndicate.

Every large business organization has one or more scapegoats or whipping boys—individuals who rightly or wrongly are targets for blame, even abuse. The individual chosen for the satisfaction of this need is likely to be a ruthless power-seeking person who recognizes that he is hated but is not emotionally disturbed by the brickbats tossed against him behind his back. Top management men are not ordinarily disturbed by the employees' hatred toward the scapegoat member of their group —they know that many employees have unconscious needs for such an outlet. Subconsciously, too, perhaps some feel that if one member of management is the unofficial whipping boy, the other members are likely to miss some of the mudballs that might legitimately be thrown at them!

The new employee who is unaware of the ways in which needs for aggression are expressed is likely to misunderstand the fellow employee who advises him to "tell the boss off." Many a novice has caused trouble for himself by listening to the fellow employee who advised him to loaf on the job and to resist the boss. This kind of unsophisticated youth believes the pseudo "big shot" when he describes how he put the boss into his place! Of course when the youth and the bad counselor are in the presence of the boss, the newcomer discovers that the loudtalker is actually meek as a lamb.

Ideally, no one should have destructive aggressive tendencies. Practically, all persons have them to some extent, but most people keep them repressed. When repressed, they are likely to appear in disguised forms, most commonly in psychosomatic or other functional disorders.

When tensions are strong enough and suppressed, they are a factor in headache, stomachache, ulcers, and other ailments. This is especially likely to occur with people who are under constant pressure but cannot speak out for some reason. Bank officers and public officials who have to be "nice" to everybody occupy this kind of situation. If a person in this kind of situation "blows up" occasionally, he should be forgiven.

Some children are reared in this controlled manner. The child from infancy on is taught not to show his anger openly. He is not allowed to quarrel with brothers and sisters, to express jealousy, or to say, "I don't like you!" He is taught that it is wrong even to *think* these things. In adulthood, this kind of upbringing in regard to the firm control of aggressive feelings becomes an unconscious part of his psychic life. Consciously, he may not feel angry. He may not even realize that he denies his angry feelings. When, on occasion, he is provoked to anger he unconsciously feels guilty about his feelings of hostility which he dare not express. On the job, he may be easy to get along with; he never picks a fight, he never questions his supervisor's commands, and he does not argue when he is passed over for a promotion which he believes that he deserves. Even though this kind of person gets along quietly with everyone, he seldom develops close friendships. He usually has no deep interests outside the job. Eventually, however, the pent-up angry feelings take their toll. He has no safety valves through argument or an absorbing interest. He becomes an asthmatic, ulcer, migraine, or some other variety of patient whose ailment cannot be cured by medicines.

Frustration arouses energy. If this energy cannot be expressed, by prompt satisfying means of expression, it is nonetheless discharged somehow. If you are reprimanded but cannot talk back, you may later yell at someone for a minor misdeed. You may berate a waitress or yell at other drivers of cars you pass on the way home. Of course, if you are married, you can take out your irritation on the wife or the children!

Momentary and short-lived flareups of this kind are common to all of us. When, however, the aggression evokes feelings that are out of all proportion to the situation, we say that hostility is expressed. It is a common and important problem in industry, for unlike anger it tends to linger on. For example, we may find the man who dislikes everyone, supervisors and co-workers alike, because he feels that they are "out to get him," or are "constantly picking on him." He is the person who does everything with a chip on his shoulder. Such expressions of hostility are found not only on the employee level, but among management men, too. For instance, there are days when everyone tries to avoid the boss because rumor has it that he is "on the warpath."

We can often find ourselves being hostile to someone for no apparent reason. By stopping and thinking for a moment we may see that perhaps we are transferring frustrations from other experiences into hostility toward others. Thus by looking for the causes of hostility in ourselves and in those around us, we will be taking a constructive step toward more satisfactory relations with others.

Need for security

This term applies to the individual's seeking for certainty, stability, and predictability in life. Commonly, it is applied to the desire for economic security as in the preference for having a steady income and a pension in old age. Emotional insecurity is deeper than economic insecurity. It often arises in broken home situations where the child's world, particularly his relations with parents, are undependable. In adulthood, such a person tries to protect himself and his position. He likes routine, regular schedules, and obedience to precedent. The term also applies

Motivation—Increasing Your Sensitivity

to stability in social relationships as exemplified by the person who avoids the making of new friends but clings tenaciously to a few old friends.

Employees who feel insecure are likely to have extra tensions which in some cases, are relieved by criticising the company. Older employees who resent their lack of progress often express themselves caustically toward management. Managements know this and try to have new and young employees work with employees who are not soured on the company. This is one of the factors involved in the first assignment of a capable new employee: are his associates old employees who feel defeated or are they well-adjusted men who enjoy the challenge in their jobs?

"Here's Mr. Apgar, Ed—set your watch for 7:32." SOURCE: by Jeff Keate. Reproduced by permission of The McNaught Syndicate, Inc.

The "touchy" employee is a problem commonly encountered by almost every supervisor. This kind of employee is overly sensitive to any comments about his work, however well meant or constructive. The touchy employee magnifies or misinterprets incidental remarks that he hears even though not directed to him nor applicable to his situation.

Of course such a person is exceedingly insecure. He needs constant reassurance and approval. Some supervisors try to assure the individual of his value to the organization at every opportunity. They ask his advice about the work and praise him in the presence of more well-adjusted friends who "go along" with the ego-building praise.

Every alert supervisor does some of this kind of catering to the insecure person in his group. When, however, the task proves to be endless because the need is never satisfied or resolved, the supervisor gives up the attempt to satisfy the insecure person's needs and concentrates on

Motivation—Increasing Your Sensitivity **447**

the work rather than the person who does the work. Some of these super-visors become cynical about the values of human relations skills—their answer is likely to be: "Aw, I fed so-and-so compliments every day for years but he never changed. I got tired of wetnursing him along. From now on he's got to get his ego built somewhere else."

One answer to the discouraged supervisor might be to the effect: "Sure, you have to keep it up, maybe all your life. Your job in super-vision is not to cure people of their peculiarities but to get along with them, day in and day out, as they are—not as they ought to be."

The need to overcome guilt feelings and protection

The process of ascribing to another person or institution the burden of our own repressions is commonly referred to as *projection*. The person who perceives in other people the traits and motives which he cannot admit in himself is probably using the mechanism of projection.

The personnel man must occasionally deal with pathetic cases that involve projection. One employee, for example, whipped his tiny baby because it cried. The employee's wife complained to the personnel man and asked his help. He found that the man had had sexual relations with the girl before marriage and when she became pregnant, he thought he was the father. After marriage, he discovered that other men also had had intimate relations with his wife. The husband developed hatred of the baby but wanted to continue the marriage. Such impulsions are difficult for an employer to tolerate. A solution in this case was found by placing the baby for adoption through a social agency.

The student who has the barrier of failure in an examination often projects the cause to the unfairness of the teacher. The husband who slips in his marital relations may satisfy his feelings of guilt by accusing others of infidelity. The man who fails in business does not, as a rule, blame himself, but imputes his losses to the "powerful forces of Wall Street," unfair competitors, or governmental interference. An executive may project his failures to factors other than himself. If the balance sheet figures are unsatisfactory, he can blame his employees, com-petitors, or government interferences; or he can calmly analyze the situation for the causes or failure and then busy himself on an improved plan of procedure for the next fiscal period. "Passing the buck" satisfies the "passer" but does not bring objective results. The production fore-man who falls down on his schedule may have sound reasons for so doing, but it is to be expected that he will suggest that the blame should be placed on some other executive.

To avoid such excuses, forceful leaders often develop the habit of asking their subordinates to perform certain jobs and of implying, when the orders are given, that excuses are not going to be considered. This method has decided benefits, because it causes the subordinate executives to spend their mental effort in working out schemes for the accomplishment of the desired end rather than in seeking excuses of the projectionist's kind. The executive who insists upon results, the results he wants, may develop the reputation of being hard-boiled, but his methods are sounder psychologically than those of the other man who accepts the excuses of poorly-adjusted employees. Any organization that is made up of a large number of people who find it easy to excuse poor work on their part is a weak organization.

Our everyday human relations in business do not enable us to know how an individual's feelings of guilt arise. That kind of probing is in the province of the trained psychotherapist. We can, however, see the outward manifestations as exemplified by the persons who wash their hands many times a day because they are afraid of contamination by dirt. Dirt symbolizes some factor in their guilt. Some wear gloves to overcome the fear. Compulsive habits of tidiness and accuracy often have their origins in guilt feelings. Compulsive spenders, habitual gamblers, and givers of extravagant gifts are likely to be motivated by an underlying feeling of guilt or some other inadequacy.

Similar but less important compulsions are counting the number of steps in every stairway, counting the cracks in the sidewalk, counting the letters in street signs, and putting dots inside all the "o's" on a printed page. Some count their change numerous times every day.

Need for recognition, acceptance

It is evening. A husband and wife are sitting in the living room. He is tired from the day's work. She takes a cigarette and insists that he walk across the room to light it for her even though a lighter is within her reach. Obviously she has strong needs for recognition and acceptance.

Each one of us has feelings of inadequacy, hunger for acceptance by others, and a desire for recognition. In our yearnings, we make demands on others, buy products, and go to certain places that appease our unconscious needs. Sometimes these inner strivings cause us to change friends, change neighborhoods, and change churches. We can see these strivings at work in the youth who must use profanity, drink to excess, or join a tough military outfit in order to prove that he is a man!

The young college man who joins a business organization wants to feel that he is accepted, not only by his fellow workers, but also by the executives. If he has a strong need for acceptance by those of higher status, he is apt to try to become "chummy" with executives before he has earned their friendship. He may, for example, meet an executive a few times, note that his friends address him by a certain nickname, and then imagine that he, too, has acquired the privilege of addressing the executive by his nickname. Of course the older man resents it because such familiarity must be earned—not assumed by the beginner. The smart young man keeps on addressing the boss as "Mr." even though the boss addresses the young man by nickname.

Defensiveness

The most common description of the defensive person is "He has a chip on his shoulder." This pattern is self-protective. The person who has difficulty in admitting to others or himself some inadequacy in his personality may try to guard it from scrutiny by others. He develops some modes of behavior that shield or appear to shield him. These protective forms of behavior are called *defensive mechanisms.* He uses them to protect himself from anxieties and his associates soon learn to avoid any mention of those inadequacies for which he adjusts by defensive behavior. They know that any mention of his defect, real or imagined, is likely to result in exaggerated behavior or withdrawal from the social situation.

Painful and unpleasant topics of importance to us are likely to bring out defense mechanisms, such as anger over a situation in which we have played an unintelligent part.

> "Never talk to Oliver Gaskell about his son!" one of the new executives of the pottery plant was warned. "If you want to get along with the old man, don't mention Junior unless he brings it up first."

Why should Gaskell, Sr. become angry when someone discusses the son? Does he, perhaps, realize that he is responsible for wrecking his son's life, forcing him away from medicine into a career the son finds distasteful and in which he cannot be successful? Or does he secretly think of his son as a weakling, a failure? In either case, is he not trying to close his mind to a painful idea? When someone mentions his son, he uses anger as a defense.[13]

---

[13] John Perry, *Human Relations in Small Industry* (Small Business Administration, Washington, D.C.), March 1954, p. 8.

The one situation in business where defensiveness is most often evident is in the ways certain employees react to criticism of their work. When the supervisor points out an error, the non-defensive person accepts it objectively. In contrast, the defensive employee tightens up and refuses to admit the error, however small. He may even refuse to admit the error when it is clearly evident that he made it, and offers far-fetched explanations instead.

The defensive person asserts his innocence even when not accused as exemplified by one executive who said of his secretary: "She is so defensive that if you told her it was raining outside, she'd say it wasn't her fault."

A common example of defensiveness in social situations is the very dignified gentleman who seems to wear an armor plating of dignity as a protection against criticism and social inadequacy. As one humorist said: "Don't mistake dignity. Lots of times it enables a man who says nothin', does nothin', and knows nothin' to command a lot of respect!"

Everyone is certain to meet this type of dignity. It is protective. The individual avoids risks of social failure by means of a manner which causes others to treat him with the kind of respect his manner demands. In business, his associates sense his sensitiveness. They defer to him when in his presence but they avoid his presence whenever possible. He is a lonely person and can be "reached" only when he is in circumstances where he feels secure from criticism. In previous generations, many of these dignified gentlemen held executive jobs. Today, if circumstances place them in executive positions, they are likely to be poor leaders. Modern business requires the ability to give and take criticism without excessive defensiveness.

Coping mechanisms

Even though much of an individual's behavior is an attempt to satisfy his needs, we must not imagine that he is the helpless victim of his need drives. He has many coping mechanisms. *Coping mechanisms* are related to the defense mechanisms. The defense mechanisms indicate how the individual adjusts to conditions that arouse his anxieties. The coping mechanisms indicate how he utilizes positively both his potentialities and his defense mechanisms in his life and work situations. From this standpoint, each person exhibits two varieties of behavior: one variety develops from needs to which he adjusts inadequately as in defense mechanisms, the others are expressions of ways in which he channels his tensions and need outlets into the means of making a living,

living with others, and living with himself. The human relations specialist sees examples every day of individuals who exhibit markedly disturbed personality patterns, inability to live with themselves, but they function effectively in work and certain other situations.[14] They have good coping mechanisms.

Our major question about the individual's characteristic behavior should not be: "How normal or abnormal is he?" but rather "Are his coping mechanisms enabling him to function effectively in certain situations under certain conditions?" If the answer is "Yes," we want to note the favorable situations and conditions. In everyday practice, almost every intelligent executive does this. He knows that certain defensive or other inadequately adjusted persons do very good work and live happily when conditions are favorable to their needs.

Also, we need to realize that the employee's needs may change as he undergoes new experiences such as "shock" arising from a tragic experience. The earlier need drives may be modified by later needs even though the earlier patterns tend to remain in modified form.

The important objective for the human relations leader in business is to produce a satisfactory balance between the employee's needs and the full range of satisfactions which may be gained from his work. Management must keep the needs of employees in perspective with the needs of the company; both are evolving in accordance with their established patterns.[15]

The supervisor who knows the dominant needs of his individual employees can often find ways to define work assignments in terms of their needs. The insightful supervisor can add to his work instructions statements about the need satisfactions that will accrue to the successful worker. A capable foreman will often explain to an emotionally insecure employee that accomplishment of a difficult assignment will make the employee's status so secure that he will be recognized by management as an especially valuable employee.

One basic conclusion from the study of the worker's needs is that we are not utilizing sufficiently his need to be needed, to make a contribution, to feel that he is a worthy participant in a great enterprise. He does not want to be used merely as a means to an end but as a partner in the attainment of worthwhile ends.

---

[14] See Daniel Brower, "The Applicability of Projective Techniques to Personnel Appraisal," *Personnel Psychology,* Summer 1955.

[15] For suggestions as to how this can be done, see Robert Saltonstall, "What Employees Want from Their Work," *Harvard Business Review,* November-December 1953.

For All Students

Harrell, Thomas W., *Industrial Psychology*. New York: Rinehart & Company, Inc., 1958, Chapter 10. Deals with motivations and work, and wage incentives.

Pressey, Sidney L., and Raymond G. Kuhlen, *Psychological Development Through the Life Span*. New York: Harper & Brothers, 1957. An excellent volume on the subject.

For Advanced Students

Atkinson, John W., *Motives in Fantasy, Action and Society*. Princeton, N. J.: D. Van Nostrand Company, Inc., 1958. Presents a series of 46 articles that survey progress made in developing methods for measuring socially meaningful motives.

Lindzey, Gardner, editor, *Assessment of Human Motives*. New York: Rinehart & Company, Inc., 1958. Nine distinguished psychologists present a cross-section of thinking on problems of research in human motivation.

Maslow, A. H., "A Dynamic Theory of Human Motivation," *Psychological Review*, July 1943, pp. 370-396. Presents a hierarchy of needs, an early study.

Stacey, Chalmers L., and Manfred F. DeMartino, editors, *Understanding Human Motivation*. Cleveland: Howard Allen, Inc., 1958. A book of readings.

For Men in Business

McGregor, Douglas, *The Human Side of Enterprise*. New York: McGraw-Hill Book Co., Inc., 1960. Attempts to build a bridge between the manager and the social scientist. Stresses individual motivation rather than authority.

Marrow, Alfred J., *Making Management Human*. New York: McGraw-Hill Book Company, Inc., 1957, Chapter 8. A psychologist who also heads up a company discusses why people work.

Smith, Henry Clay, *Psychology of Industrial Behavior*. New York: McGraw-Hill Book Company, Inc., 1955, Chapters 4-8. Deals with obstacles to need satisfaction, job anxiety, job satisfaction, employee adjustment, and human engineering.

QUESTIONS ON THE CHAPTER

1. What is the significance in the example of the alert executive who reacts to a useless suggestion submitted by one of his employees?
2. Comment on the assumption that sensitivity to individual needs is limited to educated persons.
3. Differentiate between the need for achievement in college men and in college women.
4. How may an ambitious employee cope with his desire for advancement through problem-solving?

5. How does increasing age affect achievement needs?

6. What is the difference between the aggression drive and the constructive drive?

7. Give the several definitions of the need for security.

8. Why does a person tend to use the mechanism of projection?

9. Describe the characteristics of the man with "a chip on his shoulder."

10. In what way are coping mechanisms related to defense mechanisms?

11. Which important worker's need should be taken into consideration more often by business executives?

12. Of all the ideas presented in the chapter, which one had most value for you?

13. How did the chapter contribute to your future relations with (a) your supervisors, (b) employees whom you may supervise?

PROBLEMS AND PROJECTS

For All Students

1. Examine several old magazines that publish human interest cartoons. Clip some that amuse you. Can you recognize any relationships between your own psychological needs and the ideas or characters in the cartoons? How might this insight be of value to you when you supervise others?

2. Give an example of an embarrassing situation which you brought about because of your failure to sense some other person's unspoken needs.

For Advanced Students

3. Make a study of problems involved in developing standard labels of needs. See footnote 6 in the early part of this chapter regarding Chris Argyris' ability to obtain high predictive validity scores from an apparently inconsistent list of needs.

4. Of course much behavior takes place as the result of joint effects or interactions of several motives. This fusion has been recognized for years. See H. A. Murray, *et al., Explorations in Personality.* New York: Oxford University Press, 1938. However, little research on fusions has been reported. Why not?

For Men in Business

5. Discuss the influence of psychological needs in customers. To see an example, visit a hearing-aid sales office. There you can note customers whose need for personal attention seems to be greater than their need for an instrument to overcome loss of hearing. Can you cite similar examples in other businesses?

6. Describe some examples of effects of needs in the employment of workers. For data on the subject, see "Joblessness and Family Status—A Case Study," *The Management Review,* American Management Association, Inc., April 1956, p. 266.

V ERY PROBABLY, SOME OF YOUR INTEREST IN STUDYING HUMAN relations stems from your difficulties in dealing with problem persons. Each one of us meets some people who are maladjusted, neurotic, suspicious, unkind, sarcastic, opinionated, or destructive. As employees they not only lower morale and retard production but they also add to our burdens. Sometimes we react to them by ignoring them, sometimes by trying to change or improve them. In the end, we may conclude that since we cannot ignore or change them, our best policy is to strengthen ourselves so that we can endure them without too much emotional strain on our part.

Dealing with difficult people can strengthen you

Each one of us has need for the ability to objectify and understand problem persons in order that we may treat them intelligently and rise above being hurt by their orneriness. The qualities we develop in ourselves are more important than the few modifications we can help bring about in others. You should not look upon most difficult people as persons whom you should "cure" or change. Instead, look upon them as opportunities for strengthening yourself. Each difficult person has certain inherent rights to become and be what he is—why should you

25

Problem Employees
Whom You May Meet in Business

assume that every one should do or be what you choose for him? This does not mean that you should ignore the difficult person. Perhaps you can understand him, work with him, and thereby enable yourself and him to grow to a higher level of maturity.

One of the most helpful points of view for us to acquire is that problem people are not wholly bad. Even the most cussed have some good characteristics. They are cussed only in "spots." They have the same psychological needs as the well adjusted but they use inappropriate behavior to satisfy their needs.

Vocational self-sabotage

Anyone who does vocational counseling of adults is certain to meet individuals who have high intelligence, pleasing personalities, seemingly good habits, and many good character qualities; but who always manage somehow to fail in their vocations. In contrast with them, other individuals of less intelligence, more irritating personalities, and poorer personal habits manage to succeed, regardless of their opportunities. Both types are difficult to explain as long as we use quantitative approaches only. When, however, we think in terms of unconscious motives, we get plausible explanations. We discover that many of the men who always manage to fail are really expressing an unconscious urge toward self-sabotage in their vocation.

Failure enables the maladjusted person to accomplish aims that are more important to him than success. Such aims have been revealed by Friend and Haggard in the systematic investigation of two classes of unemployed adults: those *high* and those *low* on eight basic criterion items of occupational adjustment. One of the striking differences between the two groups was described, in part, in their findings.

> Topping the many sharp contrasts in personality, the stronger tendency of the *Lows* to defeat themselves and spoil their job chances stands out as an indicator of adjustment at work. It is often evidenced by excessive drinking, quarreling, and illness. The *Lows* seem to marry the wrong person and to have families so large that they experience difficulty in supporting them. Correlational and other special analyses of the extent of the tendency toward self-sabotage link it with the extent of the following attitudes: parental rejection, antagonism toward the father, resentments both of dependence and domination of families, rigidity, buried fear of failure, and self-attack, unrealistic thinking about jobs, ambivalence, and reliance on pull. . . . Although the relationships suggested are not necessarily causal ones, these factors do seem to serve as devices through which the maladjusted individual accomplishes an aim. They seem to be ways of settling early parental scores; or of handling the guilt

which demands constant failure; or of protecting himself against fears of being unable to cope with work. . . . This extreme type of "vicious-circle" behavior seems related to the well-known proclivity of those seriously disturbed emotionally (the *Lows*) to make things generally hard for themselves—a trait which is slight in the *Highs*.[1]

Whatever the explanations that may eventually be found most appropriate for the understanding of capable adults who manage to fail, the fact is that they do manage to fail in spite of apparently excellent outward reasons for success. The only helpful psychological explanation, thus far, is that they themselves are unconsciously sabotaging their own efforts in order to attain aims more important to themselves.

The person who, for example, has a strong drive to dominate or control others may try to do so by being a tactful executive or he may be merely abusive and sarcastic. Both positive and negative value kinds of behavior may originate from the same kind of basic need. Criminals have the same inner needs as good citizens but the criminals satisfy their drives through behavior that is dangerous to society. They have not learned the art of satisfying their own needs through service to others.

When we deal with problem people we should observe the characteristic ways they use in dealing with life's situations. We may, for example, note that a person expresses egotistical behavior. Most people say that he "*is* conceited." Instead, we should say to ourselves that he "*uses* conceit" as his characteristic way of dealing with others.

The people who use poor techniques in dealing with life's situations are everywhere. We cannot escape them. They are found in the primitive societies of Africa and Australia as well as in America. Many savages as well as civilized persons fail to gain happiness and serenity. The faultless, guiltless persons of the world cannot be found in the sunny, palmtreed islands of the South Pacific any more easily than in our own cultures.[2] Perfection in humanity cannot be found by going to some new environment. Instead, we have to find examples of fine ways of dealing with life's situations among the persons wherever we are.

After all, most people try to live what they think is the good life. Most employees are anxious to please, to do a good day's work even though a small percentage, estimated as ten per cent by one executive, may loom too large in our thinking. This executive stated his observations, in part, as follows:

---

[1] Jeannette G. Friend and Ernest A. Haggard, "Work Adjustment in Relation to Family Background," *Applied Psychology Monographs*, No. 16 (Stanford University Press, Stanford, California, 1948), pp. 58-59.

[2] Fereidoun Estandiary, "Is It the Mysterious—or Neurotic—East?" *The New York Times Magazine*, March 24, 1957.

Problem Employees

People are the same everywhere I have been. I have found employees in all parts of the country equally competent and willing to turn out a good day's work, but wherever I have gone I found my "Ten percenters." My experience has proved that regardless of what you do for your employees about 10% will never be satisfied. . . .

Regardless of how good the conditions or how good the wages these "Ten percenters" can never be satisfied. Maybe this is exaggerated a little but these are the only people I can't seem to please or become friendly with. I don't hold any grudge against these people—I feel sorry for them. Complaining and being dissatisfied is their petcock and method of emotional relief. Other people get the same by being loyal, happy and complimentary. The way I get around this situation and the reason why I don't have ulcers is I overlook their shortages. My deepest concern is for the other 90%.

There is no use worrying about getting rid of this 10% because you will get another 10 just as bad. You will always have them—it just seems to be the law of averages. You will find them in all departments and in all walks of life. Some employers have been condemning the whole 100% because of the "Ten percenters." In visiting plants around the country I have noticed everyone is always ready to complain about their 10% group but fail to give credit that is due the other fine 90%. [3]

Some problem persons make important contributions

In business, it would be easier to deal only with well-adjusted mature individuals, but we have to recognize that some very great contributors are maladjusted and immature. Many problem persons have certain strong traits that offset some of their bad ones. In one of our leading corporations, there is an unofficial company policy "never to stop hiring a screwball" if the man shows a quick mind, a knack for ideas, and ambition. [4]

Findings from the extreme stress conditions of war vindicate this policy. Of all those who have broken down in action under stress, the contributions of those who have done so in wartime have been given special study. The investigations indicate that, as a group, the psychological patients of our recent wars served as long and as well as the average soldier. Before the breakdown took place, official evidence indicates that in a very large proportion of cases, the man did credit to himself and his unit. Statistically, the proportion of men with neuroses who received decorations for valour showed little difference from the proportion of other soldiers who received decorations. Indeed, there is

---

[3] William S. Sadler, Jr., "Human Evaluation and Business Profits," *Mechanical Bulletin 578* (American Newspaper Publishers Association), July 3, 1956, pp. 47-49.

[4] See *Business Week,* August 2, 1959, p. 57.

Problem Employees

"Two years ago they'd of fired me for goofing off. Now they promote me for 'creative thinking'." SOURCE: by Angelo. Courtesy Sales Management (January 3, 1958).

considerable evidence to indicate that some measure of mental peculiarity may endow a man with extra spirit, conscientiousness, and additional grit.[5]

Executives who direct engineers and research workers know that a preconceived pattern of personality adjustment does not hold for all occupational groups. They know, for example, that the compulsive-looking, tense, rigid, introverted person, not infrequently found among expert research men and engineers, might erroneously be considered as maladjusted. Clinicians realize that such a picture often contributes to successful functioning in engineering and research.

Psychiatrists recognize that most persons in business have their peculiarities as individuals. Emotional problems that are handicaps in one job may or may not be handicaps in another job. As one practitioner in the field of the problem person in industry has stated:

> . . . it is widely accepted today that a "healthy family background"—whatever that is—is the Golden Key to productivity, happiness, and success in most (if not, in fact, *all*) occupations and activities. Yet there is mounting evidence that *it is not at all necessary to have a "healthy family background" to perform successfully in business and industry today.* Indeed, there is considerable evidence that many people are outstanding in their jobs or professions precisely *because* they come from psychologically unhealthy homes. . . .
>
> There is, of course, a considerable body of sociological literature demonstrating that city slums, generally regarded as a breeding-ground of poor home environments, produce more than their share of delinquents. But the same literature also reveals, upon closer inspection, that city slums have provided certain individuals with powerful motivation to

[5] See several authors in Emanuel Miller, editor, *The Neuroses in War* (New York: The MacMillan Company, 1940).

Problem Employees

"make something of themselves," and that many men and women from the slums have risen to the top in their businesses, or professions.

In the same way, from families which are clearly not ideal, we may get both delinquents and top executives. . . .

Of course, it should be acknowledged that not everyone who has an emotional problem or a psychiatric syndrome is a desirable person occupationally. Further, it should be emphasized that, although emotional disturbances may be assets, they are not assets in every type of job; frequently they are assets in only one or a very few jobs. In other words, emotional disabilities may sometimes be outright handicaps because of the individual himself, because of the job he is in, or even because of the emotional disabilities of his superior.

Purely for financial reasons—but not ignoring the humanitarian and morale factors—we must raise the question of what can be done with such people. Facing this issue involves many factors, including timing of action. For instance, one company sent eight superintendents to us at Stevens' Laboratory of Psychological Studies; all were chemists or chemical engineers. Their question to us was: "Are any of these men salvageable?" It turned out that two of the men were "salvageable." Among the others were two men over 60 who had been considered unsatisfactory for more than 15 years.[6]

Generally, psychological disability is not synonymous with occupational disability.

Enlightened managements realize that it is management's task to discover the maladjusted individuals, to correct any work conditions that contribute to maladjustments, and to decrease the harmful influences of psychoneurotics who inoculate large groups of otherwise efficient workers. The main channel for providing favorable influences is through selecting and guiding the supervisors and foremen. To many employees, they are "the company." They can, at times, reduce or accentuate the individual employee's anxieties and fears.

The neurotics in industry [7]

The neurotics (also called psychoneurotics) are emotionally immature individuals. A neurotic is likely to be a nuisance to himself, to others, or to both. The kind that is a nuisance to himself is the more common. He fixates the attention upon himself and has emotional reactions out of proportion to his difficulties. Frequently his symptoms are a direct appeal for sympathy and attention. Or he may be setting up an excellent alibi

---

[6] Frederick J. Gaudet, "The Problem Employee: Some Points of Confusion," *The Personnel Function: A Progress Report*, Management Report No. 24, Personnel Division, American Management Association, Inc., New York, 1958. Reprinted with special permission of the AMA.

[7] For a related description of neurotics in business, see pages 343-345.

Problem Employees

for possible failure in a given situation. His lowered efficiency and emotional distortions affect other employees around him. The morale and working efficiency of the whole group may be lowered seriously by the continued presence of just one neurotic.

The neurotic who is a nuisance to others is likely to be arrogant, demanding, or just plain cussed. He has trouble getting along with his associates: he gets angry easily, is irritable, hostile, and faultfinding.

The alert management notes that emotional upsets appear in greater numbers in specific departments than in others. This may be due to a maladjusted supervisor who keeps his subordinates emotionally upset. The foreman may have a disrupting effect by exerting excessive or constant pressure on the employees. He may criticise too much. He may praise certain employees and ignore others. He may lean over them at work and tell them how to do work which they know well. He may find fault with incidental details. He may insist that everything must be done his way even though the employee knows a better way. Studies have shown that poor supervisors take their sickness rates with them when they move from one part of an organization to another.[8]

Interestingly, too, neurotic employees tend to gravitate toward other neurotics. They seem to feel that they are among persons of their own kind. Neurotics attract neurotics in industry as well as in marriage. When management spots such a situation, the maladjusted persons are not promptly fired because the typical neurotic does good work or, at least, has learned how to give the impression that he is doing good work. As an employee, he tends to punish himself. He feels that he is not doing his job well. He needs constant reassurance that his work is passable. He may be especially agreeable toward others, but he has personal problems that are overwhelming, problems that his well-adjusted associates usually ignore.

Neurotics differ from psychotics. Psychotics must or should be hospitalized. They cannot hold jobs. Neurotics seldom receive hospital treatment. They can and do hold jobs. Many, but not all, psychotics are out of touch with reality. Neurotics live in touch with time and place, but do not enjoy it. As one humorist expressed this difference: "A psychotic thinks that 2 and 2 make 5. A neurotic knows that 2 and 2 make 4 but he is unhappy about it!"

Contrary to general belief, many neurotic workers are valuable workers, likely to be among the most conscientious members of the company's workers. Many neurotics when working individually give as good an occupational performance as non-neurotics. Certain jobs lend

---

[8] See Alan H. Owen, "What Do We Mean by Neurotic Absenteeism?" *Personnel Management Abstracts,* Spring 1957.

Problem Employees

themselves to a person who is excessively suspicious as long as he has good control over his judgment. Many neurotics are submissive people who will do extra hours of work, because they are afraid to say "no." Others are extreme perfectionists who turn out accurate reliable work at the price of tremendous internal discomfort if it is not perfect.[9]

The complainers

Any executive who keeps in touch with the feelings of his employees is likely to find that he has some gripers in his department. One of the most common variety is the employee who constantly complains that he works too hard. He imagines that he is doing more than he should. If job descriptions have been written for each job, he will use the description of duties as evidence of the claim that he is asked to do tasks that he should not be expected to perform. If the job description has the statement, "Performs other related duties as assigned," this part of the description is overlooked by the complainer.

To the executive who looks upon complaints as symptoms, the claim that the employee works too hard usually means that the executive has failed to give the employee ego involvement in the work. The employee who identifies with his superiors and the company tends to see his tasks in terms of his own ego needs. He has few complaints even when invited to express them.

Investigators who have studied complaints of employees have found that the complaints may be classified into three major groups:

1. Those which can be clearly seen and agreed upon such as a broken tool. Sensory experience can define them.

2. Experiences or conditions which cannot be clearly seen and agreed upon, such as, "The room is too hot."

3. Complaints in which sensory experiences play a small role but hopes and fears are involved. Conditions complained about are expressions of the sentiments of the person, such as complaints about wages, supervision, or advancement. Complaints of this third group are the most disturbing. These are likely to be symptoms of some deeper or symbolical need rather than justifiable complaints about objective matters that are easily verified.[10]

We should also view some complaints as tension releasers. Perhaps,

---

[9] See S. L. Warner, "Spotting the Neurotic and Helping the Maladjusted," *Personnel Journal*, September 1957.

[10] See F. J. Roethlisberger and W. J. Dickson, *Management and the Worker* (Cambridge: Harvard University Press, 1939), pp. 255-69.

Problem Employees

From "The 'Worry-Go-Round'," a booklet prepared and distributed by The Connecticut Mutual Life Insurance Company. Copyright 1955 by The Connecticut Mutual Life Insurance Company.

for some individuals, gripes are just another variety of goose pimples or allergies! As one physician has well stated:

> Many of us react to being chilled with goose pimples. Some persons react to emotional tension in the same manner. Around the bottom of each hair on the body is a tiny muscle, and it is this muscle that our nerves activate under certain conditions of stress and strain. Actually "goose pimples" can be as much a tension outlet as hysterical crying or over-eating.
>
> Another way to relieve tension would be to regrow our prehensile tail. It has been shown that monkeys do not suffer from mental ailments or strokes because wiggling their tails seems to relieve them of pent-up emotional disturbances. In surveying the emotionally disturbed in mental hospitals, it has been reported that persons with asthma or hay fever are rarely found to be patients in these institutions. The belief is that certain allergic symptoms may be the method whereby some "normal" people blow off steam.[11]

A common reason for the dissatisfaction voiced by a disgruntled employee is likely to be his pay, but it is not usually the basic motivating

---

[11] Edward R. Pinckney, M.D., "From A Doctor's Notebook," *Blue Print for Health,* Fall 1958. Dr. Pinckney is Director of the Comprehensive Medical Clinic, Northwestern University Medical School.

Problem Employees 463

factor. Insufficient salary is repeatedly used as a pet peeve but this claim often turns out to be a means of release from some troublesome but submerged and unidentified irritation. The lack of money is a real problem with many people and it does cause worries, but it also symbolizes or covers up the seat of many a complainer's troubles. Frequently, other factors are involved in the frustrations which the lack of money symbolizes. (See page 411.)

Many complaints about wages are not cured by wage increases. Too many executives take for granted the idea that everyone wants more money and that if employees are given more money, they will be happy. Desire for more pay may really mean that the employee believes that his foreman does not give sufficient recognition for years of service, or that a certain rate of pay symbolizes answers to status needs.

If the foreman does get a raise for the complainer, he will be treating symptoms rather than causes. Logic and fact will not satisfy the dissatisfied employee who is seeking emotional satisfactions. Logic merely disgruntles him more. The supervisor is more likely to be helpful by evaluating the worker's need for a feeling of worthwhileness. Perhaps he needs recognition as a person, new assignments that challenge him and that may lead to a higher rate of pay. Certainly, the supervisor should let the complainer air his grievance before he offers logical answers.

Well-adjusted happy people accept or improve difficult conditions. Unhappy inadequately adjusted persons are seldom satisfied with the job or life, but some of the tensions involved in their complaints can be re-directed into useful satisfactions.

Complaints should be examined for their direct objective meaning and any causes for complaints in groups 1 and 2 should be corrected when possible. Complaints that are in group 3 must often be approached with insight into their obscure meanings.

The ideological "expert"

Of all the problem persons in industry, one of the most baffling is the employee who has developed some elaborate scheme for interpreting the world or some complex aspect of life. He usually has only a smattering of knowledge of a favorite field of study such as philosophy, economics, or political science, but he becomes convinced that his superficial explanations and remedies would, if accepted by others, solve the world's ills. He expends much time and effort in explaining to others his panaceas. Those who listen do so out of courtesy rather than interest.

He may, for example, have a line of reasoning that divides the world into two conflicting groups: (1) the employers or managers and (2) the workers. He can take any event in his work surroundings and translate it into the differences which he sees in the goals of managers and workers. Even the most altruistic action by the company is interpreted as an attempt to gain ends that benefit the managers at the expense of the workers.

Men of this kind are likely to be lonesome, isolated from their immediate social world. They have few satisfactory relations with their colleagues. Hence, they move from one job to the next and each job is terminated by a crisis caused by misunderstanding on the part of those whom he perceives as exploiters or at best as stupid. Even though some member of management such as the personnel manager may appreciate the nature of the employee's unconscious motivations, he cannot redirect his drives into constructive channels. The self-styled "expert's" drives continue to be expressed through warped thinking. Eventually he may find himself dropping to the lowest levels of jobs or even placed in an institution where he can continue to "preach" until he reaches the end of his wasted life.

The ideological expert should not be confused with the temperamental artist. He usually applies his energies to an ideal greater than himself and he makes contributions which are beneficial rather than beyond man's needs.

The problem drinker

Many persons still think of the employee with a drinking problem as something of a moral degenerate. Some managements try to deal with him by giving him numerous "last chances" and eventually using discharge when admonitions fail. Fortunately, however, new attitudes toward such employees are emerging, particularly among members of management.

Many companies now look upon alcoholism as a form of illness. They think of alcoholics as sick rather than morally corrupt individuals. They believe that many can be cured, and that the company can assist in the curing process. They believe that it is better policy to try to rehabilitate the problem drinker than to fire him. They think in terms of therapy rather than punishment. They have worked out specific personnel programs and procedures toward this end.[12]

Several big corporations have created their own rehabilitation pro-

---

[12] See Harrison M. Trice, "Identifying the Problem Drinker On the Job," *Personnel*, American Management Association, Inc., May 1957.

grams or joined with other companies in community-type clinics. Consolidated Edison Co. of New York, has been one of the pioneers. In 1952, they underwrote the cost of setting up a consultation clinic at New York University-Bellevue Medical Clinic. In later years, they have been joined by other companies such as Bell Telephone Laboratories, Metropolitan Life Insurance, and *The New York Times*. Several companies of other areas also have extensive programs of their own for rehabilitating alcoholics. Some companies have informal programs or they refer their workers to clinics, to psychiatrists, and to organizations such as Alcoholics Anonymous, Boston's Committee on Alcoholism, and Cleveland's Center on Alcoholism.

Of course these companies and organizations are not trying to help the employee who goes on an occasional binge but the worker whose job suffers from his drinking.

Psychiatrists who work in the clinics realize that they have no one cure for alcoholism. They seek to find the causes for the drinking. Causes are likely to be so deep-seated in the mental life that special training and clinical practice are necessary for giving helpful treatment. They cannot transfer their clinical techniques to personnel men of industry so that they can give treatment, but they can help educate supervisors in regard to the "covering-up" aspect of the problem.

Anyone who has dealt with problem drinkers knows that friends often cover up for the drinker. When he is absent on a Monday morning, his wife reports him "sick with a cold." The fellow worker at the next desk or the next machine does his work for him on his bad days. The supervisor, who likes the drinker as a person, overlooks his absenteeism, especially if he is a good worker on good days. These loyalties all help to keep the alcoholic or incipient alcoholic from getting prompt remedial attention.[13] The "cover up" practice is the reason many managements imagine that they have "no alcohol problem." These pre-alcoholics are usually viewed as social drinkers by most members of management.

Managements of large companies have found it helpful to brief supervisory personnel on the signs to watch for, such as frequent absenteeism (usually beginning on Monday), irritability, and sloppy appearance. Supervisors are also warned that sheltering the problem drinker does him a disservice.

The problem drinker, when spotted, is usually given a friendly talk by his supervisor or by a member of the firm's counseling staff. They refer him to the plant's doctor, local clinics, or rehabilitation groups. These programs are voluntary, but the worker who refuses help gives

---

[13] "The Drunk: He's Management's Baby," *Business Week*, March 13, 1954, pp. 103-108.

466   **Problem Employees**

management little choice but to discipline him by short layoffs or by eventual discharge.

SIX FACTS ABOUT THE PROBLEM DRINKER

Recent studies of alcoholism have dispelled many previously held notions about this problem. Here are some facts uncovered by research during the past few years:

1. *In the early and middle states of alcoholism, the problem drinker continues to work.* Very few active industrial workers are to be found in the lost-week-end category. Because of the general failure to recognize incipient alcoholism as well as the alcoholic's own attempt to cover up, employers are usually unaware of the presence of a problem drinker in the work force.

2. *On the average, 3 per cent of the work force are problem drinkers.* Though this is an over-all estimate, it indicates the extent of the problem.

3. *Alcoholism develops during the productive years.* The great majority of problem drinkers are in the 35-50 age group—the period when a company expects the most effective work from an employee.

4. *The problem drinker is often a long-time employee with skills, experience, and management know-how.* One large company found that 82 per cent of its problem drinkers had been on the payroll for 10 years or more.

5. *Alcoholism creates hidden costs for the employer.* These include reduced efficiency and absenteeism, errors in handling company business, loss of training investment, and loss of customers.

6. *The problem drinker exists at all levels of employment.* He is not confined to the unskilled category and is as likely to be found among executives as in the rank and file.

Alcoholism: The early signs

By his behavior, both on and off the job, the incipient alcoholic can be identified *before* he becomes a problem to himself, his family and his employers.

There are certain clues, this study shows, which suggest that the employee has progressed beyond the social-drinking stage: increased absenteeism, uneven work pace, temperamental and physical irregularities.

If this evidence is reinforced by unusual drinking behavior off the job and domestic, financial, and community problems, it is highly *probable* that a drinking problem exists.

Though only a doctor or a psychologist can make the final diagnosis, management in general should be alerted to these signs. Many employees who are now struggling with a full-fledged drinking problem might have been rehabilitated much earlier if their bosses had recognized their behavior for what it was.

SOURCE: Harrison M. Trice, "Identifying the Problem Drinker On the Job," *Personnel*, American Management Association, Inc., May 1957, pp. 527, 533.

Counseling problem employees

Everyone who works in business, whether he is a top executive or on some other level, takes some personal interest in each of his work associates. He usually knows each working associate by name, and to some extent each one's personal problems. If he is an executive, he often lends money, helps find a doctor, or obtains legal advice for the benefit of the employee.

As an executive, he finds that this kind of close acquaintance with each employee, however well-meaning, also involves certain difficulties as indicated by this example:

> An employer learned that one of his young, unmarried women employees was pregnant. He talked it over with her, knowing she had no family nearby. She was frightened and helpless, feeling desperate.
>
> He arranged for her confinement and subsequent care of her child. When she was able to return to work, he rehired her.
>
> One month later she quit.
>
> This seemed to him like the rankest kind of ingratitude. Someone with greater understanding of psychology would see the outcome as inevitable. The girl felt a deep sense of guilt. She could not stand working in a place where her boss, and possibly others, knew her secret.[14]

The more experienced executive in human relations would not have handled this kind of situation himself. He would have recognized that if he wants the employee to be able to continue to work with her fellow employees and supervisors, she should be able to do so without the usual feeling of guilt. Astute executives who learn about acute problems of an embarrassing kind usually arrange for someone to help the person with minimum dangers of embarrassment. When they deal with embarrassing situations, they operate behind the scenes.

Most executives follow the policy: "Stay out of private lives." An employee's private life is *his* private life. The employee's life away from the plant is his own. The only occasions when attempts to regulate his life are justified, occur when an employee says or does something outside the company that injures the company's business or reputation.

The good supervisor is a good listener

Many employees, particularly those in repetitive and routine work, tend to become preoccupied with personal problems. If the supervisor

---

[14] John Perry, "Human Relations in Small Industry," Small Business Administration, Washington, D.C., March 1954, p. 58.

can get the employee to talk about his problems and the supervisor listens, this may be sufficient in itself to relieve him of many of his symptoms. The employee perceives his difficulties in better perspective and he decides how he himself will deal with his problems more objectively and constructively.

The supervisor need not, and in most cases should not, give very much advice. Nor should he try to solve the employee's problem for him. He should be supportive in his attitude toward the employee and his problem. He should listen with an understanding ear but encourage the employee to develop his own solution or action plan.

As someone has said: "A good listener is not only popular everywhere, but after a while he knows something."

Psychologists have found the *nondirective* interview especially helpful in dealing with individuals who have difficult problems.

In the nondirective technique, the counselor allows and encourages the individual to talk freely about those things which worry him. The counselor does not have a set of questions to which he wants answers. He does not try to get the individual to see things the same way the counselor sees them. His objective is to get the person to talk as freely as possible about the things which matter to him.

This technique is more difficult for the counselor than most supervisors appreciate. The person with a problem feels some embarrassment in telling another person about feelings which are often considered wrong. Nondirective counselors must be systematically trained in the interviewing technique before they can function properly.[15] (See Chapter 17.)

Diagnosis of psychoneurosis should remain in the hands of the expert psychiatrist. Supervisors should be trained concerning symptoms, but they should not try to become practicing psychiatrists. A little knowledge of psychiatry can be a dangerous thing.

Signs that alert the supervisor to the employee's need for special treatment are the following: if he is frequently absent from work, if he is irritable, if he is prone to accidents, if he becomes angry or excitable, if he has widely fluctuating moods, if his work pace varies greatly, or if he cannot get along with other people.

The psychiatrist must make his diagnosis in terms of the individual's family background, education, health, training, social relationships, and general history, past and present. His interpretation depends upon what he can learn about the individual. If he has accurate background information about the patient, he can better interpret and weigh the vari-

---

[15] Methods in dealing with problems of individual adjustment may be found in Carl Rogers, *Counseling and Psychotherapy*, Boston: Houghton Mifflin Co., 1942.

ous combinations of factors that must be considered in the treatment. Supervisors and personnel men can furnish much helpful information to the psychiatrist to aid him in his diagnosis.

Managements that decide they need a counseling program usually develop one of two general categories of counseling programs. (1) They use presently employed personnel who have demonstrated their qualifications for counseling, or they hire a trained counselor and place him under the general supervision of the personnel manager. This kind of counselor is more likely to be a friendly listener who saves time of busy executives than a therapist. (2) They utilize an outsider, a professional counselor, who does not come under any jurisdiction of the company. He is employed on a fee basis as a consultant. Most companies do not attempt to provide a counseling service. They simply refer the troubled employee to a consultant. The consultant does not, in most cases, cure the problem person but his counsel often enables management to reach an intelligent decision as to what action, if any, shall be taken in regard to the problem employee.

For your further consideration

The presence of problem people in business should accentuate your interest in human relations. Difficulties in dealing with them should stimulate you as a student to study the social sciences as thoroughly as you can. You should not, however, imagine that taking a few courses in abnormal psychology or a related subject will enable you to be a therapist. The treatment of the maladjusted and mentally ill requires years of special training. Experienced psychiatrists will, for example, tell you that the proper treatment of the mentally ill requires a medical degree plus several years of clinical experience under supervision.

Even though you do not wish to become a professional psychotherapist, you can improve your insight into the needs and problems of problem persons. You can increase your helpfulness to the therapists. You can also become a more intelligent friend to those who need special understanding. And in the process you too will attain a higher level of maturity that will strengthen you as well as those who are problems to themselves.

COLLATERAL READINGS

For All Students
Hepner, Harry Walker, *Psychology Applied to Life and Work*. Englewood Cliffs, N.J.: Prentice-Hall, Inc., 1957, Part Two. Presents an easily-

understood description of adjustments of problem persons in business and elsewhere.

Uris, Auren, "What You Can Do About Your Problem People," *Factory Management and Maintenance,* October 1958. Describes several types of problem employees and solutions that may be tried. Also includes a self-test for the employee who would like to know whether he is a problem employee.

For Advanced Students

Rogers, Carl R., *Counseling and Psychotherapy.* Boston: Houghton Mifflin Company, 1942. A classic in the field. Counseling is presented as a process that can be learned, tested, and refined.

Shaffer, Laurance Frederic, and Edward Joseph Shoben, Jr., *The Psychology of Adjustment.* Boston: Houghton Mifflin Company, 1956. Presents a comprehensive scholarly treatment of adjustment and adjustment patterns.

For Men in Business

Troubled People on the Job, American Psychiatric Association, Committee on Occupational Psychiatry, Washington, D.C., 1959. Distributed by Mental Health Materials Center, 104 East 25th St., New York, N. Y. Designed to help the supervisor deal with the problem employee. Offers pointers on recognizing symptoms of mental illness and tells where he can get professional aid.

"What You Should Know about Mental Illness," interview with Dr. Winfred Overholser, *U. S. News and World Report,* November 18, 1955, pp. 126-142.

QUESTIONS ON THE CHAPTER

1. Why should an untrained individual not attempt to "cure" a problem person?
2. Can the same basic need lead to both positive and negative value kinds of behavior? Give an example.
3. Who are the "ten percenters," and should they be eliminated?
4. Why is a healthy family background not the only Golden Key to success in all occupations and activities?
5. In what ways is the neurotic employee a problem to those around him?
6. Differentiate between the neurotic and the psychotic in industry.
7. Describe the most disturbing of the three major groups of complaints.
8. Why is it undesirable to "cover up" for a problem drinker in a company?
9. What are some early signs of alcoholism which management should watch for?
10. Explain the interview technique most applicable in dealing with persons who have problems.

11. When a management decides to have a counseling program, what two forms is it likely to take?

12. Of all the ideas presented in the chapter, which ones are of most interest to you?

13. How did the chapter contribute to your future relations with (a) your supervisors, (b) employees whom you may supervise?

PROBLEMS AND PROJECTS

For All Students

1. Describe the characteristic behavior of several problem persons whom you know. To what extent does the content of this and the preceding chapter add or fail to add light on each described person's behavior?

2. Describe some variety of behavior on your own part that has been a problem to others. Suggest possible causal or related factors. Can you suggest ways in which you might redirect your behavior into positive channels?

For Advanced Students

3. Make a study of mental health clinics and published materials on mental hygiene. Describe publications of the National Association for Mental Health, Inc., 10 Columbus Circle, New York, and other organizations that can furnish objective information.

4. Interview several men in business in regard to specific problem employees with whom they have dealt. Write descriptions of each person's behavior as reported to you. Then investigate the literature for light on the problem persons.

For Men in Business

5. Perhaps you have heard the statement: "The bartender is the poor man's psychiatrist." What counseling facilities, better than those of the typical bartender, are available in your community or nearby?

6. Assume that the constant use of excessive profanity is a problem in certain departments of your company. Some employees seem to try to outdo their associates in offensiveness. Tell how you would introduce the subject at a foremen's meeting in order to bring about improvement.

PART 6

You and Your Advancement
in Business

M ANY A STUDENT CAN MAKE A HIGH GRADE IN A COURSE ON
human relations but he is unable to carry on a conversation
with the janitor—the janitor prefers to talk to more interesting
people! The academic student, science scholar, the introverted
research man, even the alert extroverted administrator, may
have need to improve their social skills. Certainly, book learning
must be supplemented with daily intelligent practice in dealing
with people if we want to make our relations effective to all
concerned. Human relations skills can be sharpened especially
when we ourselves determine to do the sharpening.[1]

A nationally known consultant in personnel management
phrased well the inadequacy that many of us feel in regard to
social skills:

> We hear a lot about "working with people" and "social skills"
> and their importance in business today. There are many niceties
> in dealing with people that come naturally to some people and
> are acquired "the hard way" by most of us. These small "social
> lubricants" contribute a great deal to the smoothness and pleas-
> ure with which a day's work can be accomplished. I envy those
> people to whom these little niceties of human communication
> come easily for I am rather impersonal and logical.[2]

---

[1] Robert L. Katz, "Human Relations Skills Can Be Sharpened," *Harvard Business
Review,* July-August 1956. The author, a professor of business administration at
Dartmouth College, reports his findings of a survey of several company training
programs in human relations. He concluded that despite the many shortcomings in
such training programs, human relations skills can be improved.
[2] Ned Hay, "Editor to the Reader," *Personnel Journal,* October 1956, p. 163.

26   Developing Your Social Skills
in Business

Social skills are essential to the ability of each person who is expected to lead a work group and get willing cooperation from the workers. His skills in human relations are likely to be as necessary as his technical knowledge about the job itself. Social skills are, however, more difficult to impart than technical skills. No one can be taught how to handle an employee's grievance or to inspire men merely by being told how to do it.

Even though executives recognize the difficulty in teaching social skills, they attend the many seminars and workshops in better management currently conducted throughout the country. The programs range in length from a day to a year. Many of the programs include sessions in human relations.[3] Generally, courses in human relations are attended not so much as a result of definitely proven effectiveness as the hope that some benefits will accrue.

The need for sensitivity training

Training in sensitivity to social situations may take either of two directions: increased insight into one's own motivations, or greater understanding of the other person's characteristics. The first objective is by far the more difficult. Only a few business groups have made systematic attempts to achieve it. The process is slow, time consuming, and the benefits are often difficult to measure. And yet some persons never can become effective in their human relations—the barriers to their development in this field of action are so deepseated within themselves that they cannot function effectively in social situations. Examples are the extremely rigid personality, the introvert, and the defensive person. They need much courage to gain insight into their motivations and to overcome the inhibiting influences within themselves. Most others as

---

[3] F. J. Roethlisberger, George F. F. Lombard, and Harriet O. Rankin, *Training for Human Relations* (Boston: Division of Research, Graduate School of Business Administration, Harvard University, 1954). This monograph is an interim report on a Ford Foundation sponsored study of advanced training and research in human relations. The staff in charge of this venture started with the hypothesis that human relations skill develops only from experience in concrete situations requiring this skill and cannot be developed at the verbal level. The investigators planned a training program designed to give concrete experience in human relations. Each trainee was to have experience as an observer, as a member, and as a leader of small groups. Each trainee was to have experience also as a counselor and as a recipient of counseling. This was the "experimental design." "That they did learn something was for us a *fact*. They told us so!" "They" refers to "trainees"; "us," to "staff." Perhaps the main finding was that individuals learn human relations in different ways. See William McGehee, *Personnel Psychology*, Summer 1955, pp. 279-81.

well as those mentioned find it easier to try to change the other person than to change themselves. Thomas G. Spates has stated:

> From my own study of the work of the social scientists, clinical psychologists and psychiatrists, and from my own experiences, the conclusion is overwhelmingly clear that the most important field for future action for all of those who direct the work of others is to know and understand themselves and their impact upon those whose work they direct. That is the latest major development in the evolution of personnel administration.
>
> That new and important item, so far as I have been able to find out, has not yet been put on the agenda of a management meeting. I've tried to get it there, but in vain. A few months ago I made the recommendation to an audience composed almost entirely of personnel specialists. Within an hour they were asked to record on questionnaire what, as a result of their participation in this particular meeting, they would like to see on the agenda for next year's meeting. Not a single one recommended that next year's meeting include even preliminary discussion of knowing and understanding themselves and their impact upon others. I wonder how you would account for the difficulty of getting this important phase of administration on the agenda. My explanation is this: consciously or unconsciously we realize that knowing and understanding ourselves as others see us calls for more courage and more perseverance than any project we have yet undertaken.[4]

Even though we do not have the courage to understand ourselves as others see us, we can increase our sensitivity to the ways other people feel.

The socially sensitive person recognizes the "mental set" of each person whom he meets. As commonly used, the term "set" is applied to a relatively restricted temporary attitude, or to momentary states of readiness.[5]

A good example of the need for recognizing mental set occurs when we try to teach the older worker. To begin with, the instructor should try to sense whether his pupil has any resistance to learning because his self-esteem makes it difficult for him to admit to himself that the instructor has superior skill. Perhaps the worker is proud of having learned to perform skillfully an operation by hand and resents learning how to operate a machine which displaces his skill. Older men are proud of

---

[4] Thomas G. Spates, Professor Emeritus of Personnel Administration, Yale University, "Crisis and Promise in Collective Bargaining and Interpersonal Relations," address delivered in January 1958, at the University of Michigan (Bureau of Industrial Relations, University of Michigan, Ann Arbor, Michigan).

[5] The word "stereotype" is applied to an intense and rigid attitude. The word "prejudice" applies to an attitude still more rigid and intense and one generally based on false information. The term "opinion" is generally used to describe an attitude that is or has been expressed and that is based more on objective conditions than a "stereotype" or "prejudice." "Set" is a temporary mental state that favors the selection of certain stimuli or facilitates a particular type of response.

their abilities in performing the line of work they know and regard a transfer to some other work as unfair disregard of their skills. Also, many an older man is conscious of his long years of experience and rebels against being returned to the rank of novice, particularly when he must take instruction from a younger person.

Young people as well as older employees must be treated in accordance with their mental set. The smart mother who has dinner prepared and announces it to her two small boys may find that they are wearing space helmets and just about ready to take a flight to the moon! She doesn't say: "Come on kids, forget that stuff—dinner's ready!" Instead she says, "The moon? How wonderful! Tell me about it while you're eating dinner. You could go after dinner, couldn't you?"

Likewise the alert supervisor who wants a certain employee to do a task but finds him talking with several other employees does not say: "Come on, Joe. Do this job." Instead, he realizes that the employee has a certain mental set in his conversation. The supervisor breaks it respectfully by explaining to the several men: "Say, fellows, I've got to get a job done quickly and need Joe's help. Do you men mind if he breaks off with you now so he can help me? Come on, Joe, let's get going."

Obligations should be felt but not mentioned

People in business have so many mutually shared experiences that individuals are constantly doing favors for each other. A supervisor, for example, helps an employee get a pay raise, allows him to leave work early in order to take care of a personal matter, or arranges to get him a discount on the price of an appliance for the home. The one who has granted or arranged the favor may be conscious of his kindness to the employee but he should not mention it to him. Ideally, he should not even be so conscious of it that the employee can sense his consciousness!

The supervisor who does favors for employees cannot, if he is sensitive to the feelings of his employees, remind the employees that they are obligated to "put out" for him because of the favors. Nor can he grant favors in order to get back more than he gives. If he gives favors in a calculating manner, to make employees feel obligated, they will sense it and convince themselves that the obligation really does not exist. The usual reaction of the obligated employee is "I don't owe him a thing."

Social skills must be adapted to the relations between the individuals

The typical college student who takes a summer job with an outdoor construction gang may hear the men cuss each other out in rather caustic terms. They call each other nasty names but remain friends. The student naturally tends to assume that he can apply the same terms to the men without objection on their part. To his surprise, he is usually given a first-class verbal lacing by the first man toward whom he expresses friendliness in the same phrasing used by the members of the gang to each other. To them, he is a newcomer, an outsider on a different level from themselves. Later, when he has proved himself and become an accepted member of the group, he is privileged to treat the men in the same manner in which they treat each other.

Anyone in a supervisory position must be especially sensitive to differences in degree of acceptance by members of the group. Even though his employees use sarcasm freely with each other, he is not privileged to use sarcasm with them. Sarcasm from someone at the men's own level is quite a different matter from sarcasm from a supervisor.

Corporation presidents become acutely aware of these differences in status levels when talking with subordinates.

Sensitivity to the feelings of others is one of the commonest perplexities of presidents and other members of management. When they make decisions and inform subordinates of the decision, they soon become "concerned about hurting people," "hesitancy to hurt others," and "personal loyalties." This is one of the greatest handicaps in making decisions in a logical manner—their question is likely to be not "What is the logical decision?" but "How will those affected by the decision react to or take the decision?"

Of course sensitivity to people is largely a matter of feeling developed through many years of experience with people. Many a student of the social sciences fails to appreciate this principle. He imagines that the ability to classify the behavior patterns such as compensation, projection, identification, and others is all that he needs to learn. To the mature specialist, such labels are merely incidental to becoming acquainted with the dynamics in human behavior.

The cataloging of a person's peculiarities, when told to the other person, usually arouses antagonisms. We do not like tags. The fact that an especially loquacious person uses talkativeness as a form of defense does not mean that you should tell him so. You should avoid mention of the label, but increase your efforts to make his defensiveness unnecessary when he is with you.

Developing Your Social Skills in Business   **479**

DETOUR

The Executive Skill Game

The elevator operator addresses you by your first name in front of the boss.

You are invited to lecture to a business course. Advance 5 miles.

You casually mention that you have been invited to a director's cocktail party. Advance 4 miles.

You develop an ulcer. Advance 3 miles.

You admit to never having gone abroad on a business trip.

You let it be known that your brother-in-law is the assistant director of internal revenue. Advance 5 miles.

You address the Chairman of the Board by the wrong name.

Your protege loses a big customer.

Remain behind 8-ball for one turn.

DETOUR
The Executive Skill Game

DETOUR, THE EXECUTIVE SKILL GAME, is the exciting new way to practice and analyze the skills necessary for advancement in management. A few pleasant and profitable minutes spent with this game will enable the aspiring executive to test his ability to get ahead in business today.

Rules

1. Any number can play; for most realistic results, loaded dice should be used.

2. Players move in turn, each advancing the number of miles indicated by their throw of the dice.

3. Any player landing on a town moves ahead the number of miles indicated on the sign.

4. Any player landing on a Detour square loses status to the end of the detour road.

SOURCE: *The Management Review (December 1957). Courtesy American Management Association, Inc.*

Selling as a means of learning social skills

Many a retiring or socially inadequate college student has been advised: "Get a selling job—it will help you learn how to get along with people." Certainly some salesmen are highly alert to the little cues that indicate the prospect's unvoiced antagonisms, feelings, and questions. One salesman, for example, notes the position of the prospect's hands: if the hands are open, he is supposed to be receptive; if closed, antagonistic.[6] This salesman believed in the value of his system of observation but no one, so far as known, has ever made a scientific study of the validity of his method. Perhaps it would stand up under scientific analysis, perhaps not. Generally, when scientists have investigated the validity of such systems of analyzing people as used by salesmen, they have found that the system, *per se*, proved to be only slightly better than chance in its objective soundness. However, they also found that when a salesman used a system, any system in which he believed, he became a better salesman than he had been. This indicates that the use of a system for analyzing people gives the salesman more confidence in himself and he does a better selling job! It's the self-confidence, not the system, that counts.

Generally, experience indicates that the typical observer of people concentrates on details such as clothing and bodily features. Observation of a person's clothing will suggest whether the person is neat in his appearance, but the neatness may apply to appearance only, not to every activity. Some stenographers are well groomed but turn out poorly typed letters. If, however, the supervisor is impressed by her personal neatness, he is likely to be more patient in teaching her how to produce acceptably typed letters.

Most of us observe the other person's eyes on first meeting. The fact that they are shifty does not mean that the person is evasive or dishonest, but he may be more submissive than the average person. If his gaze is direct and piercing, he is likely to be above average in aggressiveness. To keen observers, the mouth, especially when the person is in sleep or in repose, is especially indicative of the individual's degree of happiness.

Observing and understanding is a continuing process. Few reliable conclusions can be made on a first meeting. Most good judges of people want to observe and be with the person on a number of occasions so that they may add to and modify first impressions.

The student of human relations should, of course, realize that cues

---

[6] Lloyd A. Pender, "Watch Your Prospects' Hands," *Specialty Salesman,* January 1957.

or clues such as those mentioned above are often learned in a mechanical manner only. Students have a tendency to note one bit of behavior that in some cases is significant and conclude that the individual observed has the specific trait or problem that is, in some cases, related to the cue. The person trained in human relations seldom jumps to conclusions so quickly—he wants to see a pattern. Any one cue must fit into a larger pattern before it is accepted as significant.

Listening is a social skill

Most persons assume that socially skilled persons do a lot of talking and that they dominate conversations. On the contrary, they are more likely to be good listeners than loquacious talkers. They not only listen in order to learn the other person's points of view but they also listen "between the lines" in search of the meaning that is not necessarily put into spoken words.

The good listener pays attention to nonverbal communication: facial expressions, gestures, tone of voice. He knows that these add meaning to the spoken words. He asks himself, "Why does the talker purposely emphasize certain phases of the subject? Why does he avoid other phases?"

According to surveys reported by Ralph Nichols, Department of Rhetoric, University of Minnesota, the average industrial executive spends at least 70 per cent of all his working moments in verbal communication. His communication activities are divided as follows: 9 per cent of this time is devoted to *writing*, 16 per cent to *reading*, 30 per cent to *talking*, and 45 per cent to *listening*.

While the executive is listening, he can study the visitor and his state of mind.

Seminar discussions led by Nichols revealed that executives in attendance did not consider listening to be a passive affair. As one put it, "You don't just sit there and say nothing. That is not enough. It requires real effort to concentrate carefully on what the speaker is saying, to miss no point he is making, to put in just the right question at the right time, and to give proper voice inflection to these queries. And you must do all these things while another part of your mind is busy studying the visitor and deciding what you are going to say after he has finished speaking. That's listening!"

Another executive put it this way,

> It takes a lot more out of you to *listen* well for an hour than it does to *talk* well for an hour. This is particularly the case should the visitor's

Developing Your Social Skills in Business 483

attitude be antagonistic, or when you find yourself altogether opposed to the ideas he is presenting. Such situations call for the exercise of real effort in repressing your natural desire to argue with the visitor.[7]

Researches concerning the art of listening have shown the importance of attitude while listening: a facial expression that denotes interest, physical relaxation on the part of the listener, meeting the eye of the speaker squarely but without antagonism, and careful avoidance of any movement or mannerism that would distract the visitor's attention from his own recital.

Braille by Heart

Could I not see, were wholly blind,
  I still could trace
  Upon your face
The telltale imprints of your mind.

—Merhl Norton Doren,
  Ogdensburg, N. Y.

The questions asked by the listener should be brief and slipped into the visitor's recital without interrupting his train of thought. These may be along the lines of "How?" and "Why?" They lead the speaker to discuss phases of the problem he has failed to cover and encourage him to think. They may even make it possible for him to work out his own solution to the problem that occasioned the interview.

Listening as well as talking is an art. Sometimes it is even effective in dealing with a hostile person. One corporation president has described his technique in controversies:

The next time you find yourself confronted with a serious difference of opinion, try "sitting out" the controversy. Just sit and listen to all the arguments of the group or an individual. If you can become an active and absorbing listener, you may sometimes be able to dissolve the whole problem or dispute without saying a word!

Here is how it works for me: The proponent for some opposing view enters my office and proceeds to advance his views. I simply listen intently to everything he has to say. He continues to expound on his story until he expects me to introduce a counterargument, but I say nothing. Then I suppose he feels tempted to mention my side of the case or at least to refer to it in some way. And so he ventures into my viewpoint and finds himself talking about the things which I now do not have to mention. He believes he is doing a fine job—and so he is—until he finally

---

[7] Alfred M. Cooper, "The Executive Art of Good Listening," *The Office Economist*, September-October 1958. Copyright © 1958 Art Metal Construction Company, Jamestown, N. Y. and Ralph G. Nichols, "Listening Is a 10-Part Skill," *Nation's Business*, July 1957, p. 58.

concludes that there are perhaps two sides to the controversy after all. On a number of occasions I have seen situations completely solved, believe it or not, in just this way. I simply allowed the other fellow an opportunity to talk himself out of his own erroneous position.

We cannot always tell the other fellow what our story is—he will not believe us. But when he comes to that same realization by way of his own route and reasoning, he informs himself. In that respect an intelligent listener is actually a communicator, isn't he? Since it is natural for men to want to talk, I find that listening is one of the most valuable executive techniques I can use.[8]

In addition to the open hostility in controversy, hostility often occurs in the form of "unvoiced threat." An easy place to note unvoiced threats is an office where two women have been working together for years. A new girl, younger, better dressed, having more education, and greater appeal to men is hired to work with the two older women. The new girl is likely to be a terrifying threat to the two older women and they usually make life miserable for the newcomer unless management defines the new girl's status in a manner that removes the threat. The supervisor can also eliminate the threat feeling by having the women participate in the hiring of the new girl. If the two older women are made to feel that they helped select the new girl and that they are responsible for her, they are apt to "mother" and protect as well as advise her.

Another situation where threat is obvious occurs when management places a young well-trained specialist in a department headed by a less-trained executive. The department head usually says to himself, "Is this new guy really here because he has been selected to take over my job?" Again, management can remove the feeling of threat by defining the man's status and by increasing the department head's feeling of security by conferring with him about the best way to utilize the specialist.

The typical college girls' social affair reveals threat when a new girl appears to have special appeal to any girl's boy friend. Everyone present may be "awfully" friendly—so friendly that the threat is veiled but obvious to the alert observer.

Consciousness of threat can be developed by keen observation and by listening for "between the lines" meanings.

Situational allergies often reveal repressed dislikes. An example is a sneezing fit brought on by having to look at other people's travel Kodachromes or to their home movies. Certain individuals who hate to attend committee meetings blow their nose repeatedly even though the room is free of drafts. The person who develops a coughing spell and

---

[8] Robert C. Hood, President, Ansul Chemical Co., in an address before the California Personnel Management Association. Reported in *The Management Review*, American Management Association, Inc., May 1956, p. 405.

"Listen, Dear—the Boss insists on coming for dinner. Hide the TV set, park the car in the next street, don't serve anything fancy, wear something old. . . ." SOURCE: by Hank Baeb. Courtesy The Office (July 1956).

HANK BAEB

must leave the room may not want to be there even though he feels obligated to be present. The astute host either makes it easy for him to be excused or gets him to participate in the discussion to the extent that his attention is directed to the main topic and away from his affective reaction to the situation.

Helping others to save face

When the situation is embarrassing to the other fellow, making it easy for him to "save face" is an old axiom of the socially skilled person. The supervisor who discovers that an employee has made a mistake

---

WORDS TO THE WISE

Here is a "thought-provoker." In human relations the
—five most important words are "I am proud of you."
—four most important words are "What is your opinion?"
—three most important words are "If you please."
—two most important words are "Thank you."
—smallest word is "I."

From *Mill & Factory*. Reprinted in *The Management Review*, American Management Association, Inc., May 1955, p. 320. Original author unknown.

can treat the error objectively but still allow the employee to feel that he is not disgraced. This applies also to the employee who has prevaricated in order to make himself appear more important. Unless a lie is a legal offense, the liar should, in most cases, be allowed to save face. After all, many untruths are really just phases of gossip; if all gossips were to be jailed, we would have more jails than residences.

In business, many executives are skilled in enabling employees to save face. Supervisors who have responsibility for checking an employee's work can check openly but a great deal of checking is also done casually. The executive who has an extra sensitive stenographer need not check her typing—he can instead check his dictation!

The production manager of a plant, for example, knew that union members were restricting production. He proved to the head of the labor union that the men were not producing as much as the same kind of equipment was producing in competitors' plants. To enable the union leader to save face, the production manager offered to attach an inexpensive facilitating device to each machine to help the men produce more. The device itself had little value but it gave the union head a reason for asking the men to raise their production instead of restricting it to abnormally low levels. The new mechanical device allowed the men to save face.

The supervisor who has the knack of making men feel honorable in his presence and gives them ego involvement in their work will often find that his men are willing to help him in an emergency. Moreover they will also help him to save face by compensating for any lack of technical knowledge on his part with their productive shop know-how. An awful lot of everyday human relations in business consists of saving face and is practiced by employees for the benefit of executives as well as by executives for the benefit of employees.

Remembering names and faces

Each one of us has need for a good memory, especially memory for names and faces. It is an art that adds more charm to the personality than many other skills.

Many people think that the ability to remember names and faces is some kind of inborn gift. Actually any one who wishes to do so can acquire the habit. The main factor in its learning is to determine to remember names and faces. Certain persons such as the personnel man need this ability. They practice it until they master the ability. Here are several simple rules which, if practiced, are bound to produce marked improvement:

1. Be sure that you get the name correct. If in doubt, ask the person how he spells it even though it is a simple name such as "Brown" or "Smith."

2. Use the stranger's name several times during the first conversation.
3. Associate some pertinent facts about the person with the name—his occupation, color of eyes, way he shakes hands, manner of speaking, and so on.
4. While still with him, look away from him and visualize him.
5. After he has left you, visualize him again and repeat his name to yourself and the pertinent facts you noted.
6. At the end of the day, visualize all the faces and say all the names of the persons whom you met that day.
7. Practice constantly, again and again.
8. Take pride in your ability to remember names and faces. Utilize the ability whenever you can.

Accurate and frequent observations are essential. Avoid generalities such as "A fat lady of about thirty" or "A grey-haired old man." Be specific. Add details.

Add associations such as "The fat lady of thirty who talked so much about the fine qualities of her husband that I wondered whether she fears that she may lose him" and "The grey-haired old man who bragged about the important job he had years ago with the XYZ Corporation."

The ability to remember names also involves our emotions at the time when we wish to use the name. No doubt you have had the unpleasant experience of being unable to recall the name of an old acquaintance when you wanted to introduce him to someone. This inability is accentuated when you are more concerned about the impression you are making than about enabling both persons to have a pleasant experience. To avoid such embarrassing situations, concentrate, in advance of the introductions, on the ways in which you can help the two strangers have a pleasant meeting. Transfer your self-centered thoughts into thinking about the pleasures which the two may gain through mutual acquaintance.

Skill in ending the interview

One of the most frequently mentioned questions asked by young executives who are called upon by customers, applicants, and friends is "How do you get rid of the guy, tactfully, who stays with you too long?" Most of these visitors have a normal business reason for calling. They must be treated respectfully. Typically, too, the visitor often keeps on talking long after the business transaction has been completed.

The oldtimers in management learn the art of easing these overstayers out of the office in a manner that maintains cordial relations between host and guest. They do it simply by telling a story or humorous incident. When both are laughing, the host stands up and the guest rises without realizing that he has risen. The host moves to the door and continues talking in a manner that keeps their conversation mutually interesting. Usually, the guest leaves in a good mood.

Some executives and personnel men have this problem so frequently that they train their secretaries and other staff members to speed the visitor's departure by reminding him of his overlapping appointments.

Keeping the secrets in business

People who work in the business world soon learn that certain topics are "off limits" for discussion with outsiders. Other topics may be discussed only with certain members of the organization, and some should never be mentioned to anyone within or without the company. Every employee has an unwritten assignment to learn what may and what may not be discussed. The employees, of course, discuss certain topics through the grapevine rather than openly. These are topics that interest the employees: scraps of information about the likelihood of layoffs, reasons for failure to get an order, and personal matters such as scan-

"*Well, how was I to know the client was with us in the elevator?*" SOURCE: Tide (*November 30, 1951*), *since absorbed by* Printers' Ink.

dalous conduct, real or imagined, on the part of members of the organization.

The most important secrets are not those of the grapevine variety but facts that provide a competitive advantage: technical discoveries that improve the product, marketing plans for the next year, and financial data which, if known to a competitor, would enable him to underbid the company in presenting his bid for a contract.

Executives soon learn which employees are too gabby in the restrooms, at social affairs, or with members of the family. Those employees are not entrusted with information that must be kept under cover until the stipulated release date. Mimeograph machine operators, secretaries, research men, and accountants are always under some observation in order that loose talkers, informers, and talebearers may be spotted. Most smart employees learn to avoid the giving of "classified information" when asked for it by a simple statement such as "I have no special knowledge about that part of the business" or "Mr. Blank heads up that work—he can tell you more about it than I can."

Sometimes managements must code secret information, record the name of every person who handles it, and set aside certain offices as "off limits" to everyone except to designated personnel. Security measures similar to those used by governments are at times necessary in business.

Speak of your company and work associates with pride

Even though certain company matters should not be discussed with outsiders, the employee who likes his company should speak well of it to others. If he does not like his job or the company, he should do what the college student does who does not like his college—transfer to another institution as soon as possible. Only the inadequately adjusted person remains with a college or a company that he does not respect.

One of the characteristics of the well-adjusted person is that he habitually speaks well of the institutions to which he belongs: his family, community, and the company that employs him. This does not mean that he is blind to their shortcomings. But he respects his colleagues and the institutions to which he and they belong. He speaks well of them whenever the opportunity arises. After all, some admirable persons belong to each institution.

It is, of course, easy to parrot the gripes of those employees whose unconscious needs for aggression are expressed against the employer. But when they do, they merely make some people unhappy. Criticism against the institution to which one belongs decreases the stranger's respect for the griper rather than the institution toward which the fault-finding is directed. We can see examples of this in college. Every college student is likely to be asked during vacation by someone in his hometown: "Well, Bill, how do you like your college?" If the student answers: "Aw heck, the place stinks!" the listener is likely to say, "That's too bad." What he probably thinks, however, is "Maybe it's Bill, not the college, that stinks."

The employee who takes an objective, sincere pride in his company and its products is more likely to develop himself and contribute to the company's success than the chronic faultfinder.

The titles used in conversation

In a few companies, the president makes a fetish of having everyone use first names and nicknames in conversations in the office and plant. This is disliked by many employees who prefer to recognize the greater responsibility and status of major executives by referring to them as "Mr." In some firms, almost everyone is addressed as "Mr." regardless of his job status.

Generally, secretaries and young men use the "Mr." even though the supervisors use first names and nicknames in addressing the secretary or the young man. The practice is similar to that of the college classroom where few students would ever thing of addressing the teacher as "Bud," "Bill" or "Hank" even though the teacher addresses students by their first names.

Incidentally, many American college students do not know the difference between the titles: "Doctor" and "Professor." The doctorate is a title conferred on anyone who has completed a specific program of graduate study. It has no professional status other than that. The title of "Professor," in contrast, has professional status. It indicates professional achievement. The full professorship is attained in the larger institutions only after years of professional work. To become a full professor, the teacher, who may or may not have a doctorate, must start as an instructor and advance to the assistant professorship, the associate professorship, and finally to the full professorship. The last-mentioned level is normally accorded to those few men whose colleagues meet in a formal meeting and vote as to whether he, in comparison with other teachers of the subject, is one of outstanding ability among his colleagues in the nation. Generally, the younger faculty members can be addressed as "Doctor" because they have not as yet risen to the full

HOW'S YOUR ETIQUETTE?

You know, of course, which fork to use when, and how to make introductions without stumbling, but are you up on the intricacies that make the rules of etiquette as fascinating as they are maddening? To find out, test yourself with these 22 questions. [See answers, page 496.]

	true	false
1. When walking or sitting with two women, the man should place himself between them.	—	—
2. A man should offer his arm when walking with a woman at night but not in the daytime.	—	—
3. An engaged man may give his fiancée a fur stole but not a fur coat.	—	—
4. A bride's linen is always marked with her initials as an unmarried girl.	—	—
5. At weddings it is proper for each bridesmaid to be escorted down the aisle by an usher.	—	—
6. A recent death in the family automatically rules out a church wedding.	—	—
7. It is proper to telegraph either formal or informal invitations.	—	—
8. Typewriting personal letters, even long ones, is not in good taste.	—	—
9. A married woman never, never signs a letter with "Mrs."	—	—
10. Letters to teen-aged boys are addressed: "Master John Jones."	—	—
11. Butter plates are always used at a luncheon, never at a formal dinner.	—	—
12. Napkins are folded flat and laid on the plates at a formal dinner.	—	—
13. A hostess is served before any guest.	—	—
14. A guest may ask for anything that is not served.	—	—
15. At the start of a meal, shake out your napkin and lay it on your lap.	—	—
16. It is good manners to leave a portion of food uneaten on your plate.	—	—
17. You may properly use your knife or a crust of bread as a food pusher.	—	—
18. Never use bread to sop up gravy or sauce.	—	—
19. Head lettuce may be cut only with a fork.	—	—
20. A woman never takes off her gloves to shake hands.	—	—
21. The host at a cocktail party should be prepared to serve almost any drink.	—	—
22. The christening gift from a godparent is always something in silver.	—	—

SOURCE: *Changing Times*, The Kiplinger Magazine, January 1958.

professorship. The older men of distinction are full professors and should be addressed as "Professor."

These differentiations are fairly well standardized in the older and larger institutions of this country and in most European nations. In some universities, particularly the newer ones, the differentiations are not well standardized. One of America's leading universities, for example, is especially confusing to the student—every faculty member regardless of degrees or academic rank is customarily addressed as "Mr." The student in college and the employee in business should use as his guide the customary titles used by his superiors rather than the titles that are used by his colleagues—his colleagues may be out of line with the right practices.

Of course when a man is truly great, no title should be used. A title would be superfluous for an Albert Schweitzer or a Winston Churchill! The same principle applies to the great scientist or teacher.

Social skills are learned through daily contacts

A student who realizes that he ought to improve his social skills is likely to learn rules or to assume that when he gets into business, he will develop the human relations skills needed by the effective executive. If he postpones his practice that long, it may be too late. The way to learn how to get along with the boss and employees is to get along with people. To get along well with the boss is easy for the student who has learned to get along with his fellow students and work associates. The best laboratory for learning these skills is with members of the family, companions, sales clerks, policemen, janitors, waitresses, and others whom we meet every day.

COLLATERAL READINGS

For All Students

Hepner, Harry Walker, *Psychology Applied to Life and Work.* Englewood Cliffs, N.J.: Prentice-Hall, Inc., 1957, Chapter 9. Offers suggestions for personality development.

Laird, Donald A. and Eleanor C., *Sizing Up People.* New York: McGraw-Hill Book Company, Inc., 1951. Presents many helpful suggestions for developing social skills.

For Advanced Students

Gardner, Eric F., and George G. Thompson, *Social Relations and Morale in Small Groups.* New York: Appleton-Century-Crofts, Inc., 1956. Presents research in this area.

Heider, Fritz, *The Psychology of Interpersonal Relations.* New York: John Wiley & Sons, Inc., 1958. The behavioral sciences are gaining in significance in our understanding of the interactions of people in the work situation.

For Men in Business

Luken, H. E., "A New Approach to Training in Leadership Skills," *Advanced Management,* July 1958. Report of an important pilot project that was conducted, known as "The Society for the Advancement of Management Workshop in Leadership Skills." The staff members who conducted the workshop were members of the National Training Laboratories of Washington, D.C.

Pigors, Paul, "Of Giving Orders and Getting Results," *Personnel,* American Management Association, Inc., March-April 1960. Offers suggestions to first-line supervisors in the principles of effective order giving.

QUESTIONS ON THE CHAPTER

1. What attempts are made to teach social skills?
2. What are two important phases of sensitivity training?
3. Differentiate between the terms "set" and "prejudice."
4. Discuss sensitivity to cues in the behavior of the other person. A system of interpreting cues as used by a salesman may not be valid but it may, nonetheless, be effective. Why? When does a cue become significant?
5. Describe some of the practices essential to effective listening.
6. Discuss sensitivity to "unvoiced threats."
7. Give examples of the executive's way of "saving face" of an employee.
8. How is the communication time of an average industrial executive divided?
9. Define situational allergies.
10. Why is it beneficial for a supervisor to make his men feel honorable in his presence?
11. What are some of the factors involved in learning to remember names and faces?
12. Describe a method of easing overstayers out of an office.
13. Discuss the importance of keeping business secrets.
14. Why should an employee speak of his company and work associates with pride?
15. What is the best "laboratory" for learning how to get along with the boss and employees?
16. Of all the ideas presented in the chapter, which ones are of special value to you?
17. How did the chapter contribute to your future relations with (a) the men who supervise you, (b) employees whom you may supervise?

For All Students

1. Describe a personal experience which indicated that your social skills were inadequate in the situation. What did you learn from it?

2. The skilled conversationalist tells his listeners when he changes topics by making a "switch comment" such as "Let me change the subject for a moment?" Suggest additional switch comments that may be made to help the listeners.

For Advanced Students

3. Social skills are not taught as formal courses in many colleges or if given, do not receive academic credit. Ask several faculty members for the reasons.

4. Assume that training in social skills should be given to trainees for management and supervision. Consult the available literature for descriptions of such programs, the methods, objectives, and so on.

For Men in Business

5. Interview several friends in regard to their failures in social skills in business. An example might be: A research specialist made a study of a problem and wrote a report on his findings. Later, he learned that his supervisor resented the writer's use of his name on the report without mention of the supervisor's name.

6. Every person has some "blind spots" in his thinking, certain topics that he cannot discuss objectively. Usually, his associates recognize these blind spots and adjust their thinking to them. Think of the supervisors and executives under whom you have worked. Describe some of their blind spots and possible stages in their development.

ANSWERS TO ETIQUETTE TEST:

1. False. It is preferable that the man stand or sit so that he can speak to both women without turning away from one.
2. True. But he may offer help, even in daylight, if the woman is aged or the way very rough.
3. True. A stole is adornment, but a coat is wearing apparel, and he can't appear to be supporting her—yet.
4. False. Nowadays trousseau linen is marked with the initials of the bride's given name, her maiden name and her husband's last name.
5. False. The processional would look as if there were several brides and bridegrooms.
6. False. A wedding during mourning should be smaller and quieter, but it may be in the church.
7. True. And just handing over a list of names and a form invitation to Western Union is convenient.
8. False. Typewritten personal letters are polite, but messages of congratulation or condolence must still be handwritten.
9. True. But she may put "Mrs." in parentheses or add her full married name in parentheses below the signature.
10. False. After the age of 12, boys are given no titles. When they finish high school, they get the "Mr."
11. True. Butter plates are for informal service only.
12. True. Fancy folds are in bad taste. And napkins at a formal dinner are never put beside the plate, as at a luncheon.
13. False. This custom is held in horror. The ranking feminine guest should always be served first—never the hostess, unless she is the only woman.
14. False. A guest should not ask for anything except possibly water— especially any item that has not already been offered.
15. False. Don't make like a headwaiter. Lay your dinner napkin, folded double, on your lap.
16. False. The practice is wasteful. If you eat properly, you won't have to prove you are not a glutton.
17. True. Bread is the preferred pusher, but a knife may be used if handled properly.
18. False. You may sop up gravy with a bit of bread if you use a fork to transport it to your mouth.
19. False. The old rule grew out of an effort to protect silver from salad dressing vinegar, but this solicitude for silver has gone out of style.
20. True. On the other hand, men must apologize if they keep on their gloves when shaking hands.
21. False. One or two kinds of drinks are sufficient. Avoid the bartender's professional-sounding "What'll you have?"
22. False. Gifts in silver are traditional, but nonsilver things may be just as appropriate.

Want to argue about any of these pronouncements? *Changing Times* bows before the authorities Emily Post and Amy Vanderbilt and the editors of other etiquette books, such as *Vogue* and *Esquire*.

SOURCE: *Changing Times,* The Kiplinger Magazine, January 1958.

Most young men who study business look forward to advancement. They expect to attain jobs on the department head level, or higher still, in top management. Some, of course, will become specialists rather than executives but their jobs too will be on the department head level or possibly higher.

Any personnel man or management consultant who interviews applicants and employees learns to think of the abilities of men in terms of the individual's age when he begins to "level out" in his growth. (See chart on next page.) Many men who enter business level out fairly quickly after they leave school or college. They take various jobs that enable them to make a living but all the jobs are on about the same difficulty and pay level. Many of these men work as semi-skilled mechanics, routine clerical workers, retail sales clerks, order-taking salesmen, bookkeepers, typists, and in similar low skill, low pay jobs. They grow very little in ability through the years. Some realize that they do not want to put forth the effort to lift themselves to a higher ability level and therefore join labor unions because the union will get them a few nickels more per hour.

Contrast these lower-level workers with the high grade professional man who keeps on growing all his life (or until he reaches senility). The normal well-motivated physician, lawyer, engineer, or teacher, if his standards for himself are at all worthwhile, is constantly challenging himself to learn more, to increase his ability, to improve his judgment, and to handle

27 Your Own Advancement in Business

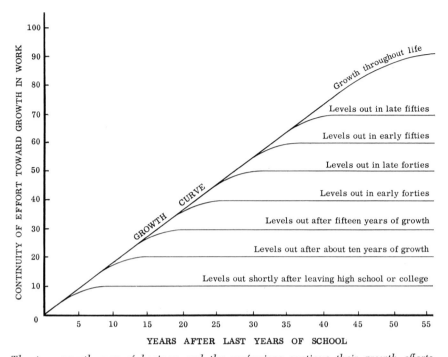

The true growth men of business and the professions continue their growth efforts throughout life. Others level out in their efforts to seek growth, many early in life. Those who drop out early hold the lower level jobs.

Anyone who interviews an adult applicant tends to note the approximate stage in his life history when he leveled out in his developmental efforts. Also, the human relations specialist who interviews employees finds that many employees would like to continue to grow in their work but they do not know how to go about it. They need and would like to have counsel and encouragement from their supervisors.

more difficult responsibilities than he is handling in the current year. These growth men seek to know the latest technical information. They tackle problems more difficult than any they have tackled before. They associate with other growth men in their field. They think in terms of problems and methods of dealing with them—not in terms of nickels more per hour worked. Most of these men do not know exactly how much money they make nor do they care about their titles. They know that more money and titles come to them as by-products of their greater abilities. They do not, as a rule, seek money or status as an end in itself. They seek growth for themselves because true growth brings the many satisfactions of greater service that come to the person of inner maturity.

The mature men in business, particularly those on the executive levels, realize that they must function anonymously rather than in a spectacular manner. Crawford H. Greenewalt, president of du Pont, has well stated that ". . . achievement in the executive field is much less spectacular than comparable success in many of the professions—the scientist, for example, who wins the Nobel Prize, the headline name who is elected governor, the skillful politician, the articulate college president. In fact, the more effective an executive, the more his own identity and personality blend into the background of his organization. Here is a queer paradox. The more able the man, the less he stands out, the greater his relative anonymity outside his immediate circle." [1]

Young men who note the by-product benefits of high income and social status that come to some of these growth men tend to see only the incidental signs of better income and higher status. They make the mistake of thinking of wealth and status as ends in themselves. As a result, they strain too hard and when the wealth and status do come to many of these, they find the rewards empty and meaningless. The great religionists and philosophers of the past have known this for many centuries but most young men have to re-discover this old truth for themselves.

The men who have not as yet learned the principle that inner growth usually precedes and gives rise to achievement are the over-anxious, tense men who have caused observers to imagine that personal advancement in business invariably involves the development of ulcers. Occasionally a college man will even say to himself: "No ulcers for me—I'll settle for less and enjoy life instead." They choose a way of life even worse than one involving ulcers when they decide to vegetate rather than grow.

Most normal men must work in order to be happy. People need work almost as much as they need food; without it they're devoured by discontent. They become defensive and embittered when they cannot respect themselves because of their own lack of growth through work.

People who think they hate to work should recognize it as the thing they need in order to find contentment. The man who goes to work for years often discovers when he retires that working was one of his finest privileges. He wants to continue to work.

The housewife who groans over the chores of raising a family realizes later—after the children have left home—that those were among the happiest years of all. What a pity she didn't know it at the time!

The daily enjoyment of working is part of growing up. Unfortunately, many people never learn it and so they never achieve the peace of mind and contentment that might be theirs.

Young men who apply for jobs are apt to say: "I'm looking for an opportunity," or "I am a financial man. I'd like to be considered for any

---

[1] Crawford H. Greenewalt, *The Uncommon Man.* New York: McGraw-Hill Book Company, Inc., 1959, p. 66.

spot you have in the treasurer's or controller's line." Or "I'm good with people. I can sell anything. If you have a sales opening or a public relations spot, I'd be a natural."

These men are misdirecting their thinking. They have not thought through the problems and responsibilities of the fields they are applying for. They are thinking of themselves more than of the contribution they can make to a future employer. They are thinking in terms of job vacancies, the kinds of jobs that are most plentiful on the lowest level of the chart on page 498.

Vacancies in business that are worthy of a growth man arise as a result of some need that has developed in the business.

Responsibility is more often assumed than it is granted. The growth man is aware of problems rather than vacancies. He knows the problems of business and says: "I believe that I can help you in regard to your problems in accounting, (selling, public relations, or other specific field)."

Admittedly, advancement can be overemphasized. Each job itself

Ladder of Success

When I was starting out, and young,
My foot was on the bottom rung,
And then, by standing on my toes
And straining hard, one step I rose.

So I was on my way. I lifted
My foot and thought myself quite gifted.
I bent my knee, I took a flier,
And there I was, up one rung higher.

Sometimes the chap above me stepped
Upon my hands. I nearly wept,
But using muscles, mind, and will,
I kept on climbing, climbing still.

Now that I'm almost up the ladder
I should, no doubt, be feeling gladder.
It is quite fine, the view and such,
If just it didn't shake so much.

SOURCE: by Richard Armour, The Management Review (October 1957). Courtesy American Management Association, Inc.

Your Own Advancement in Business

should be rewarding and satisfying, not just another step up the promotion ladder. When promotion is sought merely in order to satisfy ego needs, failure to attain it causes frustration. (See poem, "Ladder of Success.") It may also lead to the wrong kind of competitive spirit in which a man becomes ruthless in his desire to get ahead at the expense of his fellow workers.

Fortunately for the ambitious young man, most companies have a shortage rather than a surplus of promotable men. The annual growth pattern of American business means that we have a need for about 5 per cent more able men each year. In addition about 42 per cent of all top management personnel are in the age bracket from 55 to 65—their retirement is necessary within 10 years. Death, disability, and turnover continue apace. The sum total of these demands makes the finding of an available supply of persons who are promotable to executive jobs difficult for many managements.[2] The effectiveness and growth of an organization depend upon the upward career orientation of its members.

Marks of the growth man

The growth man is easily recognized by executives and personnel men. He has a pattern of greater ability each year than the previous year. Whether in college or at work, he develops his abilities through regular reading of the journals in his field, (see the "Periodical Check List," page 502) purchase of technical books, membership in business or professional organizations, and attendance at some meetings where he can exchange ideas with men who are working in his field. He likes to associate with people who are more competent than he. When he seeks a new employer, he looks for a job in a growth company. He has a disdain for unemployment compensation and for jobs that pay income in the form of tips for service.

He is honest in his financial dealings. He seldom borrows money but when he does, he pays his debts. Nor does he help himself to an employer's property such as postage stamps or supplies. When he is an applicant for a job and is invited to visit an employer's premises at the employer's expense, he includes on his expense report only those costs which actually pertain to the trip. If he visits several employers on the same trip, he prorates the costs among them.

He can be entrusted with records of a confidential nature. As a student, he can work in a professor's office and not steal copies of exams. When

---

[2] See C. Wilson Randle, "How To Identify Promotable Executives," *Harvard Business Review*, May-June 1956.

Periodical Check List

Where to Find Articles on Manpower Management, a Quick Guide and Selector

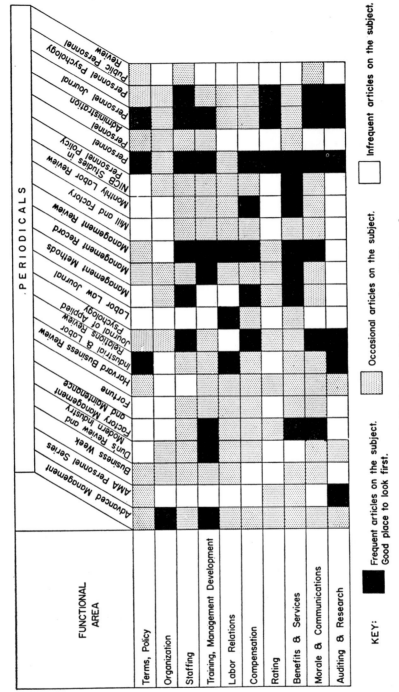

SOURCE: The Manpower Management Five-Foot Shelf, Bulletin 19 (November 1956), published for Industrial Relations Center, University of Minnesota, by the University of Minnesota Press, Minneapolis, p. 24. Prepared by Herbert G. Heneman, Jr., with the assistance of Roberta J. Nelson and Georgianna Herman.

he takes an examination, he need not be proctored because he depends entirely on his own knowledge to answer questions. He finds few courses dull because he is anxious to learn about every field. Even though some courses are difficult for him, he studies them in the hope that eventually he can master whatever they offer.

As an employee, he believes that plain old-fashioned hard work is still one of the most important ingredients for success in business. He has a desire to excel rather than get by. He rarely thinks about the number of hours he works. Instead, he thinks in terms of getting the job done. If it is necessary to work overtime or skip lunch, he does so without feeling heroic or imposed upon.

As a young employee, he takes advantage of opportunities to learn more about the company's equipment and methods. If he is a technical man who works for a manufacturing company where operating equipment must be repaired over weekends and holidays, he arranges to spend some time with the repairmen so that he can see the company's dismantled machines. He wants to know how the equipment really operates.

In his conversations, he uses reasonably good English. He would not be guilty of an error such as "He don't speak very good English!" In one survey that included a poll of 40,000 people, seven of every ten put good grammar and correct pronunciation first as characteristic of a well-educated person. Second on the list was the ability to meet people, and third was the ability to say what you mean. Only one of every 20 people polled considered the amount of money a person makes an indication of how well educated he is.[3]

Advancement through a company or through a "function"

Some ambitious men identify with a company. They study the company and try to move upward through the various supervisory and managerial levels. If they find it necessary or expedient to move from one company to another, they still think in terms of advancing in the company where they are employed.

Certain others, fewer in number, identify with a specific field of business such as accounting, production, finance, or some other function. The functions in which they excel may be technical research, operational analysis, coordinating, evaluating, promoting, interpreting, or teaching. As functional specialists, they are not likely to be especially loyal to any

---

[3] See *Changing Times*, The Kiplinger Magazine, September 1956, p. 18.

company that employs them nor are they emotionally disturbed if they happen to be laid off or discharged. They are like scientists—loyal to the science rather than the company or institution that employs them.

Two types of men are active at the executive level in American industry: (1) the "company" man and (2) the "profession" man. The first is essentially job directed, security-oriented. The emphasis in his thinking is not on analyzing but on achievement, action, accomplishment.

The second is function-oriented. He is analytical in his approach to a problem. Many of these men become consultants to business. Some do become executives in companies but they are likely to move to other companies where they can practice their chosen specialization in a new setting.

Of those who seek to gain advancement through a company, a special variety consist of those individuals who become known as a "second man." They always remain in staff jobs or as assistants to higher executives. They are like the nice girl who is often a bridesmaid but never a bride.

Many of these second men are very intelligent and have had excellent formal training in our graduate schools of business. Because of their extra formal training they can easily get well-paying staff jobs. However, they tend to remain on the staff or assistant level simply because they have learned how to deal with business problems on paper but they have not learned how to handle the actual responsibilities in engineering, production, sales, finance or any other field. They are excellent statistical analysts and report writers but untested performers on the firing line. They also fail to develop strong ties of full colleagueship with other action-minded executives.

In the course of time, a few of these educated second men recognize their predicament and wish that they had passed up the plush staff job in order to earn their spurs on a line job but they cannot afford to quit a well-paying staff job to go down the scale to a lower-paying line job. They usually remain where they are, as assistants to executives, while men from the line move past them into jobs of greater actual responsibility. Fortunately for them, some of these second men are sufficiently intelligent and mature to continue to grow as professional specialists rather than general executives. Because of their strong intellectual rather than action interests, they lead a very satisfying work life as second men.

Pathways to advancement are not well defined

Young people who wish to advance in the professions can follow a definite educational program that will lead to admission to the profession.

Unfortunately for the recent graduate, the pathways to advancement in business are not as clearly marked as the grades and semesters in grammar school, high school, and college. In school, the pupil moves from one grade or year to the next higher stage. The levels or stages in business are not definite and have no time table. Working hard on the job does not always assure promotion. This fact has been illustrated by the old example of the employee who had served loyally for many years and was disgruntled when he was not given a salary increase. He decided to needle the boss about it by reminding him: "I have had 20 years of experience here; that's worth a raise, isn't it?" "No," replied the boss, "you have had one year's experience 20 times."

Of course many employers allow employees to expect promotion as the result of mere length of service. They continue to give increases in pay without much regard to improvement in the quality of the job performed. Relatively few employers have definite salary standards nor do they communicate to the employee evidence of his progress or lack of it.

In some crafts, it is possible to take certain steps necessary for progress from one level to another. Young people enter an apprenticeship program which they must complete before they can be accepted as journeymen. The crafts are limited largely to the shop. To advance in the business fields studied in college, the ambitious young man must move out of the craft level if he wants to move up the promotional ladder.

Many factory jobs are blind-alley jobs which do not lead to anything better without training. To advance, the young man who finds himself in a craft job in a factory must take more technical training for engineering or for business. If he has extra ability in human relations, however, he may be able to move on to the upper levels of management through supervisory functions.

The benefits of an "adviser"

One of the best pieces of advice to the ambitious young employee is "Work for an executive who likes you." This should not be confused with the "drag" idea. Drag is usually applied to the situation where family or financial connections cause an older executive to feel obligated to help a young person advance. He feels that to please someone else he should open doors and smooth the way for the young man even though he has little real liking for him or respect for his potentials. He may even resent the obligation. Many sons of men whose fathers hold important positions recognize the possible resentment and decide to retain their own self-respect by working in companies where the management has no obligatory feelings of responsibility toward them.

When a young man finds that an executive likes him, the executive rarely says: "You are the kind of young fellow whom I admire. I'll help you to advance." The astute executive does not want to do so much for his assistant that he becomes his "crutch." He does want to be a guide and stimulator, but no commitments are made or assumed. Instead, the alert young man becomes aware of the executive's tendency to give him special or difficult assignments. As part of an assignment, the older man gives advice, praise, and reprimands. The smart young man is pleased when he finds that a top management man is sufficiently interested in him to bawl him out! If no one takes the trouble to put him on the carpet for an obvious failure, that should be more discouraging than a first-rate reprimand.

The typical growth man tries to associate himself with a boss who is a good teacher. A good teacher is hard and demanding, but if the pupil admires him, both benefit from the relationship, particularly the pupil. He learns to recognize his strengths and weaknesses. He soon reaches out for more responsibility. He learns to delegate some of his work to others. He improves his communications skills. He grows intellectually as well as professionally.

The young man can, however, "select" an adviser. His work is bound to have some direct and indirect relationships with able members of management. The young man can ask him a definite question he can answer, in his field, and one that applies to work rather than himself as a person. A genuine interest in work and a desire to learn always impresses an older man. Without being aware of it, the older man acquires a protegé, but the young man should never think of himself as a protegé. (As a student, you can develop this kind of relationship while you are in college—with one of the professors.)

Dangers of over-identification with management

As Diogenes stated: "A man should live with his superiors as he does with his fire; not too near, lest he burn; nor too far off, lest he freeze."

The ambitious junior executive may identify so fully with management that he forgets his team responsibilities. This is especially likely to happen if the junior knows that he has developed the good will and admiration of a top level senior. The junior no longer feels obligated to maintain cordial relations with colleagues on his own level. After all, he knows the boss likes him—why should he bother about the fellows on his level? So he thinks, but this kind of thinking has its hazards as stated by one executive who was asked to write his evaluation of a promising junior executive:

> Junior Executive "Y" has always identified himself with management. He thinks of himself as a member of middle management and as eventually becoming a member of higher management. In general, this is a good tendency. The tendency, however, has also caused him to acquire a handicapping characteristic—he has identified himself so decidedly with management that he has not developed the knack of gaining the spontaneous good will of the colleagues on his own level. I do not think that any one could point to any serious deficiency or defect in his business behavior but many of the men on his own and on lower levels of supervision seem to have a lukewarm attitude toward him. They sense that he is not one of them. If, for example, he is late in coming to a meeting, some of the others will assume that he feels he does not have to be on time even though they are expected to be on time.
>
> "Y" is intelligent and adaptable. If he were to make up his mind that he should get the good will of his colleagues as well as members of management, he could do it.

Keep the boss informed

A good rule for all men is "Do not let the boss be surprised." If he is taken by surprise about anything that happens in his department, or is about to happen, he is jolted. He expects his people to keep him fully informed about any happenings that involve his responsibilities. To the executive few things embarrass him as much as reports from outsiders of important events that happen in his area, especially when the "news" is indicative of failure on the part of some member of his department.

The head of a department or division needs to know at all times what is going on in his area of responsibility, and he also wants to know what progress is being made with specific plans, projects or programs. If he knows which plans are going well, he can concentrate on other matters that need extra attention.

In modern managements, a great all-controlling leader is seldom found. However, the top executive must be consulted, and subordinates are expected to carry out his policies. The subordinates want to perform as expected but at times the subordinate must make a decision without knowing whether his decision would be approved by his superior. The superior may be absent or pre-occupied with a critical issue. The subordinate therefore worries as to whether he should postpone action or take action and later appear to be guilty of insubordination. This means that he should confer with other members of the team who can advise him and give him support in case the superior is later displeased with the subordinate's action.

Keep your superior informed, but use discrimination. Do not waste his time with trivialities. Bear in mind, too, that whenever your boss asks for your opinion, he wants your opinion, not necessarily an agreement with his own.

Be a member of the team

One of the best comments on the part of management in regard to a subordinate is "He is one of us. He is on the team. We can depend upon him."

The good team member demonstrates his team spirit most frequently by the way he presents new ideas. He follows the lines of organization. He knows that suggestions should be approved by lower levels of authority before the upper levels will give them much consideration.

Presenting important suggestions to management requires special skills. The originator has a tendency to overestimate rewards and to underestimate costs and difficulties. An extreme overstatement can produce a loss of confidence so great that the suggested idea is never considered. Overstatement, rather than *wrong* statement, may be disastrous.

The suggester's personal role is important. The right man should be chosen to push the idea. Sometimes a smart suggester realizes that he is not the man who can sell or execute his idea. He therefore makes a "gift" of it to the person who can develop and present it most effectively.

The employee who regards his immediate superior with a suspicion that he is throwing cold water on his efforts and trying to keep him down is wasting his time, and may build up an antagonism that will destroy the boss' confidence in him. One of the major criteria in evaluating a subordinate's loyalty and cooperation is the way he presents suggestions. If it is obvious that the subordinate's first thought is to assist the superior in promoting the interests of the firm rather than his own, he thinks of the subordinate as a member of the team. Besides, the boss knows that if an idea is important, he himself must sell it to several persons higher up and lower down in the hierarchy of operational direction. The boss must be sure the idea is sound before he will want to sell it to other members of management.

Selling an idea to management

Employees on almost all job levels of a company have asked the question, "How can I sell an idea to management? —management ought to make certain changes but I do not know how to convince them of the need." Members of middle management, too, ask the question even though they have daily working contacts with the men to whom they refer. Getting acceptance of an idea from top management is no more difficult than getting an idea across to a parent, spouse, or neighbor. In each case, we have to consider the personalities of the individuals, their psychological needs, and their work interests. This kind of person-to-person persuasion is dependent upon our social skills as discussed in Chapter 26. To gain acceptance by management of a plan of action, certain factors should be considered:

1. Instead of trying to *sell* something to management, as though the seller and management had opposing interests, assume that both have common business objectives. Both are members of the same team regardless of differences in rank. The first requirement is to overcome any tendency to think of yourself as an outsider who must battle an entrenched management. Such thinking tends to bring out latent difficulties in communication. Bear in mind that management and men are not ordinarily on two sides of a fence.

2. Present your plan with the expectation of bringing about exchange of ideas rather than an immediate acceptance of the plan. The act of persuasion has the double aspect of having two minds consider an idea. Important plans often require discussion and lengthy consideration. Without deliberation, management is likely to do too many things in the half-cocked manner.

3. Communication to be easy must be frequent rather than spaced by long intervals of silence. People must deal with each other so often that each party to a question feels that he knows how the other individual is likely to conduct himself in the future. An idea that comes from a person unknown to us is likely to be weighed more carefully than the same idea from a person whom we know and respect.

4. Present your plan in oral as well as in written form. A salesman could not hope to make many sales by means of written reports only. If he uses printed material in his interview, he depends mainly upon his oral presentation—the printed material has the secondary function of backing up the oral presentation. Visual materials should not be handed out until the oral presentation has been completed.

An oral presentation is better if it can be developed step-by-step, without the detours which interruptions often bring. On the other hand, questions asking for clarification often help to strengthen interest. They give the opportunity for additional stress on points that may be bothering the approving authority and tend to prevent his closing his mind to later refinements on a crucial point. Accept questions as you go along.

Your Own Advancement in Business

If you find that this breaks the thread of your presentation, you can always suggest that you go completely through the rest of it and then go back for questions. Many of the most likely questions will be answered by later material in your presentation.

5. Consider the climate in which the idea is offered. A management that is aggressive and determined to be the leader in its industry is more likely to be receptive than one which is "hanging on" until the head of the firm dies or retires. The best way to learn whether the climate is warm or cold is to raise the problem which the plan will solve before presenting your solution. If management's interest in the problem can be aroused, you may be able to get their blessing in the search for a solution.

The first supervisory job

Executives are developed from men and women who have demonstrated ability as supervisors. An employee's first important chance for advancement comes the day he is placed in charge of a small group of fellow workers. The young man who proves that he can supervise 20 people may expect a chance to show what he can do with a hundred and possibly, in time, a thousand. If he can prove that he has what it takes to handle even a small group of people, he is in direct line for the bigger executive jobs. Supervisors do not automatically slide into executive jobs, but they do have extra opportunities to demonstrate their growth potentials.

The supervisor must win people's respect. If he is too genial (a common defect in new supervisors) he should tighten up. He must learn how to be firm, play fair with everybody, and keep his word. Fraternization with a select few is bound to bring about criticism of favoritism. The new supervisor must find ways to avoid this criticism even though some of his old friends may accuse him of going snobbish now that he has become a "little boss."

The transition from worker to supervisor is often one of the most difficult for the young employee. He must make certain adjustments in the way he thinks and works. He must renounce his earlier habit of doing all the work himself—he must turn it over to others, and take on the specific functions of supervising. He must learn to see his role as one of getting others to perform their responsibilities rather than do the work for them. At the same time, he must be able to learn from the fellows who sweep the floors, operate the machines, do the clerical tasks, sell the products, and collect the bills as well as from his colleagues in management. He can learn from the machine operator with a sixth grade education and from the foreman who is a member of the old school. They all have a great deal to teach him. And he must show them that they can depend upon him.

One of the greatest needs of major executives is for subordinates upon

---

Table 27-1

WHAT FACTORS INFLUENCE THE JOB SELECTIONS
OF YOUNG ENGINEERS AND SCIENTISTS?

In a McGraw-Hill survey, 2,596 recently-hired engineers and scientists employed in 57 companies listed the factors they had considered before accepting a position. The replies of the younger engineers and scientists—those with less than five years' experiences—have great significance.

Potential growth of the company was listed by more young engineers and scientists than any of the 42 other items on the list as a factor that influenced greatly their decision in accepting a position: challenging opportunity was second, the company's prestige and reputation ranked third, progressive research and development program was fourth, but starting salary ranked only seventh.

Factors Influencing Decision Greatly	Per Cent Listing Factor
Potential growth of company	55
Challenging opportunity	53
Company's prestige, reputation	44
Progressive research and development program	41
Geographic location	37
Permanent position	35
Starting salary	34
Educational facilities in vicinity	33
Regular salary increases	31
Chance to work on specific project, or in certain field	27
Company's facilities (laboratories, technical libraries, etc.)	25
Tuition for graduate study	25

Based on replies by recently-hired engineers and scientists with less than five years' experience to questionnaire distributed by McGraw-Hill Classified Advertising Division.

SOURCE: "Is Industry Creating A New Breed of 'Bonus Babies'?" Classified Advertising Department, McGraw-Hill Publishing Company, Inc., July 1957.

Your Own Advancement in Business

whom they can place absolute reliance, knowing that responsibilities given to those individuals will be properly handled. Such people are identified quickly. When the executive must be away from the job, he wants to have the comfort of complete assurance that there are people on the jobs under his supervision and that they will carry on normally. This is a basic quality that managers look for in people they hope to promote.

Most companies do not have a systematic method for training their oncoming generation of executives. They do, however, have a selection plan of the "progressive hurdles" type. Under this procedure, a growth man is given a number of assignments or "hurdles" to overcome. If he makes good on the first test, he is advanced to more difficult ones. If not, management loses interest in his potentials for advancement to the top.

Another testing procedure is to pick prospective future managers for jobs that carry "Assistant to" or "Acting Director" titles. Important committee assignments may be used as testing grounds. In these assignments, candidates are given ample chance to show their abilities. If they fail, little harm has been done. But most managers believe that a man must be held responsible for certain accomplishments during the test period. Otherwise there is no real test of his ability.

Ambitious men who are promoted to greater responsibilities often wonder why they are not given the title that usually goes with the new responsibilities. Failure to grant the title usually means that management wants to try out the promoted man before giving him the full title. Top management does not like to be put in the position of having to back out of a bad situation.

Some want the veneer but not the discipline of growth

If a survey were made of young men and each were asked whether he considered himself a growth man, most would answer in the affirmative. The answer would not have much meaning for some men. Many young men want the appearance and illusion of growth but they do not care to discipline themselves enough to earn it.

> One of America's leading manufacturing concerns prided itself on its comprehensive approach to selecting and training college graduates for executive work. Recently, however, the company's critical review of its experience shook this pride. This company had centered its recruiting activities in eastern colleges that made a special effort to attract a large number of young men from families distinguished for their wealth and social position. It had induced many of the most likely graduates to

512   **Your Own Advancement in Business**

work for the company. Yet the review showed that most of these promising young men were not so promising after five years—that many of them would not rise to the top, or even close to the top. This selection program was almost doomed to failure from the start. For, if reaching the top in business requires an overriding commitment to work, these young men were not likely to fill the requirement. They came from upper socio-economic groups. Long weekends and vacations were embedded in the family value structure. Most of them married girls from the same groups, and these wives were more interested in having their husbands home on week-ends than in having them fight for the presidency of the firm. Thus these men were willing to work—but not as they would have had to work in order to reach the top.

A major steel company, realizing these facts, scours midwestern state universities for its engineers and future production executives. The company's rationale is simple: The farm boy is accustomed to working till the job is done; if he has to begin at 5 or even 4 A.M., he will do so; and if he has to keep going until 10 P.M. or midnight, he will not feel abused.[4]

Obviously, an intelligent athlete would not expect the social status of his family or his own easygoing efforts to train him for competence in his chosen sport. He would take for granted the need for continuous effort regardless of social relationships or congenial hours for himself or his family. Industry and business require the same kind of devotion to daily performance for the attainment of superior competence and recognition. The qualities often considered in hiring the college graduate are indicated by the guide for company interviewers, pages 514-515.

Education in relation to advancement

Anyone who associates with college students has met the senior who has decided to continue his education by going to a graduate school. Graduate work, he claims, will increase his chances for advancement. In some cases, as in research, graduate work is essential. It is helpful in many fields. For action fields, however, such as production, marketing, and retailing, a decision to do graduate study may mean that the individual is either thinking of himself as a staff specialist or simply postponing the day when he must enter the hurly-burly world of business. By continuing as a student, he can let his personality remain as it is.

Of course, he should seek to do good work in his studies regardless of his underlying motives. Superior scholastic ability in college is related to success in later occupational life but it is not the only factor so related.

Richard Husband, Dartmouth graduate, class of 1926, made a survey of the 368 members of his own graduating class and carefully compared

---

4 Eli Ginzberg, "Perspectives on Work Motivation, *Personnel,* American Management Association, Inc., July 1954, pp. 44, 45.

Rating Scale for Recording Interview with Applicant

Applicant's Name———————————————————————— Date————————————

College or University————————————————————————————————

After a careful appraisal of the applicant you have just interviewed, consider each of the points listed below. Place a check-mark (√) on the line above the comment which in your opinion best describes this applicant. Rate each applicant immediately after the interview. Do not check those items on which you have not had the opportunity to formulate an opinion.

---

(1) Consider his judgment. Does he appreciate the relative value of important and unimportant material? Is he diplomatic in what he says and does?

| Seems to be inaccurate in judgment. Spends time on unimportant details. | Is somewhat undependable in judgment. Often wastes time on non-essentials. Says wrong thing frequently. | Uses good judgment on simple problems, but sometimes gets confused on more complex problems. | Is level-headed. Recognizes important material. | Is accurate and prompt in judgment. Spends time on important material. Says and does right thing at right time. |

(2) Consider the possibilities of his becoming a leader. Has he a past record of successful leadership? Will he inspire confidence and respect?

| Has been a follower. Lacks desire and ability to lead. | Wants to be a leader, but never has been. Lacks ability to inspire confidence and respect. | Was leader in minor affairs. Probably will not develop further leadership powers. | Has been leader in minor affairs. Will develop. Has knack of inspiring cooperation. | Has demonstrated leadership ability. Inspires respect and confidence. |

(3) Consider his initiative. Does he impress you as having drive and force? Is he a "self-starter"?

| Apparently has little initiative. Will need detailed instructions to carry out ideas. | Will be content to let others go ahead. Has ability, but no drive. | Will keep going at a satisfactory level if some one starts him. Needs prodding. | Apparently is very resourceful in carrying out other persons' ideas. | Is a "self-starter." Will attack own and others' problems with drive and enthusiasm. |

(4) Does he appear to be well-informed in his major field? Can he talk intelligently about what he has been studying and doing?

| Is unable to talk about his field of specialization. Does not display knowledge of his field. | Talks glibly about field, but does not appear to know very much about it. | Somewhat hesitant in talking about his field. Appears to have only average grasp of the material. | Does not talk about field easily, but gives impression of knowing it well. | Talks easily and intelligently about his field. Appears to know it thoroughly. |

(5) Consider his ability to express himself. Are his statements clear and simple? Does he use good English?

| Gets tangled up frequently. Has poor command of English. | Is hesitant in expression. Frequently uses poor English. | Is somewhat hesitant in expression, but uses good English. | Has fairly easy, informal expression, but occasionally makes a grammatical error. | Expresses self easily and accurately. Uses good English. |

(6) Consider his ability to conduct himself appropriately in the interview. Is he receptive? Does he make valuable contributions?

| Is not receptive. Makes no valuable contributions to the interview. | Doesn't react to questions well. Must be prodded into saying anything. | Listens fairly well, but makes only a few contributions to the interview. | Is receptive, but makes only average contribution to the interview. | Listens carefully and asks intelligent questions. Makes valuable contributions. |

(7) How does his appearance impress you? Consider his facial expression, physique, carriage.

| Physique and carriage are not impressive. Creates poor effect. | Physique and carriage are satisfactory, but bears some marked physical disfigurements. | Has fair physique and carriage. General appearance is not outstanding. | Has good physique and carriage. General effect is fairly good. | Is well-built. Carries self well. Creates a favorable lasting impression. |

(Over)

SOURCE: *Richard S. Uhrbrock,* Recruiting the College Graduate: A Guide for

Below are some statements which might be made concerning the applicant you have just interviewed. Consider each statement.

Place a check-mark (√) in front of the statements which describe the man most accurately.

Check not less than five and not more than ten of the statements.

Check only such statements as you yourself would make in describing the applicant you have just interviewed.

_____ Does not know how to work.

_____ Talks disrespectfully of former employers.

_____ Would become dissatisfied readily.

_____ In the long run could not stand the competition.

_____ Is easily discouraged.

_____ Lacks force or drive.

_____ Suggests instability of emotional control.

_____ Is shy, embarrassed, ill-at-ease.

_____ Has reached his upper level of development.

_____ Does not seem to know what he wants.

_____ Is probably not a good team-worker.

_____ Would have difficulty in finding common ground with workmen.

_____ Tries to impress others too much.

_____ Is slow to express own ideas during interview.

_____ Is too much concerned with his appearance.

_____ Prefers to be a follower rather than a leader.

_____ Expects too rapid advancement.

_____ Is a little slow to catch on.

_____ Is too much interested in initial salary.

_____ Is not so mature as the average for his age.

_____ Does not impress one strongly one way or the other.

_____ Gives impression of being opportunist.

_____ Has had too much training for this job.

_____ Will be a good prospect if permitted to work in his narrow range of interest and training.

_____ Is not so good as some, but is acceptable.

_____ Knows what he wants to do about as well as the average.

_____ Would be good on specific assignments.

_____ Is outspoken in his opinions.

_____ Has not formed definite goals as yet, but will as he matures.

_____ Is a plugger who will work his way up slowly, but surely.

_____ Obviously is in need of coaching but it would be worthwhile.

_____ Is not brilliant, but is able above the average.

_____ Does not appear to be afraid of work.

_____ Would probably cooperate well.

_____ Is a better man than the average we have hired in past years.

_____ Is a careful and systematic thinker.

_____ Has a good foundation for further development.

_____ Possesses considerable initiative.

_____ Will get along well with associates.

_____ Looks like a "live-wire."

_____ Is self-confident, yet conservative, in his opinion of his own abilities.

_____ Has an analytical mind.

_____ Has a well-rounded personality.

_____ Asks pertinent, intelligent questions.

_____ Sets a definite goal for himself and works toward this end.

_____ Gives impression of possessing ability to handle people.

_____ Is a good prospect for executive development.

_____ Compares favorably with the best men we have hired.

_____ Is best prospect I have seen in some time.

_____ Is outstanding in all respects.

Would you recommend this man for employment? (Check one)

With no reservations. ☐   With reservations as listed below. ☐   Applicant rejected because

Under no consideration. ☐   of obviously poor health. ☐

I would recommend him if...

....

The applicant's most outstanding characteristics are:...

....

....

The applicant's weakest points are:...

....

....

Signature of Interviewer.

Company Interviewers (1953). *Courtesy American Management Association, Inc.*

their records in college with their standing in the world 30 years later. In the main, his findings indicated that an outstanding college record is certainly no bar to success in later life.

He found that activities afforded another significant clue: the more activities, the higher the later income. He concluded that companies would be well advised to look for "the man in the top quarter of almost anything: . . . Actually, *it does not seem to make much difference in what field, or fields, he made his mark.* Together or singly, in sum, grades and extracurricular activity furnish an excellent predictor of later success." [5]

Many able men of business did not go to college. Some learned more outside, on their own, than they would have if they had gotten a diploma. The diploma *per se* is not important. The test of a man is what he can do and what he is worth to his society. Where he acquired his training and his ability is incidental. One investigator, for example, found that of the fellows of one professional society, roughly 6 per cent have no college degree, 28 per cent have a bachelor's degree, 32 per cent a master's degree, 34 per cent a doctor's degree, and 7 per cent an honorary doctor's degree.[6] Perhaps the best evidence of potential ability is past ability and the urge to improve oneself, to grow.

And finally

A man's search for growth may be directed toward material possessions and social status or toward growth as a person. If you seek inner maturity for yourself, you will be inspired by your work relations with people. You will discover that the basic patterns in human behavior as exhibited in business are remarkably stable through the ages in the history of man. And when you study business, you will also want to study the classics. You will want to learn about history, literature, and art as well as about business in order that you may integrate the past with the present and the future. Of course you will never learn all that you would like to know nor attain the full maturity that you desire but you will enrich your living through the delightful neverending quest.

---

[5] Dr. Richard W. Husband, "What Do College Grades Predict?" *Fortune,* June 1957, p. 158.

[6] See Harley Iams, "How to Attract and Select Creative People," *The Management Review,* American Management Association, Inc., December 1958, p. 5.

COLLATERAL READINGS

For All Students

Havemann, Ernest, and Patricia S. West, *They Went to College*. New York: Harcourt, Brace & Company, 1952. A comprehensive study of interest to most students.

Shepherd, H. D., V. A. Musselman, and E. H. Hughes, *Introduction to Modern Business*. Englewood Cliffs, N.J.: Prentice-Hall, Inc., 1955. Examine this and/or other introduction-to-business books available to you for additional suggestions.

For Advanced Students

Roe, Anna, *The Psychology of Occupations*. New York: John Wiley & Sons, Inc., 1956. This book is intended for upper-class students. Presents research findings.

Taylor, Erwin K., "The Unsolved Riddle of Executive Success," *Personnel*, American Management Association, Inc., March-April 1960. We still have a great deal to learn before we can pinpoint what makes a man a success in his particular field.

For Men in Business

Guide to Intensive Courses and Seminars for Executives (Annual). American Management Association, 1515 Broadway, Times Square, New York 36, 59 pp., 75¢. Courses and seminars for executive and management development conducted regularly by educational institutions, associations, and consultants. Also list of universities sponsoring evening classes or periodic conferences.

Paneral, Allen J., "Educational Assistance Programs," *Journal of the American Society of Training Directors*, September 1958. A large number of companies have set up plans whereby their employees may undertake further educational course work with some form of employer reimbursement. This article gives the results of a questionnaire survey conducted by Loyola University of Chicago.

QUESTIONS ON THE CHAPTER

1. Discuss the "leveling out" of men in regard to their occupational growth.
2. Explain Greenewalt's paradox about the anonymity of the effective executive.
3. Describe the personal benefits that come to the man who enjoys his work.
4. Describe the marks of the growth man.
5. Differentiate between the "company" man and the "profession" man in business.
6. What are some of the effects of favoritism on advancement?
7. Compare the effects of definite steps for advancement in education with the poorly defined pathways for advancement in business.

8. What method does a good team member use to demonstrate his team spirit?

9. How may an ambitious person gain the benefit of an adviser?

10. When a worker advances to the position of supervisor, how is his role changed?

11. How should an employee "sell" an idea to management?

12. Explain the "progressive hurdles" type of selection plan.

13. According to the McGraw-Hill survey what were the two most important factors which young engineers considered before accepting a position? What ranked seventh?

14. Discuss education in relation to advancement.

15. Of all the ideas presented in the chapter, which ones are of special interest to you?

16. What did the chapter contribute to your future relations with (a) the men who supervise your work, (b) employees whom you may supervise?

PROBLEMS AND PROJECTS

For All Students

1. If, as a student, you can still elect certain courses before graduating, discuss the possibilities with others. Give reasons for any decisions.

2. Have you established friendly relations with any members of the faculty or with business executives? A growth man does. If you have not as yet done this, describe how you plan to do so in a sincere manner.

For Advanced Students

3. Before you finally leave school, you should prepare a resumé of your job qualifications. List the main characteristics an employer would want to know. Discuss your first draft with others and prepare a final copy for future use.

4. Plan a direct mail campaign for getting a job. Write a letter of application to be sent with your resumé. Ask others to review and suggest improvements in your job-getting program.

For Men in Business

5. Assume that you have left school and taken a job at a salary somewhat higher than the salaries of employees who have been working in the company for several years. Assume that some of the employees know your salary and resent the difference because you are a newcomer. Some employees show their resentment to you. What might you do to make the situation tolerable for both of you?

6. Look over the suggestions for advancement presented in this chapter. Which ones have you already fulfilled? Describe any specific plans you have for gaining advancement where you are now working. Discuss them with several friendly colleagues.

A

Abegglen, James, 221
Agan, Miles G., 196
Allen, Louis A., 170, 264
Anderson, David R., 379
Andrews, Kenneth R., 237
Anthony, Edward L., 377
Appley, Lawrence A., 7, 48, 49
Arensberg, Conrad M., 295
Argyris, Chris, 15, 156, 381, 382, 383, 392, 440, 454
Asch, Solomon E., 74
Atkinson, John W., 453

B

Balinsky, Benjamin, 315
Barnard, Chester I., 100
Bayton, James A., 139
Becker, E. R., 352
Beecher, Mathew J., 198
Bellows, Roger M., 107
Bendix, Reinhard, 221
Benge, Eugene J., 266
Benjamin, Hazel C., 136
Berdie, Ralph F., 305
Bernberg, Raymond E., 264
Bernhardt, K. B., 91
Bing, Ralph A., 151
Bittel, Lester R., 111
Black, James M., 256
Blake, R. R., 333
Bloeth, William, 417
Blough, Roger M., 396
Boulding, Kenneth E., 100
Bradford, Leland P., 200
Brady, Joseph V., 221
Brinker, Paul A., 267
Broehl, Wayne G., Jr., 216
Bromley, Dorothy Dunbar, 96
Brooks, Joseph, 297
Brower, Daniel, 452
Brown, J. A. C., 277
Bruce, M. M., 239
Bryant, William Cullen, 436
Burger, Ruth, 315
Burck, Gilbert, 414
Burtt, Harold E., 237
Bush, George P., 429

C

Cady, E. L., 221
Campbell, McCoy C., 246

Cannell, Charles F., 307, 308, 309
Cantor, D. C., 100
Cantor, Nathaniel, 23
Carey, John L., 391
Chalmers, W. Ellison, 295
Cifrino, Paul, 25, 26
Coch, Lester, 52, 73
Cole, G. D. H., 220
Conarroe, R. R., 222
Conner, George A., 389
Cooper, A. M., 239, 484
Covner, Bernard, 330
Craf, J. R., 62
Crain, G. D., Jr., 133
Creaghead, Robert M., 272
Curtice, Harlow H., 148

D

Dalton, Andrew J., Jr., 292
Dalton, Melville, 181
Danielson, Lee E., 233
Davies, Daniel R., 180
Davis, Keith, 62
DeMartino, Manfred F., 453
Dent, James K., 227
Diamond, Evan D., 245
Dichter, Ernest, 436
Dickson, W. J., 33, 37, 462
Dodge, J. M., 4
Doren, Merhl Norton, 484
Doty, Roy A., 206
Dover, C. J., 106
Drucker, Peter F., 3, 15, 378, 386
Dubin, Robert, 100, 294
Dyer, Frederick C., 200

E

Edwards, A. L., 440
Eitington, Julius E., 81, 268
Emmons, Russell J., 295
Evans, Chester E., 226
Estandiary, Fereidoun, 457

F

Fear, Richard A., 314
Feldman, Sidney, 348, 349, 358, 361
Filley, Alan C., 148
Finn, David, 139
Fleishman, Edwin A., 237
Floor, L., 229

Name Index

Rousseau, J. J., 220
Rowland, Virgil K., 327
Ryder, Claire F., 361

S

Sadler, William S., Jr., 458
Saltonstall, Robert, 452
Sammons, Marg, 119, 371
Sayles, Leonard R., 82, 239, 288, 289
Schleh, Edward C., 198
Schoenfeld, Erwin, 62, 313
Schrieber, Albert N., 190
Schutz, William C., 156, 215
Schwartz, W. L. K., 181
Seashore, Stanley E., 52, 60, 63, 78, 228
Segal, Stanley J., 392
Seligson, Harry, 225
Selvage, James P., 415
Sessions, Robert, 441
Shaffer, Laurance Frederic, 471
Shartle, Carroll L., 172, 173, 305
Shaw, Gerald H., 320, 334
Sherman, E. L., 278
Shepard, Clovis, 277
Shepherd, H. D., 517
Shoben, Edward Joseph, Jr., 471
Silver, Bernard, 55
Sloan, Alfred P., Jr., 4, 186
Slote, Clair Trieb, 371
Smigel, Erwin O., 132
Smith, E. Everett, 181
Smith, Henry Clay, 100, 453
Smith, John H., Jr., 131
Smith, R. M., 353, 371
Smith, Robert W., 151
Smith, Stanley E., 314
Smuts, Robert W., 26
Snegireff, Leonid S., 361
Soik, Nile, 333
Spates, Thomas G., 477
Spector, A. J., 27
Stacey, Chalmers L., 453
Stagner, Ross, 31
Stanley, J. D., 82, 201
Steckle, L. C., 239
Steiber, Jack, 294
Stern, George, 142
Stessin, Lawrence, 119, 370
Stogdill, Ralph M., 82, 172
Stolz, Robert K., 423, 427
Strauss, George, 241, 288, 289
Strong, Lydia, 209, 211
Strother, George B., 256
Stroud, Peggy V., 15
Sunderlin, Donald H., 248
Suojanen, Waino, 352

T

Tallman, E. Lee, 392
Taylor, Erwin K., 223, 236, 517
Thistlethwaite, Donald L., 142
Thompson, George G., 494
Thornton, G. R., 299
Trice, Harrison M., 465, 467

U

Uhrbrock, Richard S., 514
Uris, Auren, 12, 471
Urwick, Lyndall F., 24

V

VanZelst, Raymond H., 69, 70
Vicary, James M., 107
Vollmer, Howard M., 232, 362

W

Waddell, Richard L., 229
Wald, Robert M., 206
Walker, Charles R., 41, 44, 69, 71
Walker, Ross G., 112
Walton, C. W., 391
Warner, S. L., 462
Warner, W. Lloyd, 221
Weimer, Arthur M., 15
Weschler, Irving R., 264, 277
West, Patricia S., 517
White, George R., 376, 397
Whitehead, Alfred North, 7
Whitehead, T. N., 35, 36, 37, 39
Whyte, William H., Jr., 220
Wickert, Frederic R., 53, 55
Wiggers, Raymond P., 214
Williams, Douglas, 125, 126, 152
Willson, James D., 391
Wolf, William B., 44
Woodward, Walter P., 218
Worbois, G. M., 270
Worthy, James C., 42
Wrape, H. Edward, 32
Wright, Moorhead, 187, 326
Wyshak, Grace, 361

Y

Yoder, Dale, 27, 255
Yonge, K. A., 314

Z

Zaleznik, A., 19, 20, 27, 28, 76, 77, 95, 239, 439
Zander, Alvin, 333

A

A-Bomb, Hiroshima, 271
Absenteeism of women, 361
Accountants:
  as technical men, 377
  industrial, 379
Accounting:
  and financial reporting, 400
  influence on executives, 378
  as tool of communication, 376
ACTION, 135
Advancement, personal, 497, 503, 513
"Adviser," benefits of, 505
Ages:
  and absences of women, 361
  of management men, 150, 175, 319
Aggression needs, 443
Alcoholics, 465
American Thermos Products Company,
  The, 269
Analysts, financial, 175
Appraising:
  the employee, 317
  employee opinion study, 320
  of managements, 174
  purposes of, 318
  recommendations for, 330
Assistants to the president, 169
Attitude surveys, 263
Audits, 380
Authority symbols, 95
Automation, 71, 351
Automobile, as status symbol, 97

B

Bank-wiring room, 37
Barrington Associates, Inc., 179
Baxter, Don, Inc., 271
Bernhardt, K. B., chart, 91
Big business, hostility to, 132
Boards of directors, 163
Borg-Warner Corporation:
  and research, 427
  training program, 177
"Braille by Heart," 484
Brand images, 122
Broadcast personality, 129
"Brown's Job," 205
Budgets, 380
"Bumping," 289

C

Capitalism, employee reaction to, 125,
  396
"Captive employees," 248
Carrot-and-stick theory, 12
Chamber of Commerce, U. S., 126
Charts:
  changing department head, 194
  "Exec-Chart," 92
  leveling out, 497
  organization, 82, 161, 173
  restriction of production, 73
  Stromberg-Carlson Company, 196
Chesapeake & Ohio Railroad, 54, 229
Cinder I and II, 136
Cities Service Company, 425
"Clerical bandits," 348
Cliques, 37, 74, 82, 345
Coaching employees, 235, 317, 327
Collective bargaining, 291
College graduates:
  factors in job selection, 511
  interviewing, 300, 313, 514
  and old employees, 251
Colonial Insurance Company, 41
Committees:
  as management tool, 116
  participation in, 59, 116
Communication:
  barriers to, 105
  for cost control, 387
  to employees' wives, 367
  nonverbal, 102
  participation, 111
  regarding employer's finances, 395
  in research organizations, 422
Community leaders, 133
Company-group feeling, 79
Complainers, 462
Connecticut Mutual Life Insurance Company, 463
Consultants, 178, 470
Controllers, 384
Conversation, titles used, 491
Coping mechanisms, 451
Corporate image:
  definition, 121
  effects of, 122
  estimates of, 123
Counseling problem employees, 468
Cultural influences, 144, 305
Cybernetics, 351

Subject Index

D

Decision-making, 53, 59, 130, 148, 189, 211, 341, 479
Defensiveness, 450
Department head, effects of changing, 193
Depth of management, 176
"Detour, Executive Skill Game," 480
Director of industrial relations, 242
Disciplining employees, 232, 260
Dishonesty, of employees, 348, 388
Dispensary visits, 261
Dominant personality, influence of, 173
Drinker, problem, 465
Duplication of ourselves, 301

E

Education, relation to advancement, 513
Embezzlers, 389
Employees:
  and financial reporting, 400
  and job satisfaction, 266
  liking for employer, 9
  moving to suburbs, 261
  opinions of profits, 126
  reactions to supervisors, 230
  reasons for quitting, 53
  respect for leadership, 293
  unvoiced grievances, 262
Etiquette:
  for meetings, 118
  test of, 492
"Evolution of an ad man," 98
"Executive Appraisals" (poem), 327
"Exec-Chart," 92
Executives:
  accessibility to employees, 154
  characteristics of, 204
  definition, 203
  earnings, 211
  "Executive Skill Game," 480
  as exemplar, 215
  guide for evaluating, 91
  health of, 217
  interviews, 307
  loneliness of, 178
  magazine list for, 502
  promotability, 319
  psychological roles, 214
  relations, 213, 507
  signs of decline, 219
  status signs, 91
  training of, 187
  vacations, 209
  wives of, 365
  work patterns, 209

Exit interviews, 273, 310
Expense accounts, 212, 390

F

Family controlled companies, 149, 176
"Favorites of the court," 192
Featherbedding, 290
Finance:
  analysts of companies, 404
  definition of, 394
  reports to employees, 399
Financial reports:
  rating the company, 175
  to employees, 111
Financiers on boards, 165
Foremen (see Supervisor)
Fringe benefits, 7, 274, 370

G

Game approach to training, 189
Gas mask plants, 42
General Electric Co., 127, 186, 328
German Nazis, 96
Gilbert Youth Research Co. survey, 124
Glasses, wearing, 299
Grapevine, 110
Grievances:
  classification of, 462
  of office workers, 342
  unvoiced, 262
Group:
  cohesiveness, 77
  criticisms, 81
  dynamics, 65 f.
Growth:
  companies, 151
  curve for individual, 498
  marks of, 501
Guilt feelings, 448

H

Halo error, 298
Harwood Manufacturing Co., 51, 56
Hawthorne studies, 33 f.
Hiring:
  questions for, 67 (see also "Interview")
"How's Your Etiquette," 492
Human relations:
  in accounting, 375 f.
  definition of, 3
  in finance, 394 f.
  objectives in study, 11, 18
  problems of presidents, 167
  in research, 416 f.
  stages in development, 7

Subject Index   **525**